R.J. Unstead's
DICTIONARY OF HISTORY

R.J. Unstead's DICTIONARY OF HISTORY

WARD LOCK LIMITED · LONDON

Acknowledgments

The drawings for the *Dictionary* were prepared by
Peter Dennis, Enzo di Grazia, David Eaton, Lorraine
Johnson, Vanessa Luff, Elly Robinson, Jim Robins and
Jenny Thorne. The maps were prepared by Design
Practitioners Ltd.

The illustration on p. 44 (right) is reproduced by courtesy of
the Trustees of the British Museum. That on p. 69 by
courtesy of the Mansell Collection, and that on p. 241 (right)
is taken from Joseph Needham's *Science and Civilisation in
China* (Cambridge University Press).

The colour plates are reproduced by courtesy of Werner
Forman (p. 81), Denver Public Library (p. 100), Giraudon
(p. 99), Imperial War Museum, London (p. 182), The
National Maritime Museum, London (pp. 82, 181) and
Scala (pp. 199, 200).

FOREWORD

When I decided to try to compile this dictionary of history, I began by making a list of people and events and movements that I thought would be useful to readers and browsers who, for one reason or another, are interested in finding out about the past. The list included lots of kings, queens, emperors, leaders, wars and treaties, because these have generally seemed to be important and have affected people's lives and the course of events. Unless the book was to be too heavy to hold, there had to be limits: politicians only came in as a rule if they could be termed statesmen; there could be but a few battles and explorers, with one or two top-ranking inventors and scientists, but there was no room for writers, artists or musicians.

I soon found that one entry led to another. **CORTES, Hernando**, for instance, called for AZTECS; **GRANT, Ulysses S.**, for MEXICAN WAR, CIVIL WAR, American, LINCOLN and LEE; **MAO TSE-TUNG** for the LONG MARCH; **MARY QUEEN OF SCOTS** for REFORMATION and so on. Throughout the dictionary the use of capital letters indicates an entry elsewhere in its alphabetical position. This means that if you are interested in the Elizabethans you will be led from the article on **ELIZABETH I** to articles on HENRY VIII, EDWARD VI, MARY I, Lord BURGHLEY, MARY QUEEN OF SCOTS, ARMADA, DRAKE, HAWKINS and others, and these will in turn lead to further related articles.

I hope that the dictionary will help you to find your way about in history and to understand the past better.

R. J. Unstead

A

ADAMS, John (1735–1826), second President of the United States of America. Born in Massachusetts, John Adams was educated at Harvard and became a lawyer. He actively opposed British colonial rule and helped to draft the DECLARATION OF INDEPENDENCE. After serving as ambassador to Holland and Britain he became Vice-President, 1789–97, and succeeded George WASHINGTON as President in 1797.

During Adams's term American relations with France were strained almost to the point of war, but he managed to avoid its actual outbreak, while building up a strong fleet that captured nearly two hundred French vessels. He concluded a treaty with France in 1800.

An aristocrat rather than a democrat, Adams was generally unpopular at home, being held responsible for the Aliens and Sedition Acts, which gave the President dictatorial powers. He was defeated in the 1800 Election by Thomas JEFFERSON.

ADENAUER, Konrad (1876–1967), German statesman who played a dominant role in West Germany's recovery after the Second World War. A lawyer by profession, he was an outstandingly energetic Lord Mayor of Cologne from 1917 until 1933, when the NAZIS removed him from office and twice sentenced him to terms of imprisonment. At the end of the war the Americans reinstated him as Lord Mayor, and after he had founded the Christian Democratic Union party he became Germany's first post-war Chancellor.

From 1949 until his retirement in 1963 he practically ruled the country, making it his policy to rebuild Germany's economy and bring her back into partnership with other European nations. Thus he supported NATO and the founding of the Common Market (EUROPEAN ECONOMIC COMMUNITY), established friendship with the USA, made a treaty with France and visited Moscow in order to open diplomatic relations and to obtain the release of German prisoners-of-war.

AFGHAN WARS. During the era of British rule in India the British were much concerned about the security of the North-West Frontier. Beyond the frontier lay Afghanistan, whose warlike tribesmen seemed likely to come under Russian influence. These fears led to the First Anglo-Afghan War, 1839–42. British and Indian troops invaded Afghanistan, where the existing ruler was removed. This caused a major revolt, in which the British garrison was wiped out while retreating from Kabul, only one man surviving to reach Jellalabad. After a relieving force had recaptured Kabul the British decided to leave the country.

The Second Afghan War lasted from 1878 to 1881. British troops occupied Kabul and expelled the pro-Russian ruler, but in a general uprising the British were defeated at Maiwand and General Roberts made a famous march from Kabul to relieve the garrison at Kandahar. Having made a friendly agreement with a new ruler, Abd al-Rahman, the

British again withdrew, feeling that they had now created a buffer state between India and Russia.

In 1919 occurred the Third Afghan War when the Amir Amanullah sent troops to invade India, but these were speedily repulsed and a treaty was signed in which the British recognized Afghanistan's independence.

AFRICAN INDEPENDENCE. At the outbreak of the Second World War Liberia was the only country in Africa free from European rule or 'protection'. However, the inter-war years had seen the rise of national movements in Tunisia, Morocco and Egypt, with stirrings among the peoples of West Africa and the Kikuyu of Kenya. Furthermore, the former German colonies had been held as mandates of the LEAGUE OF NATIONS only until they were ready to govern themselves.

The Second World War shook the power and prestige of the colonial rulers and opened up prospects of independence that could not be stifled. After India, Pakistan, Ceylon and Burma had been granted independence in Asia, Africa's turn was bound to come. ETHIOPIA had indeed regained its independence in 1941, but it was ten years later that Ghana was granted internal self-rule by the British and full political independence in 1957. Nigeria followed with self-rule in 1952 and inde-

pendence in 1960. Meanwhile, in 1952 a party of officers, led by General Neguib and later by NASSER, had founded the Egyptian Republic; the former Italian colony of Libya achieved independence in 1951 and was followed by Morocco and Tunisia in 1955–6. In 1956 the Anglo-Egyptian rule of the Sudan was ended and the Republic of Sudan proclaimed at Khartoum.

These events gave a tremendous boost to nationalist movements throughout the continent. French Guinea demanded and obtained independence, whereupon the rest of the French colonies, apart from Algeria, followed suit in 1960. This was the year in which Belgium quit the Congo (now Zaïre) so hurriedly that the country soon became torn by civil war. In most cases independence was achieved without violence, though Algeria had to fight bitterly before the French accepted defeat in 1962.

The year 1961 saw the grant of independence to Sierra Leone and Tanganyika, which later was joined by Zanzibar in the union called Tanzania. 1962 brought freedom to Uganda, and in the following year Kenya, which had experienced the Mau Mau insurrection (1952–6), achieved self-government. The European-dominated Federation of Rhodesia and Nyasaland, founded in 1953, was abandoned and there came into existence the independent countries of Malawi and Zambia (1964). When Gambia gained its independence in 1965 there was little left of the former British Empire in Africa. Southern Rhodesia presented a novel problem because, while it had enjoyed self-government under white rule for forty years, the British government was not willing to grant full independence except on terms acceptable to *all* Rhodesians. Hence, in 1965 the Rhodesian government proclaimed its own independence and continued to defy Britain and the neighbouring African states.

Portugal clung on to its colonies of Angola and Mozambique in the face of costly and prolonged guerrilla warfare until 1975, when both achieved independence. By this time, apart from one or two thinly populated areas like Spanish Sahara (Rio d'Oro), Africa had freed itself of colonial rule. There remained two countries in which the black majority was governed by a white minority – Rhodesia, already mentioned, and South Africa, rich and highly developed, where the white population had adopted the policy of *apartheid* ('separate development') for its black and 'coloured' peoples.

English knight and longbowmen at Agincourt

AGINCOURT, Battle of (1415). Soon after he came to the throne HENRY V, King of England, renewed the HUNDRED YEARS WAR with France. With a large army of archers and mounted knights, he crossed the Channel to the Seine estuary and laid siege to Harfleur. The town held out much longer than he expected, and Henry was faced with the humiliating prospect of returning home by sea or boldly marching to Calais before winter set in.

He chose the latter course, only to find that the French had massed a huge army to oppose him. His own troops, short of stores and stricken by dysentery, were in poor shape when he was brought to bay at Agincourt on 25 October 1415. However, Henry was confident. He chose his position carefully where heavy ground separated the two armies, and as the French knights, weighed down by plate armour, floundered in the mud the English longbowmen poured their arrows into the dense ranks and finished the slaughter with axes and knives. The result was one of the most complete victories in history, for the French lost some 10,000 men and the English hardly more than 100.

AGRICOLA, Gnaeus Julius (AD 37–93). After service with the imperial Roman armies, Agricola was elected consul in 77 and sent as governor to the province of Britain. He was the first Roman general effectively to subdue the island and to bring peace and civilization to its southern inhabitants. Having exterminated the Druids (*see* CELTS) in Wales, he marched to Caledonia (Scotland) and defeated the northern tribesmen. Then he built a line of forts to protect the Lowlands and sent a fleet to sail round the coasts, establishing that Britain was in fact an island. Agricola encouraged the Britons to settle in towns and to adopt Roman ways, but his success as as a governor aroused the envy of the Emperor Domitian. He was recalled to Italy and made to live in retirement.

Akbar's army besieging the fort of Chitor

AKBAR (1542–1605) was the greatest of the Mogul emperors of India. A grandson of BABUR, his reign coincided with that of Elizabeth I of England. Akbar came to the throne as a boy, the kingdom being ruled for him by a cruel regent until, at eighteen, the young man took control. For ten years he extended his dominions until he ruled the whole of India except the extreme south. Then, from his capital at Agra and assisted by an able minister, Abu-l Fazl, he devoted himself to reforming the laws and providing his subjects with roads, schools, fair taxation, a police force and a system of weights and measures. The people called him 'Guardian of Mankind'. As a follower of Islam, Akbar was remarkably tolerant towards the Hindus and others, including Christians, and he tried vainly to unite his people in a new religious faith. His magnificent tomb can still be visited at Sikandra, near Agra.

Akhnaten with Nefertiti. Notice that the rays of the sun Aten end in hands stretched out to bless.

AKHNATEN, a pharaoh of the 18th Dynasty who ruled Ancient EGYPT for seventeen years until his death in about 1350 BC. As Amenhotep IV, he succeeded his father as ruler of an empire of unsurpassed wealth and extent, at a time when the priests of the god Amen-Ra possessed great power, even over Pharaoh himself. The young king came to believe in only one god, Aten, the sun god, whom he ordered his people to worship. Changing his name to Akhn-aten, he left Thebes with his beautiful wife Nefertiti to found a new capital at El-Amarna dedicated to the god. Here he devoted himself to religion, building, poetry and a new style of art far more realistic than the traditional Egyptian forms.

Meanwhile, he neglected the affairs of the empire, so that the province of Syria was lost and governors of distant garrisons begged in vain for assistance. At his death the priests of Amen-Ra recovered their power, the new capital was abandoned and a boy ruler, Akhnaten's son-in-law, became the Pharaoh TUTANKHAMUN.

ALABAMA DISPUTE. In 1862 the *Alabama*, an armed ship ordered by the Confederate (Southern) States of America, slipped away from Liverpool to join other Southern ships raiding the commercial vessels of the Northern States. After the CIVIL WAR ended, the USA claimed damages from Britain for losses inflicted by the *Alabama* and other British-built raiders. In 1871 GLADSTONE agreed to refer the dispute to arbitration and Britain was ordered to pay $15½ (£3¼) million in compensation. Gladstone's action was unpopular at home, but this was an important instance of two nations bringing a dispute to a peaceful solution.

ALBERT, Prince Consort (1819–61), was the youngest son of the Duke of Saxe-Coburg and nephew of Prince Leopold of Saxe-Coburg, who had married George IV's daughter. While on a visit to his uncle in England, Albert first met Princess VICTORIA at the age of seventeen. They were married in 1840.

From the outset Albert's position was difficult. The young Queen was popular, but the English disliked foreigners and Albert found himself distrusted by Parliament and despised by the aristocracy because he took no interest in sport or fashionable pleasures. Moreover, his self-willed little wife did

Prince Albert with Queen Victoria

ALEXANDER I (1777–1825), Tsar of Russia (1801–25), was the son of Paul I and grandson of CATHERINE the Great. Having connived at the overthrow and possibly at the murder of his father in 1801, he began his reign by introducing reforms in education and government, though he took no steps to abolish serfdom. He joined the Third Coalition (1805) against France, but after defeat at Austerlitz made peace with NAPOLEON at Tilsit, where he seemed to be fascinated by the Emperor's personality. However, serious differences arose between the two rulers and when Napoleon invaded Russia in 1812 Alexander refused to surrender. His example and the wise appointment of Kutuzov to command the Russian armies contributed to Napoleon's total defeat.

not mean him to share in her royal duties. However, Albert was more intelligent and better educated than Victoria and he gradually became her closest adviser. She adored him and as their family grew (they had nine children) she was happy to take his advice in matters which affected the country and Empire.

Albert was serious and extremely hard-working. One of his first achievements was to reorganize the royal household and put an end to extravagance and waste. He planned the family homes at Balmoral and Osborne House and took an active interest in science, trade and working-class conditions. In the face of much opposition he inspired the Great Exhibition of 1851 and helped to make it a national success. Shortly before his death he almost certainly prevented war with the United States when he changed the wording of a despatch which otherwise would have given deep offence to President LINCOLN.

In December 1861 Albert died suddenly of typhoid, leaving Victoria so overwhelmed with grief that she scarcely appeared in public for ten years.

Hailed as the saviour of Europe after WATERLOO, Alexander played a leading role at the Congress of VIENNA and genuinely believed that he stood for moderation and liberty. His 'sacred mission' was to unite Christian monarchs in the Holy Alliance. However, his increasing fear of revolution caused him to change his views, so that he put an end to further reforms in Russia and reversed many of his former measures. Alexander remains an enigma, the high-minded youth of brilliant promise who turned into a reactionary tyrant.

Alexander the Great (*left*) in battle with Darius III

ALEXANDER the Great (356–323 BC) was the son of Philip of MACEDON, who defeated the Greeks and, admiring their culture, brought Aristotle to his court to educate the young Alexander. The boy eagerly absorbed Greek ideals and showed such brilliant qualities that at sixteen he took charge of the kingdom while his father was away on campaign. Even so, his life was stormy and he and his mother were living in exile when Philip was murdered.

At once Alexander returned to seize the throne and crush the Greek city-states, which had hoped to throw off the rule of a twenty-year-old. He then announced that he would lead an army of Greeks and Macedonians against the all-powerful PERSIAN EMPIRE, which stretched from the Mediterranean to India, and avenge Xerxes' invasion of Greece one hundred and fifty years earlier.

In 334 BC Alexander crossed the Hellespont into Asia and defeated the Persian King Darius III in two great battles. He took Damascus, Tyre, JERUSALEM and EGYPT, where he stayed long enough to found the city of Alexandria. Then, having routed another colossal Persian army at Arbela, he marched eastwards to seize the treasures of BABYLON and Susa and to destroy Persepolis, the richest city in the world. Wearied by feasting and luxury, he resumed the march to the east, defeating every adversary in his path until, in India, his troops refused to go any further. Alexander reluctantly led them back, losing half his army from starvation and fatigue before reaching Babylon.

Here, with all the magnificence and despotism of an eastern potentate, he set up a sumptuous court and was busy with plans to bind his vast empire together by means of Greek culture and trade when he caught fever and died. He was only thirty-two years old.

England in Alfred's times

NORTHUMBRIA

DANELAW

MERCIA

WESSEX

ALFRED the Great (*c.* 849–900), King of WESSEX. A son of Aethelwulf, he succeeded his brother Ethelred in 871, at a time when the Danes had conquered most of England and were massing their forces against Wessex. In the first year of his reign Alfred is said to have fought them in nine battles; then, to obtain breathing-space, he made peace and built a fleet to repel the invaders at sea. However, in a surprise attack the Danes overran Wessex and Alfred was forced into hiding in the marshes of Athelney in Somerset. In 878 he re-emerged to win a great victory at Edington, after which he made the Peace of Wedmore with Guthrum, the Danish leader. In 886 England was partitioned along the line of Watling Street, the Danes keeping the part known as the Danelaw lying north and east of the line, while Alfred ruled Wessex lying to the south and west.

This agreement enabled Alfred to concentrate on rebuilding his ruined kingdom. He restored justice, issued a code of laws, constructed churches and monasteries and rebuilt London. Foreign scholars and monks were invited to the kingdom to revive learning and Alfred himself learned Latin and probably instigated the commencement of the ANGLO-SAXON CHRONICLE. To improve defence, he reorganized the army, built numbers of burghs or forts and expanded the West Saxon fleet.

When war broke out again in 892, Alfred inflicted some defeats on the Danes but was unable to put an end to the fighting. He suffered all his life from a mysterious disease and died about the age of fifty at Winchester, where he was buried in the cathedral.

AMERICAN WAR OF INDEPENDENCE (1775–81). The basic cause of the breach between the thirteen American colonies and the mother country was that the colonies had grown up and felt capable of managing their own affairs without direction from a distant government. Moreover, many of the colonists – Germans, Dutch and Irish – felt themselves to be free Americans, not subjects of the King of England. Unfortunately, GEORGE III and his ministers did not understand the situation in America but chose to tighten the reins by imposing restrictions on trade and expansion and taxes on a number of articles. In response to indignant protests all the taxes except one on tea were removed, but in 1773 occurred the BOSTON TEA PARTY, when cargoes of tea bearing the hated tax were thrown into the harbour.

Lord North then closed the port of Boston, causing the colonies to band together in a Continental Congress and to draw up a Declaration of Rights. Extra troops were sent to America, the colonists began to collect arms, and when General Gage sent a force to seize a cache at Concord shots were fired in Lexington. By the time the soldiers had returned to Boston, the war had broken out, and at Bunker Hill, 1775, the local militia showed they could fight and inflict heavy casualties on regular troops.

Congress decided to raise an army with Colonel George WASHINGTON as Commander-in-Chief, and the British made no move until 1776, when General Howe captured New York and forced Washington to retreat. By this time the Americans had issued their famous DECLARATION OF INDEPENDENCE. Apart from minor skirmishes little more happened that year, but in 1777 the British decided to concentrate their forces and destroy Washington's army. General Burgoyne would advance from Canada to meet Howe in the Hudson Valley, but, through some muddle, Howe never marched and Burgoyne's army was surrounded and forced to surrender at Saratoga. This reverse was all that was needed to

The Thirteen Colonies in 1776

CANADA

MASSACHUSETTS

NEW HAMPSHIRE

Saratoga

Boston

NEW YORK

MASS.

RHODE I.

CONNECTICUT

New York

PENNSYLVANIA

NEW JERSEY

DELAWARE

MARYLAND

VIRGINIA

Yorktown

NORTH CAROLINA

SOUTH CAROLINA

GEORGIA

One of
Washington's
Life Guards

had about 7,000 men and the British army in the north was still intact, but Yorktown was as decisive as Saratoga. It convinced the British government that it was time to end a war which many Englishmen had never wanted and which they could never win.

AMRITSAR MASSACRE (1919). In India after the First World War GANDHI organized protests against the government's new laws to suppress revolutionary activity. He was refused entry into the Punjab, whereupon serious disorders broke out in Amritsar. General Dyer ordered a ban on meetings, but on 13 April 1919 a large crowd assembled in a square. Dyer arrived with 50 soldiers and ordered them to fire. As a result 379 civilians were killed and over 1,200 wounded. This was the worst bloodshed in India since the INDIAN MUTINY and, although the British government disowned Dyer's action and removed him from active service, the massacre hardened the attitude of Indian nationalists and Gandhi began his campaign of civil disobedience.

bring Britain's enemies, France, Holland and Spain, into the war. Their combined fleets outnumbered the British navy and cut communications across the Atlantic.

However, while Washington was keeping watch on the British in the north, Cornwallis won some victories in the mainly loyalist south and presently occupied Yorktown on the coast. This gave the Americans and the French their chance to combine. While a French fleet held the sea, Washington closed in from the land and Cornwallis was trapped. He surrendered at Yorktown in October 1781. The numbers involved were small, for Cornwallis only

AMUNDSEN, Roald (1872–1928), the most persistent and successful of all Polar explorers, was born at Borge in Norway. He abandoned medical studies to go to sea and had already been to the Antarctic as first mate of a Belgian ship when, with five companions, he succeeded in finding the North-West Passage, which had baffled explorers since the time of the CABOTS.

After this success Amundsen tried to reach the North Pole, but learning that PEARY had done so he determined to make for the South Pole instead. With a team of skiers, dog-drivers and 97 Eskimo dogs aboard the *Fram*, he sailed south in 1910 and set up his base near the Bay of Whales in the Ross Sea. Months were spent in laying provision depots and placing markers until in October 1911 Amundsen set out with four companions. Their sledges, lightly loaded, were each drawn by 13 dogs, and the men on skis were attached by ropes to the sledges. In appalling conditions they made swift progress, and on 14 December Amundsen placed the Norwegian flag at the place he calculated to be the South Pole. Without delay the explorers returned safely to base.

In 1918 Amundsen took a small vessel, the *Maud*, through the North-East Passage, and later, in order to make further Polar explorations, he took up flying. Hearing that the Italian explorer Umberto Nobile had crashed his airship on the sea-ice, Amundsen took off to go to the rescue, but he disappeared and only part of his machine's wreckage was ever found.

ANGLO-SAXON CHRONICLE was a series of chronicles written in English at various monasteries, including Winchester, Peterborough and Canterbury, which provides a history of events, mainly in WESSEX, from Julius Caesar's invasion until the year 1154. It contains picturesque descriptions and poems and is most vivid when the scribe is describing events and persons of his own time, such as the character of William the Conqueror (WILLIAM I) and the anarchy of King STEPHEN's reign. The Chronicle was begun in about AD 892 at the court of ALFRED the Great, who probably encouraged the work and may have written some of it himself. No other country possesses a history of so early a date written in its own language, for Latin was almost always used for documents of every kind, and the Chronicle is valuable not only for its accounts of events in England but also for its clear vigorous prose.

ANNE (1665–1714), Queen of Great Britain (1702–14), was the second daughter of JAMES II and Anne Hyde. She was the last Stuart monarch, and although her father became an ardent Roman Catholic she herself was brought up as a Protestant. Anne married Prince George of Denmark in 1683 and they had seventeen children, of whom only one survived infancy. She seems to have been a good-natured woman without very much strength of

character, for she was greatly influenced by her favourite Sarah Churchill (the wife of MARLBOROUGH) and, after they finally quarrelled, by Abigail Masham. Her reign was notable for the political rivalry between Whigs and Tories, for the Act of Union (1707) between England and Scotland and for Marlborough's victories over the French.

Coin of Mark Antony showing a Roman warship

ANTONY, Mark (*c.* 83–30 BC), was a leading figure in the collapse of the Roman Republic (*see* ROME). After a spendthrift youth, he served with his kinsman JULIUS CAESAR in Gaul and later, in the civil war against Pompey, commanded forces for Caesar in Italy and Greece. As a consul in 47 BC he vainly tried to persuade the Romans to accept Caesar as emperor, and after his murder he delivered the funeral oration in the Forum. On the flight of the conspirators, he attained almost absolute power, but soon came up against Caesar's great-nephew Octavian (*see* AUGUSTUS). Defeated at Mutina (43 BC), he joined Lepidus in Gaul, returned to Rome with an army and came to an agreement that he, Octavian and Lepidus should share the Roman world as 'triumvirs'.

After a reign of terror in Rome, Antony defeated Caesar's assassins Brutus and Cassius at Philippi in

Greece and then went into Asia to settle a dispute with CLEOPATRA, Queen of Egypt. Captivated by her beauty, he followed her to Egypt and lived there in luxury with her until returning to Italy. It was agreed that he should take the East, Octavian the West and Lepidus Africa, and, to cement the partnership, Antony married Octavian's sister, but he soon went back to Cleopatra.

In his absence, Octavian persuaded the Senate to deprive Antony of his authority and declare war on Cleopatra. In 31 BC he defeated their combined fleets at Actium off the coast of Greece. Antony went back to Egypt, where, deserted by his fleet and army and on a false report of Cleopatra's death, he committed suicide.

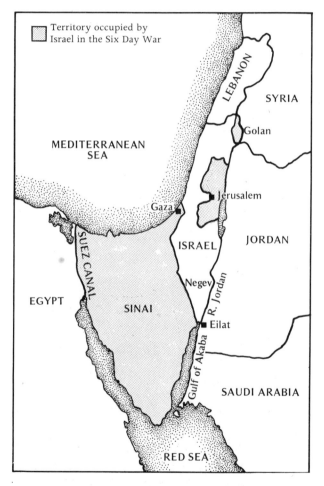

Territory occupied by Israel in the Six Day War

MEDITERRANEAN SEA

LEBANON

SYRIA

Golan

Jerusalem

Gaza

ISRAEL

JORDAN

SUEZ CANAL

Negev

R. Jordan

EGYPT

SINAI

Eilat

Gulf of Akaba

SAUDI ARABIA

RED SEA

ARAB-ISRAELI WARS. In 1947, soon after the UNITED NATIONS approved the partition of Palestine, fighting broke out between the Palestinian Arabs and the Jews. Then, on the ending of the

British mandate (1948), forces from Iraq, Jordan, Syria, Lebanon and Egypt entered the conflict, but the Israeli army struck back with such effect that by the time of an armistice in 1949 Israel had gained four-fifths of Palestine including Galilee and the Negev to the Gulf of Akaba. The war led to the flight or expulsion of a large number of Arabs, mostly to Jordan or Gaza, who became known as the Palestinian refugees.

Tension, raids and reprisals during the next eighteen years culminated in the Six Day War of May 1967. Egypt had moved troops towards the Israeli border to threaten her port of Eilat, with Jordan and Syria apparently at readiness, when Israel struck with lightning speed. The Arab air forces were destroyed and Israeli armies swiftly occupied the Sinai peninsular, the west bank of the Jordan and the Golan Heights.

A third outbreak of hostilies was the October War of 1973, when an Egyptian army entered the Sinai desert and Syria attacked the Golan Heights. The Israelis, apparently taken by surprise, fought back desperately and had recovered the lost territory by the time an uneasy truce was arranged. Negotiations for a peace settlement continued into 1976.

Arkwright with his spinning machine

ARKWRIGHT, Richard (1732–92), a British inventor, whose inventions had much to do with the introduction of the factory system. Born in poverty at Preston, Lancashire, he set up as a barber

The Spanish Armada proceeding up the Channel

in Bolton, and as a buyer of hair for wig-making he frequently visited the cottages of clothworkers. His inventive mind became occupied by the problem of how to produce cotton thread in quantity, and with the help of John Kay, a clockmaker, he built an efficient spinning-frame (patented 1769). To escape popular anger against machines, he moved to Nottingham and set up a mill driven by horses. Next, in 1771, partnered by Jedidiah Strutt, he opened a factory at Cromford, Derbyshire, where his machines used water power. In spite of rivals copying his machines and methods and the destruction of one of his mills by a mob, Arkwright made a fortune. He was knighted in 1786 and became High Sheriff of Derbyshire.

ARMADA, Spanish (1588), PHILIP II's fleet which transported an army from Spain to invade England. The fleet would have sailed in the previous year but for the heavy damage it suffered through DRAKE's attack on Cadiz. About 130 ships set out, some 40 of which were warships, the rest being merchantmen and transports carrying 20,000 soldiers and stores. The Armada was commanded by the Duke of Medina Sidonia, whose orders were to make no

attack on the English coast until contact had been made with the Duke of Parma, who was stationed in the Netherlands with an experienced Spanish army, which was to join the invasion fleet off Calais.

The English awaited the Armada's coming with a navy consisting of 36 royal warships and about 150 smaller vessels, mostly armed merchant ships and fishing boats. Lord Howard of Effingham commanded this force, which he divided into squadrons led by Drake, HAWKINS, FROBISHER and himself. Part of the English fleet, under Lord Edward Seymour, was stationed in the Downs to keep watch on Parma. The rest were based on Plymouth.

The Armada was sighted off the Lizard on 19 July advancing slowly up-Channel in a crescent-shaped formation, with the warships protecting the transports. Although the English attacked during the next eight days, they were unable to do more than damage a number of ships and were disconcerted by the excellence of the Spanish gunnery. Thus, with its formation unbroken and its main strength intact, the Armada reached anchor off Calais on the 27 July. It only remained for Medina Sidonia to make contact with Parma before undertaking the invasion.

For the English the situation was crucial. Some means had to be devised to break up the Spanish fleet, and in the night Howard sent eight fireships into the crowded anchorage. Panic ensued as cables were cut and every ship tried to stand out to sea. Dawn saw the great fleet scattered along the coast and the English sailing in to attack. The main battle took place off Gravelines and after eight hours' pounding the Armada had ceased to exist as a fighting force. The Spaniards had failed to secure a friendly port to give refuge to the damaged ships and Medina Sidonia could only try to escape by rounding the north of Scotland. The English gave chase as far as the Firth of Forth and then, short of ammunition and victuals, they were content to allow storms and rocky coasts to complete the enemy's destruction. Only 53 Spanish vessels reached home.

The English understandably rejoiced in a great victory, for they had certainly been saved from invasion, but the Armada's defeat was by no means the end of the war, nor the end of Spain as a naval power. Philip intended to assemble another armada, but although this did not come about he remained strong enough during the next decade to deny the English a second major success.

ARNOLD, Benedict (1741–1801), American general and traitor. On the outbreak of the AMERICAN WAR OF INDEPENDENCE Arnold joined the American army and so distinguished himself that he was soon promoted to brigadier-general. WASHINGTON thought highly of him and, though he was disgruntled by the promotion of junior officers over his head, he continued to serve and fought gallantly at Ridgefield and Saratoga.

In 1778 he commanded Philadelphia and then was put in charge of the vital post at West Point on the Hudson River. Here, possibly through being short of money and from a grievance over a court martial, at which he was acquitted, he entered into communication with the British, agreeing to betray West Point for £20,000. A British officer, Major André, who had been sent to see him, was captured with details of the plot hidden in his boots. André was hanged, but Arnold escaped into the British lines, where he was given a command and fought against his own countrymen. At the end of the war he went to England and he died there in obscurity in 1801.

Top of a pillar raised by Asoka for a Buddhist temple. The wheel has become the national emblem of India.

ASOKA (reigned 264–232 BC), Emperor of India, grandson of Chandra Gupta, who after ALEXANDER the Great's departure had conquered most of India. Asoka inherited his empire and for a time lived like an autocrat; however, on joining a Buddhist community he devoted the rest of his life to piety, peace

King Assurbanipal lion-hunting from his chariot

and good government. He sent missionaries far beyond India's boundaries, and it was probably through him that Buddhism became established as a religion throughout the East. Many rock inscriptions have been found in northern India which express, as edicts, his religious views and concern for his people's welfare.

ASSURBANIPAL (*c.* 669–633 BC), King of the ASSYRIANS, grandson of Sennacherib. He invaded EGYPT to put down a rebellion but subsequently lost the province. However, when his brother, ruler of BABYLON, proved troublesome, he captured and sacked the city (648 BC), and he defeated the Elamites and destroyed their capital Susa. Although he apparently made Assyria richer and stronger than ever before, the Empire was overthrown only a few years after his death. A vast library of clay tablets, covered with religious, literary and scientific writings collected during his reign, was discovered at Nineveh and is now in the British Museum in London.

ASSYRIANS originated from the northern part of the valley of the River Tigris which was known as Assur. A race of fighters and traders, the Assyrians had learnt much from the Babylonians and, in an age of cruelty, they became famous for their ferocity in war. Their expansion seems to have started under Tiglath-Pileser I (12th–11th century BC) and from about 850 BC they swept across the Middle East, capturing BABYLON and pushing westwards to the Mediterranean to take JERUSALEM, Damascus and, finally, EGYPT itself. Assyrian armies consisted of archers and spearmen supported by squadrons of horse-drawn chariots and they were the first to use siege-towers and battering-rams against walled cities.

Their capital was Nineveh, which King Sennacherib rebuilt in magnificent style, with temples and palaces faced with brilliantly coloured tiles and guarded by immense statues of winged bulls with human heads. The Assyrian Empire suddenly collapsed when the Chaldeans captured Babylon in 616 BC and then, with the Medes, utterly destroyed Nineveh.

ATHELSTAN (895–940), King of WESSEX and subsequently of England, was the son of ALFRED the Great. With his aunt Ethelfleda he defeated the Danes and later conquered most of the country. When a league of Scots, Welsh and Danes challenged him, he defeated them decisively at Brunanburh in 937. Having made England into a single kingdom, he ruled well, showing himself a friend to learning, commerce and the Church. By marrying five of his sisters to foreign princes, he made alliances and was the best-known abroad of any of the Saxon kings.

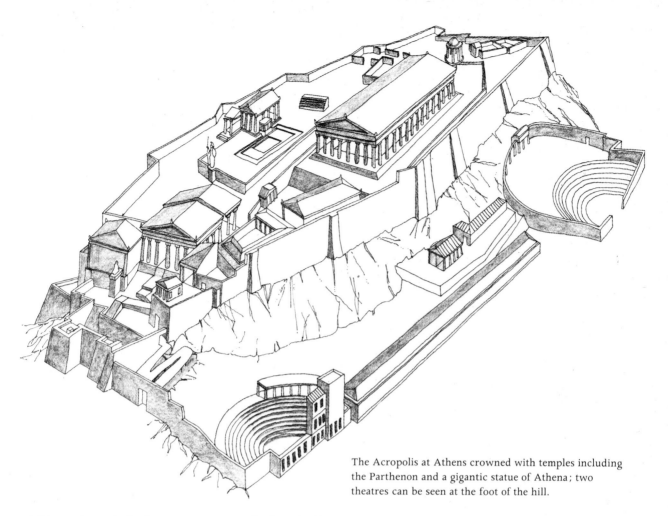

The Acropolis at Athens crowned with temples including the Parthenon and a gigantic statue of Athena; two theatres can be seen at the foot of the hill.

ATHENS, capital of ancient Attica and of modern Greece, was originally only one of many city-states, but its position and the energy of the quick-witted Athenians made it prosperous and important at an early date. Ruled at first by a succession of kings and 'tyrants', the Athenians founded a democracy in which freeborn citizens elected a council to rule them. When in 490 BC DARIUS I, King of Persia, invaded Greece, Athens defeated his forces at the battle of MARATHON. Ten years later, thanks to the leadership of THEMISTOCLES, the Athenian ships destroyed the Persian fleet at Salamis.

Athens now became mistress of the Greek world, lording it over practically all the city-states except SPARTA. Her most glorious period lasted from 480 to 430 BC, when PERICLES, aided by the sculptor Phidias, filled the city with superb temples, buildings and statues. Music and drama flourished; Aeschylus, Sophocles and Euripides wrote plays

and Athens became famous for its philosophers, historians, doctors and artists. Even in decline, it still produced such thinkers as Socrates, Plato and Aristotle.

The city's power and wealth aroused envy and some of the lesser states looked to Sparta to help them throw off the Athenian yoke. The PELOPON-NESIAN WAR between Athens and Sparta lasted for twenty-six years and ended with the surrender of Athens in 404 BC.

The city never recovered its former position, but when Greece became part of the Roman Empire (from 146 BC) Athens was celebrated as a centre of culture and education. For centuries it remained under Byzantine rule until, in the 15th century, it was captured by the TURKS and declined into poverty-stricken obscurity. Finally, it was captured by Greek patriots in 1822 and became the capital of the new kingdom of Greece that emerged in 1830.

ATTILA (c. 400–453), King of the Huns, known as the 'Scourge of God', ruled the BARBARIAN hordes of Huns from Asia. They were nomadic and skilled horsemen. With Ostrogoths, Vandals, Gepidae and Franks fighting under his banner, he devastated the Eastern Roman or BYZANTINE EMPIRE and forced the Emperor Theodosius to pay tribute. The city of Constantinople was saved by its massive fortifications. Attila then invaded Gaul, but was checked by an army of Romans and Visigoths at Châlons; he retreated to Hungary, and from there he launched an invasion of Italy in 452, ravaging the northern cities but sparing Rome, where Pope Leo I raised huge sums to buy him off. In the following year he died suddenly, possibly from poison, and the Hunnish Empire collapsed.

ATTLEE, Clement (1883–1967), Britain's second Labour Prime Minister, came from a prosperous middle-class home, and, as a young barrister, took up social work in London's East End. He became a socialist and went to live in Stepney, where, after war service, he was elected Mayor in 1919. Three years later he entered Parliament, and served in the Labour governments of 1924 and 1929–31 under Ramsay MacDonald, but he resigned when MacDonald founded a coalition government with Conservatives and Liberals. This step was crucial to Attlee's career. At the 1931 Election nearly all the Labour candidates were defeated, but Attlee was among the few who returned to Westminster. Thus he became deputy leader of the tiny Opposition under George Lansbury, and when the latter resigned over the question of rearmament Attlee became leader of the Labour Party. Its numbers in Parliament were larger after the 1935 Election, but the authority of its quietly spoken leader was never questioned.

During the Second World War, Attlee worked willingly with CHURCHILL and served as Deputy Prime Minister. In 1945 Labour won a resounding victory, and for the first time in history had a majority that enabled it to carry out socialist policies. Under Attlee's leadership the coalmines, the Bank of England, gas, electricity, civil aviation, railways, road transport and steel were nationalized. The National Health Service was introduced and independence was granted to India, Pakistan and Burma. By 1951 Attlee's ministers were ageing and tired; his party was defeated and he took up his old role as Leader of the Opposition until 1955, when he retired and accepted an earldom.

For most of his career Attlee was underrated by both his friends and enemies, but under his unassuming manner he was an astute determined politician, who was always in control of his difficult team. He was, in fact, one of the outstanding figures of the century – a good chairman rather than a brilliant general – but he got things done and played a leading part in changing Britain and the Commonwealth.

AUGUSTINE, Saint (c. 560–604), the first Archbishop of Canterbury. Augustine was an Italian monk, chosen by Pope GREGORY I to convert the Anglo-Saxons in Britain (see SAXONS). With a party of forty monks he landed in 597 at Ebbsfleet in Kent, a kingdom ruled by Ethelbert, whose wife Bertha was already a Christian. Augustine obtained permission to use a ruined Roman church in Canterbury and he presently baptized the King and converted the kingdom of Kent. He then travelled to Wales, where the Christian faith had not died out since Roman times, but, by adopting an air of superiority, he seems to have offended the Welsh bishops and they rejected his leadership. Augustine therefore returned to Kent, where he died, and his remains were eventually buried in the church of the monastery of Saints Peter and Paul.

AUGUSTUS, Caesar (63 BC–AD 14), formerly named Octavian, was the son of a niece of JULIUS CAESAR, who adopted him as his own son and heir (see ROME). At the time of Caesar's murder Octavian was eighteen, a student in Greece; he returned to Rome, won the support of the mob and the legionary veterans, drove out Mark ANTONY and defeated him at Mutina. Octavian was then made consul at the age of nineteen, but when Antony returned to Italy with Lepidus he joined them in a triumvirate, whose power soon became absolute through the massacre of their opponents. With Antony, he next defeated the republicans Brutus and Cassius at Philippi, and after Antony had gone to the East he stripped Lepidus of power, won the support of the Roman people and finally defeated the fleets of Antony and CLEOPATRA at Actium in 31 BC. With Antony's death Octavian became sole ruler of the Roman world and, as the first Emperor, he took the name of Caesar Augustus.

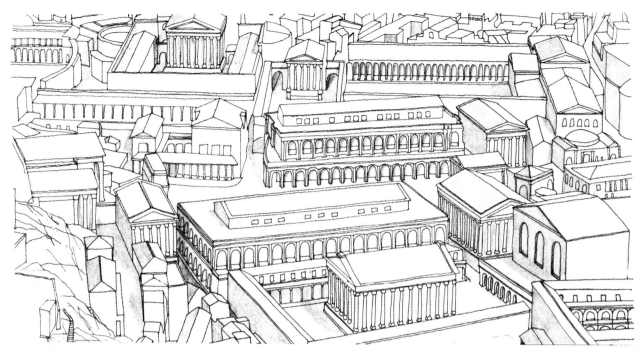

Above Temples and public buildings below the Capitoline Hill in Rome at the time of Augustus

Below Prussian 'Death's Head' Hussar. Frederick the Great used his hussars to defeat the Austrians in 1741.

During his long reign he ruled mildly and well, introducing many reforms in Rome and appointing governors of the provinces more honest and efficient than in the past. He made the Empire's frontiers secure through a series of military and diplomatic victories, though there was one crushing defeat when the legions of Varus were wiped out by German tribesmen. His greatest achievements were transforming Rome into a city of noble buildings – it was said 'Augustus found a city built of brick and left it built of marble' – and encouraging the arts. The Augustan Age came to mean an era of literature and culture.

In his private life Augustus lived simply, but his later years were clouded by ill health and domestic sorrow; his favourite stepson and two grandsons died and he adopted another stepson, Tiberius, who succeeded him as the second Emperor.

AUSTRIAN SUCCESSION, War of the (1740–48), was caused by FREDERICK the Great of Prussia's seizure of Silesia, a Hapsburg province, shortly after the Empress MARIA THERESA had succeeded to the Hapsburg possessions. Bavaria, Spain and France sided with Prussia, while Britain (with Hanover), Holland and Savoy supported Maria

Theresa. The war was a confused affair, marked by military inefficiency and changing alliances. Having defeated the Austrians at Mollwitz (1741), Frederick made a truce with Maria Theresa, enabling her to repel the French and Bavarian armies. In 1743 an Anglo-Dutch force, known as the 'Pragmatic Army', defeated the French at Dresden, but Frederick re-entered the war and forced Maria Theresa to recognize his control of Silesia by the Treaty of Dresden, 1745. Meanwhile, fighting continued in the Netherlands, where the French general Marshal Saxe defeated the Pragmatic Army at Fontenoy (1745), Rocoux (1746) and Lauffeldt (1747).

In 1745 British troops were brought home to deal with the JACOBITE REBELLION. By this time the war had become a colonial struggle between Britain and France, aided by Spain. At sea the British Navy won the victories of Cape Finisterre (1747) and Belle Ile, Admiral Vernon attacked Portobello, and in North America British settlers captured Louisbourg. These successes were offset by the loss of Madras in India. The war ended in 1748 with the Treaty of Aix-la-Chapelle, whereby Frederick kept Silesia, Louisbourg was exchanged for Madras and Maria Theresa emerged the loser.

AUSTRO-PRUSSIAN WAR (1866). The 'Seven Weeks War' was engineered by BISMARCK to destroy Austrian influence in Germany and to ensure Prussia's leadership. Having met NAPOLEON III and secured French neutrality, Bismarck made an alliance with Italy and picked a quarrel with Austria over the Duchy of Holstein (recently taken from Denmark). In the war, which broke out in June 1866, the Italians were defeated at Custozza, but Moltke's Prussian armies, making good use of railways and telegraph, decisively defeated the Austrians at Sadowa. By the Treaty of Prague in August the Emperor FRANCIS JOSEPH was forced to agree to Prussia's reorganization of Germany and to cede Venetia to Italy.

AZTECS. In about 1250 a nomadic tribe called Aztecs arrived in the Valley of Mexico, where older peoples, such as the Toltecs, had long established a flourishing civilization. Allowed to settle on some marshy islands in a lake, the Aztecs built themselves a lake-city they called Tenochtitlan. Warlike and ferociously brave, they defeated the shore people

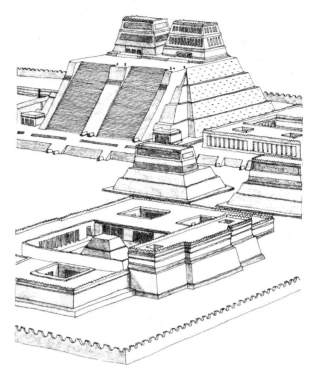

Aztec temple at Tenochtitlan (now Mexico City)

and came to rule an empire of 15 million inhabitants, who were forced to pay tribute in the form of food, gold, coloured feathers and slaves.

The Aztecs cultivated island gardens, engaged in trade and made pottery, cloth, mosaics and brilliant feather cloaks. Knowing nothing of iron or the wheel, they had no vehicles, nor indeed any pack-animals, but they studied the stars, worked out a calendar and knew a great deal about building, water-supply, farming and trade. Their city was laid out in handsome squares and broad streets bordered by canals. They built vast temples, where thousands of human beings were sacrificed to the gods, and they were obliged to wage perpetual war on their neighbours in order to obtain the captives for sacrifice.

This bizarre empire came to a sudden end in 1520 when Hernando CORTES led a party of Spaniards to the island capital, killed the Emperor Montezuma and eventually overcame all opposition. Cortes was able to carry out this astonishing feat because the Aztecs believed that he was Quetzalcoatl, the Plumed Serpent god who was destined to return and claim his kingdom. Hence resistance was half-hearted. Cortes also had firearms, horses and help from local tribes who hated their oppressors.

B

BABINGTON PLOT (1586). Antony Babington, a Catholic gentleman who had been page to MARY QUEEN OF SCOTS in captivity, plotted to murder Queen ELIZABETH and release Mary. Cipher messages were intercepted by WALSINGHAM's spies, in which it appeared that Mary approved of the plot, and this led to her subsequent execution. Babington was arrested and executed with some of his confederates in September 1586.

BABUR (1483–1530), the first Mogul Emperor of India, was a descendant of the conqueror Timur and grandfather of AKBAR. As a youth he succeeded to a small kingdom in Asia, beyond the Hindu Kush, the mountain range of Afghanistan, and after vain attempts to recover the ancestral capital of Samarkand he established himself as ruler of a number of provinces centred on Kabul. In 1526, with a small army, he invaded India and routed the forces of the Afghan Emperor at Delhi. Further victories enabled him to extend his conquests as far as the borders of Bengal and, although he reigned for only five years,

he established an empire which his successors were to develop. Babur possessed great gifts of leadership and a passion for science, art, gardens and sport. He was a poet and a writer of memoirs describing his life and conquests.

BABYLON, an ancient city and kingdom of Mesopotamia, situated on the banks of the river Euphrates, about 70 miles (113 km) from Baghdad. The first Babylonian dynasty emerged in about 2000 BC when a Semitic tribe called Amorites overran the kingdoms of Akkad and SUMER. From these tribesmen emerged the great HAMMURABI (c. 1792–1750 BC), who ruled his empire with remarkable efficiency and made the town of Babylon into a splendid capital.

About two hundred years later, when the river valley was conquered by the Kassites, Babylon was plundered and became of little importance for the next four centuries. It eventually belonged to the ASSYRIANS and had been restored by ASSURBANI-PAL when it was captured by the Chaldeans in 616 BC. Thereafter it enjoyed its second period of splendour.

NEBUCHADNEZZAR II (c. 605–562 BC) conquered the Assyrian Empire and rebuilt the city on both sides of the river. It was said to have been 15 miles (24 km) square and surrounded by a massive wall, in which were set a hundred gates. Over the city

The temple at Babylon in the time of Nebuchadnezzar II

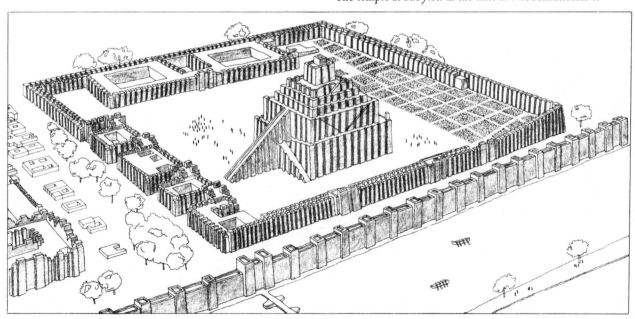

towered the vast temple of the god Marduk, and it also contained Nebuchadnezzar's fabulous palace, whose Hanging Gardens were known to the Greeks as one of the Seven Wonders of the World. The glory was short-lived, for the city was captured by CYRUS the Great in 539 BC and Babylonia was merged into the PERSIAN EMPIRE.

BADEN-POWELL, Robert Stephenson Smyth (1857–1941), a British general who served in India, Afghanistan and Africa. He made his name for his spirited defence of Mafeking during the BOER WAR, but his real claim to fame lies in the founding of the worldwide Boy Scout organization. The movement had its origin on Brownsea Island, Poole, in 1907, and in 1910 Baden-Powell's sister Agnes founded the Girl Guides.

Baird testing an experimental television apparatus

BAIRD, John Logie (1888–1946), the Scottish television pioneer, was born at Helensburgh and studied electrical engineering at Glasgow University. Poor health compelled him to give up a normal career and he retired to Hastings in 1922 to devote himself to experiments with sending and receiving television signals. In the face of dire poverty, he continued his research in Soho, London, and by 1926 was able to give the first demonstration of television to the Royal Institution. His 240-line system was adopted experimentally by the BBC in

1929 and was used when the first regular broadcasts took place in 1936. However, a rival 405-line system was adopted in preference to Baird's, but he continued his research and before his death had produced colour television.

Balboa has Indian prisoners thrown to the dogs

BALBOA, Vasco Nuñez de (1475–1517), Spanish explorer, discoverer of the Pacific Ocean and first of the *conquistadores*. He settled in Hispaniola and in 1510 joined an expedition to the American mainland as a penniless stowaway. Having overthrown the leader, Enciso, he founded the Settlement of Darien (Panama) and in 1513 led an expedition across the isthmus, where from a mountain peak he sighted the Pacific and claimed the 'Great South Sea' for Spain. He began exploration and was making plans for the conquest of Peru when Pedrarias Dávila arrived from Spain as governor of Darien. Motivated by jealousy, Dávila ordered the arrest of Balboa, had him tried for treason and executed at Acla.

BALDWIN I (1058–1118), King of Jerusalem, joined the First CRUSADE in 1096 with his older brother Godfrey of Bouillon, leader of the German crusaders. Intending to win an estate, Baldwin left the main army and with the aid of Armenian Christians made himself Count of Edessa. By cunning and audacity he ruled there for two years until, on the death of his brother in 1100, he was invited to Jerusalem to be crowned king. During his reign he captured the main coastal towns of Palestine, repelled Egyptian attacks and established himself as overlord of the other three Crusader kingdoms. He died from fever caught during a successful raid into Egypt.

BALFOUR DECLARATION (1917), made in a letter from Arthur Balfour, the Foreign Secretary, to Lord Rothschild, a prominent Jew, stated that the British government favoured the establishment of a national home for the Jewish people in Palestine. It amounted to a promise that Britain would support the Zionist cause and was made partly out of sympathy for the Jews, partly to win their support, especially in America, for the war and also to put a barrier between the French in Syria and the Suez Canal. It meant that Britain (which ruled Palestine after the war as a mandate of the LEAGUE OF NATIONS) acquired the task of fostering a Jewish national homeland in the face of mounting hostility from the Arabs.

Balkan states after the wars of 1912-13

BALKAN WARS (1912–13). In the First Balkan War Serbia, Greece, Bulgaria and Montenegro formed the Balkan League and in 1912 drove the Turks out of most of the area they had been ruling in south-eastern Europe. The European powers called the London Conference and, through Austrian pressure, insisted on the creation of an independent Albania, thus denying Serbia access to the Adriatic.

The Second Balkan War broke out in 1913, when Bulgaria attacked both Serbia and Greece but was speedily defeated when Rumania and Turkey declared war on her.

These two wars reduced the OTTOMAN EMPIRE in Europe to a small area round Constantinople and made Serbia the strongest Balkan state, one that was bitterly hostile to Austria.

BANNOCKBURN, Battle of (24 June 1314), was the greatest defeat ever inflicted on the English by the Scots. With a small army of spearmen and some light cavalry, ROBERT BRUCE took up a strong position near Stirling to await the arrival of EDWARD II's much larger army. Through bad generalship the English made no effective use of their archers, but launched the cavalry on a narrow front against Bruce's close-packed spearmen. At the height of the struggle a crowd of Scottish camp-followers was mistaken for a reserve army and the English tried to retreat, but most were trapped in marshy ground and slaughtered or were drowned in the river. Edward II abandoned his stricken army and escaped with a few knights. Bannockburn confirmed Robert Bruce as king and ensured Scotland's independence.

BARBARIAN INVASIONS. At an early date in Rome's history the Gauls or CELTS from northern Europe invaded Italy and captured Rome (*c*. 390 BC) before being driven off. A century later they flooded into Macedonia and Greece and then entered Asia Minor, where some of them settled and gave their name to an area called Galatia.

As Rome's power increased the barbarians were held in check, but the government was always aware of the menace of the tribesmen who lived just beyond the frontiers of the Empire. In a hard-fought series of campaigns (58–50 BC) JULIUS CAESAR defeated the German tribes, but even he used barbarians in his army as cavalrymen. Over the years the fighting power and discipline of the Roman legions grew weaker and the threat of barbarian invasion grew ever stronger.

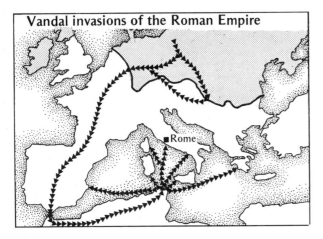

Invasions from north-west Europe

JUTES
ANGLES
SAXONS

BURGUNDIANS
ALEMANS

BRITONS
FRANKS

Rome

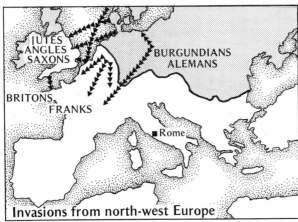

Vandal invasions of the Roman Empire

Rome

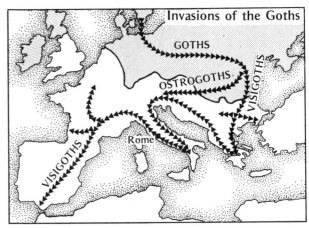

Invasions of the Huns

Rome

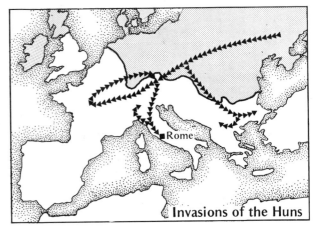

Invasions of the Goths

GOTHS

OSTROGOTHS

VISIGOTHS

VISIGOTHS

Rome

By Diocletian's reign (AD 284–305) German peoples, like the Franks, the VANDALS and the Alemans, were pressing hard along the frontier and often crossing it to live inside the Empire, while from the lower Danube the Goths were a constant danger.

At about this time barbarians of another race entered Europe from Asia. These were the ferocious Huns, who drove the West Goths (Visigoths) across the Danube into the Empire, where they defeated the Emperor Valens at Adrianople (378). From then on the Empire began to break up. Led by their king Alaric, the Visigoths advanced from the Danube into Greece, crossed to Italy and plundered Rome itself in 410. Later they settled in Spain. Meanwhile, the Franks entered Northern Gaul, the Burgundians and Alemans installed themselves in other parts of Gaul, and the Vandals crossed the Rhine and swept through Gaul into Spain and North Africa.

By this time Angles and SAXONS from Germany were invading Britain and, further east, the Huns greatly increased their power under ATTILA, but were eventually defeated at Châlons in France (451). Attila invaded Italy, but died soon afterwards and the Hunnish Empire collapsed. However, a fresh danger appeared when the Vandals crossed over from Carthage in North Africa to Sicily and Italy, capturing Rome in 455.

Some forty years later an eastern branch of the Goths, the Ostrogoths, entered Italy to displace the German ruler, Odoacer, and set up a strong Gothic kingdom under Theodoric the Great.

BECKET, Thomas (c. 1118–70), Archbishop of Canterbury, was the son of a London merchant; he studied law and was raised by HENRY II to be Lord Chancellor. As the King's closest friend and adviser Becket enjoyed great power and wealth and he was much dismayed by Henry's insistence in 1162 that he accept the vacant archbishopric of Canterbury. At once his character and way of life changed, for he saw himself now as the servant of the Church and protector of its rights. Henry, intent on increasing his control of the Church, was outraged by his former friend's attitude, and when Becket refused to accept royal demands he charged the Archbishop with treason. Becket fled abroad, but after six years Henry became alarmed lest Pope Alexander III's displeasure affect his son's succession (see PAPACY); so peace was made and Becket returned to Canterbury in triumph. Without delay he excommunicated the bishops who had obeyed the King in his absence.

News of this action was carried to Henry in Normandy, where he burst out in such a tirade of anger that four knights left the court, crossed the Channel and made for Canterbury, where they murdered the defiant Archbishop in the cathedral. The crime resulted in Henry's complete defeat and humiliation, for he had to throw himself upon the Pope's mercy and there could be no question of exercising control over the Church. Becket was canonized as Saint Thomas in 1172 and his shrine became the most popular object of pilgrimage in western Europe until it was destroyed by Henry VIII in 1538.

BEDE, the Venerable (673–735), the greatest scholar of pre-Conquest England. A monk of the Benedictine monastery at Jarrow, Northumbria, Bede spent his entire life in study, teaching and writing. His interests were extraordinarily wide, for he knew Latin, Greek and Hebrew and he studied astronomy, medicine, music and, indeed, the whole field of knowledge of his time. His writings included religious works, lives of saints, hymns and books on grammar, but his greatest work was his *Ecclesiastical History of England*, which is the source of almost all our knowledge of the country's ancient history. He completed a translation of the Gospel of St John into Anglo-Saxon just before his death.

BELL, Alexander Graham (1847–1922), the inventor of the telephone, was born in Edinburgh, where his father was a well-known teacher of elocution. In 1870 father and son went to Canada and then to Boston to set up a school for training teachers of the deaf. Alexander fell in love with a deaf girl, Mabel Hubbard, and it was through trying to make a machine to help her that he turned his attention to transmitting speech by electricity. In

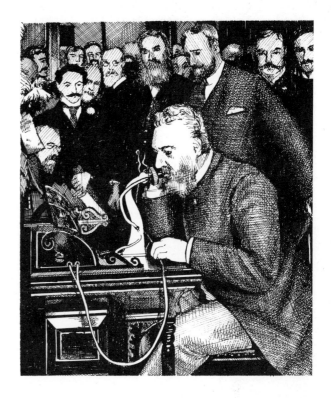

1876 he exhibited his telephone at the Centennial Exposition at Philadelphia, but he had to fight lawsuits to establish his patent and it was some time before his invention made him a rich man. He then settled himself in Nova Scotia and devoted himself to experiments and inventions mostly to do with speech and aeronautics.

BENEŠ, Eduard (1884–1948), Czech patriot and statesman, was born in Bohemia and educated at Prague, when his country-to-be was part of the Hapsburg Empire. During the First World War he worked in Paris with Masaryk for Czechoslovak nationalism, and from 1918 to 1935 was Foreign Minister of the new state. Famous as spokesman for small nations, he was elected President of the LEAGUE OF NATIONS in 1935, the year in which he succeeded Masaryk as his country's President. In protest against the Munich settlement of 1938 he resigned and went abroad, but during the Second World War he headed the government in exile in France and in England. Beneš returned to Czechoslovakia in 1945 and was elected President again, but the Communist coup of 1948 destroyed the democracy he believed in and he resigned, to die a few months later.

BEN-GURION, David (1886–1973), the creator of the state of Israel, has been called the greatest Jewish leader since Moses. He was born at Plonsk in Poland and, as an ardent young Zionist, went to live in Palestine, where he founded the first Jewish trade union in 1915. After the Turks expelled him for pro-Allied activity, he went to America to help raise the Jewish Legion and subsequently fought in Palestine against the Turks. In 1930 he became leader of the Mapai (Labour) Party, which was to be the ruling party when the state of Israel was founded in 1948. Ben-Gurion was the first Israeli Prime Minister from 1948 to 1953, and he held that office again from 1955 to 1963.

BERLIN, Congress and Treaty of (1878), dealt with the eastern situation after the Russo-Turkish War of 1877–8. By the Treaty of San Stefano Turkey had to agree to the creation of a large independent Bulgaria, and this appeared to Austria and Britain to be likely to lead to Russian domination of the Balkans. Thus Andrassy, the Austrian Foreign Minister, and DISRAELI, the British Prime Minister, demanded a European Congress to revise the treaty, and BISMARCK, anxious to keep on good terms with both Austria and Russia, invited the powers to Berlin.

Here it was agreed that Bulgaria should be reduced in size by returning part (Eastern Rumelia and Macedonia) to Turkey; Austria was to occupy Bosnia-Herzegovina, while Britain, refusing to annex Egypt, should take over Cyprus. Thus it appeared that Russian gains had been wiped out, and Disraeli went home in triumph, claiming to have brought 'Peace with honour'.

In the long run, however, the arrangements were not successful. The Balkan peoples continued to resist Turkish rule (*see* BALKAN WARS) and the increase of Austrian influence in the Balkans was to lead to the outbreak of the FIRST WORLD WAR.

BESSEMER, Sir Henry (1813–98), British inventor of the Bessemer process (1855) for making steel by driving an air blast through molten pig-iron. This greatly reduced the cost of steel manufacture and, for a time, gave Britain an industrial advantage over other countries. Bessemer, whose father was a successful inventor and manufacturer, possessed great ingenuity and commercial acumen. Having already made a comfortable income from various inventions and industrial improvements, including a method of making gold paint for lettering, he set up his own steel works in Sheffield and also licensed his new process to manufacturers at a royalty of £2 per ton. Not surprisingly, he made more than a million pounds from his inventions.

BISMARCK, Otto von (1815–98), statesman, the creator of modern Germany. By birth he was a Prussian Junker, a member of the land-owning class, and after a rather wild youth this huge ungainly aristocrat made a name for himself as an ardent supporter of the King against the Prussian liberals. At this time Germany was a collection of thirty-nine states, loosely allied in a German Confederation, which met at the Diet at Frankfurt. In 1851 King Frederick William IV sent Bismarck to the Diet as Prussia's representative. Later he served as the ambassador to Russia until the next King, William I, at hopeless loggerheads with his Parliament, made him Prime Minister in 1862.

For the next twenty-seven years Bismarck held supreme power, ruling the country autocratically and practically ignoring Parliament. From the outset his aim was to break Austria's hold on Germany and to unite all the states under Prussian leadership. So, having persuaded Austria to join Prussia in 1864 in a war against Denmark, he used a quarrel over the settlement as an excuse to attack and defeat Austria herself in the AUSTRO-PRUSSIAN WAR (1866). This victory put Austria out of Germany and united the northern states in a confederation with William I as President and Bismarck as Chancellor.

He now needed a cause that would bring in the southern states and this he achieved by engineering a war with France. A dispute over the candidature of a German prince to the Spanish throne was turned into a situation in which the French Emperor NAPOLEON III appeared to have been insulted. As before, the Army won the FRANCO-PRUSSIAN WAR in lightning style and William I was crowned German Emperor at Versailles in 1871. Bismarck, made a prince, became Imperial Chancellor; he had unified Germany and he set to work to build a powerful centralized state.

With masterly skill, he controlled the Reichstag (Parliament), solved innumerable problems raised by the states and introduced remarkable social benefits for the workers. In foreign affairs his policy now was to preserve peace, to pose as friend of both Austria and Russia, to isolate France, yet to distract her from thoughts of revenge by encouraging her to build an overseas empire. He also contrived to acquire a German empire in Africa without coming into conflict with Britain.

As long as William I lived the 'Iron Chancellor's' power was undisputed, but William died in 1888 and two years later the headstrong Kaiser WILLIAM II compelled Bismarck to resign. The old man went into retirement, fulminating against the Kaiser's policies, which would, he predicted, undo much of his work. He was right. Twenty years after Bismarck's death the state which he had created was totally defeated.

BLACK AND TANS was the name given to the security force (from the colours of its makeshift uniforms) that was recruited in England in 1920 to strengthen the Royal Irish Constabulary in its struggle with the Irish Republican Army (*see* IRISH HOME RULE). This force was recruited from ex-servicemen with a taste for fighting (the Irish believed that many came from jails), and during eighteen months of guerrilla warfare terror was met by terror. Both sides accused the other of atrocities and it seems certain that the 'Tans' behaved with shocking brutality.

Townsmen burying victims of the Black Death

BLACK DEATH. Outbreaks of plague occurred from time to time during the Dark Ages and in medieval times, but the worst outbreak in history began in about 1346 in China. The disease which became known as the Black Death was carried in the bodies of fleas which lived on black rats and the pestilence travelled along trade routes to India, to southern Russia and into Italy, where half the population of Florence died. From there it spread into France and western Europe, reaching England in 1348.

Fever, dark blotches under the skin and raging thirst preceded death. There was no cure and the disease attacked the young and the strong, wiping

Admiral Blake's flagship in battle during the First Dutch War

out whole communities in remote villages and monasteries, as well as in the insanitary over-crowded towns. At least one third of England's population perished and the disaster had serious effects upon trade, agriculture and the people's morale.

Further outbreaks of plague occurred during the next three centuries, the last serious one in England being in 1665. After that there were no more major visitations, possibly because of cleaner living con-ditions or because the black rats were killed off by the brown ones.

BLAKE, Robert (1599–1657), English admiral, possibly the greatest after Nelson that England has produced. The extraordinary feature of his career is that he lived the life of a Somerset gentleman until he was forty and had little or no experience of warfare or of the sea.

Elected to Parliament in 1640, he opposed the King and during the CIVIL WAR distinguished him-self as a general, especially in his stubborn defence of Lyme and Taunton. In 1649 he was appointed a general at sea; the fleet was then in poor condition, but in two years he destroyed Prince RUPERT's squadron and forced the Royalists to surrender their last strongholds, the Scilly Isles and Jersey. On the outbreak of the First DUTCH WAR (1652) he commanded the Channel fleet and fought engage-ments against the Dutch admirals, de Ruyter, Tromp and De Witt, usually with success.

In 1654 he sailed the Mediterranean, where he defeated the Tunis pirates and forced the Dey of Algiers to submit. Blake's last and greatest exploit was the destruction of a Spanish fleet at Santa Cruz in April 1657. His health was failing and he died on the voyage home as his ship entered Plymouth harbour.

BLENHEIM, Battle of (13 August 1704), was the first major encounter of the War of the SPANISH SUCCESSION and the greatest English victory on the continent since Agincourt. LOUIS XIV had gained the support of the Elector of Bavaria, and the French commander Tallard was assembling a large army to capture Vienna and thus knock Austria out of the war. To avert this disaster MARLBOROUGH left Holland, marched his army rapidly into Bavaria and joined forces with Prince Eugene, the Austrian commander. The French-Bavarian army had taken up position at Blenheim on a tributary of the Danube when Marlborough launched his attack, not on the French right flank, as Tallard expected, but at the centre, which broke after a desperate struggle. Marshal Tallard was captured and 25,000 of his men were killed or captured. Vienna was saved; Bavaria dropped out of the war; the French had to retire from Germany and Marlborough's reputation was made.

Boer encampment

English musketeers ford the river at Blenheim

BOER WAR (*or* South African War, 1899–1902) arose out of the long-standing feud between the Boer or Dutch settlers and the British in South Africa. Ill-feeling was made worse by the discovery of a rich goldfield in the Transvaal in 1886, because over 50,000 foreign whites (the 'Uitlanders'), most of them British, entered the province, where the Boer President Paul Kruger refused to grant them political rights. Cecil RHODES, Prime Minister of Cape Colony, hoped for an uprising of the Uitlanders, but Jameson's Raid, which was to have triggered it off, failed in January 1896. As tension mounted, the Boers bought German armaments and the British sent additional troops to the Cape.

Kruger's demand that these troops be recalled was rejected, and in October 1899 Boer armies entered British territory, won three engagements and laid siege to the towns of Ladysmith, Kimberley and Mafeking. Superior in numbers and arms, the Boers might have swept through to the Cape, but by splitting their forces and engaging in protracted sieges they gave the British time to bring in reinforcements and appoint better generals. Thus Lord Roberts and General Kitchener were able to wear down their opponents and in 1900 Kimberley, Ladysmith and Mafeking were relieved, while the main Boer army, under Cronje, was defeated at Paardeberg. Although Bloemfontein, Johannesburg and Pretoria fell, the Boer commandos continued guerrilla warfare so effectively that Kitchener had to resort to a scorched earth policy, destroying farms and interning civilians in concentration camps, where many died from disease.

The war ended in 1902 with the Treaty of Vereeniging, whereby the Boer republics became British colonies, with the promise of eventual self-government, and this was granted in 1906–7. The British also made a grant of £3 million to pay for the ruined farms.

BOLIVAR, Simon (1783–1830), hero of South American independence, was born in Venezuela into an aristocratic family. He travelled widely in Europe, where he became an admirer of NAPOLEON and a convert to revolutionary ideals. Back in Venezuela, he took a leading part in an uprising against the Spanish rulers. Though the revolt failed in 1814, he continued to organize resistance until, with his victory at Carabobo in 1821, he won freedom for Venezuela and New Granada. He joined these countries together as Colombia, of which he became President, and in 1822 he added Ecuador to the Republic.

In 1824 he drove the Spaniards out of Peru and ruled there for a time. Upper Peru was made into a separate state, named Bolivia in his honour. His dictatorial methods aroused opposition and he returned as President to Colombia, but here too his assumption of complete power alarmed the Republicans and he was compelled to resign in 1830, the year in which he died. Although he ended as a dictator, Bolivar gave his life to the cause he believed in so passionately and he is rightly regarded as the liberator of South America.

The hammer and sickle, emblem of the Bolsheviks

BOLSHEVIKS were members of the Russian Social Democratic Party, which seized power in Russia in 1917. Their leader was LENIN, and the name, meaning 'majority men' as distinct from the Mensheviks ('minority men'), arose from a division of the party at a congress in London in 1903, when Lenin obtained a majority because some of the delegates withdrew. The Bolsheviks stood essentially for disciplined revolutionary action, while the Mensheviks advocated less extreme policies. After the RUSSIAN REVOLUTION the Bolsheviks emerged as the sole party in Russia and, from 1918, changed their name to the Communist Party.

BOSTON MASSACRE (5 March 1770) was an event that increased bad feeling between the American government and the British authorities and led up to the AMERICAN WAR OF INDEPENDENCE. Revenue duties imposed by Townshend,

The new nations of South America

Great Colombia (1819–30)

VENEZUELA
COLOMBIA (NEW GRANADA)
ECUADOR
GUIANA
PERU
BRAZIL
BOLIVIA
PARAGUAY
CHILE
ARGENTINA
URUGUAY

Bolivar

the British Chancellor of the Exchequer, had been a heavy blow to Massachusetts, where a show of violence caused the Governor to ask for troops. On 5 March 1770 a crowd of youths snowballed the redcoats; someone gave the order to fire and three Bostonians were killed. Two more died later. New England seethed with anger and, although the troops were withdrawn from Boston, Samuel Adams and Paul REVERE were able to use the incident to keep alive the idea of rebellion.

BOSTON TEA PARTY (16 December 1773). To help the EAST INDIA COMPANY, the British Parliament allowed it to ship tea direct to the American colonies. Since it did not bear the English duty of one shilling a pound, the tea was actually cheaper than formerly, but it bore the hated tax of threepence a pound and the monopoly hurt both the Boston merchants and the smugglers. British tea was therefore boycotted and in Boston a group of citizens, calling themselves 'Sons of Liberty' and disguised as Mohawk Indians, boarded ships in the harbour and threw overboard 342 chests of tea. In retaliation, Lord North, the British Prime Minister, closed the port and put the town under martial law. Resentment throughout all the colonies led to the calling of the First Continental Congress at Philadelphia, when the delegates adopted measures against English goods and drew up a petition to GEORGE III stating their rights and grievances.

BOUDICCA (*or* Boadicea, died AD 61), British Queen, was wife of Prasutagus, King of the Iceni, a tribe of East Anglia in Roman Britain. At his death Prasutagus made the Emperor NERO co-heir to his property, hoping that this would secure the kingdom for his own family. However, the Roman officials ill-treated Boudicca and her daughters and ordered confiscation of the lands of Icenian nobles.

A revolt broke out, in which the Iceni were joined by other tribes, and, at the head of a large army, Boudicca defeated the 9th Legion and sacked the towns of Colchester (Camulodunum), St Albans (Verulamium) and London (Londinium), putting their inhabitants to the sword. The Roman commander Suetonius Paulinus, who had been campaigning in Anglesey, hurried south to meet the Britons somewhere in the Midlands, where he completely defeated the undisciplined tribesmen. Boudicca, who had escaped from the field, took poison to avoid capture.

BOURBON, House of, was the dynasty or family which ruled France from 1589 until 1830, apart from the years 1793–1814. The family became connected to the royal house of France in the 13th century, when the Bourbon heiress married a son of LOUIS IX. Their descendant Anthony de Bourbon became king of Navarre through marriage, and it was his son, Henry of Navarre, who succeeded to the throne of France as HENRY IV in 1589, on the assassination of Henry III, last of the Valois kings. Henry IV and the successive monarchs, Louis XIII and LOUIS XIV, raised France to heights of unprecedented grandeur, but decline set in with Louis XV and Louis XVI. With Louis XVI's execution in 1793 the dynasty was interrupted, but after NAPOLEON'S downfall a Bourbon returned to the throne in the person of Louis XVIII (1814–24). The dynasty ended when his brother Charles X was deposed by the JULY REVOLUTION of 1830.

BOXER RISING (1900) occurred in China when, under the Dowager Empress TZ'U HSI, the misgoverned country had been penetrated by Western merchants and missionaries and had recently suffered defeat by the Japanese. Widespread discontent, famine, drought and floods produced a violent anti-foreigner peasant movement and the emergence of the Boxers, a secret society whose members went in for exercises not unlike boxing

A band of Boxer rebels

and who claimed to be invulnerable to bullets. Bands roamed about killing and ill-treating foreigners, missionaries and their converts.

The Empress and the imperial troops took no steps to repress them, and in 1900 the Boxers reached Peking and besieged the foreign legations, where some five thousand diplomats, merchants, officials and guards defended their compound for fifty-five days. Western troops, joined by Americans and Japanese, managed to raise the siege and take possession of Peking, thus enabling the Allies to dictate a settlement.

The Chinese were made to execute a number of officials, to destroy forts, to permit the occupation of strategic points and to pay an indemnity amounting to £67 million. These terms intensified anti-foreign resentment and caused many young Chinese to join nationalist and republican movements.

BRINDLEY, James (1716–72), the English engineer and canal-builder, was born at Thornsett, Derbyshire, into a poor family. He received little or no education, but after serving an apprenticeship to a millwright, he became known for his skill in repairing machines and in 1752 designed an engine to drain some coal-pits. Recommended to the Duke of Bridgewater, who was anxious to improve the output of coal from his estates, Brindley advised the construction of a canal from Worsley to Manchester, and this he carried out with complete success by 1772.

His crowning triumph was building an aqueduct to carry the canal across the river Irwell. After this he began the building of the Grand Trunk Canal and completed several others, constructing in all over 360 miles (580 km) of canals.

Throughout his career he remained illiterate, solving his problems without notes or drawings, and it was said that when confronted with a difficulty he would retire to bed and work out the solution in his head. His work provided England with a valuable means for transporting heavy goods and raw materials at a time when roads were bad and railways had not yet been built. Canals therefore played an important role in the INDUSTRIAL REVOLUTION.

BRITAIN, Battle of (1940). The epic conflict in the SECOND WORLD WAR between the Royal Air Force and the German Air Force (Luftwaffe) which took place between 10 July and 31 October. As the prelude to the invasion of Britain, the Germans launched a series of attacks, with an initial force of 1,350 bombers and 1,200 fighters, against shipping, and then, from August, against airfields and finally against towns. The British air defence depended chiefly on Hurricane and Spitfire fighters, which were usually outnumbered by three to one, but had the advantage of an efficient system of radar stations, which gave warning of the approach of enemy formations.

The climax of the battle came on 15 September, when 56 German planes were shot down (due to faulty intelligence, the RAF claimed 185), and after this the Germans resorted mainly to night bombing of cities, especially London. No daylight attacks were made after 5 October, by which time HITLER had called off the proposed invasion. During the twelve-week battle 1,733 German aircraft were destroyed for the loss of 915 British fighters.

BRUNEL, Isambard Kingdom (1806–59), was the son of Sir Marc Brunel, a Frenchman who settled in England, where he became a successful architect-engineer. Isambard entered his father's office and worked with him on the construction of the Thames Tunnel, before making a name for himself as designer of the Clifton Suspension Bridge at Bristol.

Scramble! Battle of Britain pilots about to take off to attack the enemy

Brunel and the
SS *Great Britain*

He next carried out dock and harbour works at various ports and in 1833 was appointed engineer to the Great Western Railway, for which he planned the route and designed the tunnels, bridges and viaducts (*see* RAILWAYS). In order to use more powerful locomotives and to give greater steadiness and speed, he built his track on a 7-foot (210 cm) gauge.

While engaged on the railway he designed and supervised the building of the *Great Western*, the biggest steamship of her time, which crossed the Atlantic in 1838 in the record time of fifteen days. He also designed the *Great Britain* (1845), the first ocean-going screw-steamer, and his belief in big ships led him to build the *Great Eastern* (1853–8), by far the largest ship then constructed. Her commercial failure did not disprove his methods and ideas, and she was the forerunner of all big ships.

Brunel's was a many-sided genius; he took an active part in planning the Great Exhibition of 1851, and during the CRIMEAN WAR he turned his attention to gunnery and designing military hospitals. Worry over the problems of building the *Great Eastern* affected his health and he died suddenly in 1859.

BURGHLEY, Lord (William Cecil, 1520–98), one of England's greatest statesmen, was the son of Richard Cecil, a gentleman who rose high in Henry VIII's service. William was educated at Cambridge and he studied law before becoming secretary to Protector Somerset in Edward VI's reign. The Protector's downfall brought Cecil to the Tower for a time, but his known abilities soon won him the post of Secretary of State under NORTHUMBERLAND. Yet on MARY's accession he managed to secure her approval, especially since he temporarily adopted the Catholic religion. However, before her death he was in secret correspondence with ELIZABETH, and when she came to the throne in 1558 she at once chose him to be her Secretary of State.

For the next forty years Cecil retained a hold over the Queen which no one at court or in the council could shake. She relied on his advice and experience and trusted him to carry out the policies on which they were agreed. At the beginning of the reign, especially, he was exactly the minister England needed, for his watchword was caution, so the country could win time to settle the problems at home and abroad. It is not easy to decide how far he was responsible for the religious settlement, for the help given to the HUGUENOTS and the DUTCH REVOLT and for foreign policy, since he left few indications of his personal views. On occasion, as in

helping the Scots against the French in 1559–60 and in procuring the execution of MARY QUEEN OF SCOTS, he would take action from which the Queen shrank. At all times he remained her wise subtle counsellor, the quiet power behind the throne, who bore patiently with her tantrums and the irritating influence of favourites.

Elizabeth raised him to the peerage as Baron Burghley and made him Lord Treasurer; as he lay dying, she fed him herself with a spoon and afterwards, at mention of his name, she would turn aside to weep. His supreme concern had been to serve his country and the Queen. For them he did not hesitate to take harsh measures, to keep an army of spies and to deny religious toleration. He was the architect of Elizabethan greatness.

BURMESE WARS. These 19th-century conflicts caused Burma to be incorporated into the British Empire; their course was as follows:
1) 1824–6; the threat of a Burmese invasion of Bengal led to the capture of Rangoon by a British force. After further fighting the Burmese ceded territory in southern Burma and renounced claims on Assam.
2) 1852; after frontier incidents and ill-treatment of British traders, the second Burma War resulted in the British annexation of the Irrawaddy Delta. The Burmese refused to recognize this or to make a treaty.
3) 1885; King Thibaw, in collaboration with the French, imposed heavy fines on the Bombay-Burma Trading Corporation and this led to the despatch of a British-Indian army, which occupied Mandalay and deported the King. Upper Burma was annexed in 1886 and the whole country became a province of the Indian Empire.

BURTON, Sir Richard (1821–90), the eccentric British explorer, began his adventurous career in India in the service of the EAST INDIA COMPANY. Whilst there he mastered several languages and made a pilgrimage to Mecca disguised as a Pathan. In 1854 he explored Somaliland, and two years later, accompanied by J. H. Speke, he set out on a journey that led to the discovery of Lakes Tanganyika and Victoria. Speke's separate discovery of the latter, through leaving Burton when he was ill, led to a bitter quarrel. Burton also made journeys in West Africa before entering the consular service,

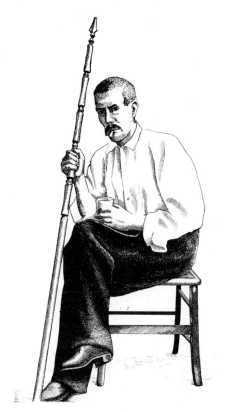

and it was as consul at Fernando Po (1861), Brazil (1865), Damascus (1869) and finally at Trieste (1871) that he wrote many of his books, including a translation of the *Arabian Nights*. Burton possessed extraordinary gifts as a scholar, linguist and adventurer; there was a savage bitter side to his nature, and he has been described as an Elizabethan born out of time.

BYZANTINE EMPIRE. Often called the Eastern Roman Empire, the Byzantine Empire came into existence in 330, when the Emperor CONSTANTINE built Constantinople on the site of the ancient city of Byzantium. He transferred the capital of the Roman Empire there and adopted CHRISTIANITY. Thus he founded a Christian empire, which preserved many of the Roman ideals for a thousand years after the Roman Empire in the West had vanished.

When the BARBARIANS overran Italy and the provinces, the Eastern emperors managed to survive. Indeed, JUSTINIAN (527–565), through the victories of his general Belisarius, recovered Italy, part of Spain and North Africa from the Barbarian tribes. But the recovery was short lived and

Byzantium suffered many reverses until, in about 610, Heraclius defeated the Persians and won back many lost territories. A worse foe soon appeared when the Arabs swept across the Empire (*see* ISLAM), but Constantinople, defended by its massive walls, survived two sieges.

From the 8th century Byzantium became increasingly Greek in spirit and was perpetually at war with the Arabs, Bulgars and Russians. Yet, although the Empire shrank in size until only Greece and Asia Minor were left, trade, art and learning flourished and Constantinople's magnificence astonished travellers from the West. In the 9th century Byzantium had to withstand attacks by VIKING marauders, but in the next century a series of Macedonian emperors won back large territories and drove the Muslims out of Asia Minor and Syria.

Once again danger threatened from the east when, from about 1030, the SELJUK TURKS invaded the Middle East, causing the Emperor Alexius to appeal to the West to save Christianity. The Crusaders restored parts of Asia Minor to the Empire (*see* CRUSADES) but the foundation of the Kingdom of Jerusalem and quarrels between the Roman Church and the Greek Orthodox Church of Constantinople led to bitter hostility. In 1204 Crusaders actually sacked Constantinople itself, and for the next fifty years westerners took control of the Empire. However, the Greek Emperor Michael Palaeologus recovered the capital in 1261, but the Empire was still beset by enemies, principally the Turks and Serbs.

During the next two centuries, when emperors were constantly elected and dethroned, civil strife and the indolence of the ruling classes led to increasing decay, so that the Turks were able to win possession of practically all the Byzantine territory. By 1453 only the great city of Constantinople was left, and the OTTOMAN Sultan Mahomet II brought up his armies for the final assault. After an eight weeks' siege the walls were breached, the last Emperor, Constantine XI, was killed and the Byzantine Empire came to its end.

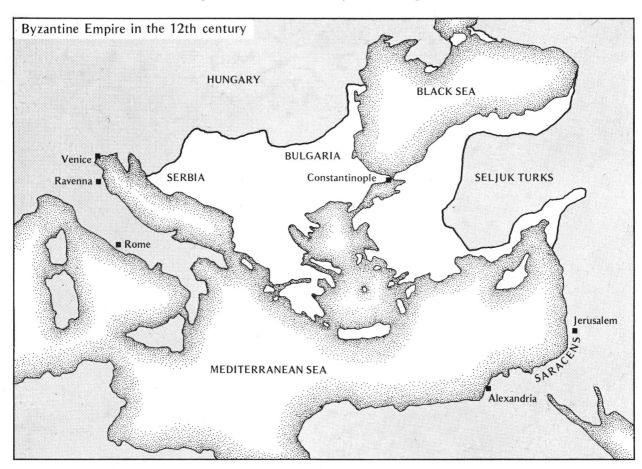

Byzantine Empire in the 12th century

C

CABAL, the (1667–73), was a group of five ministers who in CHARLES II's reign became a sort of inner circle of the Privy Council. The word 'cabal' already meant a small secret faction or clique and, by a coincidence, the initials of the five members made that word. They were Clifford, Arlington, Buckingham, Ashley and Lauderdale. This group was more or less involved in the King's scheme to do without Parliament and to betray his Dutch allies, but only the first two (who were both Catholics) were let into the secret of the King turning Catholic. The members of the Cabal were divided and jealous of each other; Charles used them as advisers chiefly to conceal his own policy, and their influence, such as it was, ended in 1673.

CABOT, John (1450–98), a Genoese merchant who settled in Bristol, was commissioned by HENRY VII to make a voyage of discovery. In 1497 he reached Cape Breton Island and sailed along the coasts of Newfoundland and Labrador. A year later he set out again, hoping to reach China and the Spice Islands, but after sailing along the eastern coast of North America as far as Chesapeake Bay he returned to England. Cabot's voyages gave England her first claims to lands in North America.

CABOT, Sebastian (c. 1476–1557), son of John, also received a commission from HENRY VII, and in 1509 he set out to find the North-West Passage to Asia. He seems to have explored the North American coast, though there is no positive proof that he did so. In 1512 he moved to Spain, where he rose to become Pilot Major, earning a reputation as a navigator and organizer of voyages of discovery. Given command of an expedition to the Pacific (1526–30), he achieved little more than exploration of some of the rivers of South America. In Edward VI's reign he returned to England, where, as Governor of the Merchant Adventurers, he organized an expedition to find a North-East Passage. Led by Willoughby and CHANCELLOR, the expedition failed in its object, but Chancellor reached Moscow and established trade with Russia.

CALVIN, John (1509–64), the French Protestant leader, was born in Picardy and from an early age he seemed certain to become a Catholic priest. As a young man, scholarly, refined and saintlike, he immersed himself in religious studies and became converted to the Protestant faith in about 1533. Forced to leave Paris for criticizing the Catholic Church, he moved to Switzerland, where at Basle he issued his celebrated statement of Protestant belief. After visiting Italy, he settled in Geneva and set about bringing the city's whole life under control of the reform movement.

Through books, fellow converts and incessant

letter-writing, he made himself the leader of the HUGUENOT party in France, and the spirit of the REFORMATION in several other countries. Ceaseless work weakened his fragile constitution and he died in 1564, shortly after preaching his last sermon. Calvin wanted to return to early Christianity. He believed that men should be good without thought of reward or punishment, though God had destined some for salvation and others for eternal damnation. He demanded strict discipline, with supervision of people's private lives and punishment for sins. Thus Calvinism has seemed to many to be a harsh, intolerant religion, but its influence was profound. It made the Protestant Church in France and the Dutch Republic. It became Scotland's national religion; it fired the English Puritans and was transported across the Atlantic into the New England colonies.

CANUTE (or Cnut, c. 995–1035), son of King Sweyn of Denmark, invaded England in 1015, dividing the kingdom with the SAXON Edmund Ironside. On Edmund's death in 1016 he became undisputed King of England. Two years later he became King of Denmark and in 1030 of Norway; thus he ruled an extensive sea-empire and was one of the most powerful monarchs of his time. He ruled England well and gained popularity by adopting Christianity and making a pilgrimage to Rome. He also appointed Saxons to positions of importance, and under his rule trade revived and contacts with Europe increased. After his death, his sons HAROLD and Hardicanute showed none of their father's ability and the sea-empire soon fell apart.

CARACTACUS (or Caratacus or Caradoc), son of Cunobelinus, was a king of south-east Britain who fought against the Romans in AD 43. Though defeated in the south, he carried on resistance in Wales and the south-west for eight years until his family was captured and he himself was betrayed to the Romans by the Queen of the Brigantes. He was taken to Rome to be exhibited to the crowds before execution, but it is said that his proud bearing so impressed the Emperor CLAUDIUS that he was set free. He died in Rome in about AD 54.

CARTHAGE was an ancient seaport on the coast of North Africa near modern Tunis. The city, founded by PHOENICIANS from Tyre in about 800

BC, owed its great wealth to the Carthaginians' enterprise as sea-traders. They built a huge fleet of ships to carry Negro slaves, ivory, precious stones and, above all, metals from Spain and West Africa to all parts of the Mediterranean.

Enormous profits enabled them to hire mercenary soldiers to control an empire that included Tunisia, Sardinia, most of Sicily (won from the Greeks) and numerous colonies along the coasts of North Africa and Spain. The Carthaginians were governed by magistrates elected annually and a council of wealthy citizens. Their art was unremarkable and in their religion they worshipped many gods and made use of human sacrifices.

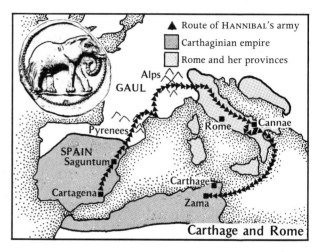

Carthage and Rome

For several centuries the interests of Carthage and ROME did not clash, but eventually, as Rome's power increased, conflict became inevitable. The long struggle, known as the Punic Wars, lasted from 264 until 202 BC and ended, despite the genius of HANNIBAL, in total defeat for the Carthaginians. When they tried to assert their independence, the city was razed to the ground in 146 BC and its territory became the Roman province of Africa.

Caesar AUGUSTUS rebuilt Carthage in 29 BC and it grew rapidly into the largest city in the west after Rome. It was finally destroyed by the Arabs in 697.

CARTIER, Jacques (1491–1557), the French navigator and discoverer of the St Lawrence River, set sail from St Malo in 1534 to look for the North-West Passage to Asia. He reached Newfoundland and sailed along the neighbouring coast before returning to France with two Indians. In 1536 he set out again with three ships and voyaged up the

St Lawrence River, aided by the Indians who acted as interpreters and informed him he was in the land of Canada, the Huron-Iroquois word for village. Cartier returned to Canada in 1541 as leader of the Roberval expedition, which hoped to find the mythical kingdom of Saguenay, supposedly rich in precious stones. The expedition failed and Cartier returned home to St Malo, where he acted as a nautical adviser until his death.

CARTWRIGHT, Edmund (1743–1823), was an English clergyman at Goadby Marwood, Leicestershire, until a chance meeting with ARKWRIGHT aroused his interest in the possibility of applying machinery to weaving. In 1785 he invented a power-loom and followed this with further inventions, including a wool-combing machine, another for making rope and various farm implements. Although he opened a factory at Doncaster, his inventions brought him no financial success and in 1809 the government awarded him £10,000 for the benefits conferred on the country by his power-loom.

CASEMENT, Sir Roger (1864–1916), was born of Protestant stock in Ireland. He entered the British consular service and spent years in Africa where, in 1903, he reported on the near-slavery conditions in the rubber trade of the Congo. In 1905 he was transferred to South America and made a similar report on conditions on the rubber stations of Peru. Whilst in the consular service, Casement had become an ardent Irish nationalist (*see* IRISH HOME RULE), and at the beginning of the First World War he went to Germany to seek support and to urge Irish prisoners to form a brigade to fight against the Allies. In 1916 a German submarine took him to

Ireland, but he was arrested on landing, tried for high treason and hanged at Pentonville on 3 August. In 1965 his remains were returned to Ireland and buried in Dublin.

CASTLES. A castle was a fortified dwelling belonging to a lord, who might be the King or a powerful noble. It served as the lord's home, as a stronghold and also as the centre of local government.

The NORMANS built castles in Normandy during the 11th century, and after they conquered England they erected many of these fortifications to hold down the SAXONS. Early castles consisted of a wooden tower on a mound (motte), which stood in a courtyard (bailey) surrounded by a palisade and a ditch. By the 12th century the wooden tower had been replaced by a stone keep, which formed the last refuge of the garrison if the outer fortifications had been overrun. The keep contained storerooms, a baronial hall, sleeping quarters, a chapel, a well and a prison; its top was crowned by battlements from which defenders could fire down at the attackers.

In time the outer fortifications became more important than the keep. The bailey walls were strengthened by battlements and towers and the gatehouse was protected by a drawbridge, a portcullis (an iron grating lowered in front of the doors) and machicolations or holes through which missiles and liquids could be dropped. Concentric castles (whose plan was learnt from the Saracens during the CRUSADES) had at least two rings of walls, the outer ones being lower than the inner ones, so that defenders could direct their fire from two or three levels.

Castles played an important role in European

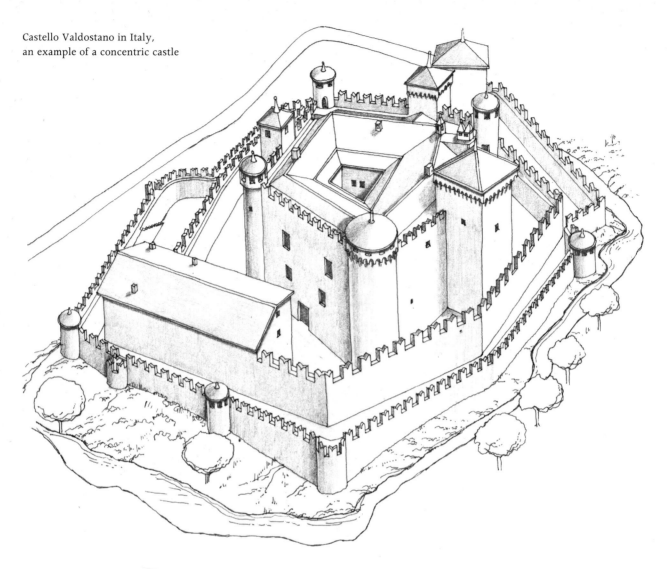

Castello Valdostano in Italy,
an example of a concentric castle

warfare until about the middle of the 17th century. By that time artillery had become sufficiently powerful to pound a castle into ruins from a safe distance.

CASTRO, Fidel (born 1927), trained as a lawyer in Cuba, where during the 1950s he became leader of guerrilla forces which waged a lengthy war against Batista, the Cuban dictator. By 1959 he had overthrown Batista and assumed power as Prime Minister. The USA did not look on him, the first Communist head of state in the western hemisphere, or his regime with favour, while Castro for his part seized American assets and nationalized foreign companies. Meanwhile, he sought aid from Communist countries, including arms from the USSR,

which enabled him to defeat a US-backed invasion attempt (Bay of Pigs, 1961). He was disappointed when KRUSHCHEV removed the atomic missiles

from Cuba in 1962. Castro appears to be an absolute ruler, concentrating all power into his own hands, but he seems to enjoy complete support from the overwhelming mass of the Cuban people.

CATHERINE the Great (1729–96), Empress of Russia (1762–96), was a German princess, Sophia of Anhalt-Zerbst, who went to Russia as a girl to be betrothed to the future Emperor Peter III. Married unhappily to this degenerate youth, she nevertheless took enthusiastically to everything Russian, learned the language, joined the Greek Orthodox Church and changed her name to Catherine. When her unpopular husband became emperor in 1762, Catherine speedily brought about his overthrow and murder. Thus, as Catherine II, she became sole ruler of Russia for the next thirty-four years. Although she had a succession of lovers, some of whom she made ministers, she really ruled the country, and the advance of Russia during her reign was due to her own intelligence, energy and cunning.

In home affairs Catherine began as a reformer, introducing a scheme to improve the lot of the serfs, but opposition from the nobles caused her to abandon this idea. In fact serfdom became worse and a revolt under the Cossack Pugachev had to be crushed. She achieved more success as a lawgiver and a reformer of provincial government.

Her foreign policy was to enlarge Russia, and in two successful wars against Turkey, thanks to the victories of her general Suvorov, she made gains that extended to the Black Sea, the Crimea and the Caucasus. She shared in three partitions of Poland and finally gained possession of that country. Catherine was a cultured woman with a keen intellect. She read widely, corresponded with Voltaire and other French thinkers, collected art treasures, wrote a number of books and imposed a new culture and manners on the Russian court.

CATHERINE DE MEDICI (1519–89), Queen of France, daughter of Lorenzo de Medici (*see* MEDICI FAMILY), was the wife of Henry II of France and mother of three French kings. During her husband's life she had little influence, but on the accession of her son Francis II (married to MARY QUEEN OF SCOTS) she became Regent and was to dominate French politics for the next thirty years. Francis died in 1560 and was succeeded by the ten-year-old Charles IX, and in 1574 her favourite son, Henry of Anjou (who had been a suitor of Elizabeth I of England), came to the throne as Henry III.

As Queen Mother Catherine's policy was to assert the authority of the Crown, which her feeble sons failed to do, and to play off the Catholic faction against the HUGUENOTS, yet to avoid civil war. This she was unable to do, and the wars of religion continued from 1562 to the end of her life. Fearing the rise of the Huguenot power, she instigated the murder of Coligny, the Huguenot leader. There followed the Massacre of ST BARTHOLOMEW (1572), when thousands of Huguenots were slaughtered. It

SWEDEN

FINLAND

Russia under Catherine the Great

– – Boundary at the beginning of Catherine's reign

St Petersburg

RUSSIA

■ Moscow

PRUSSIA

■ Warsaw

POLAND

HUNGARY

Crimea

CASPIAN SEA

BLACK SEA

CAUCASUS

OTTOMAN EMPIRE

was believed that she connived at the death of her fourth son Alençon. At her death, detested by Catholics and Protestants alike, she left the kingdom in a state of anarchy. She was a true Medici in her love of intrigue, art and magnificence.

CAVOUR, Count Camillo Benso di (1810–61), the statesman whose diplomatic skill brought about the unification of Italy, was born in Turin in the kingdom of Piedmont. After Piedmont's defeat by Austria in 1848–9 Cavour threw himself into the ideal of freeing his country from Austrian rule and uniting all of Italy. He became Prime Minister and shrewdly sent a force of Piedmontese troops to the CRIMEAN WAR, thus ensuring himself a place at the peace conference, where he cultivated the friendship of France and Britain. He met Emperor NAPOLEON III secretly at Plombières in 1858, where they agreed that France would help Piedmont against Austria, and after Cavour had manoeuvred Austria into the position of an aggressor Napoleon fulfilled his promise. With Austria defeated at Magenta and Solferino the central states of Italy joined themselves to Piedmont, but Cavour had to cede Savoy and Nice to France and leave Venetia in Austrian hands. In 1860 GARIBALDI invaded Sicily, marched to Naples and appeared to be about to invade Rome, whereupon Cavour, sensing that this would provoke an international crisis, persuaded his king, Victor Emmanuel II, to accompany Piedmontese troops through the Papal States into Neapolitan territory. Garibaldi then agreed to hand over his conquests to Victor Emmanuel, and when Cavour died a few months later the unity of the greater part of Italy had been achieved.

Woodcut from a book on chess printed by Caxton c. 1483

CAXTON, William (c. 1422–91), the first English printer, was born at Tenterden, Kent, and was apprenticed to the cloth trade. As a youth he went to Bruges, in Flanders, where he prospered, becoming the chief English merchant in the Low Countries and negotiator of commercial treaties. In about 1471 he became commercial adviser to the Duchess Margaret, sister of EDWARD IV and wife of Charles of Burgundy. Their mutual interest in books took him to Cologne to investigate the new art of printing developed by GUTENBERG, and in 1474 or 1475 Caxton himself translated and printed his first book, a French romance called *The Recuyell of the Historyes of Troye*. His second printed work was *The Game and Playe of Chesse*. In 1476 he set up as a printer in Westminster and thereafter he published some ninety books, including Chaucer's *Canterbury Tales* and Malory's *Morte d'Arthur*.

CELTS were an ancient people whose original homeland was in central Europe, east of the Rhine. From about the 7th century BC they spread into Italy, Spain and Gaul. A great wave of Celts invaded Italy in about 400 BC, sacked ROME and passed into Greece and Asia Minor. La Tène, a 5th-century BC Iron Age settlement on Lake Neuchâtel, Switzerland, has given its name to the La Tène culture, whose Celtic ornaments, weapons and art-styles have been found from Hungary to Britain.

Numbers of Celtic tribes reached Britain and are generally known as Ancient Britons. They were tall, fair-haired people, who dressed in a sleeved blouse and trousers fitting close to the ankle, with a tartan plaid fastened with a brooch. They loved jewellery, music and poetry; were expert metal-workers and good farmers.

Much given to tribal warfare, they fought with swords, daggers, javelins, bows, slings and two-wheeled chariots. The Celts of Gaul and Belgium wore plated armour or chainmail coats. Priests, known as Druids, performed magical ceremonies in which groves of oak-trees and the mistletoe played significant parts. Celtic languages have survived as Welsh, Manx, Cornish, Breton, Irish and Gaelic.

The capture of Cetewayo

CETEWAYO (died 1884), last of the Zulu kings, led armed resistance to the whites in South Africa. In the Zulu War of 1879 his warriors defeated the British at Isandhlwana and Rorke's Drift, but he was decisively beaten at Ulundi. Captured and sent to Cape Town, he was taken to England for a brief period, but was permitted to return to a portion of his kingdom in 1883. Enemies among his own people soon drove him out and he died shortly afterwards at Eshowe.

CHAMPLAIN, Samuel de (1567–1635), the French explorer and first Governor of French Canada, served in the army of HENRY IV and made a voyage to Central America before making his first expedition to Canada in 1603. At once he made friends with the Indians and explored part of the St Lawrence river. In 1608 he chose the site for Quebec and gave the city its name; then, with the Algonquin and Huron Indians, he discovered the lake that bears his name and helped his friends to defeat the Iroquois.

Encouraged by his royal patron, he continued his explorations, ascended the Ottawa River and mapped Lake Huron and Lake Ontario. Later he sent younger men to continue his work and to learn Indian ways and languages. Each year he returned to France to seek help for the colony, but in 1629 Quebec was taken by the British and Champlain was sent as a prisoner to England. When Canada was restored to the French in 1633, he returned to Quebec and died there two years later. In addition to his achievements as a pioneer and an explorer, Champlain was an accomplished writer, whose descriptions of his adventures were published after his death in six volumes.

CHANCELLOR, Richard (died 1556), a young sea-captain, was briefed by old Sebastian CABOT for a voyage in search of the North-East Passage. In 1553 he sailed in the *Edward Bonaventure* with two other ships of the Merchant Adventurers Company under the overall command of Sir Hugh Willoughby. A storm separated the ships and Chancellor alone reached the agreed rendezvous. Unknown to him Willoughby had perished, but Chancellor entered the White Sea and reached Archangel. A journey by sledge took him to Moscow, where he was received by the Tsar IVAN the Terrible, who agreed to open trade with England.

Chancellor returned to London, where the Muscovy Company was formed to pursue this trade, but

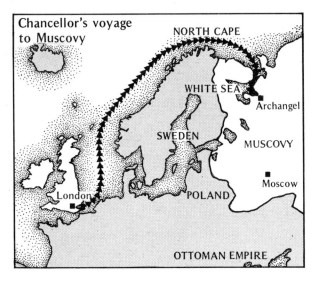

Chancellor's voyage to Muscovy

NORTH CAPE

WHITE SEA
Archangel

SWEDEN

MUSCOVY

Moscow

London

POLAND

OTTOMAN EMPIRE

Coin of Charlemagne

on his way home from a second voyage to Russia his ship was wrecked off the coast of Scotland and Chancellor was drowned.

CHARLEMAGNE (Charles the Great, c. 742–814), King of the Franks, was the son of Pepin the Short, whose realm included most of modern France and western Germany. In 772 Charles led a campaign against the heathen Saxons who had been raiding his borders, and for the next thirty years he was to be engaged in subduing these warlike tribesmen. In 773, at the request of Pope Hadrian I, he defeated the Lombard kingdom in northern Italy, but returned in 775 to deal with a Saxon rebellion and decided to convert the tribes by force. Missionaries baptized the pagans on pain of death and when they revolted under Witikind in 782 Charles took a terrible vengeance, massacring the nobles, dispersing tribes and extending his domains to the Elbe.

Earlier that year he had invaded Spain to attack the Saracens (see ISLAM), but during his withdrawal his rearguard suffered a disastrous defeat at Roncesvalles, where his knights Roland and Oliver perished. Eventually he fortified the frontier and obtained a strip of territory called the Spanish March. Bavaria was added to his possessions in 788 and, after that, the territory of the dreaded Hungarian Avars, whom he exterminated.

As champion of Christendom, he went to Rome in 799 to save Pope Leo III from his enemies and to restore him to the papal throne (see PAPACY). On Christmas Day 800 Leo crowned him Emperor of the HOLY ROMAN EMPIRE. For the next fourteen years Charles concentrated on ruling and touring his domains, which now stretched from Brittany to the Elbe, from the North Sea to the Mediterranean. He divided the Empire into counties, each ruled by a count, and he also appointed envoys called *missi* to carry out tours of inspection.

A giant of a man, with colossal energy and a sharp inquisitive brain, he built churches, monasteries, schools and a splendid palace at Aachen, working ceaselessly to instil order and justice into his unruly subjects. Everything interested him, from peasant farming to religious debate, and he loved discussion with scholars like Alcuin, the English monk who became his chief adviser. During his long reign Charlemagne brought order and Christian culture to the West, but after his death the Empire, divided among his three sons, soon fell apart.

CHARLES I (1600–49), King of Great Britain (1625–49), succeeded his father JAMES I in 1625, the year in which he married the French princess Henrietta Maria. From his youth Charles was dominated by the unpopular Duke of Buckingham, after whose murder in 1628 he was increasingly influenced by his wife, a devoted but foolish woman.

Three parliaments were summoned and dissolved in the first four years of Charles's reign and then, for eleven years, he contrived to rule without one, raising money by various devices, and using the courts of the Star Chamber and High Commission to fine and punish his subjects. His own unpopularity was matched by that of his ablest supporters, Archbishop LAUD and Thomas Wentworth, later Earl of Strafford. Laud's attempt to impose the English Prayer Book on the Scots led to the COVENANTERS' protest and the Bishops' War of 1639. Charles was forced to call the Short Parliament. Its dissolution still left him with no money to pay off the victorious Scots, so the Long Parliament met to demand Strafford's death and Charles was

During the war Charles displayed personal courage but ruined every chance of victory by indecision and by his fatal tendency to accept the worst advice. After Naseby (1645) his cause was hopeless and he left Oxford to surrender to the Scots, who handed him over to Parliament. After several months of captivity he escaped to Carisbrooke Castle, but its governor kept him in close confinement. Nevertheless, he still hoped to renew the war with Scottish help, until CROMWELL speedily crushed these hopes and demanded the King's death.

At his trial Charles faced his accusers with superb dignity and he went bravely to the scaffold on 30 January 1649. The 'Royal Martyr', as he is often called, was a strange mixture; handsome, dignified, brave, a good husband and father, a lover of art and a sincere Christian, he was also a man whom no one could trust; he broke promises, betrayed his friends and only showed resolution when he had ruined his cause through double-dealing and hesitation.

CHARLES II (1630–85), King of Great Britain (1660–85), joined his mother in Paris towards the end of the CIVIL WAR, but after his father's execution he went to Scotland to be crowned King at Scone. With a motley army he marched into England, only to be completely defeated by CROMWELL at Worcester (1651). After many adventures he escaped to France and spent the next nine years wandering about in penniless exile. In 1660 the nation, weary of military despotism, welcomed him enthusiastically and he began his reign determined to enjoy himself and never to go on his 'travels' again. He married Catherine of Braganza in 1662.

His first government, 1660–7, under the Earl of Clarendon, avoided any great persecution of Cromwell's supporters but provided an intolerant religious settlement (the Clarendon Code). Parliament kept the King short of money and the country was humiliated in 1667, when the Dutch admiral de Ruyter destroyed shipping in the Medway (*see* DUTCH WARS). Two other disasters of this period were the Great Plague and the FIRE OF LONDON.

In 1670 Charles signed the secret Treaty of Dover with LOUIS XIV, agreeing to make war on the Dutch and to declare himself a Catholic, in return for a pension that made him independent of Parliament. After the inconclusive Third Dutch War (1672–4)

terrorized into agreeing to his execution. Laud was imprisoned and although Charles accepted all of Parliament's demands John PYM insisted on drawing up the Grand Remonstrance, a list of all the King's faults and illegal acts. By this time a King's Party had formed and Charles, emboldened, went in person to the House of Commons to arrest the Five Members who persistently opposed him. His failure to do so was the signal for both sides to prepare for hostilities and the CIVIL WAR broke out in August 1642.

peace was made with Holland and Charles's niece Mary married William of Orange.

At home Charles had to weather a stormy period, during which Parliament passed the Test Act (1673), excluding Roman Catholics from office, and the Earl of Shaftesbury led the hostile 'Country Party'. Anti-Catholic hysteria reached its peak during the affair of Titus OATES and the Popish Plot (1678–80), but Charles shrewdly bided his time until he was able to outmanoeuvre Shaftesbury and, with another subsidy from Louis, dissolve Parliament

and reign for the rest of his life without obstruction.

Charles was by far the ablest of the Stuarts. His indolent charm and innumerable love affairs concealed great intelligence and political skill. At heart an absolute monarch, he knew when to give way and when to act ruthlessly, and while he gave the impression of minding his own pleasures more than public business he left the country stronger and more prosperous than he had found it. He was a great sportsman, a lover of ships and a patron of science, navigation and architecture.

CHARLES V (1500–58), Holy Roman Emperor and King of Spain, was the son of Philip of Burgundy and Joanna, daughter of FERDINAND AND ISABELLA of Spain. As a child his father's death brought him the Netherlands (1506); at seventeen he was ruler of Spain, and at nineteen the death of his grandfather, the Emperor Maximilian, gave him the HOLY ROMAN EMPIRE.

His dominions were enormous, including as they did Spain, the Americas, part of Italy (Naples, Sicily, Sardinia), the Netherlands and the HAPS-

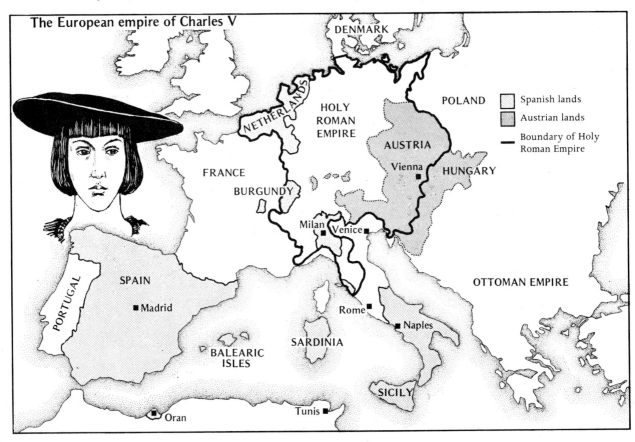

The European empire of Charles V

Spanish lands

Austrian lands

Boundary of Holy Roman Empire

BURG possessions in Germany and Austria. Thus he had to try to rule an empire of many races with different forms of government, and during his reign he had to contend with the enmity of France, the rise of Protestantism (*see* REFORMATION) and the menace of OTTOMAN (Turkish) power in Europe.

In the early part of Charles's reign he was at war with FRANCIS I of France, whom he defeated and captured at Pavia (1525). His troops sacked Rome and imprisoned Pope Clement VII, so that by 1529 (Peace of Cambrai) Charles was master of Italy. In 1535 he captured the pirate stronghold of Tunis, crushed a rising in the Netherlands in 1540 and was soon at war again with France. Having imposed the Treaty of Crespy (1544) on his enemy, he turned to deal with the German Protestants, who had formed the League of Schmalkald against him. Helped by Maurice of Saxony, he defeated the League at Mühlberg (1547), but Maurice later deserted him, so that by the religious peace of Augsburg (1555) he had to give up his gains and recognize the Protestant religion.

Disappointed and broken in health, Charles gave the Netherlands and Spain to his son PHILIP. He then resigned the imperial crown to his brother Ferdinand and retired to a monastery in Spain, where he spent the last three years of his life in complete seclusion.

CHARLES EDWARD STUART (1720–88), known as 'the Young Pretender' and 'Bonnie Prince Charlie', was the son of James, 'The Old Pretender', and grandson of James II. In 1744 he headed a projected invasion of England, which failed, and in the following year, without French support, he landed at Eriskay in the Hebrides with a few companions (*see* JACOBITE REBELLION OF 1745). His courage and youthful charm soon won over the Highland chiefs, and the clansmen flocked in when he raised his father's standard. On 17 September 1745 Edinburgh surrendered and Prince Charles held court at Holyrood. There followed the victory over Cope at Prestonpans and the march to England at the head of six thousand men. Though there was alarm in London, the English Jacobites did not rise, and at Derby the Highlanders refused to go any further. On the retreat northwards Charles beat the government forces at Falkirk, but the Duke of Cumberland pursued him into the Highlands and totally defeated

his army at Culloden Moor on 16 April 1746. For five months Charles lived as a hunted fugitive with a price of £30,000 on his head, but no one betrayed him and in September he reached safety in Brittany. He stayed in France until his expulsion in 1748 and later settled in Italy, where he died, a childless unhappy drunkard.

CHARTISTS were supporters, mainly working men, of a reform movement which arose in England in about 1838, though its origins went back to 18th-century radicalism. Workers had been disappointed that the 1832 Reform Act did not give the vote to the working class, and in 1838 the People's Charter was drawn up by members of the London Working Men's Association and six radical MPs. The Charter demanded six reforms: 1) Household suffrage, whereby the head of every household would have the vote, 2) secret ballot, 3) abolition of property qualification for MPs, 4) payment of MPs, 5) equal electoral districts, 6) annual parliaments.

Mass meetings were held and petitions to Parliament drawn up, but the movement was weakened by internal differences. One party, under William Lovett, believed in peaceful agitation, but the 'Physical Force Party', under Feargus O'Connor, advocated violence. The government imprisoned some of the leaders and Chartism died down until 1848, when O'Connor announced a great demonstration to be held on Kennington Common, with a procession and a monster petition to Parliament. The government banned the procession and the Duke of WELLINGTON posted troops to guard London, whereupon O'Connor gave way and the whole movement collapsed in ridicule.

Chartism disappeared partly because of improved conditions of labour and partly because its demands were granted (other than the one for annual parliaments) by various Reform Acts.

CHATHAM, Earl of (William Pitt the Elder, 1708–78), was educated at Eton and Oxford and as a young man became a cornet in the Dragoons. His military career was brief, for he entered Parliament, where he opposed Sir Robert WALPOLE and earned the dislike of GEORGE II for supporting Frederick Prince of Wales. This fact hampered his progress until 1746, when he became Paymaster-General of the forces, an office in which he distinguished himself by refusing the usual opportunities to make money. For his bitter attacks on the Newcastle-Fox coalition, he was dismissed in 1755, but the inefficiency of the Newcastle government after the outbreak of the SEVEN YEARS WAR led to him becoming Secretary of State, with the Duke of Devonshire as nominal head of government. The King soon found an excuse to dismiss Pitt, but with the country indignant and the war going badly it was impossible to form a government without him.

The solution was to let Newcastle control Parliament, while Pitt had a free hand to manage the war, and with enormous energy and self-confidence ('I know that I can save this country and no one else can') he took up the task of defeating France in a worldwide struggle.

Pitt's strategy was to strike hard and often at France, to wage war at sea in order to safeguard British interests in America and India and to support FREDERICK the Great in Europe with massive subsidies of gold. To carry out his aims, he personally appointed officers of his own choice, men like Amherst and WOLFE, Boscawen and Keppel; he replaced the Duke of Cumberland by the brilliant Ferdinand of Brunswick. His reward was a whole string of victories on the continent, at sea, in Canada and India, but at the zenith of his triumphs George II died, in 1760, and the new King, GEORGE III, wanted peace. Pitt therefore resigned and was granted a peerage as Earl of Chatham.

In opposition he grumbled about the terms of the Treaty of Paris (1763) and supported John WILKES and the American colonies in their fight against the Stamp Act. He returned to office for two years, but his health was too bad for him to be more than an absentee Prime Minister and he resigned in 1768. Though he opposed the war with the American colonies, he tottered into the House of Lords in 1778 to speak vigorously against granting them independence. Taken ill during his speech, he collapsed and died shortly afterwards.

Pompous and overbearing, Chatham was nevertheless one of Britain's greatest statesmen and orators; he combined outstanding administrative ability with honesty unusual at that time and the gift to inspire men. It was said 'No man ever entered his closet who did not feel himself braver at his return than when he went in'.

CHIANG KAI-SHEK (1887–1975), the Chinese statesman and general, was educated at military schools in China and Japan. He came under the influence of SUN YAT-SEN and took part in the 1911 Revolution, later becoming commander of the Whampoa Military Academy, where he trained officers on Russian lines. After Sun Yat-sen's death in 1925 he assumed leadership of the Kuomintang (People's National Party) and conducted successful campaigns against the war-lords, but he became increasingly hostile to the Communists in the Party

and in 1926 and 1927 took savage measures to destroy them. As a result MAO TSE-TUNG and a few survivors fled to the mountains to found the Red Army and plan their own revolution.

From 1928, as President of the Chinese Republic, Chiang achieved an uneasy unification of the country, but in the early 1930s he was still so occupied with the Communists and other rebellious subjects that he had no time to deal with the Japanese, who were extending their power in northern China. In 1936 Chiang was kidnapped at Sian, where he was persuaded to agree to co-operate with the Communists in resisting the invaders, but the Japanese succeeded in occupying all China's northern, eastern and southern provinces. Chiang retired to the west to continue the struggle as Commander-in-Chief, though once America and Japan were at war in the Pacific he tended to concentrate on keeping the Kuomintang forces intact instead of launching vigorous counter-attacks.

This inactivity and the dominance of corrupt right-wing elements weakened his appeal to the people, and in the Civil War which began in 1946 the Kuomintang steadily lost ground. In 1949 he resigned the presidency and went to Formosa (Taiwan), taking with him the Nationalist army, navy, and airforce. There he maintained himself with American help, while the Chinese mainland came completely under Communist rule.

CHINA: the Dynasties. Settlements dating from about 4000 BC have been excavated, while the so-called Painted Pottery culture occurred from about 2200 BC. Chinese history is supposed to begin with the *Hsia* dynasty (2205 BC to about 1765 BC), of which our knowledge is shadowy, but it was

followed by the *Shang* dynasty (*c.* 1765–*c.* 1027 BC), during which time a writing system developed.

Succeeding dynasties were as follows:

c. 1027–254 BC, *Chou*: a race of conquerors from the north-west. Emperors ruled the country; Confucius lived and taught; this feudal age ended with the Warring States period.

256–206 BC, *Ch'in*: Great Wall of China built.

206 BC–AD 220, HAN: a period of expansion when science and literature and art flourished.

AD 220–580, *'The Six Dynasties'*: China's Dark Ages.

580–618, *Sui*: the Emperor restored.

618–907, T'ANG: an age of brilliant achievement.

907–960, *'The Five Dynasties'*.

960–1279, SUNG: art, literature and printing flourished.

1279–1368, YÜAN or Mongol: expansion of commerce; Kublai Khan, MARCO POLO.

1368–1644, MING: a native dynasty noted for peaceful arts.

1644–1912, *Ch'ing* or Manchu, a dynasty of invaders from the north-west; expansion under K'ang Hsi, followed by penetration of China by Western powers and an era of decline.

1912, The first Republic.

CHRISTIANITY, its early development. The spread of Christianity outside Palestine began with the journeys and preaching of St Paul. The new religion advanced rapidly through Syria and Asia

Early Christian mosaic showing the Last Supper

Minor to Greece and Italy; it also reached Egypt at an early date. Belief in a saviour-god appealed to many people, especially to the poor and oppressed, but the early Christians had to suffer persecution because the Roman authorities regarded the religion as a dangerous superstition. They connected it with the Jewish rebellion and with opposition to accepted ideas, such as worship of the Emperor.

Persecution occurred in the reigns of NERO (54–68), Domitian (81–96) and TRAJAN (98–117) and then, after a period of quiet, thousands of Christians were put to death during the half century from about 250 to the abdication of Diocletian in 305. However, the Emperor CONSTANTINE became a Christian, granting religious freedom to all his subjects (313), and during the reign of Theodosius the Great (379–95) Christianity was made the state religion.

Despite persecution, Christianity had gone on spreading throughout the Empire and beyond, into lands of the so-called barbarians. It reached Britain, probably through Roman soldiers, as early as the 1st century and found its first martyr there in St Alban (c. 304). Christian churches were built and bishops appointed, but all were overwhelmed by the Anglo-Saxon (see SAXONS), except in Wales and parts of the west country, where the faith survived.

St PATRICK (c. 385–461), probably born on the borders of Wales, took Christianity to Ireland, where he established the Celtic church, and it was from Ireland that St Columba (563) went to Iona to convert Scotland. Thus Christians were worshipping God in Wales, Ireland and parts of Scotland years before St AUGUSTINE reached Canterbury (596). But St Augustine's mission, coming as it did from Rome, broke the isolation of the Church in Britain and led to it coming under the authority of the Pope. From Britain missionaries such as St Boniface (c. 675–754) went to Germany to convert the heathen.

In Western Europe Christianity survived the break-up of the Roman Empire, preserving learning, authority and culture. MONASTERIES of a kind existed from early times and in the 6th century St Benedict founded the Benedictine Order, which quickly established its 'houses' throughout the continent.

During the 8th century Christianity was threatened by two forces, Mohammedanism (ISLAM) and the heathen Saxons. However, in 732 Charles Martel, King of the Franks, beat the Saracens at Tours, and drove them back into Spain, while his grandson CHARLEMAGNE waged war on the Saxons for over thirty years (772–804), compelling them by force to adopt Christianity. By the second half of the 10th century the Christian Church was established throughout Europe, with the Pope's authority accepted by kings, bishops, abbots, monks and priests (see PAPACY). The long struggle between Pope and Emperor was yet to come.

CHURCHILL, Sir Winston Leonard Spencer (1874–1965), was the son of Lord Randolph Churchill and an American mother, Jennie Jerome. After doing badly at school, he managed to enter Sandhurst, and as a young officer saw active service in India and with the Nile Expeditionary Force of 1898, when he fought hand to hand at the battle of Omdurman. As a newspaper correspondent in the BOER WAR he was captured, but made a dramatic escape and returned to London a celebrity. He entered Parliament as a Conservative in 1900, but quarrelled with the party over tariff reform and joined the Liberals, with whom he held office as Colonial Under-Secretary (1906–8), President of the Board of Trade (1908–10), Home Secretary (1910–11), and First Lord of the Admiralty (1911–15). The fleet's excellent state of preparedness at the outbreak of the FIRST WORLD WAR was largely due to his vigorous naval policy. Made the scapegoat of the disastrous Dardanelles campaign of 1915, he resigned and joined the army in France. In 1917 LLOYD GEORGE, who had always recognized his ability, made him Minister of Munitions, where he was an outstanding success. Later, as Secretary for War, he was responsible for sending troops to aid the anti-BOLSHEVIK forces in Russia.

After Lloyd George's downfall Churchill disagreed with the Liberal Party's attitude to the minority Labour government and rejoined the Conservatives, becoming Chancellor of the Exchequer under Baldwin from 1924 to 1929. For the next ten years he was out of office and politically isolated owing to his fierce opposition to the official policy of granting self-rule to India, but he occupied his time painting, writing history and, after the rise of HITLER, warning the country of the danger of German rearmament. His career appeared to be finished until, on the outbreak of the SECOND WORLD WAR in 1939, the Prime Minister, Neville Chamberlain bowed to public demand and brought him back to the Admiralty.

In May 1940 Churchill, who had held almost every office of state, became Prime Minister at the age of sixty-five. For the next five years, through a period of unparalleled disasters to the achievement of final victory, he rose to every occasion with unfaltering courage and matchless oratory. Thanks to the radio he was able to speak directly to the people, and he gave Britain leadership such as she has never perhaps had in all her history. Among his most striking achievements were his realization of the strategic importance of the Middle East and Mediterranean operations and his friendship with F. D. ROOSEVELT, which made for the 'special relationship' between Britain and America. Despite his unchanged views on Communism, he pledged all possible aid to Russia when Hitler launched his invasion, and throughout the war this indomitable old man made journeys about the world to confer with fellow-leaders, besides visiting war fronts and scenes of disaster at home. As the war drew to its end, he realized more clearly than Roosevelt the true nature of STALIN's interest in the countries of Eastern Europe (see COLD WAR).

At the General Election of 1945 the electorate rejected the Conservatives, and the great leader went into opposition for the next six years. During this period he wrote his classic work *The Second World War*, saw his paintings hung in the Royal Academy and made his historic 'Iron Curtain' speech at Fulton, Missouri, where he warned the world of the Communist menace. He was Prime Minister again in 1951, but his health declined and he resigned in 1955, though he remained in Parliament until 1964. He died in the following year.

Often described in his lifetime as 'the greatest living Englishman', Churchill had faults; he was autocratic, often inflexible and difficult to work with, as his Service chiefs well knew, but he was also a rich and vivid personality, brave, generous-hearted, possessed of phenomenal energy and remarkable gifts. Above all, he loved his country and served it all his life.

Merchant ship in the heyday of the Cinque Ports

CINQUE PORTS were originally five ports of south-east England – Hastings, Romney, Hythe, Dover and Sandwich. To them were later added the 'ancient towns' of Rye and Winchelsea. Each Cinque Port, except Winchelsea, had a number of subordinate towns attached to it, called 'limbs'. From Edward the Confessor's time, their function was to provide ships for the defence of the realm; by Edward I's reign the number was 57 ships for 57 days without payment. In return the Cinque Ports had many privileges, including freedom from taxation, the right to make their own by-laws and to seize anything of value cast up by the sea. The highest officer was the Lord Warden, who was also Constable of Dover Castle, with his official residence at Walmer Castle.

Creation of a regular navy in Tudor times lessened the importance of the Cinque Ports, but they retained some of their privileges for many years and returned sixteen members to Parliament until as late as 1835. The ancient courts of Shepway, Brotherhood and Guestling still meet and the Lord Warden still exercises certain powers, but the appointment is now purely a mark of honour. King George VI appointed CHURCHILL Lord Warden of the Cinque Ports in 1941.

CIVIL WAR, American (1861–5). The causes of this tragic conflict lay in the deep-seated antagonism between the cotton-growing, slave-owning Southern States of America and the increasingly industrialized Northern States. Northerners disliked SLAVERY; some wanted it totally abolished and many felt that it should not be introduced into the new territories being opened up in the West. The South relied on slave labour and feared that the thrusting energetic Northerners would dominate the United States both politically and in economics. In 1860 the election of Abraham LINCOLN as President, a Republican opposed to extension of slavery, caused South Carolina to leave the Union. Six other states (Mississippi, Florida, Alabama,

Georgia, Louisiana and Texas) followed suit to form the Southern Confederacy, with Jefferson DAVIS as President. To preserve the Union by force of arms Lincoln called for 75,000 volunteers, and the war began in April 1861 when Confederate forces captured Fort Sumter.

For four years eleven Southern states, with a population of 9 million (of whom one third were Negroes), fought twenty-three Northern (Federal) states, whose population totalled 22 million. The North possessed far greater resources in wealth, raw materials, shipping, railways and industrial capacity, while the South had practically no industry or skilled workers. However, initially at least, they had the better commanders, a tradition of military service and tremendous determination and endurance.

Much of the war took place in the state of Virginia, where the Confederate forces, commanded by two soldiers of genius, Robert E. LEE and 'Stonewall' JACKSON, generally concentrated upon holding Richmond, their capital. In a number of battles, Bull Run, the Seven Days, Antietam, Chancellorville and Fredericksburg, the Confederate armies held or defeated their opponents, but the North with superiority in manpower and materials could

Ironclads on the Mississippi shelling a Confederate post. They were used by Grant to support his forces.

replace their heavy losses and, thanks to Lincoln's steadfastness, surmount their many setbacks.

Meanwhile, in the west the Union general Ulysses GRANT won many successes, and after Admiral FARRAGUT had captured New Orleans the South lost control of the whole of the Mississippi. At sea, despite Confederate raiders, the Union navy held control and prevented war materials from Europe reaching the South in significant quantity. In 1863 General Lee advanced north of Washington and Lincoln sent General Meade to intercept him. They met at GETTYSBURG, where in an indecisive battle Lee lost a third of his splendid army. This was the turning point. The Southerners could not make good their losses but they fought on, and in a series of desperate battles in Virginia inflicted terrible damage upon Grant's armies. Meanwhile, the Union general Sherridan devastated the Shenandoah Valley and Sherman marched through Georgia, destroying everything in his path. When the Confederates were forced to abandon Richmond, the end had come and Lee surrendered to Grant at Appomattox on 9 April 1865.

In many ways the American Civil War was the forerunner of 'modern' wars. In the deployment of troops, cavalry and artillery there was little change from Wellington's day, but in the use of railways and the electric telegraph, in the involvement of civilians, in the intensity of hatred, in the numbers of troops and the appalling casualties, this was a modern war. Both sides introduced conscription, the North enlisting 2 million men, while, from a smaller population, the South enlisted between 700,000 and a million. Close order fighting and improved rifles caused heavy casualties (over 500,000 died in the war) and this led to increasing use of trenches.

CIVIL WAR, English (1642–9), between Royalists and Parliament, began when CHARLES I raised his standard at Nottingham on 22 August 1642. The first major battle took place at *Edgehill*, where the Earl of Essex barred the King's route to London; the battle was drawn and Charles withdrew to Oxford, which remained his headquarters until 1646. Essex and the train bands of London stopped a Royalist advance on the capital at *Turnham Green*.

In 1643 the Royalists planned to capture London by a three-pronged attack; the Earl of Newcastle would drive down from the north, Sir Ralph Hopton

A Royalist cavalry regiment with its colonel's standard

would come from the south-west and the King from Oxford. The plan almost succeeded. Newcastle beat Lord Fairfax and his sons at *Adwalton Moor*, Hopton beat Waller at *Roundway Down* and Prince RUPERT captured Bristol. The Royalists held all the north and the west, except Hull and Gloucester; East Anglia stood firm for Parliament and the year ended with the indecisive battle of *Newbury*, where Essex extricated his army from a tight corner.

By now Parliament had made an alliance with the Scots, and in 1644 the Royalist fortunes declined. The Scots and the Fairfaxes besieged York, which Rupert daringly relieved, but then rashly offered battle at *Marston Moor*. CROMWELL's cavalry and Scottish pikemen won an overwhelming victory and the north was lost to the King. In the west, however, Essex lost most of his army at *Lostwithiel* and Charles won the second battle of *Newbury*.

These setbacks brought Cromwell to the fore as a stern critic of his fellow-commanders. Through his urging the New Model Army was formed and he got rid of soldiers like Essex through the Self-Denying Ordinance, which barred peers and MP's from holding army commands. Fairfax nevertheless made Cromwell head of the cavalry and at *Naseby* (June 1645) Parliament won a decisive victory and this was followed by further success at *Langport*, while Rupert surrendered Bristol. After the Scots had cleared the north and Cromwell mopped up in the south, Oxford fell in June 1646 and the King fled to the Scots at Newark. They handed him over to Parliament and thus ended the First Civil War.

Through 1647 Parliament and the Army tried to come to terms with Charles, whose policy was to play off one side against the other, while he got in touch with the Scots, promising to introduce Presbyterianism into England in return for their support, which would be helped by a Royalist uprising. When he got wind of these plans, Cromwell acted swiftly ; Royalist risings were crushed by the New Model Army, while he defeated the Scots at *Preston*. There was now, in his opinion, only one way to deal with the King, and on 30 January 1649 Charles was beheaded in Whitehall. The Civil War had ended and the victor was not Parliament, but Cromwell and the Army.

CLEMENCEAU, Georges (1841–1929), French statesman, took a medical degree and studied in the USA before entering national politics, where he made a reputation as a radical. So fierce was he in debate and so adept at bringing about the fall of ministries that he became known as 'the Tiger'. As Premier of France, 1906–9, he introduced social reforms and took a firm attitude towards Germany, whom he had never forgiven for annexing Alsace-Lorraine in 1871 at the conclusion of the FRANCO-PRUSSIAN WAR. After 1914 he was a strong critic of the way the war was being run, and when he became Premier and Minister of War in 1917 he revived failing morale and inspired France to resist the final German onslaught. As president of the Peace Conference, he played a large part in dictating the terms of the Treaty of VERSAILLES, yet he did not manage to satisfy those Frenchmen who wanted still harsher terms. Thus he resigned in 1920 and spent his retirement writing his memoirs.

CLAUDIUS (10 BC–AD 54), Roman Emperor from AD 41 to 54 (*see* ROME), was the nephew of the Emperor Tiberius. A sickly, neglected child, he devoted himself to study and writing, but after the murder of Caligula, who had succeeded Tiberius, the Praetorian Guard found Claudius in hiding and proclaimed him emperor. He showed unexpected energy and ability, extending citizenship to provincials and improving administration and the city of Rome. He resumed Caligula's plan for the conquest of Britain and himself visited the island shortly after its invasion by Aulus Plautius. Claudius died from poison, which, it was said, was administered to him by his wife Agrippina.

CLEOPATRA was the name of many queens of Egypt, of whom the best-known was the daughter of PTOLEMY XI. Born in about 69 BC, she became at seventeen joint ruler of Egypt with her brother Ptolemy XII. Two years later, driven out by his guardians, she had taken refuge on the borders of Syria when she first met JULIUS CAESAR. Fascinated by her beauty, he made war on her behalf, defeated and killed Ptolemy and restored her to the throne with a younger brother. She soon got rid of him by poison and went to Rome to live with Caesar until his murder in 44 BC, when she returned to Egypt with their son Caesarion. In the civil war that followed this masterful woman became the ally and mistress of Mark ANTONY, but Octavian (later Caesar AUGUSTUS) defeated them at Actium and Antony committed suicide. Cleopatra then tried to win over Octavian, but failing to do so and in order to avoid being taken captive to Rome she killed herself in 30 BC by placing an asp in her bosom.

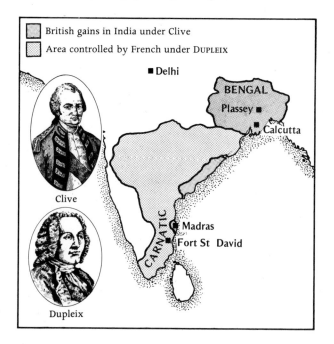

British gains in India under Clive

Area controlled by French under DUPLEIX

Clive

Dupleix

CLIVE, Lord Robert (1725–74), the founder of British India, was born in Shropshire, where his wild behaviour in boyhood caused his despairing family to send him to India as a clerk in the EAST INDIA COMPANY. At Madras, bored and lonely, he became so depressed that he twice attempted suicide.

Rivalry between the French and British East India Companies was intense, and when the SEVEN YEARS WAR broke out in Europe the fighting spread to India. The French made good progress and captured Madras in 1746; Clive was taken prisoner but he escaped to Fort St David, where he joined the Company's army and quickly showed that he was a born soldier. Promoted captain, he proposed a plan to relieve the beleaguered British garrison at Trinchinopoli by making a diversionary attack on Arcot, capital of the Carnatic. With only 500 soldiers he captured the town and held it for fifty-three days against a French and Indian army of 10,000 men. This feat restored British prestige and turned the tide of war in their favour.

Clive returned to England a hero, but he soon spent the fortune he had made and in 1756 was back in India as Governor of Fort St David. Learning that Surajah Dowlah, the new Nawab of Bengal, had captured Calcutta, he marched north to retake the town and to win the brilliant victory of Plassey (June 1757) against enormous odds. He then dethroned Surajah Dowlah in favour of Mir Jaffa, who paid him nearly £250,000.

From 1757 to 1760 Clive was Governor of Bengal and again from 1765 to 1767, when he restored a troubled situation and by firm rule put an end to widespread corruption. Bengal passed under British control, but Clive had made many enemies among Company officials and he came home to face charges of dishonesty.

Though the enquiry found that he had made a fortune by dubious means, Parliament resolved that he had rendered 'great and meritorious services to this country'. Clive, however, had become ill and depressed during the proceedings and he committed suicide in 1774, when only forty-nine years of age.

COLD WAR is the name given to the hostility, just short of outright warfare, which has existed between the two super-powers, the USA and the Soviet Union, since the end of the SECOND WORLD WAR. The Cold War can be said to have begun in 1945 at the Potsdam Conference, when the three leaders of the Allied powers, STALIN, President Truman and CHURCHILL (who was succeeded by ATTLEE), met to discuss the shape of the world after the war. On almost every question – in particular Poland, treatment of Germany and the administration of Berlin – there was virtually no agreement. As Soviet-installed puppet governments took over power in Poland, Hungary, Czechoslovakia, Rumania, Bulgaria and East Germany, the USA and her allies ('the West') began to take steps to try to halt the spread of COMMUNISM. In most cases this took the form of massive financial help to rebuild shattered economies and to lay the foundations of prosperity in emergent countries.

Among important happenings of the Cold War have been the Marshall Plan, which from 1948 distributed millions of dollars to aid recovery in Europe, the Berlin Airlift (1948), when the Western Allies flew supplies into occupied Berlin after the Russians had cut land routes from West Germany,

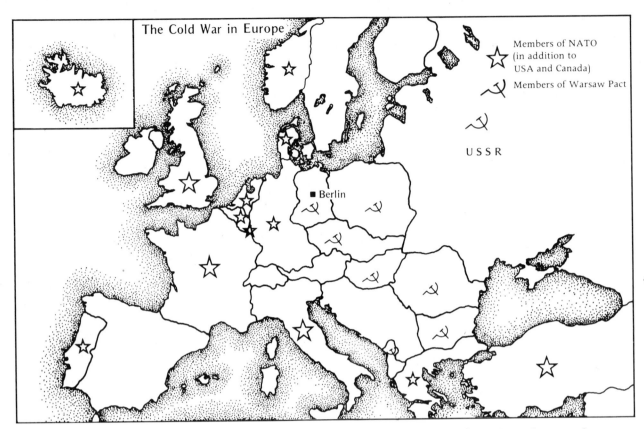

The Cold War in Europe

Members of NATO
(in addition to
USA and Canada)

Members of Warsaw Pact

USSR

Berlin

and the formation of NATO (North Atlantic Treaty Organization) by the West as a defence against aggression. The Soviet Union countered these moves with the Cominform, an information bureau to spread propaganda and organize Communist activities, and the Warsaw Pact (1955). This latter was a treaty of mutual defence among Communist countries.

In Asia American help to CHIANG KAI-SHEK could not stay the triumph of MAO TSE-TUNG and the Communists, but in the KOREAN WAR (1950–3) the Communist invaders from the North were driven back. When Hungary (1956) and Czechoslovakia (1968) attempted to rid themselves of Soviet domination, Russian troops speedily crushed those who had been bold enough to demand freedom.

The Cold War came perilously close to real warfare in 1962, when the Russians began to instal nuclear missile bases on the island of Cuba, only 130 miles (210 km) from the American mainland. The situation was extremely tense, but at the eleventh hour the Russian leader KRUSHCHEV came to an agreement with President KENNEDY and the missile sites were dismantled.

From time to time efforts have been made to ease the tension between the two great powers and their allies and to agree to coexist peaceably. By the mid-seventies, however, the Cold War with its moves, countermoves and ceaseless propaganda, showed little sign of abating.

COLUMBUS, Christopher (c. 1446–1506), was born in Genoa, the son of a wool-carder. He went to sea at about the age of fourteen and made a number of voyages, one of which may have been to Iceland. In 1477 he was wrecked on the coast of Portugal and went to live in Lisbon, where he found work as a chartmaker.

For a number of years he had believed that Asia could be reached by sailing westward and he put his theory to King John II of Portugal in the hope of being provided with a fleet. The King was interested, but a committee of geographers rejected the project, so Columbus moved to Spain to seek support there at the court of FERDINAND AND ISABELLA. Though he obtained an introduction to Queen Isabella and aroused the interest of influential people, he could not get a definite offer of help

and, in despair, he sent messages to HENRY VII of England and to the French court, but without result.

After seven years his luck changed and on 3 August 1492 he set out from Spain, in command of the *Santa Maria*, 100 tons, and two caravels, the *Pinta* of 50 tons and the *Niña* of 40 tons. Queen Isabella granted him governorship of all lands he might discover and the title Admiral of the Ocean Sea. The little fleet reached the Canaries on 6 September and thence sailed westward. Columbus had underestimated the world's circumference and had overestimated the size of Asia, so the voyage took longer than he had anticipated and he had to soothe his frightened crews and deceive them by concealing the distance sailed.

However, on 12 October, the New World was sighted. It proved to be an island in the Bahamas, which Columbus named San Salvador and he went ashore to claim it for the King and Queen of Spain. Convinced that he had reached the fringe of China, Columbus sailed on and discovered Cuba and Hispaniola, but, after the *Santa Maria* went aground, he decided to return to Spain in the *Niña*.

Received with enthusiasm and loaded with honours, he at once made plans for a second expedition and set out again in September 1493. This time

he discovered Jamaica and other islands but the task of governing quarrelsome, greedy colonists proved too much for him and he was back in Spain in 1496. A third voyage took him to Trinidad and the mainland of South America, but again he fell foul of the colonists; a governor was sent out to supersede him and he himself came home in chains. Restored to favour, he made his fourth and last voyage in 1502, when he explored the Gulf of Mexico and landed at Honduras, Costa Rica and Panama. He died at Valladolid in Spain, moderately wealthy and still convinced that he had reached Asia.

COMBINATION ACTS were passed in 1799 and 1800, during PITT's premiership, to prevent workmen from combining together in trade unions, even if their object were merely to gain better wages and hours. These acts did not create new offences, but strengthened old laws against 'combination' and were intended to make it easier to enforce the law. They were passed because of general alarm at the spread of revolutionary ideas. In 1824, through the efforts of Francis Place and Joseph Hume, the Combination Acts were repealed, so that it became legally possible to organize trade unions.

COMMUNISM may have existed in certain forms, e.g. in religious communities, in early times, but in modern terms it dates from the publication of the *Communist Manifesto* of 1848. This was a political pamphlet written by Karl MARX and his friend Frederick Engels in London. Its influence spread throughout the 19th century, as it reached many countries and helped to found Communist parties and the international Communist movement.

The pamphlet, published first in German and later in English (1850), describes history as a class struggle and sees progress only when an exploited class overthrows its oppressor. Marx and Engels called for the overthrow of the capitalist system in Europe and its replacement by a system in which workers would own and control the means of producing wealth. There would emerge a society in which wealth would be shared according to the principle 'from each according to his ability, to each according to his needs'.

The first Communist revolution came, not as Marx had expected in an industrial country, but in Russia in 1917 (*see* RUSSIAN REVOLUTION).

Although Communist parties were founded in many countries between the wars and were quite strong in Spain, France and Italy, Communism had no significant success outside Russia until after the Second World War. In differing forms Communist regimes have been set up in practically every country of eastern Europe and also in China, North Korea, Vietnam and Cuba (*see* COLD WAR). In Communist theory the state is seen to be the enemy of human freedom, but in practice all aspects of life appear to come under state control.

CONSTANTINE the Great (*c.* 288–337), the first Christian Emperor of ROME, was acclaimed emperor at York by the soldiers after the death of his father Constantius (306). He had to overcome a number of rivals before being recognized by the Eastern Emperor Licinius. After a long period of uneasy peace, he defeated Licinius in 314 to become sole emperor. The principal events of his reign were his conversion to CHRISTIANITY in about 312, his grant of toleration to Christianity throughout the Empire, the Council of Nicea (325), which unified the Church, and the founding of Constantinople (*see* BYZANTINE EMPIRE), completed in 330.

COOK, James (1728–79), British naval captain and explorer, was born in Yorkshire of poor parents, who apprenticed him to a haberdasher. He soon changed his trade and at fifteen was at sea in a Whitby collier that carried coals to London. He rose to become mate and in 1755 joined the Royal Navy, where he made his mark as surveyor of the St Lawrence River, prior to Wolfe's capture of Quebec.

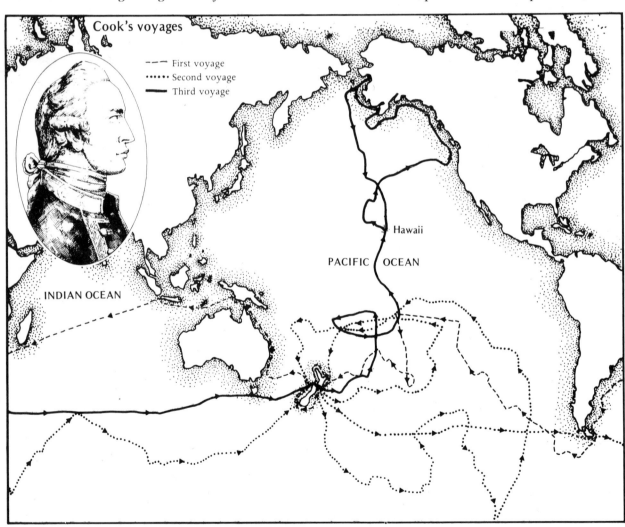

Cook's voyages

--- First voyage
····· Second voyage
— Third voyage

INDIAN OCEAN

PACIFIC OCEAN

Hawaii

In 1768 he was given command of an expedition to Tahiti to observe the transit of the planet Venus, after which he charted the coasts of New Zealand, explored the eastern coast of Australia from Botany Bay northwards, narrowly escaped disaster when his ship, the *Endeavour*, was holed on the Great Barrier Reef, and reached England after three years. On this voyage he lost more than a third of his crew from scurvy and Cook, a stern but humane commander, afterwards compelled his sailors to adopt a diet which included fresh fruit and vegetables and to obey strict rules about cleanliness on board.

In 1772–5 Cook spent three years exploring the south Pacific; he sailed far into Antarctic waters and revisited New Zealand, before returning home without the loss of one man through scurvy.

His third great voyage began in 1776, when with the *Resolution* and the *Discovery* he sailed to New Zealand, Tahiti and the Sandwich Islands, before turning north to California and into the Arctic Ocean in vain quest of a North-West Passage. Back in the Pacific, he revisited Hawaii, which he had discovered in the outward voyage. Friendly relations were established with the natives, but when Cook went ashore to investigate the theft of a ship's boat, a dispute arose and, as he was about to be taken off to his ship, he was struck down and killed.

COPERNICUS, Nicolas (1473–1543), the founder of modern astronomy, was born in East Prussia, then a part of Poland. Brought up by his uncle, a bishop, he studied at the universities of Cracow and Bologna, lectured in mathematics at Rome and studied medicine in Padua. Although never a priest, he became a cathedral canon, besides acting as doctor and general assistant to his uncle. His favourite study was astronomy and he arrived at his theory that the sun is the centre of the planetary system in 1530. His book *De Revolutionibus*, which sets out his theories, was published in the year of his death.

CORN LAWS in Britain, controlling the import and export of grain, date back to Edward III's reign. Export was generally forbidden, but in the latter part of the 17th century bounties were given to farmers to encourage production and Britain often sold surplus corn abroad. During the French Wars (1793–1815), when it was difficult to buy foreign corn, prices rose high and farm rents followed. At the end of the war farmers and landlords were alarmed by the prospect of cheap imported corn, so Parliament (dominated by aristocratic landlords, whose wealth depended on farm rents) passed the Corn Law of 1815. Foreign corn could not be imported until the home price of wheat reached 80 shillings a quarter, a high level that caused distress to the poor, since their staple food was bread. From 1828 the Corn Laws were changed to allow import below the 80 shilling level on a sliding scale of duties.

Agitation mounted and the Anti-Corn Law League was formed in 1838 to campaign for the repeal of laws which not only affected the poor but harmed trade, since other countries needed to sell grain to Britain in order to buy her manufactured goods. Generally speaking, the Whigs were for repeal, while the Tories opposed it; the most famous Anti-Corn Law spokesmen were Richard Cobden and John Bright. The Tory Prime Minister PEEL gradually became a convert to Free Trade, and the Irish potato famine of 1845 (when the corn crop in England was ruined by a wet summer) convinced him that he must open the ports to foreign grain. In 1846 he announced the repeal of the Corn Laws, thereby earning the hatred of his own party. In fact

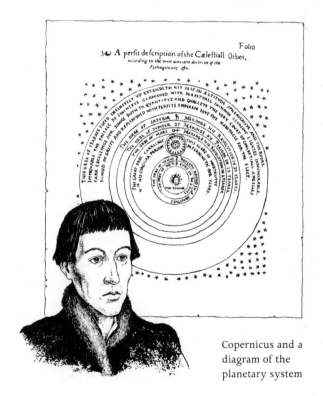

Copernicus and a diagram of the planetary system

61

The meeting of Cortes and Montezuma

the effect of repeal was not dramatic, for corn prices fell only slightly and farming did not suffer the ruin that had been forecast.

CORTES, Hernando (1485–1547), the conqueror of Mexico, was born in Spain and went to Hispaniola in the West Indies as a young man. He distinguished himself in the conquest of Cuba and was chosen to lead an expedition to the then unknown country of Mexico. In 1519 he set out with about five hundred adventurers, whose firearms were to give them a decisive advantage over their adversaries, and he also had cannons, mastiff dogs and sixteen horses, all terrifying to the Mexicans.

After burning his ships at Vera Cruz to convince his men there was no turning back, Cortes advanced inland, defeating the Tlaxcalans and then making an alliance with them against the AZTECS. At Tenochtitlan (Mexico City), the Aztec capital, he was welcomed by the Emperor Montezuma, who believed the Spaniard to be a god named Quetzalcoatl whom he was powerless to resist. Cortes captured the Emperor and began to rule, but when he went back to the coast to deal with a rival expedition the Aztecs rebelled. He returned to lead a desperate retreat from the city and then raised an army from neighbouring tribes, built a fleet of ships to cross the lake that protected Tenochtitlan and in 1521 attacked and destroyed the capital.

Cortes governed Mexico for five years until enemies secured his recall to Spain; however, he returned to Mexico later, where he ruled his vast estates, explored the coastline and discovered Lower California in 1536. He returned to Spain in 1540 and died there, neglected, in 1547.

COVENANTERS were ardent supporters of the Presbyterian Church in Scotland. Their religion was based on the teachings of CALVIN and John KNOX. They got their name from the National Covenant of 1638, an oath or promise signed by multitudes of Scots who bound themselves to resist King CHARLES I's attempt to introduce a new Prayer Book in Scotland.

In 1643, during the CIVIL WAR, the Scots also signed the Solemn League and Covenant, agreeing to send an army to help Parliament against the King, while Parliament promised to establish the Presbyterian Church in England and Ireland. This promise was never kept.

After the Restoration of 1660 CHARLES II showed no intention of observing the Covenant; instead he restored the hated bishops and took away the right of congregations to choose their own ministers. In defiance the Covenanters held open-air meetings among the hills, and when fined for doing so and attacked by dragoons they took up arms in rebellion. In 1666 more than thirty were hanged and several hundreds were transported to Barbados to work on the sugar plantations.

These measures only intensified the Covenanters' stubborn defiance. Government troops tried to suppress the illegal meetings, but in 1679 the rebels murdered Archbishop Sharp and actually held Glasgow for a few days. They were then completely defeated by the Duke of MONMOUTH at Bothwell Brig. On the accession of the Catholic JAMES II of England in 1685 the Covenanters' plight became worse than ever, for their conduct was declared treasonable and yet another rebellion, led by the Earl of Argyll, failed miserably. However, the flight of James II in 1688 and the arrival in England of William of Orange (WILLIAM III) brought persecution to an end. The Presbyterian Church was restored and there was no further need for the Covenanters to defy the government.

CRANMER, Thomas (1489–1556), Archbishop of Canterbury, attracted HENRY VIII's attention when, as a don at Cambridge, he suggested that the question of the royal divorce might be put to the universities of Europe. Henry made him a royal chaplain and sent him abroad to Italy and Germany, but summoned him home to become Archbishop of Canterbury. In May 1533 Cranmer pronounced Catherine of Aragon's marriage to Henry null and void; later he annulled Henry's marriage to Anne Boleyn, divorced him from Anne of Cleves and

informed him that Catherine Howard was a sinner unworthy to remain his Queen.

Cranmer promoted the translation of the Bible and, although he personally did not support the dissolution of the monasteries, he agreed to all the measures which separated England from Rome, serving Henry with the utmost docility to the end of the King's life.

During the rein of EDWARD VI Cranmer moved along with the tide of the REFORMATION, being mainly responsible for the issue of the First English Prayer Book and for religious changes expressed in the Second Prayer Book. He had bishops imprisoned and, subservient as ever, he complied with the dying King's wish to divert the succession from MARY to Lady Jane GREY. On Mary's accession he was arrested, tried for treason and condemned to death, but first he was made to sign a confession denying his Protestant beliefs. This he did, but as his end drew near he took back the denial and at the stake bravely thrust into the fire his right hand that had signed the confession.

British infantry at the Battle of Alma

CRIMEAN WAR (1854–6) arose out of the so-called 'Eastern Question'. European powers, principally France and Britain, became alarmed at the prospect of Russian expansion to the Mediterranean at the expense of Turkey, then ruler of most of the Balkans. A Franco-Russian quarrel over the Holy

Places in Palestine caused Tsar Nicholas I to proclaim himself protector of Christians in the Turkish Empire and to send troops to occupy two Turkish provinces at the mouth of the Danube. In March 1854 France and Britain declared war on Russia.

The campaign, confined to a small area round the port of Sevastopol on the Black Sea, was remarkable for the blunders of the military commanders and for the bravery of ill-equipped, inexperienced troops. The Allies laid siege to Sevastopol and repulsed Russian attempts to relieve the port at Balaclava (where the Charge of the Light Brigade took place) and Inkerman. The British soldiers suffered great hardships from cold and disease until Florence NIGHTINGALE reorganized the military hospital at Scutari and PALMERSTON (who had succeeded Lord Aberdeen as Prime Minister) brought a more energetic direction to the war effort. In September 1855 Sevastopol was captured and the new Tsar, Alexander II, agreed to make peace.

By the Treaty of Paris Turkey kept her European possessions and promised to protect her Christian subjects, while Russia agreed that the Black Sea should be closed to warships. These results had no permanent value, but NAPOLEON III had gained the military 'glory' he wanted and CAVOUR, by bringing Piedmont into the war, won a seat at the peace conference and Napoleon III's friendship. Thus, with French support, he was soon to realize his ambition to free Italy from Austrian rule.

CROMWELL, Oliver (1599–1658), was born in Huntingdon, the son of a country squire. As a young man he became an ardent Puritan, and after marrying a merchant's daughter he entered Parliament in 1628. During the eleven years when no parliament met he lived quietly at home, but took his seat in the Long Parliament of 1640. There, through his fervent speeches, this plain man in sober ill-fitting clothes emerged as a leader of the extreme Puritans. When the CIVIL WAR broke out, he helped to secure East Anglia for Parliament and fought at Edgehill as a captain of horse. With no previous military experience, he nevertheless saw the weakness of the parliamentary army and he went back to East Anglia to raise and train a disciplined force of cavalry devoted to him, to the Bible and to Parliament's cause. At Marston Moor, 1644, Cromwell and his Ironsides turned defeat into victory. His criticisms of fellow-generals then led to

the formation of the New Model Army and at Naseby, 1645, he played a major part in destroying the Royalist infantry. He and Fairfax then cleared up pockets of resistance to bring the war to an end.

In the ensuing quarrel between Parliament and the Army, Cromwell took the Army's side, crushed a Royalist rising in Wales and defeated the Scots at Preston in 1648. Convinced that God's will required the execution of the King, he signed the death warrant that took CHARLES I to the scaffold.

The Irish campaign of 1649 left a terrible stain on Cromwell's reputation. At his orders hundreds were put to the sword at Drogheda and Wexford and this merciless cruelty can only be explained by his fanatical conviction that he was God's servant sent to root out Roman Catholicism. Next he destroyed CHARLES II's alliance with the Scots by his victories at Dunbar and Worcester (1651). He was now the most powerful man in England and in 1653, having lost patience with the corrupt Rump Parliament, he forcibly dissolved the House and replaced it with an assembly known as Barebone's Parliament. When this proved unworkable, the Army drew up the Instrument of Government to make Cromwell Lord Protector. After quarrelling with his first Parliament, he put the country under the rule of eleven major-generals, but they proved so unpopular that he called a second Parliament, which offered him the crown. This he refused, though for the remainder of his life he was in fact king in all but name. Although he introduced a measure of religious toleration, restored order and encouraged trade, his rule was mainly unsuccessful, for it rested upon force and he, the one-time Parliament-man, had become a greater tyrant than Charles I had ever dared to be.

In foreign affairs he pursued a vigorous policy, trying to form a Protestant League of Europe, capturing Jamaica and winning victories in Flanders and at sea against Spain, so that England became respected abroad as she had not been since Tudor times. The strain and difficulties of his position told heavily on Cromwell's health; he had a morbid fear of assassination and the death of his favourite daughter grieved him deeply. He had striven earnestly for his country's welfare but he knew he had failed to establish a system that would last and he died, worn out and dispirited, on 3 September 1658.

A crusader dedicates himself to God's service

CRUSADES. The First Crusade was proclaimed in 1095 by Pope Urban II, who called on Christian princes to recover Palestine from the SELJUK TURKS. The People's Crusade, made up of thousands of peasants, set off under Peter the Hermit and other popular leaders, only to perish on the way. Meanwhile, four feudal armies from France, Germany and Italy crossed into Asia Minor and fought their way into Palestine, where they captured JERUSALEM in 1099. Four Christian states were set up – the Kingdom of Jerusalem, the County of Tripoli, the Principality of Antioch and the County of Edessa – in which the leading Crusaders became feudal landlords, ruling large estates.

The Second Crusade (1147–9) set out after the Turks had overrun Edessa in 1144. Louis VII of France and Conrad III of Germany suffered heavy losses in Asia Minor, and after they failed to capture Damascus the Crusade petered out.

A new Muslim leader arose in the person of SALADIN, who defeated the Crusader knights and took Jerusalem in 1187. Pope Gregory VIII then proclaimed the Third Crusade, whose leaders, PHILIP AUGUSTUS of France, the Emperor Frederick Barbarossa and RICHARD I of England, set out for Palestine by different routes. Barbarossa was drowned in Asia Minor and Richard, after many delays, eventually joined Philip at Acre. The city was captured in 1191, but quarrels between the French and the English caused Philip to withdraw his forces and return to France. Richard defeated Saladin at Arsuf but was not strong enough to recapture Jerusalem. Having made a truce, he departed for England, leaving the Crusaders in possession of little more than a coastal strip of Palestine.

The Fourth Crusade (1202–4), raised by Pope INNOCENT III, was a disgrace to Christianity. An army from France and Flanders, destined to be shipped from Venice to Egypt, was diverted to Constantinople. There the Crusaders became involved in a local quarrel, which resulted in them capturing and looting the city. Although this outrage tarnished the Crusader movement, an upsurge of religious fervour caused thousands of children from France and Germany to set off on the Children's Crusade of 1212. Many died on the way, were lost or sold into slavery and none ever reached Jerusalem.

The Fifth and Seventh Crusades were attempts to win back the Holy Land from Egypt, where LOUIS IX of France (Saint Louis) captured Damietta in 1249, but he was later defeated, made prisoner and ransomed. He embarked on the last Crusade in 1270, accompanied by Prince Edward, afterwards ED-WARD I of England. Louis died at Tunis and, although Edward reached Acre and fought there, the Crusade ended in failure.

In 1229, however, FREDERICK II of Germany had actually regained Jerusalem, more by cleverness than by force of arms, and had crowned himself King. However, he returned to Europe and the city was soon lost. The great Crusader fortress of Krak fell in 1271 and when the Sultan Al-Ashraf captured Acre in 1291, the crusading movement, apart from a few small expeditions, had come to its end.

Custer's Last Stand

CUSTER, George (1839–76), US general, served in the Federal army during the CIVIL WAR and won a reputation as a dashing cavalry leader. After the war he led an expedition that defeated the Cheyenne INDIANS, and in 1876 he was in South Dakota where the Sioux had been granted a reservation. Discovery of gold in the Black Hills brought white men flooding in and the Indians took up arms. Custer had advanced ahead of General Terry's army with a force of cavalry to Little Big Horn river, where he moved against what he thought was a small number of Indians. He met instead the main forces of the Sioux warriors under their chiefs Sitting Bull and Crazy Horse, who on 25 June slaughtered Custer and his column of 264 to a man. 'Custer's Last Stand' thereafter became one of the most celebrated incidents in American frontier history.

Persian soldiers from the time of Cyrus the Great

CYRUS the Great (*c.* 580–529 BC), founder of the PERSIAN EMPIRE, was king of the small vassal state of Ashan when in about 553 BC he rebelled and overthrew Astyges, King of the Medes. Opposed by a coalition of powers, including Egypt, Babylon and the city-states of Asia Minor, Cyrus defeated Croesus, the wealthy King of Lydia, and added western Asia Minor to his empire. He next destroyed the mighty state of BABYLON in a single campaign (539 BC) and permitted the Jews, whom NEBUCHADNEZZAR II had transported into captivity, to return to Palestine.

When he died in battle against nomad tribes of the East, his empire stretched from the Aegean and the borders of Egypt to the river Indus. As a conqueror, his success seems to have been due to his use of mounted archers supported by cavalry wings. His claim to greatness rests on the humanity with which he treated his subjects. He did not execute captive kings or destroy cities; he respected native customs, while to the Persians his memory was cherished as 'the father of the people'.

D

DAMPIER, William (1652–1715), the English mariner, was born in Somerset and went to sea at an early age, voyaging to Labrador, Jamaica and the East Indies and serving in Prince RUPERT's squadron against the Dutch. In the West Indies he joined the buccaneers and took part in piratical expeditions along the coasts of Central and South America. After many adventures he returned to England, published a book about his travels and was sent in 1699 by the Admiralty to explore the unknown land of Australia.

He reached the barren coast of Western Australia, but through lack of water sailed away from Dampier Bay to Timor. He explored the coast of New Guinea, gave his name to Dampier Strait and Archipelago and was wrecked on the voyage home on Ascension Island. In 1703–7 he was engaged in a largely unsuccessful privateering expedition against Spain, but on his last voyage (1708–11), as pilot to Captain Woodes Rogers, he won a share in booty worth £170,000 and took part in the rescue of the castaway Alexander Selkirk, later immortalized by Defoe as Robinson Crusoe.

DANTON, Georges (1759–94), one of the leading figures of the FRENCH REVOLUTION, played only a minor role in the early stages and it was not until

1792 that he had risen to the post of Minister of Justice. His oratory inspired the French to drive back the Prussians when they tried to restore the monarchy, and he later voted for the execution of the King. He controlled the Committee of Public Safety, and as leader of the party known as the 'Mountain' he was responsible for its victory over the more moderate Girondins. Although he wanted to end the Terror, he was unable to restrain his bloodthirsty followers and his enemies persuaded ROBESPIERRE that his death would win popular support. Tried by a revolutionary tribunal which he had himself created, he was condemned to death and guillotined with fourteen others.

DARIUS I, known as 'the Great', was King of the PERSIAN EMPIRE from c. 522 to 485 BC. A warrior and a wise ruler, he divided his empire into twenty provinces or satrapies, campaigned towards the borders of India and turned north to invade Russia. Obliged by the cold to retreat, he decided to crush the rising power of the Greeks, but, through the heroism of the Athenians, his army was defeated at

The great staircase of Darius's palace at Persepolis

MARATHON (490 BC). He intended to launch a more powerful invasion but was called to deal with a rebellion in Egypt. He died in 485, leaving his plans to his son Xerxes.

DARWIN, Charles (1809–82), the British naturalist, whose theory of evolution shook the Victorian

Darwin and the *Beagle* in Sydney Harbour

world, arrived at his conclusions through observations he made when serving as naturalist in HMS *Beagle* on her voyage (1831–6) to South America and the Pacific. His principal works, *Origin of Species* (1859) and *The Descent of Man* (1871), aroused widespread opposition because his theories contradicted the Biblical account of the Creation; and to the popular mind it appeared, wrongly, that he claimed that man was descended from the ape.

DAVID (*c.* 1000–*c.* 960 BC), Hebrew king, was a shepherd boy who became the favourite of King Saul and, later, his enemy. For a time he was the fugitive leader of a band of followers, but after the deaths of Saul and his son Jonathan in battle David was acclaimed King of Judah. He gradually subdued Israel to the north, captured JERUSALEM and made it the capital of the united kingdom. There followed a series of wars against the Philistines and the peoples of Moab, Ammon and Edom, in which David was generally victorious. His later years were troubled by his rebellious sons Absalom and Adonijah, both of whom died, so the crown was left to Solomon.

Great seal of
David I of Scotland

DAVID I (1084–1153), King of Scotland, was the son of Malcolm III and Queen MARGARET. After the deaths of his brothers, he gained the whole kingdom in 1124 and, as an English baron, he swore fealty to his niece the Empress MATILDA and supported her in the civil war against STEPHEN by invading England. Defeated at the Battle of the Standard, 1138, he returned to Scotland and devoted himself to reforming the kingdom and introducing feudalism on Norman lines. He founded bishoprics and several monasteries, including Melrose Abbey and Holyrood. He is regarded as one of the greatest Scottish kings.

DAVIS, Jefferson (1808–89), President of the Confederate States in the American CIVIL WAR, served for seven years in the US Army, became a cotton-planter in Mississippi, fought in the MEXICAN WAR and entered the US Senate in 1847. As leader of the Southern democrats, he passionately asserted the rights of the slave-holding states to leave the Union and form a separate nation. When Mississippi joined the Confederacy, he hoped for high military command and was dismayed to find himself elected President in February 1861.

During the Civil War Davis worked heart and soul for the Southern cause, but he had to contend with much criticism, and as Commander-in-Chief he stuck obstinately to a defensive strategy that proved disastrous and he was inclined to retain inefficient commanders. Still, he had courage and to the end refused any terms short of Southern independence. After Richmond fell, he was captured and imprisoned at Fortress Monroe for two years. Never brought to trial, he went to Canada for a time after his release and then retired to Mississippi, refusing to take any further part in politics.

DECLARATION OF INDEPENDENCE. On 10 May 1775 the Second Continental Congress of the American colonies met at Philadelphia in order to organize the revolution. In June Congress appointed George WASHINGTON Commander-in-Chief of the American forces and the delegates next carried a motion that the colonies were 'Free and Independent States'. On 4 July 1776 came the historic Declaration of Independence, written largely by Thomas JEFFERSON and setting forth the details of the alleged 'absolute tyranny' of King GEORGE III. Among the striking utterances of the Declaration the most famous words are as follows:

We hold these truths to be self-evident, that all men are created equal, that they are endowed by their Creator with certain unalienable Rights, that among these are Life, Liberty and the pursuit of Happiness – That to secure these rights, Governments are instituted among Men, deriving their just powers from the consent of the governed – That whenever any Form of Government becomes destructive of these ends, it is the Right of the People to alter or abolish it, and to institute new Government. . . .

DEPRESSION, the Great, is the name given to the economic collapse which began in 1929 and lasted well into the 1930s in most of the countries of the world. It is also known as the Slump, and 1931–3 is generally regarded as the period when the effects of the Depression were at their worst.

In October 1929 prices on the New York Stock Exchange fell dramatically and on 'Black Thursday', 24 October, 13 million shares changed hands. Panic set in, business collapsed and by 1931 over three thousand banks had failed. Unemployment reached between 12 and 14 million in America during 1932–3. The causes of the collapse were many and are still debated; there had been reckless share-buying, much of it on borrowed money; American productivity had outstripped wages; farming was already depressed; wealth was concentrated into comparatively few hands, yet taxation favoured the rich and the Republican government was not disposed to control business and financial activities.

The effects of the American collapse spread rapidly across the world, because many countries, struggling to recover from the First World War, relied heavily on American loans, which now

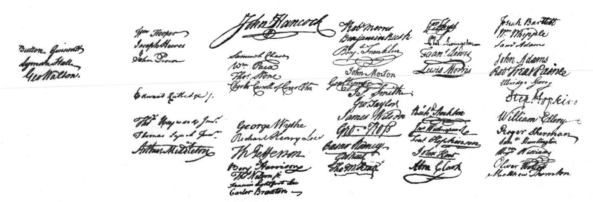

The signatures from the Declaration of Independence

ceased. Austria's leading bank failed, Germany soon had 6 million unemployed and the way was clear for the rise of the NAZI Party. Britain's heavy industries practically closed down and unemployment reached almost 3 million. France, which seemed more self-sufficient than many countries, eventually suffered like the rest, while in Latin America, Eastern Europe, Japan, Australia and the West Indies, prices of agricultural products and manufactured goods fell disastrously. As unemployment increased, people bought less, so trade declined and more businesses closed down.

A slow recovery began to take place in the mid-thirties. In America Franklin D. ROOSEVELT launched the New Deal in 1933 to tackle the Depression by a programme of public works and government aid to business, farming and industry. Unemployment was reduced (though not cured), and as confidence began to return conditions improved. However, most of the world was still suffering from the economic and social effects of the Depression when the Second World War broke out in 1939.

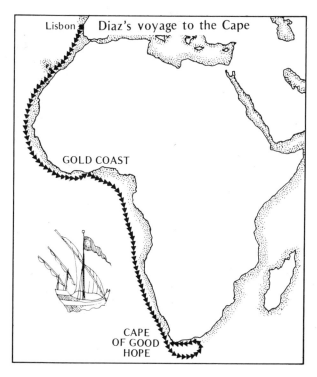

Diaz's voyage to the Cape

DIAZ, Bartholomew (c. 1455–1500), the Portuguese discoverer of the Cape of Good Hope (1488), seems to have been a cavalier at the court of King John II of Portugal. After commanding a vessel that sailed to the Gold Coast, he left Lisbon in 1486 with three ships to continue the work of African exploration. Blown considerably south of the Cape by a storm, he turned east and then north and so struck the southernmost point of Africa. Although his men insisted on returning, he sailed far enough to establish that the coast ran on in a north-easterly direction. By tradition, he gave the Cape the name of Cape of Storms and this was changed to Cape of Good Hope by King John. Some authorities, however, think that Diaz himself gave it its present name. He seems to have gained little reward for his discovery and he perished in a storm in 1500 when serving with Cabral, the discoverer of Brazil.

DISRAELI, Benjamin, Earl of Beaconsfield (1804–81), British politician who is regarded as the founder of the modern Conservative Party, entered Parliament as a Tory in 1837. A Jew, a dandy, a wit and a novelist, he did not at first commend himself to the House, but by sheer brilliance he forced himself into prominence and led the attacks on PEEL in the CORN LAW debates. After Peel had been driven from office, Disraeli became virtual leader of the Tories, whom he adroitly persuaded to accept Free Trade, extension of the franchise and social reforms. He was three times Chancellor of the Exchequer (1852, 1858–9, 1866–8) and twice Prime Minister (1868 and 1874–80).

During his career he achieved a number of striking triumphs, such as the 1867 Reform Act (when he 'dished the Whigs'), his purchase of half the SUEZ CANAL shares (1875), proclaiming Queen VICTORIA Empress of India (1876), and dominating the Congress of BERLIN (1878), when he brought

England 'Peace with honour'. His second premiership saw the passing of the Trade Union Act, the Public Health Act (1875), the Artisans Dwelling Act and the achievement of a ten-hour factory day, for Disraeli had strong sympathies with the working people, as can be seen in his novel *Sybil*.

In foreign affairs he was an ardent patriot, who pursued imperialistic policies in Afghanistan and Zululand; he annexed the Transvaal in 1877 and, unlike his great rival GLADSTONE, took a pro-Turkish line in Eastern affairs. A man of great charm, he won Queen Victoria's confidence and drew her back into public life; she raised her beloved 'Dizzy' to the peerage as Earl of Beaconsfield in 1876.

DOLLFUSS, Engelbert (1892–1934), Austrian politician who became Chancellor in 1932, when his country was in dire economic and political trouble. He did not want Austria to be dominated by Italian Fascism or absorbed into Germany; he was opposed to the Austrian NAZIS, but accepted help from the right-wing force, the Heimwehr. Finding parliamentary government impossible, he dissolved the Assembly and ruled by decree, trying to deal with his opponents by banning the Austrian Nazi Party and crushing a socialist uprising with gunfire. In July 1934 a group of Nazis invaded the Chancellery in Vienna and murdered Dollfuss.

DOMESDAY BOOK (*or* Doomsday Book, 1085–6), was a survey of England ordered by William the Conqueror (WILLIAM I). Officials were sent to all parts of the country to ascertain, with the help of juries, the exact state of the land as it was on the day of Edward the Confessor's death. The survey recorded who owned every piece of land, its value, method of cultivation, number of inhabitants, their classes, work, numbers of ploughs, cattle, sheep, pigs, the amount of woodland and even the location of fishponds. The information was transferred to two large volumes (now in the Public Record Office in London) and was probably intended to tell William all he wanted to know about his kingdom and its ability to pay taxes.

DRAKE, Sir Francis (1540–96), the Elizabethan sailor, was born in Devonshire and brought up at Chatham, in Kent, where he learned seamanship at an early age. In 1567 he commanded a ship in a slaving expedition of his cousin John HAWKINS, and at San Juan in the West Indies narrowly escaped with his life after a treacherous attack by the Spaniards. In revenge he made three voyages to the West Indies between 1570 and 1573, during which he sacked Portobello and Vera Cruz and accumulated a fortune.

In 1577 he set out on a buccaneering expedition, made his way through the Magellan Straits into the

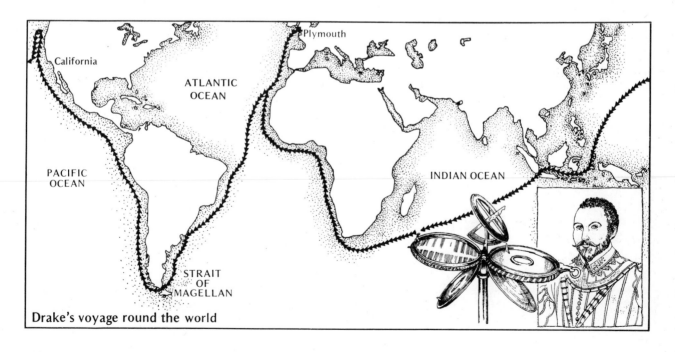

Drake's voyage round the world

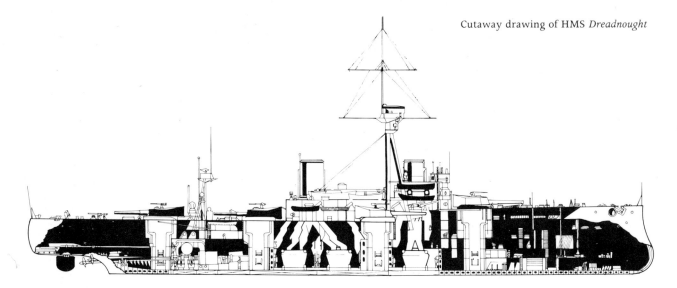

Pacific, where he robbed Spanish ships, claimed California for the Queen as New Albion and brought the *Golden Hind* across the Indian Ocean, round the Cape of Good Hope and back to Plymouth to complete the greatest voyage yet accomplished by an Englishman. ELIZABETH knighted him on the deck of his ship.

When open war broke out with Spain, Drake commanded a fleet that made attacks on Spanish coastal towns, including Cadiz, where he inflicted such damage on shipping and stores that the ARMADA was delayed for a year. In 1588 he was second-in-command against the Armada and played a major part in its defeat at Gravelines. Next year he failed in an attack on Lisbon and retired to Devonshire, but reappeared in 1595, when he and Hawkins sailed to the West Indies. Nothing went right for them and Drake, taken ill with dysentery, died and was buried at sea. Extraordinarily brave and resourceful, Drake was a hero to his own countrymen and a common pirate to the Spaniards; even by them he was described as 'sharp, well-spoken, boastful and not very cruel'.

DREADNOUGHT was the name of a class of super-battleships which began with HMS *Dreadnought*, built at Plymouth in 1906 to counter the growing strength of the German navy. She was armed with ten 12-inch guns, more than twice the number carried by any previous vessel; the first capital ship to have steam turbines, her speed was 21 knots and she could burn oil as well as coal. Able to out-gun any other ship, she made all existing battleships obsolete, including those of the British Navy. The appearance of HMS *Dreadnought* therefore brought about huge building programmes by Britain and Germany in the years preceding the FIRST WORLD WAR.

DREYFUS AFFAIR (1894–1906) was a notorious case of injustice, which aroused passionate feelings in France for more than a decade. Captain Alfred Dreyfus, a Jewish officer on the French General Staff, was accused of passing military secrets to Germany; after a secret trial by court martial, he was found guilty and sentenced to life imprisonment on Devil's Island. His condemnation aroused anti-Jewish feelings throughout France, but an intelligence officer named Piquart presently pointed out the inconvenient fact that secrets were still being leaked. The Army sent him out of the way to Tunisia. However, Dreyfus's brother managed to secure evidence that pointed to a Major Esterhazy being the traitor, but Esterhazy was acquitted by a court martial.

At this Emile Zola, the novelist, published a letter accusing the military authorities of persecuting an innocent man; although Zola was charged with libel and found guilty, he succeeded in bringing the case into the open and it now developed into an impassioned struggle between Right and Left. The Dreyfusards (socialists, radicals, intellectuals) decided that the Anti-Dreyfusards (Army chiefs, the Church, royalists) were bringing the Republic into disrepute, and amid street clashes and a violent press campaign CLEMENCEAU demanded justice for Dreyfus.

Eventually it was shown that he had been convicted on a document forged by an officer named Henri, who committed suicide. As a result Dreyfus was retried at Rennes in 1899, but the army again obtained a conviction. President Loubet then granted him a free pardon, and after some years of agitation the decisions of both courts martial were quashed in 1906. Dreyfus and Piquart were reinstated to the army and awarded promotion.

DUNDEE, Viscount (John Graham of Claverhouse, 1649–89), Scottish soldier, who after service in France and Holland was given a captaincy to suppress the COVENANTERS in south-west Scotland, who were in rebellion against CHARLES II's refusal to accept Presbyterianism. Claverhouse was much hated for the severity with which he used his dragoons to break up gatherings and prayer-meetings. Made Viscount Dundee by JAMES II, he raised 3,000 Highlanders after the King's flight and met General Mackay's government troops in the Pass of Killiecrankie, where the clansmen swept the regulars from the field. In the moment of victory, however, Dundee was killed and, with no one to hold them together, the Highlanders soon dispersed.

DUNKIRK, a fortified Channel port, formerly belonging to the Spanish Netherlands, until captured by an Anglo-French army in 1658. The French ceded it to England, but Charles II sold it back and the port subsequently became a haven for French privateers which attacked English shipping.

In 1940, during the SECOND WORLD WAR, the British Expeditionary Force retreated to Dunkirk after the Germans had broken the Allied line, and from its beaches some 330,000 men were rescued by naval vessels and more than six hundred small boats which put out from England. The British were justly proud of the courage and resource that saved their army but, as Churchill reminded them, 'wars are not won by evacuations'.

DUPLEIX, Joseph (1697–1763), went to India as a young man in the service of the French East India Company and showed such ability that in 1742 he was appointed Governor-General of French India. His aim was to destroy English influence, and by supporting one native prince against another he gained control of most of southern India and practically made the Carnatic a French province. High-handed and quarrelsome, he was nevertheless unlucky to come up against a man so brilliant as CLIVE, who defeated his plans and restored British prestige. Ordered home in disgrace by an ungrateful government, Dupleix died in poverty, after having spent his life and a fortune in his country's service.

DURHAM REPORT (1839) was prepared by Lord Durham, who was sent to Canada to investigate the causes of the 1837 rebellion, an uprising in the provinces of Ontario and Quebec. He recommended the union of Upper and Lower Canada under a two-chamber parliament and this was carried out at once by an Act passed by the British Parliament in 1840. The Report also recommended that the Canadians should have internal self-government, the Crown concerning itself with foreign trade, foreign affairs and public lands. In practice self-government came about during the Governor-Generalship of Lord Elgin (1846–54), Durham's son-in-law. The importance of the Durham Report is that it laid down colonial self-government as the object of British imperial policy, as was soon to be seen in the granting of self-government to New Zealand in 1852, Cape Colony in 1854, and most of the Australian colonies in 1856.

DUTCH REVOLT. The NETHERLANDS or Low Countries became the property of the Dukes of Burgundy in the 14th century and in 1477 came under HAPSBURG rule on the death in battle of Charles the Bold. The country enjoyed great prosperity for a time, but on the accession of PHILIP II of Spain (1555) the Dutch suffered religious persecution, with the introduction of the INQUISITION and the tyranny of a standing army.

Spanish soldiers subdue
rebellious Dutch villagers

During the long War of Independence the out-standing Spanish generals were the Duke of Parma and the hated Duke of Alva, while the Dutch hero was William, Prince of Orange, known as WILLIAM THE SILENT. At times the Dutch cause seemed hopeless, and on one occasion William could only repel the enemy by flooding the countryside. However, the Spaniards were unable to break the Dutch resistance, which was carried on after the assassination of William the Silent (1584) by his sons Maurice and Frederick. The Dutch received a certain amount of help, though never enough, from ELIZABETH I of England and from companies of English volunteers. The war came to an end in 1648, when by the Treaty of Münster Spain recognized the independence of the Netherlands, i.e. of the seven northern Dutch-speaking provinces.

DUTCH WARS, fought in the 17th century between England and Holland, were caused by rivalry over commerce and shipping. In the First Dutch War (1652–4), eight battles were fought in the English Channel and the North Sea between fleets commanded on the English side by Admiral BLAKE

and on the Dutch side by Tromp and de Ruyter. Honours were fairly even, but the English gained favourable terms when peace was made.

The Second Dutch War (1664–7) was a continuation of the first. CHARLES II's brother, James Duke of York (later JAMES II), commanded the English fleet, which was victorious at the Battle of Lowestoft in 1665, but two years later the Dutch sailed up the Medway and inflicted heavy damage on English warships at their moorings. However, by the Peace of Breda (1667) England gained the settlement of New Amsterdam, now renamed New York.

In the face of the threat of conquest by LOUIS XIV, the Dutch found an unexpected ally in England, but later, as part of the secret Treaty of Dover with Louis, Charles II agreed to reopen the war with Holland. In the Third Dutch War (1672–4) the principal engagements were the battles of Sole Bay, in which York drove off de Ruyter, but suffered heavy losses, and the Texel, in which Prince RUPERT was repulsed in an attack on the Dutch coast. With the war not going well, Parliament refused to grant money to Charles II and the war came to an end in 1674.

E

EAST INDIA COMPANY. The English Company was founded in 1600 for trade with India and the East Indies. It was given a monopoly of trade, which was expected to be mainly in spices, but the

An English 'nabob' (merchant)

hostility of the Dutch (who massacred a number of English merchants at Amboyna in 1623) kept the Company out of the East Indies and caused it to confine itself to India. There, during the 17th century, three main trading stations (or 'factories') were established at Madras, Calcutta and Bombay, with the Company building forts to protect its warehouses, raising troops and conducting peaceful trade on a fairly small scale.

In the next century rivalry between France and Britain spread to India, and thanks to the victories of CLIVE the Company emerged as the ruling power in Bengal and an influential force in other areas. Great riches were acquired, often by dubious means, by its officials, who as 'nabobs' were detested for their arrogant opulence when they retired to England. Despite these private fortunes, the Company was almost bankrupt in 1773, when the British Parliament passed a Regulating Act whereby the Company had to consult the government on political matters; there was to be a Supreme Court of English judges and a Governor-General (WARREN HASTINGS), aided by a council of four. This was the beginning of the British government's involvement in Indian affairs. PITT's India Act of 1784 set up a Board of Control to manage political, financial and military affairs. Gradually the Company lost its power and became a body of officials carrying out administration for the government. Its commerce came to depend chiefly on the tea and opium trade with China. Finally, after the disaster of the INDIAN MUTINY (1857), the last powers of the Company were abolished and rule was wholly taken over by the British government.

EASTER RISING (April 1916) took place in Ireland, mostly in Dublin. The Act giving IRISH HOME RULE had been passed in 1914, but was postponed owing to the outbreak of the First World War. John Redmond called on the Irish Volunteers to fight on the side of the Allies, but a minority, led by Eoin MacNeill, refused to do so. Among them was a smaller group, the Irish Republican Brotherhood, whose leaders, Tom Clarke, Padraic Pearse and James Conolly, planned an armed uprising to take place at Easter 1916. Just before that date a German ship, laden with arms, was intercepted by the British, and Sir Roger CASEMENT was captured after coming ashore from a German submarine. MacNeill, as Chief of Staff of the Volunteers, there-

The attack on Dublin Post Office

fore countermanded the plans for the uprising, but the militants went ahead, and on Easter Monday a force of about 1,500 men captured Dublin's General Post Office, from whose steps Pearse proclaimed the Irish Republic.

The rising was easily crushed; it lasted only six days, for the Irish people gave it little or no support. However, the British authorities reacted with astounding folly, executing Pearse, Conolly, Clarke and other leaders, not together but in ones and twos over a period, and imprisoning or deporting hundreds of others. Thus they created heroes and martyrs, and swung Irish opinion away from John Redmond and Home Rule to the Republicans.

EDGAR (944–75), King of England, son of Edmund I of WESSEX, was a powerful king whose reign was looked upon as a golden era of peace and good government. Much of this was due to his chief minister, Saint Dunstan, Archbishop of Canterbury. Edgar is said to have demonstrated his supremacy by being rowed on the river Dee at Chester by a crew of six sub-kings, or eight according to some sources.

EDISON, Thomas Alva (1847–1931), the world's most prolific inventor, was born in Ohio. At twelve he was working as a railroad newsboy when he obtained some old type and printed his own news-

paper on the train. Soon after he learned telegraphy he invented an automatic repeater and followed this with the printing-telegraph and various other innovations in telegraphy. He improved BELL's telephone by using a microphone, invented the phonograph or gramophone in 1877, perfected the incandescent electric light bulb, constructed the first power station and then turned his attention to developing a high-speed camera for motion pictures. At one time he was working on no fewer than 45 inventions and altogether he patented 1,300.

EDUCATION ACT (1870), the greatest landmark in the history of English education, was prepared by W. E. Forster, a member of GLADSTONE's government. It allowed the Churches to continue to run the 'voluntary' schools and gave them six months to build new ones, but in areas where there were not enough school places locally-elected 'School Boards' were to levy rates to build schools, and they could if they wished make education compulsory in their areas. Parents would pay a fee of up to 9 pence a week, though those who could not afford it would be granted a free ticket. Thus the Act itself established neither free nor compulsory education; it provided for elementary, not secondary, education. Compulsory schooling for all children under twelve was introduced in 1880, and from 1891 most elementary schools became free.

A ragged school before the 1870 Education Act

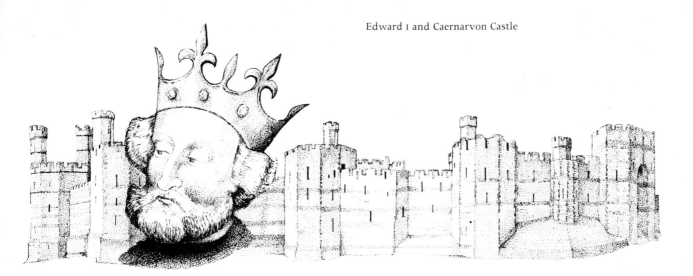

EDWARD I (1239–1307), King of England (1272–1307), was the son of HENRY III. In the latter part of his father's troubled reign, he led the Royalist forces in the baronial war and was captured at Lewes (1264), but he escaped and defeated de MONTFORT at Evesham in 1265. From then on he was the real ruler of the kingdom, restoring order so effectively that he was able to go on CRUSADE in 1270. After he became king, Edward introduced legal reforms (he is sometimes called 'the Lawgiver'), mostly to strengthen the royal authority, and he made use of Parliament chiefly to grant him money.

In two campaigns of 1277 and 1282 he defeated LLEWELLYN II and conquered Wales, after which he built a chain of massive castles in the north to keep the Welsh in subjection. He next turned his attention to Scotland, when invited to settle the disputed succession; he chose John Balliol as king and was recognized as Scotland's overlord. However, his high-handed treatment of Balliol caused the Scots to rebel and, although Edward was victorious at Dunbar (1296) and Falkirk (1298), he was never to complete the country's conquest. He set out again on campaign in 1307 to deal with ROBERT BRUCE but died before he reached Scotland.

Edward I was one of the ablest medieval kings, brave, devout, an efficient ruler and a good general, though hot-tempered and sometimes cruel. In 1290 he expelled all the Jews from England.

EDWARD II (1284–1327), King of England (1307–27), abandoned the Scottish campaign on the death of his father EDWARD I and returned to London, where he showered gifts and honours on his favourite Piers Gaveston. A group of nobles, the Lords Ordainers, raised a rebellion and executed Gaveston, but meanwhile ROBERT BRUCE had made such progress in Scotland that Edward was compelled to lead the English army north in hope of saving Stirling Castle. His total defeat at BANNOCKBURN (1314), together with his poor generalship and cowardice, aroused the contempt of everyone, including his wife Isabella of France. However, Edward had found new favourites in Hugh Despenser and his son and had overthrown the Ordainers, when Isabella and her lover Mortimer landed in Suffolk from France with an army. Edward fled to Wales, where he was captured and put to death in Berkeley Castle.

EDWARD III (1312–77), King of England (1327–77), came to the throne as a boy after the murder of his father EDWARD II. In 1330 he overthrew his mother, Isabella of France, and her lover Mortimer and began to rule, at once proving himself an altogether more resolute character than his father. He was a successful warrior, brave, courteous, the pattern of chivalry, but he was also vain, selfish and pitiless. He avenged the humiliation of BANNOCKBURN by defeating the Scots at Halidon Hill (1333) and forcing Edward Balliol to do homage; later he was victorious at Neville's Cross (1346), where David II was captured.

The HUNDRED YEARS' WAR with France began in 1338 and brought the triumphs of Sluys (1340) and Crécy (1346) and the capture of Calais and

Poitiers (1356). By the Treaty of Brétigny (1360) Edward gave up his claim to the French throne in return for recognition as sovereign of Aquitaine, Ponthieu and Calais. This was the peak of his reign; thereafter his fortunes declined, as his son EDWARD THE BLACK PRINCE went warring in Spain and ruined his health, while the French, led by du GUESCLIN, regained almost all their lost territories. Edward sank into a feeble old age, dominated by his avaricious mistress Alice Perrers; the Black Prince was too ill to rule in his stead and control fell largely into the hands of a younger son, JOHN OF GAUNT.

At home the most disastrous episode of the reign was the BLACK DEATH (1348–9), which was followed by the Statute of Labourers (1351), an attempt to freeze wages. Edward regulated the wool trade and encouraged cloth manufacture; his constant need for money enabled Parliament to strengthen its position by, for example, insisting on its right to grant customs duties known as tonnage and poundage. The Commons also asserted their right to impeach ministers and the Lords confirmed their right to trial by peers alone.

EDWARD IV (1442–83), King of England (1461–83), son of the Duke of York, was placed on the throne during the Wars of the ROSES by WARWICK 'the Kingmaker'. He angered Warwick by secretly marrying Elizabeth Woodville, a Lancastrian widow, and in the course of their quarrel forced him to go abroad, where Warwick and HENRY VI's wife, Queen Margaret, hatched a plan to put Henry back on the throne. Edward fled to Flanders, but soon returned to defeat and kill Warwick at Barnet

(1471). After this victory his reign was peaceful, for despite his indolence and love of pleasure, Edward was extremely able; he mastered the nobles, encouraged trade and the merchant class and also patronized CAXTON the printer.

EDWARD V (1470–83), King of England (April–June 1483), was only thirteen when his father EDWARD IV died suddenly. His uncle Richard of Gloucester took charge of him and lodged him in the Tower of London with his younger brother Richard. Gloucester then usurped the throne as RICHARD III, declaring that the boys were illegitimate. Neither was seen alive after October 1483 and two skeletons were discovered beneath a staircase in the Tower in 1674. They were later confirmed to have been boys of about their age and to have been strangled.

EDWARD VI (1537–53), King of England (1547–53), the son of HENRY VIII and Jane Seymour, came to the throne at the age of nine. A council of ministers was to govern during his minority, but power passed first to his uncle Protector Somerset and after him to the Duke of NORTHUMBERLAND. Edward, an intelligent and precocious boy, was given a good education and a thorough grounding in the Protestant faith, so that he came to dread

Catholicism, and during his reign Protestant zealots seized what remained of Church property. At sixteen Edward developed tuberculosis, and as he neared death Northumberland had no difficulty in persuading him to agree to leave the kingdom to the Protestant Lady Jane GREY instead of to the rightful Queen MARY.

EDWARD VII (1841–1910), King of Great Britain (1901–10), was the eldest son of Queen VICTORIA and Prince ALBERT. As Prince of Wales he became leader of a fashionable set, a lover of sport, gambling and pretty women. For many years his disapproving mother refused to let him play more than a trivial role in state affairs; however, on becoming King he soon established himself as a popular monarch, and through his visits to France helped to foster Anglo-French friendship. He was on good terms with Tsar NICHOLAS II and paid visits to the Austrian Emperor FRANCIS JOSEPH and to Kaiser WILLIAM II, his nephew, though their relationship was far from cordial. His travels and European contacts brought him the name of 'Edward the Peacemaker', though his influence on British foreign policy was much exaggerated.

EDWARD VIII (1894–1972), King of Great Britain (1936), eldest son of GEORGE V, won wide popularity as Prince of Wales, through his tours abroad, his charm, and sympathy with the unemployed. He succeeded to the throne in January 1936 and abdicated the following December without having been crowned. He wished to marry Mrs Wallis Simpson, an American lady who had divorced two husbands and when Baldwin, the Prime Minister, informed him that she would not be acceptable as Queen to the country and the Dominions Edward abdicated. He married Mrs Simpson in Paris and, as Duke of Windsor, lived abroad for the rest of his life.

EDWARD THE BLACK PRINCE (1330–76), eldest son of EDWARD III, was known in his lifetime as Edward of Woodstock, and it is not certain how or when the name of Black Prince arose. A gifted warrior, he commanded a wing at Crécy (1346) during the HUNDRED YEARS' WAR, when he was only sixteen, conquered much of France, won the Battle of Poitiers (1356), and at Nájera (1367) in Spain recovered Castile for Pedro the Cruel. He ruled Aquitaine, where, in dealing with rebellious subjects, he allowed his troops to carry out a merciless massacre at Limoges (1370). His health was ruined in Spain and he returned to England where he died. His son became RICHARD II.

EDWARD THE CONFESSOR (c. 1002–66), SAXON King of England (1042–66), son of Ethelred the Unready, spent his early life in exile in Normandy while England was ruled by CANUTE and his sons. On the death of Hardicanute Edward was elected king; he tended to favour his Norman friends and advisers but nevertheless married the daughter of Godwin, the powerful Earl of Wessex. In his later years he devoted himself to religion and built Westminster Abbey. His cousin William Duke of Normandy (later WILLIAM I), visited him in 1051 and afterwards claimed he had promised him the crown, but on his deathbed Edward named HAROLD, son of Godwin, as his heir.

EGYPT. The ancient Dynasties were as follows:
Early Dynastic Period (c. 3100–c. 2686 BC): the 1st Dynasty was founded by Menes, in whose reign and during the 2nd Dynasty Upper and Lower Egypt were unified.
Old Kingdom (c. 2686–c.2181 BC): the period of the 3rd–6th Dynasties, which saw the great era of

PYRAMID building, the cult of Ra and Osiris and the rise of the nobles.

First Intermediate Period (c. 2181–c.2133 BC): comprising the 7th–10th Dynasties, a time of chaos and petty kingdoms.

Middle Kingdom (c. 2133–c.1786 BC): the 11th Dynasty (rise of Thebes) and the 12th Dynasty (period of expansion, conquest of Nubia, irrigation, building, literature and art).

Second Intermediate Period (c. 1786–c. 1567 BC): the 13th Dynasty (60 kings and a breakdown of central authority); 14th Dynasty (76 rulers and civil strife); 15th Dynasty (6 Hyksos kings, invaders who ruled the Delta and Lower Egypt); 16th Dynasty (the lesser Hyksos); 17th Dynasty (at Thebes; war with the Hyksos).

New Kingdom (c. 1567–c.1085 BC): saw the zenith of Egypt's power and wealth during the 18th Dynasty, with Imperial expansion, Karnak, burials in the Valley of Kings, Thotmes I, Queen HATSHEPSUT, advance to the Euphrates, Amen-hotep III, temple of Amen-Ra at Luxor, AKHNA-TEN's heresy and TUTANKHAMUN; 19th Dynasty (RAMESES II, battle of Kadesh, Abu Simbel); 20th Dynasty (RAMESES III, war with Libyans and Peoples of the Sea, decline of Thebes, Empire lost).

Late Dynastic Period (c. 1085–332 BC): comprising the 21st–31st Dynasties (lack of central authority, invasions from Libya, Nubia, and Ethiopia. In 671 Esarhaddon, the Assyrian, captured Thebes. Saite Period of revival. In 525 Cambyses of Persia conquered Egypt).

Ptolemaic Period (332–30 BC): ALEXANDER the Great ended Persian rule and made Egypt a province of the Macedonian Empire. PTOLEMY Soter established the Ptolemaic Dynasty, under which Egypt flourished until it became a Roman province in 30 BC.

EISENHOWER, Dwight D. (1890–1969), American soldier and 34th President of the United States, attended the US Military Academy, was chiefly engaged in training troops during the First World War, and at the outbreak of the SECOND WORLD WAR had only risen to the rank of lieutenant-colonel. Thereafter he gained rapid promotion and, as Allied Commander-in-Chief, North Africa, concluded the desert campaign and directed the invasion of Italy. Made Supreme Commander, he was responsible for the NORMANDY INVASION in 1944 and for the defeat of Germany in the west. After governing the US occupation zone (1945), he became Supreme Commander of NATO forces in Europe (1951–2). Eisenhower was a gifted organizer rather than a great soldier in the field, a man whose tact and firm resolve made him the ideal choice as Supreme Commander of a difficult team of Allied generals.

Nominated by the Republican Party, he was elected US President in 1952 and again in 1956. During his term of office he had to deal with the ending of the KOREAN WAR, the Indo-China problem, disarmament and control of nuclear weapons. At home, opposed by the Republican right wing and a Democratic majority in Congress, he was criticized for tending to allow himself to be carried along by events, rather than shaping vigorous policies. He may have lacked the professional politician's cunning, but he was a figure who inspired respect and affection in his own country and throughout Western Europe.

ELIZABETH I (1533–1603), Queen of England (1558–1603), was the daughter of HENRY VIII and Anne Boleyn. During her childhood she received a good education and learned to speak several languages, but in the reigns of her brother EDWARD VI and her sister MARY I, she came under suspicion of being involved in treasonable plots and was closely watched and kept in semi-captivity. In 1558 she succeeded to the throne of an impoverished divided country, menaced by France and Spain. With the able assistance of her chief minister, William Cecil (later Lord BURGHLEY), she overcame all her difficulties, making a religious settlement that went some way towards satisfying both Protestants and Catholics, and fending off England's enemies, while building up the country's strength and restoring its navy. As regards France, she was lucky, for the ambitious Henry II died and the country became involved in a religious war, so she was able to conclude a peace treaty and to help destroy French influence in Scotland. Later, she kept MARY QUEEN OF SCOTS, the Catholic claimant to her throne, prisoner for many years, only agreeing to her execution (1587) when war with Spain had become inevitable.

Towards Spain her policy was to keep up the pretence of friendship and to appear to consider

Opposite TUTANKHAMUN King of EGYPT with his queen depicted on his golden throne

marriage to PHILIP II, while giving 'undercover' help to his Protestant subjects in the Netherlands during the DUTCH REVOLT and encouraging her 'sea-dogs' to pursue their piratical expeditions. When war finally came and the ARMADA sailed, Elizabeth's display of defiant courage inspired and united her people.

At home her reign was notable for an increase in prosperity and the formation of trading companies, for attempts to solve the problems of vagrancy and unemployment, for the Queen's crafty management of her parliaments and for a flowering of the arts of music, poetry and drama. The achievements of Shakespeare, Marlowe, Jonson, Spenser and the composers Dowland and Byrd are the glories of the Elizabethan period. DRAKE, HAWKINS, FROBISHER and RALEIGH founded a seafaring tradition that led to England's subsequent naval superiority. Towards Ireland Elizabeth's policy was one of cruel suppression, which aroused bitter hatred of English rule.

Elizabeth was possibly the greatest and best-loved of all the English monarchs. She was intelligent, self-willed, brave and astute, besides being vain and maddeningly capricious; much of her success as a ruler arose from her cleverness in adopting delaying tactics; towards the question of her marriage and in her foreign and religious policies she avoided decisions for as long as possible. Though she had a weakness for favourites like LEICESTER and ESSEX, she never allowed them to influence the nation's affairs, for she kept her own counsel, trusting no one entirely, except perhaps Cecil. Above all she possessed a dazzling personality that won men's devotion; she expressed this herself when she said to her last Parliament, 'This I count the chief glory of my crown, that I have reigned with your loves'.

ERASMUS, Desiderius (*c.* 1466–1536), the Dutch scholar, was the most celebrated man of letters of his time and a leading figure in the RENAISSANCE or Revival of Learning (i.e. the rediscovery of Greek and Latin literature) in the late 15th century. Between 1499 and 1517 he paid several lengthy visits to England, where he was the friend of MORE, Colet, Grocyn and other scholars. He taught at Cambridge and was given a rectory and a pension, but he hoped for better financial support and left to settle finally at Basle.

Opposite Queen ELIZABETH I

Erasmus wrote many books, including *Adagia, Handbook of a Christian Soldier, Praise of Folly* and the New Testament in Greek. With wit and audacity he ridiculed the follies and superstitions of the Church, pouring scorn on priests, even on the Pope and cardinals. Among his targets were kings, statesmen, lawyers, merchants and fellow-scholars. Yet he was not a religious reformer and was troubled to find himself blamed for spreading ideas that paved the way for LUTHER's all-out attack on the Catholic Church. He hoped that ridicule and commonsense would goad the Church into mending its ways and he disliked Luther and his teaching.

Section of the Vinland Map, thought to have been made in Leif Eriksson's time. Vinland is in the north-west.

ERIKSSON, Leif (early 11th century), was the son of Erik or Eric the Red, a Norwegian or VIKING chief who explored Greenland in 982–5 and founded a colony there. In about 1002 Leif sailed from Greenland and came to an unknown land to the west, which he named Helluland (Slateland). This may have been Labrador. Sailing south, he came to Markland (Forestland), possibly Nova Scotia; and then to Vinland, so called because he found grapes growing wild. Some say this must have been New England. At all events, Leif Eriksson is reputed to be the first European to set foot in North America.

ESSEX, 2nd Earl of (Robert Devereux, 1566–1601), was a soldier, courtier and favourite of Queen ELIZABETH. He showed dash and courage during LEICESTER's expedition to the Netherlands (1585) and in DRAKE's attack on Corunna (1589), and he commanded an English force sent to assist the French Protestants at Rouen and the land forces at the sack of Cadiz in 1596. His expedition to the Azores was a failure, but Elizabeth made him Governor-General of Ireland, where he concluded a truce with the rebel leader Tyrone (1599). Having returned unbidden to London, he was charged with desertion and imprisoned for a year; then, having failed to regain Elizabeth's favour, he hatched a mad plot to raise the Londoners and force the Queen to dismiss BURGHLEY and other ministers whom he blamed for his downfall. Arrested, he was found guilty of high treason and executed in the Tower.

ETHIOPIA, or Abyssinia, is a mountainous country of north-east Africa, which managed to remain independent until 1935. The Emperor Menelik had defeated an Italian army at Adowa in 1896, a reverse which the Italians did not forget. From 1930 Emperor HAILE SELASSIE introduced reforms into his backward country, but owing to MUSSOLINI's aggressive colonial policy he was faced with growing friction on his frontiers with Italian Somaliland and Eritrea. A border clash at the oasis of Wal-Wal gave Mussolini the excuse he needed. While the LEAGUE OF NATIONS postponed discussions, Italian troops invaded Abyssinia in October 1935, and modern aircraft, tanks, poison gas and motorized transport proved too much for defenders armed with spears and obsolete rifles. General Badoglio captured Addis Ababa, the capital, in May 1936, when King Victor Emmanuel of Italy was proclaimed emperor and poor Haile Selassie went into dignified exile. Five years later, during the Second World War, Ethiopians and British troops defeated the Italian garrisons in Abyssinia and Haile Selassie regained his throne in May 1941.

EUREKA STOCKADE (1854) was an episode during the Australian GOLD RUSH when miners on the Ballarat goldfield in Victoria staged a minor rebellion. Their grievances centred on the authorities' strict enforcement of miners' licence fees. A wooden stockade was built, in which a party of about a hundred and fifty diggers, led by Peter Lalor, an Irishman, was attacked and overwhelmed by a force of armed police and soldiers. About thirty miners were killed and their leaders were tried for treason and acquitted. Lalor became a popular hero, an MP and Speaker of the Legislative Assembly.

The Eureka incident was often acclaimed as a fight for liberty that launched Australian democracy. This is probably an exaggerated view, though the rebellion did bring about some reforms and most of the men's demands were granted. The hated monthly licence was replaced by an annual 'miner's right' costing only £1, and this was the qualification for a vote in the colony's elections.

EUROPEAN ECONOMIC COMMUNITY, known as the EEC or Common Market, was established by the Treaty of Rome (1957), signed by the Netherlands, Belgium, France, West Germany, Italy and Luxembourg. These countries founded a common market in which to trade freely with one another. There was also to be free movement of workers and capital. These arrangements were intended to lead eventually to political unification of Europe, though this aim was resisted by France.

Britain did not join the Community because of doubts about political union with European countries and concern for Commonwealth ties. Instead, with Austria, Denmark, Portugal, Sweden, Norway and Switzerland, she joined a looser association called European Free Trade Association (EFTA).

EEC policy is decided by the Council of Ministers, consisting of a representative from each member country, and put into effect by the Common Market Commission. The European Parliament supervises the Community's general affairs.

Despite differences on agricultural policy, the EEC was strikingly successful, and in 1961 and again in 1966 Britain applied for full membership. By the Treaty of Rome decisions had to be unanimous, and French opposition, personified by de GAULLE, was sufficient to keep Britain out. Some of her EFTA partners and Ireland also applied for membership. The retirement of de Gaulle brought a change of attitude in France, and in 1973 Britain and Ireland were admitted to membership.

F

FARADAY, Michael (1791–1867), is generally considered to be the greatest physical scientist of the 19th century. He began his career as assistant to Sir Humphrey Davy, whom he eventually succeeded as professor of chemistry in the Royal Institution. He made many discoveries in electricity and magnetism, invented the dynamo and transformer, studied the manufacture of optical glass and discovered the condensation of gases into liquids by pressure.

FARRAGUT, David (1801–70), the first American admiral, joined the US navy as a midshipman and at the outbreak of the CIVIL WAR although a Southerner by birth, continued to serve the Federal government. Appointed rear-admiral in command of the Union fleet, he forced a way past the defences of New Orleans (1862) and captured the city, thereby winning control of the lower reaches of the Mississippi. Later, on the rivers of the west, he made skilful use of his ships to aid the Union armies. In 1864 he won the Battle of Mobile Bay and captured Mobile, the South's second port. Congress created for him the ranks of vice-admiral and admiral.

FASHODA INCIDENT (1898) occurred shortly after the British had captured Khartoum. British control of Egypt and the Sudan upset the French plans to extend their dominions from the Sahara to the Red Sea. Major Marchand was therefore sent with a small force to set up the French flag at Fashoda on the Upper Nile. A larger British force arrived, commanded by General Kitchener, who requested Marchand to withdraw, pointing out that the Egyptian government could not allow a foreign power to control the upper waters of its river. For several weeks France and Britain stood on the brink of war, but the French, finding no support from Russia or Germany, eventually ordered Marchand's withdrawal.

FERDINAND AND ISABELLA. By their marriage Ferdinand II of Aragon (1452–1516) and Isabella of Castile (1451–1504) united the two kingdoms and became joint founders of the kingdom of Spain in 1479. Ferdinand, a shrewd and cunning ruler, broke the power of the nobles, suppressed the bandits and introduced many reforms. After ten years of war, he conquered Granada, the last kingdom of the MOORS in Spain; a peace was made with them but later the Moors were treacherously treated, causing these clever industrious people to leave the country. The INQUISITION was established in Spain and Jews were expelled from the country.

Meanwhile, Queen Isabella gave support to COLUMBUS, enabling him to set out on his immortal

Ferdinand and Isabella enter Granada after it had been captured from the Moors

voyage in 1492 and to win for Spain an empire in the New World. In 1500 Ferdinand took part in the conquest of Naples and he later added Navarre to his possessions to make himself master of the whole of Spain. Isabella died in 1504 and Ferdinand in 1516; their daughter Catherine of Aragon became the wife of HENRY VIII of England. Ferdinand was succeeded by his grandson, the Emperor CHARLES V.

FEUDAL SYSTEM, or feudalism, was the system of holding land which began to develop in western Europe after the break-up of the Roman Empire. It existed in CHARLEMAGNE's time and was widespread from the 10th to the 15th centuries; the NORMANS organized feudalism very efficiently in England and southern Italy.

The system grew up in times when no man owning an estate could feel safe; so he would go to some greater lord and surrender his land to him, promising to fight for him when necessary, in return for being allowed to live on his land and to be helped in defending it. A similar system grew up for lesser men; villagers would be allowed to hold their strips of land in the common fields in return for cultivating the lord's land, thus providing him and his followers with food. Every man who gave or granted land was called a *lord*; every man who held land was called a *tenant* or *vassal*. In England, after the Conquest, all land belonged to the King, whose barons were his *tenants-in-chief*.

Lords and vassals had duties towards each other. The vassal gave *service*, such as fighting, garrison-work or field labour, and he also had to make certain payments called *aids*. The principal occasions for making money payments were when the lord's eldest son became a knight, when his eldest daughter married and when the lord was captured and needed a ransom. For his part, the lord was bound to protect his vassals and give them justice in his court.

A vassal's estate was called a *fief*, and on his death it normally passed to his eldest son, who had to pay to the lord a sum called a *relief* before inheriting the land. He also had to perform the ceremonies of *homage* and *fealty*, kneeling down and swearing to be faithful and true to his lord.

The Feudal System gradually broke up in the 15th century for a number of reasons, such as the increase in coinage, which enabled men to pay rents and lords to hire soldiers for pay. The growth of towns and trade, the deaths of many nobles in civil wars, improvement in law and order all helped to bring about the disappearance of feudalism, but it was a gradual process and, in some countries, such as France, the peasants, in particular, continued to carry out feudal duties until the end of the 18th century.

FIELD OF THE CLOTH OF GOLD (1520) was a spectacular conference near Calais between HENRY VIII of England and FRANCIS I of France, so-called because of the extravagant display put on by the two monarchs. War was about to break out between Francis and the Emperor CHARLES V, and WOLSEY arranged the meeting to demonstrate his master's importance as an ally. In fact this was no more than a piece of showmanship, for England was certain to side with Charles V, since he was the nephew of

Henry's wife, Catherine of Aragon, and, as ruler of Flanders, he controlled the wool trade. Furthermore, Wolsey hoped that Charles would get him elected Pope.

FIRE OF LONDON (1666), also known as the Great Fire, started on 2 September in a bakery in Pudding Lane. Fanned by an east wind, it devastated practically all the old city of London, destroying in four days over 13,000 houses, St Paul's Cathedral, the Guildhall, the Exchange, some eighty parish churches, besides inns, shops, markets and halls. The fire was finally checked by blowing up houses in the path of the flames. There were very few deaths, but over 200,000 people were made homeless and, at a time when fire insurance was unknown, property losses amounted to millions.

Within days, plans were afoot to rebuild the city and CHARLES II summoned Wren, the architect, and John Evelyn to discuss the matter with him. A Proclamation was issued, which, if obeyed, would have brought into being a city with wider streets and a 'fair quay', running the length of the north bank of the Thames. However, the citizens mostly persisted in rebuilding on the old foundations of their houses, though in brick instead of timber.

Wren rebuilt fifty-two of the destroyed churches and St Paul's Cathedral. A Frenchman persisted that he had started the fire as part of a Catholic plot and, although he was obviously innocent, he was executed. Near London Bridge a stone column called the Monument commemorates the Great Fire.

Tanks entering a devastated village on the Western Front

FIRST WORLD WAR (1914–18) arose out of rivalries and tensions that had dominated European politics for more than twenty years. On 28 June 1914 the Austrian Archduke Franz Ferdinand was assassinated at Sarajevo by a Bosnian Serb. Austria issued an ultimatum and declared war on Serbia on 28 July. Russia, in order to support Serbia, mobilized her armies, whereupon Germany declared war on Russia and on her ally France. Upon the Germans refusing to respect Belgian neutrality, Britain declared war on Germany on 4 August.

German armies drove through Belgium and into France in a great sweep that was to encircle Paris. However, in September the French halted them on the Marne, and at Ypres the British prevented a breakthrough to the Channel. The opposing armies then dug themselves into lines of trenches, which eventually stretched from the Belgian coast to Switzerland. Meanwhile, the Russians attacked East Prussia and were heavily defeated by the Germans at Tannenberg, but they beat the Austri-

ans in Galicia and the Serbs recaptured Belgrade.

During 1915 the French and British suffered terrible losses trying to break the deadlock of trench warfare. Aiming to capture Constantinople, the British tried to force the Dardanelles by naval action alone; troops were then landed at Gallipoli, but the operation ended in complete failure. Italy entered the war and began a drawn-out struggle with the Austrians on the Isonzo front. Bulgaria joined the Central Powers, Serbia was defeated and the Russians endured enormous losses on the Eastern Front.

1916 saw the German assault on Verdun, where the French armies were almost bled to death. To relieve the pressure, the British under HAIG attacked on the Somme, using tanks for the first time, but making small gains at appalling cost. The Russians advanced into Galicia, only to be driven back, while Rumania, which had joined the Allies, was also defeated. In May occurred the one great naval battle of the war, when at Jutland the German fleet had the better of a sharp engagement, but withdrew as the British Grand Fleet approached. A British force had to surrender in Mesopotamia, but in Africa the Allies overran all the German colonies.

Three momentous events dominated 1917: the Germans began unrestricted submarine warfare, the United States joined the Allies and the RUSSIAN REVOLUTION put an end to Russia's war effort. On the Western Front the failure of Nivelle's offensive on the Aisne led to mutinies in the French army, while the British suffered horrifying losses at Passchendaele. The Italians were heavily defeated at Caporetto.

Strengthened by transfers from the East, the Germans launched the offensive of March 1918 to end the war. It almost succeeded. The Allies were forced to retreat when their line was broken and it needed desperate resistance to halt the enemy advance. The French general Foch took supreme command and in July began a counter-attack, which, once started, kept up a remorseless pressure on the Germans. As they fell back, their allies broke. Bulgaria surrendered first, then Turkey in October and Austria on 3 November. The war ended when Germany was granted an armistice on 11 November 1918. It had lasted over four years, had cost the lives of 8 to 10 million men in battle, of millions more from hunger and disease and had brought about the collapse of four empires.

FLEMING, Alexander (1881–1955), Scottish bacteriologist, who discovered penicillin in 1928 at St Mary's Hospital, London. It took years before this powerful antibiotic could be produced in quantity, but this was eventually achieved thanks to the work of Professors Florey and Chain, so that penicillin saved countless lives during the Second World War. Fleming and his two colleagues were jointly awarded the Nobel Prize for medicine in 1945.

FLINDERS, Matthew (1774–1814), English navigator, served in the British Navy and in 1795, as a midshipman, made his first exploration of the south-east coast of Australia with George Bass. Together they also sailed round Van Diemen's Land (Tasmania). In 1801 he began a thorough exploration of the coast of Australia, much of it totally unknown, and when he reached Sydney two years later, he had completed the circumnavigation of the continent. On his return to England, he was wrecked and held prisoner by the French at Mauritius for six years. A skilled chartmaker, he investigated the effects of iron on ships' compasses and published books and maps of his voyages.

FLODDEN, Battle of (1513), a disastrous defeat of the Scots by the English, during the absence of HENRY VIII, who was campaigning in France with WOLSEY. JAMES IV, the ally of France, crossed the Border and took up a strong position near the river Tweed, but he was outmanoeuvred by the Earl of Surrey, who marched round to the rear of the Scots. James then moved to a new position and ordered the Scots to charge downhill at the English, who won a complete victory. James himself was killed, together with 13 earls and some 10,000 of their followers. This was the last notable victory for the longbow and one of the first for the cannon.

FLORENCE, the chief city of Tuscany in Italy, stands on both banks of the river Arno. It originated as a Roman colony and became important in the 12th and 13th centuries as a military and trading

The burning of Savonarola in Florence

power. Its citizens, who acquired great skill as jewellers and cloth manufacturers, threw off the rule of the nobles and governed themselves through the rich burghers and their trade GUILDS. As the city grew in prosperity, it became filled with splendid churches, palaces and libraries. Florentine bankers became the leading financiers of Europe, establishing banks in many countries and lending money to kings, sometimes with disastrous results, as when EDWARD III defaulted and brought ruin to the leading bankers of the city. However, the MEDICI FAMILY prospered and from 1434 became virtual rulers of Florence.

Under Cosimo de Medici and his grandson Lorenzo the Magnificent (died 1492) the city reached its peak of splendour; it had already produced Dante, greatest of the medieval poets, Petrarch and Boccaccio, and now, in the 15th century, it became the heart of the RENAISSANCE, the greatest literary and artistic centre of Italy. Under the later Medicis decline set in and the monk Savonarola headed a brief revolt against the Florentines' greed and sinfulness, but the people soon abandoned him and he was burnt at the stake in 1498. Florence did not recover her financial and artistic leadership, which passed to VENICE and Rome. In 1530 the city was captured by an army of the Emperor CHARLES V. Handed over to the Pope, Florence ceased to be an independent republic and became merely the capital of the Duchy of Tuscany.

FORD, Henry (1863–1947), was born in Michigan, the son of a farmer. He started work in a machine-shop in Detroit, became a steam-engineer with the Edison Company and in 1893 studied a small petrol engine on exhibition at the World's Fair in Chicago. He decided to apply a petrol engine to a 'horseless carriage', and by 1896 he had built in his shed at home his first motorcar, a 2-cylinder–4 hp machine which had four bicycle wheels and a tiller for steering. In 1899 he started the Detroit Automobile Company with some backers, but soon launched out on his own to build and drive a successful racing car. This led to the founding of the Henry Ford Company and production, from 1908, of the famous Model T Ford, a car that was cheaper and more reliable than any of its rivals. In 1909 he built 10,600 cars; in 1914, 248,300; so successful was his

Ford's Model T was the first family car.

assembly-line production that by 1925 he was producing 10,000 cars a day, and when he abandoned the Model T in 1927 he had made 15,000,000 of them. He then shut down his vast plant to retool for the new Model A, and he did so again in 1932 for the V8. During the SECOND WORLD WAR Ford built the huge Willow Run aircraft factory, which turned out a Liberator bomber every hour; he had by then expanded his motorcar business into a world-wide organization with factories in many countries. He also built Fordson farm tractors and civil aircraft.

Henry Ford was a brilliant engineer and businessman, who pioneered mass-production and a new industrial outlook. His method was to cut the price of the car, step up sales, and improve production efficiency to increase output still further; thus he built the world's greatest one-man industrial organization, made an astronomical fortune and left a huge trust fund, the Ford Foundation, to promote social welfare.

FRANCIS I (1494–1547), King of France (1515–47), a Renaissance monarch whose reign was dominated by his rivalry with the Emperor CHARLES V. At twenty-one he won the brilliant victory of Marignano (1515) and gained control of northern Italy; he hoped to become Holy Roman Emperor, but on Charles V's election in 1519 he declared war on him. Francis failed to win HENRY VIII of England as an

ally and was himself defeated and captured at Pavia in 1525. Released a year later, he continued the war but had lost all his Italian possessions by 1529. Nevertheless, he kept up hostilities against Charles and the Pope, even allying himself with the German Protestants and the Turks in hope of breaking the imperial power. He never succeeded and was obliged to make peace at Crespy in 1544. Francis ruled his country as an absolute monarch, strengthening the crown and its control of the Church. Brilliant, erratic and pleasure-loving, he fostered learning and art, acquired many treasures in Italy and summoned Italian artists to his Court. During his reign, the HUGUENOTS (Protestants) in France were treated with savage cruelty.

FRANCIS of Assisi, Saint (1182–1226), son of a rich merchant, spent his youth enjoying himself until a severe illness and a dramatic meeting with a leper caused him to change his way of life. Taking a vow of poverty, he devoted himself to prayer, to

St Francis greeting St Dominic

helping the poor and working among lepers. His example attracted followers and, although he was reluctant to do so, he obtained the Pope's authority to found the Order known as the Franciscans or Grey FRIARS. He organized his disciples into bands of missionaries and he himself went to Egypt to ask the Sultan to promise better treatment for Christians and to allow Franciscans to guard the Church of the Holy Sepulchre in Jerusalem. The simplicity and beauty of his character and his love of all creatures made St Francis the best loved of all the saints. The Franciscan Order, which still flourishes, has for centuries continued to train missionaries and help the poor.

FRANCIS JOSEPH (*or* Franz Josef, 1830–1916), Emperor of Austria (1848) and King of Hungary (1867), devoted his long life to ruling the Austro-Hungarian Empire as an absolute monarch. After suppressing the REVOLUTIONS OF 1848 he made a close alliance with the Church and obstinately opposed liberal reforms and the demands of the various national groups in the empire, particularly

the Czechs and Slavs, for greater independence. His aim was to create one unified state, but he had to endure the loss of Austrian influence in Italy (1859) and in Germany (1866) after defeat by Prussia (*see* AUSTRO-PRUSSIAN WAR). However, he became Germany's ally, looking for support for his policy of expansion into the Balkans, where he annexed Bosnia-Herzegovina in 1908. The Austrian attack on Serbia in 1914 led immediately to the outbreak of the FIRST WORLD WAR. Two years after his death the empire which he had tried for so long to hold together fell to pieces.

FRANCO, Francisco (1892–1975), Spanish general and dictator, was born in Galicia, the son of a naval paymaster. He attended the military school at Toledo, from which he passed out as an infantry officer to serve in Morocco, where the Spanish Army conducted a series of campaigns lasting from 1912 to 1927. Franco proved himself as an able and brave officer. Without the benefit of influence or fortune, he became the youngest captain, the youngest major and, in 1927, the youngest general in the army. Called upon by the Republican government to deal with an uprising by coalminers in northern Spain in 1934, he crushed the movement with ruthless efficiency. He was then made Chief of General Staff, but lost that post in 1935 when a Popular Front government came to power. Sent into virtual exile as military governor of the Canaries, he had become convinced that Spain's greatest enemy was Communism. It is not clear when he joined the right-wing plot against the government, but on the day of the army revolt he flew from the Canaries to Morocco, where he speedily took command and transferred considerable numbers of troops into southern Spain. General Mola, commander of the Nationalists in the north was killed, so it was Franco who at Burgos in 1936 was proclaimed Head of State and Generalissimo. He took the title of El Caudillo or Leader.

During the SPANISH CIVIL WAR, which lasted until March 1939, Franco directed the strategy that brought victory to the Nationalists, though he himself did not actually take command in the field. Slow and cautious, he was greatly helped with armaments and planes from HITLER and MUSSOLINI and also by the quarrels between the various political groups of the Republic. Thus from 1939 Franco ruled Spain as a dictator. In 1940, after France fell, he met Hitler at Hendaye and the world assumed that he would repay his debt by joining Germany in an attack on GIBRALTAR. He declined to do so and skilfully contrived to keep Spain out of the war.

After the defeat of Hitler and Mussolini he was looked on as the surviving Fascist dictator, and for more than a decade Spain remained isolated. In this situation Franco held to his course, ruling through a Council of Ministers, retaining the support of the Army, the Church, the monarchists and propertied classes and permitting little in the way of free speech or opposition. It must be said, however, that the people's standard of living rose, and after a century of civil wars and army revolts this harsh, colourless dictator had given Spain, by 1975, no fewer than thirty-six years of peace and stability.

FRANCO-PRUSSIAN WAR (1870–1) had its origins in the rivalry between France and the North German Confederation, dominated by Prussia after the defeat of Austria in the AUSTRO-PRUSSIAN WAR (1866). The immediate cause of the war was the candidature of a German prince for the Spanish throne; he withdrew, but the French Emperor NAPOLEON III insisted on an assurance from the King of Prussia that the candidature would not be renewed. The King reported his interview with the French ambassador in a telegram ('the Ems Telegram') to BISMARCK, who doctored the text to make it appear that France had been insulted. France declared war on 19 July 1870 without having made adequate preparations; the German army, on the other hand, was in the highest state of readiness and quickly moved half a million men to the frontier.

The main French army under Macmahon suffered a series of defeats in August and was forced to surrender at Sedan on 1 September. Napoleon III was captured. Another French army surrendered at Metz and Paris endured a grim siege lasting three and a half months. The city surrendered on 28 January 1871 and peace was signed at Frankfurt in May. France had to surrender Alsace-Lorraine and pay an indemnity of 5 billion francs. The end of the war was marked by a revolutionary outburst in Paris, quelled by the regular army; the French Second Empire came to a disastrous end and Napoleon III never regained the throne but died in exile. For Bismarck the success of Prussian arms enabled him to create a unified Germany.

FRANKLIN, Benjamin (1706–90), the American statesman, writer and scientist, was born at Boston, Massachusetts. At twelve years of age he was apprenticed to the printing trade, and as a young man worked as a printer in Philadelphia and in London, where he spent two years. He returned to America in 1726 to run the *Pennsylvania Gazette* (1729) and to first make a name for himself by publishing *Poor Richard's Almanac* (1732), a kind of magazine full of homely sayings and funny quips, which had a big circulation for years. He began to take an interest in public affairs and became clerk to the Assembly, postmaster of Philadelphia and, in 1753, joint controller of the Colonial Postal Services. Self-educated and bursting with ideas to improve his fellow human beings, he founded societies, organized America's first circulating library, a hospital, fire-fighting measures, volunteer regiments, street-cleaning and street-paving; he also founded an academy which developed into the University of Pennsylvania. Turning his attention

Benjamin Franklin used a kite with a key on the string to prove his theory about lightning and electricity.

to science, he made researches that proved the distinction between positive and negative electricity and that lightning and electricity are identical. Always practical, he suggested the use of lightning conductors for tall buildings. Further, he discovered the course of the Gulf Stream and the paths of storms across North America. His scientific papers aroused great interest in England and France and he was made a member of the Royal Society.

In 1757 this gifted ingenious man was sent to England to put Pennsylvania's case against the Penn family in a dispute over taxes; he succeeded in his mission and during a five years' stay received honorary degrees from Oxford and Edinburgh. In 1764 he was back again to contest Parliament's taxing of the colonies; he appeared before the House of Commons and put the case so well that the Stamp Act was repealed in 1766. He himself was still a loyalist, but as the difference between the British government and the colonies became more bitter, he gave his mind and energies to serving his country and he took a leading part in drawing up the DECLARATION OF INDEPENDENCE.

After war broke out, he was sent in 1776 as delegate to Paris, where his reputation as scientist and philosopher, together with his dignified yet warm, humorous personality, brought him popularity and success. He secured the treaty of alliance with France that contributed greatly to America's victory and achievement of independence. He stayed on in Paris as United States minister and negotiated commercial treaties with Prussia and Sweden before returning home in 1785. He was now world famous and a national hero beloved by all classes. Elected President of the state of Pennsylvania, he helped to draw up the constitution of the United States, while still writing scientific papers and working in Congress for the abolition of SLAVERY up to the time of his death.

FREDERICK II (1194–1250), Holy Roman Emperor (1215–50), was known as 'Stupor Mundi' – 'the Wonder of the World'. Son of Emperor Henry VI and Constance, heiress of Sicily, he became king of Sicily in 1198. Pope INNOCENT III helped him to become Holy Roman Emperor by excommunicating Otto IV, and Frederick succeeded in 1215. At once he began to try to bring all of Italy into the Empire; the Pope's power was to be curtailed and Frederick would rule a new Empire, with Rome as its capital.

Castle of Frederick II in southern Italy and his seal

After warring with the Pope and his allies for several years he went off on CRUSADE in 1228, succeeding where many had failed, for, by means of a treaty with the Sultan of Egypt, he won possession of Jerusalem and crowned himself King of Jerusalem.

During his absence Pope Gregory IX devastated his lands in Italy, but on his return Frederick recovered them all and made peace with the Pope. However, rebellions broke out in both Germany and Italy and after suffering a heavy defeat at Parma, Frederick died at Fiorentino. His brilliant gifts as a linguist, poet and patron of the arts and science fascinated his contemporaries but no one understood him and he failed to realize his plans for Italy.

FREDERICK the Great (1712–86), Frederick II, King of Prussia (1740–86), was the son of Frederick William I, a tyrant who ruled his people and his family with almost insane brutality. Frederick's love of music and literature so enraged his father that the young man resolved to escape to England. He was apprehended, forced to witness his companion's execution and treated like a criminal. Later, however, at his château Sans Souci Prince Frederick was able to surround himself with writers, musicians and scientists and to enjoy French culture.

On his father's death Frederick, at the head of the splendid Prussian army, seized Silesia, a province belonging to MARIA THERESA the Empress of Austria, and this led to the War of the AUSTRIAN SUCCESSION (1741–8). After a victory at Mollwitz and further fighting, he managed to keep the province, but in 1756 the SEVEN YEARS WAR broke out, in which France, Austria, Sweden and Russia attacked Prussia, whose ally was Britain. In this war Frederick won a worldwide reputation as a general, gaining brilliant victories at times (as at Rossbach, 1757, over the French and at Leuthen, 1757, over the Austrians), at others staving off disaster by masterly retreats and somehow scraping together yet another army when he appeared to be about to be overwhelmed.

All seemed to be lost as his enemies closed in and GEORGE III withdrew British support (chiefly in gold), when the death of the Tsarina Elizabeth brought about a change in Russian policy. The Russians quit the war and their exhausted allies followed suit, so that by the Treaty of Paris, 1763, Frederick kept Silesia and after twenty years of war turned his energies to rebuilding his ruined country.

Frederick the Great at the Battle of Rossbach

Living like a pauper and working with ferocious intensity, he restored Prussia's trade and agriculture, founded schools and improved justice and the roads. Hence in 1772 he was strong enough to snatch more territory when he divided Poland between himself, CATHERINE of Russia and Maria Theresa.

This cold ruthless autocrat always retained his interest in the arts, but his claim to greatness lies in his military and political skill. He made Prussia into a great Power.

FRENCH AND INDIAN WARS (1754–63) is the name given to the last struggle between the British and French colonists in North America. Planning to link up their lands in Canada with Louisiana in the south, the French had built a line of forts (Niagara, Crown Point, Frontenac, Ticonderoga and Duquesne) which infringed on the Ohio lands claimed by Virginia. Governor Dinwiddie sent Lieutenant-Colonel WASHINGTON to warn the French to leave; he defeated a French and Indian force at Great Meadows (1754) but had to surrender at Fort Necessity. A British force under General Edward Braddock was beaten at Fort Duquesne in 1755, where Washington distinguished himself.

The outbreak of the SEVEN YEARS WAR intensified hostilities, and in 1756–7 the French general Montcalm captured Fort Oswego and Fort William Henry; however, the British took the great port of Louisbourg on Cape Breton Island and Fort Frontenac on Lake Ontario (1758). Fort Duquesne fell and General Amherst won the battles of Ticonderoga and Crown Point (1759). WOLFE captured Quebec in 1759 and Montreal surrendered in the following year, so that French Canada was now in British hands. The war was formally ended by the Treaty of Paris, 1763.

FRENCH REVOLUTION (1789). When Louis XVI agreed to summon the States General, or parliament, in May 1789, France was practically bankrupt and seething with discontent. Unsuccessful wars, help to the American colonies and royal extravagance had emptied the Treasury; the monarchy was despised, the nobles hated and the Church widely unpopular. The peasants endured unjust taxation and feudal oppression, while the middle classes resented having little or no say in the government. When, after 175 years, the States General did meet, the two upper 'estates', the nobles and the Church, opposed the third estate, or commons, whose representatives broke away, proclaimed themselves the National Assembly and swore never to disband until they had made a new constitution.

While they debated, food riots broke out in Paris, where, on 14 July, a mob captured the Bastille, an ancient prison that seemed to stand for the authority of the rulers. Its fall sparked off violent disorders throughout the country, and in many places peasants attacked manor houses and destroyed feudal rent-rolls. In October the Paris mob marched to Versailles and brought back the

The fall of the Bastille

Royal Family to semi-captivity in the capital. After this the Assembly abolished feudal privileges and dues, nobility and Church property. Although the King accepted the Declaration of the Rights of Man, the Assembly came to be dominated by fanatical Republicans and Louis's attempted flight abroad made him yet more unpopular. In 1791 the National Assembly gave way to the Legislative Assembly, in which a struggle developed between the moderate Girondins and the 'Mountain' or extremists, consisting of the JACOBINS led by ROBESPIERRE and the *Cordeliers* led by DANTON. War broke out with Austria in 1792 and some early reverses so infuriated the Paris mob that they stormed the royal palace, massacred the Swiss Guard and abolished the monarchy. The revolutionary armies soon beat the Prussians at Valmy (September) and the Austrians at Jemappes (November), but hysterical fear of the Royalists led to the September Massacres, when hundreds of suspects were guillotined. The extremists, now in control, declared a Republic and executed Louis XVI in January 1793 and Queen MARIE ANTOINETTE soon afterwards.

The Committee of Public Safety, which took over the government, put down a Royalist rising in western France (la Vendée) and defeated the Republic's enemies in the field. But Robespierre, who held complete power for a year, was not satisfied; he brought in the Reign of Terror, which only ended when he himself was guillotined in July 1794. Affairs now became less violent and a committee of five called the Directory ruled France for the next five years, pursuing a middle-of-the-road course until it was overthrown by General Bonaparte (NAPOLEON I) in 1799.

The French Revolution was one of the most momentous events in the world's history and its effects are with us today. Its course was marked by tyranny and horrifying brutality, yet the ideals of Liberty, Equality and Fraternity did survive to provide inspiration for later European reformers.

FRIARS were members of religious Orders known as mendicant (i.e. begging), because they lived by begging alms and owned no property. Unlike monks belonging to such orders as the Benedictines and Cistercians (*see* MONASTERIES), friars did not belong to a particular house, but spent most of their time out in the world, preaching and helping the poor and the sick. The 13th century was the great

Friar preaching to an Italian confraternity

age of the friars, when the Franciscans (Grey Friars), Dominicans (Black Friars), Carmelites (White Friars) and the Augustinian or Austin Friars were well-known figures throughout Europe. Besides these there were several other Orders, such as the Servites, the Trinity or Red Friars and the Crutched Friars or the Friars of the Holy Cross. Friars brought religion into the growing towns before the regular clergy were active there. By adopting a life of poverty, helping the poor and often criticizing the Church's wealth in their preaching, they won widespread popularity.

FROBISHER, Sir Martin (*c*. 1535–94), Elizabethan seaman, who in 1576 sailed in search of the North-West Passage and reached what is now Baffin Island, Canada, where he named Frobisher Bay. He made two more voyages of exploration and brought back 200 tons of what was thought to be gold ore, but the stones proved worthless. In 1586 he was vice-admiral to DRAKE's expedition to the West Indies and he commanded one of the four squadrons that fought the Spanish ARMADA. He died of wounds received when fighting to prevent the Spaniards from taking the French port of Brest.

Reputed to be a 'rough captain' with no courtly manners, ELIZABETH liked and trusted him as one of her leading 'sea dogs'.

Elizabeth Fry reading to prisoners in Newgate Gaol

FRY, Elizabeth (1780–1845), British prison reformer, was a Quaker married to a wealthy merchant. After her first visit to Newgate Prison, she spent her life improving the lot of women prisoners by visiting them, arousing public sympathy, writing pamphlets and urging reforms. She concerned herself with the condition of women convicts transported to Australia and, through visiting continental prisons, was regarded in Europe as an expert on prison reform.

FULTON, Robert (1765–1815), American steamboat pioneer, went to England as a young man, where he studied canal-building. In France he invented a submarine, the *Nautilus*, in 1801 and designed a small steamboat, which was tried out on the Seine. Returning to America, he worked on canal construction before building the *Clermont*, a steamboat powered by a Boulton and Watt engine, which in 1807 made the 150-mile (240 km) trip from New York to Albany on the Hudson River. He also built the *Fulton* for the US government, a paddle-steamer which was the first steam warship.

Fulton's *Clermont* on the Hudson River in 1810

Opposite The FEUDAL SYSTEM in France: peasants working on the Lord's domain

G

GALILEO Galilei (1564–1642) was born at Pisa and as a student came to disbelieve the ancient and hallowed teachings of Aristotle. When only nineteen, he realized the laws of the vibrations of a pendulum and its value in measuring time. He became a professor at Padua University, lecturing in mathematics and astronomy and he invented the thermometer, constructed his own telescope and proved that heavy and light bodies fall at the same velocity. Believing in the theories of COPERNICUS, he came into conflict with the Church, since these were condemned by the INQUISITION. However, he made his peace, pretending to accept the view of the Church and thereby saving himself from being burned at the stake. After a brief imprisonment he was given a light sentence and was permitted to carry on his scientific researches at Florence.

GANDHI, Mohandas K. (1869–1948), Indian national leader, generally known as Mahatma, 'great soul', studied law in England and went to South Africa in 1893, where he campaigned for political and social justice for the Asiatic immigrants. He returned to India in 1914, and after the war, as national leader opposed to the British authorities, he introduced, first, his non-co-operation policy and, later, civil disobedience. In spite of his own belief in non-violence, his followers frequently took part in riots and strikes and Gandhi spent several terms in prison. His prestige

Opposite Pioneer emigrants to the West crossing the plains beneath the Rocky Mountains (*see* GOLD RUSH, Californian)

made him the guiding spirit of the INDIAN NATIONAL CONGRESS, yet he was only once president (1925) and often held himself aloof from its activities. In the 1930s he went into religious retreat for a lengthy period, but so great was his hold on the people's affection that the national leaders had to consult him constantly.

As a social reformer, Gandhi campaigned for the untouchables, for a return to simple village industries, such as hand-spinning, and for friendship between Hindus and Muslims. There were strange contradictions in his principles; the opponent of modern industry accepted help from Indian big business; the saintly mystic was also a cunning politician and a hard bargainer. But he never wavered from his belief in non-violence and the essential goodness of man.

When the Second World War broke out, he felt that Hitler was the aggressor, but that only a free India could give Britain moral support. He therefore demanded complete independence and, in face of the threatened Japanese invasion, proposed that Indians should offer no resistance. He was interned from 1942 to 1944 and at the end of the war took a large part in the negotiations for independence. When it came, the prospect of a bloody conflict caused him to preach brotherhood between Hindus and Muslims, an attitude which angered extremists. He was assassinated by a Hindu fanatic at Delhi on 30 January 1948.

The manner of his death emphasized his failures. In spite of his saintly example, he did not succeed in restraining violence, industrialization or religious intolerance; nevertheless, he was the most influential figure India has produced for centuries.

GARIBALDI, Giuseppe (1807–82), the Italian patriot, was born at Nice, son of a sea-captain, and he himself was a sailor before taking up his remarkable career as a nationalist. His part in an unsuccessful rising at Genoa caused him to flee abroad in 1834 and he spent the next twelve years in South America, fighting as a guerrilla leader on the side of popular movements against oppressive rulers.

Back in Italy he led a volunteer army with the utmost courage against the French and the Austrians in the REVOLUTIONS OF 1848, but again had to go into exile, this time to the USA. He lived there for several years and made enough money to return to Italy and buy the island of Caprera, which was

Garibaldi and his Redshirts land in Sicily in May 1860

thenceforward his home. In 1859 he commanded the Alpine infantry against the Austrians and, after peace, landed in Sicily with his One Thousand Redshirts and in a brilliant campaign defeated the Neapolitan army and took control of the island. He next expelled Ferdinand II from Naples and was intending to invade the Papal States and liberate Rome when King Victor Emmanuel II arrived with the Sardinian army. To bring about the union of Italy, Garibaldi was persuaded by CAVOUR to agree that his conquests should become part of the Italian realm, so he disbanded his volunteers and retired to Caprera.

His adventurous career was not yet ended. In 1862 and 1867 he made two attempts to capture Rome, but was prevented from doing so on both occasions. During the AUSTRO-PRUSSIAN WAR of 1866 he and his volunteers attacked the Austrians, and in 1870, during the FRANCO-PRUSSIAN WAR, he raised a force to help the French in Burgundy and inflicted several defeats on the German troops. By this time Garibaldi was a legendary figure, beloved by the Italian people and famous throughout the world. When he visited London in 1864, he was welcomed with such enthusiasm by the working class that the government nervously cancelled his projected tour of the provinces. After Rome became the capital of Italy (1871), he entered Parliament as deputy for the city and was eventually persuaded to accept a pension and a large gift in return for his services to his country.

GAULLE, Charles de (1890–1970), French soldier and statesman, fought in the First World War and was captured by the Germans. As a professional soldier between the wars he put forward theories about the use of tanks which were not accepted by his superiors. In 1940, a general in command of an armoured division, he opposed an armistice, escaped to England and put himself at the head of the Free French forces. Proud and aloof, he was often at odds with the Allies, who did not readily accept him as the true leader of France. However, when liberation came, he entered Paris at once and became head of the provisional government. As President he succeeded in restoring France to the

status of a great power during the post-war settlement and, his task done, he resigned in 1946. In the troubled years that followed, many people still regarded him as the strong man of France and in 1958 he was swept into power by a popular movement.

As President of the Fifth Republic, he settled the Algerian war (1962) by accepting defeat (*see* AFRICAN INDEPENDENCE). He gave independence to French colonies and made moves for friendly relations with Germany and Russia. His aim was to make France strong and to give her an independent role in world affairs; thus he vetoed Britain's entry into the Common Market (EUROPEAN ECONOMIC COMMUNITY), established considerable dominance over his Common Market partners, especially as regards agricultural policy, withdrew from NATO (1969) and insisted on France producing her own nuclear weapon. At home he strove for economic growth and the fostering of national pride, and in these aims he was mainly successful; but his regime was shaken by widespread strikes and student riots in 1968 and he resigned in the following year.

Volunteers manning a London bus during the General Strike

GENERAL STRIKE (1926) in Britain lasted for nine days, from 4 to 13 May. Its cause was a dispute between the Miners' Federation and the coal-owners, who, owing to the bad state of the industry, proposed to cut wages. The Trades Union Congress agreed to support the miners with a sympathetic strike by workers in transport, heavy industry, printing, building, gas and electricity. Other unions would be held in reserve. The general strike began on 4 May and Britain came near to a complete standstill. However, the Conservative Government had prepared emergency plans, so that it took over broadcasting, issued a newspaper, used the navy to man power stations and set up food depots, while volunteers manned buses and lorries. There was very little disorder.

Meanwhile, Sir Herbert Samuel produced a memorandum containing proposals to settle the miners' dispute and this was accepted by the TUC. Unfortunately, the miners (who were not represented on the negotiating committee) rejected it. Nevertheless, the TUC leaders decided to call off the strike. They did not want a head-on collision with the government nor a protracted strike, for they feared extremists taking over the unions and they were dismayed by widespread talk that the strike was illegal. To many workers its abrupt ending seemed to be a complete surrender and the miners felt they had been betrayed.

GENGHIS KHAN (1162–1227), founder of the MONGOL Empire, was the son of Yesukai, chief or khan of one of the many nomad tribes which inhabited the plains of eastern Siberia. Yesukai was murdered and his son, then named Temujin, had to fend for himself and learn the military and political skills that were to make him leader of all the tribes. By 1206 he had defeated all his rivals and was proclaimed the Great Khan at Karakorum, sacred meeting-place of the Mongols. He then took the name of Chinghis or Genghis Khan. At the head of hordes of well-mounted tribesmen, he swept into China as far as Peking and then, leaving one of his generals behind as viceroy, turned westwards to extend his conquests across Afghanistan and Persia to the shores of the Black Sea, where he decisively defeated the warlike TURKS. In his old age he retired to Mongolia and devoted himself to ruling his vast empire through his four sons; he set up a system of staging-posts and royal messengers to keep himself informed and he issued a code of laws, the Yassa, which was obeyed by the Mongols for generations. He died on campaign against a rebellion in northern China. His grandson, Kublai Khan, founded the Mongol (or YÜAN) Dynasty of China.

GEORGE I (1660–1727), King of Great Britain (1714–27) and Elector of HANOVER, came to the throne on the death of ANNE because he was descended from James I and was a Protestant. His mother Sophia was the daughter of Elizabeth of Bohemia, herself the daughter of James I. George was unpopular in England; he much preferred Hanover and went there as often as he could. Unable to speak English, he gave up attending cabinet meetings, but conferred privately with his ministers in French, since they could not speak German. A dull plain man, who imprisoned his wife for life and loathed his own son, he had shrewd knowledge of European affairs and plenty of common sense. The chief events of his reign were the JACOBITE REBELLION OF 1715 and the SOUTH SEA BUBBLE of 1720, which brought WALPOLE to the fore.

GEORGE II (1683–1760), King of Great Britain (1727–60) and Elector of HANOVER, was the son of GEORGE I. At his accession it seemed certain that he would dismiss WALPOLE, whom he disliked, but Queen Caroline, more intelligent than her coarse pompous husband, persuaded him to let Walpole continue in office. George often visited Hanover, which he preferred to England, and his concern for his family homeland involved Britain in continental campaigns during the War of the AUSTRIAN SUCCESSION. The last English king to lead his army in battle, he fought bravely at Dettingen (1743). He detested Pitt (later Earl of CHATHAM), who had ridiculed him and his beloved Hanover, but was compelled by the government's resignation to let him hold office in 1746. Eleven years later, when the SEVEN YEARS WAR was going badly, he reluctantly accepted Pitt as Secretary of State in charge of the conduct of the war and thereafter they worked loyally together.

GEORGE III (1738–1820), King of Great Britain (1760–1820), was the son of Frederick Prince of Wales and grandson of GEORGE II. Brought up as an Englishman, he said he 'gloried in the name of Briton' and at his succession he was determined to be a king, not a puppet controlled by Parliament. At once he began to reverse George II's policies by choosing his own ministers and bringing the SEVEN YEARS WAR to an end. He built up a party of 'King's Friends' and seemed to be succeeding in his aims when there arose the fatal dispute with the American colonies. To the end he believed that he was right and the colonists wrong, and it was his obstinate refusal to make concessions that led directly to the AMERICAN WAR OF INDEPENDENCE and to an alliance of nations against Britain.

The loss of the American colonies lessened but did not destroy George III's influence and prestige. For one thing, most of his countrymen had agreed with his attitude. In 1783 he was able to overthrow the alliance of Charles James Fox and Lord North and make PITT the Younger the equivalent of Prime Minister, even without a majority in the Commons. Here, too, he had the public's support. He asserted himself again in 1801, after Pitt put through the Act of Union with Ireland, promising to bring in

Catholic Emancipation. George flatly refused to agree, saying that to do so would violate his coronation oath to uphold the Protestant religion.

Though stubborn, George III was shrewd, hardworking and devoted to what he thought were the country's best interests. He married Charlotte of Mecklenburg, by whom he had fifteen children, and they lived happily and simply at Windsor, where he took a keen interest in his model farm in the Great Park. Known as 'Farmer George', he was genuinely popular in the country, especially after the outbreak of the FRENCH REVOLUTION. He suffered from bouts of insanity and in 1811 became permanently mad, so that his reign effectively ended and his son, later GEORGE IV, was appointed Prince Regent.

George IV and his pavilion at Brighton

GEORGE IV (1762–1830), King of Great Britain (1820–30), was the eldest son of GEORGE III. As Prince of Wales, or 'Prinny', he became a byword for his love affairs, extravagance and cultivation of Whig friends hostile to his father. He married Caroline of Brunswick, whom he soon deserted; she disappeared abroad, but the country was shaken by the scandal of the 'Queen's Affair' when she returned in 1820 before the coronation to contest her divorce. George, for long an object of ridicule, became so unpopular that the monarchy seemed in danger; however, it survived, and during his reign he avoided conflict with his ministers, most of whom he heartily disliked. His one virtue was his interest in art, music and architecture; he bought many paintings and was responsible for the building of Regent Street and Brighton Pavilion and for the enlargement of Windsor Castle.

GEORGE V (1865–1936), King of Great Britain (1910–36), succeeded his father EDWARD VII. During his reign there occurred the FIRST WORLD WAR, war in Ireland, the first Labour Government, the GENERAL STRIKE, mass unemployment and the economic crisis of 1931. Throughout this period of profound change the King played the part of a constitutional monarch, taking the deepest interest in the country's affairs, consulting his ministers and accepting their guidance. Stolid, unimaginative, a martinet to his family, a lover of country life, he and his wife, Queen Mary, came more and more to stand for stability in a changing world. At the Silver Jubilee celebrations of 1935 the nation demonstrated its loyalty with an outburst of enthusiasm that surprised the modest conscientious man who had done his duty for twenty-five years.

GEORGE VI (1895–1952), King of Great Britain (1936–52), second son of GEORGE V and Queen Mary, came to the throne on the abdication of his brother EDWARD VIII. In his youth he joined the navy, served at the Battle of Jutland (*see* FIRST WORLD WAR) and, as Duke of York, became well-known for his welfare work for boys' clubs. Thanks to his modesty, devotion to duty and the help he received from his wife Elizabeth, the monarchy recovered from the abdication crisis, and during the SECOND WORLD WAR he and the Queen, who had remained in London during the bombing, became immensely popular. He died suddenly and was succeeded by his elder daughter as Queen Elizabeth II.

GERONIMO (1829–1909), leader of the Apache INDIANS and the last one to put up armed resistance to the white man. From 1884 to 1886 he and his band of warriors made raids across the south-western States and into northern Mexico, tying down a large force of American troops. After his capture Geronimo was exiled to Florida, but he was eventually released to become a stock-raiser and a public celebrity.

GESTAPO, the Secret Police of NAZI Germany, was organized soon after HITLER came to power in 1933 and lasted until Germany's defeat in 1945. Its leader, Heinrich Himmler, established the Gestapo in every German state to deal with anti-Nazi organizations and persons suspected of political offences. The power of the dreaded Gestapo rested on the fact that it was above the law. There was no superior authority to keep its activities in check, to question its decisions or reprimand its officers. Gestapo officers could decide what was a political offence; they could arrest a person who had committed no legal offence and could rearrest acquitted persons and those who had served prison sentences. In effect they had the power to send anyone to the concentration camps without trial.

GETTYSBURG ADDRESS (19 November 1863) was a speech delivered by Abraham LINCOLN at the dedication of a national cemetery on the battlefield of Gettysburg. There, in the previous July, the Federal Army under General Meade had defeated the Confederates, led by General Robert E. LEE, with huge losses to both sides.

At the ceremony Edward Everett spoke for two hours. Then Lincoln stepped forward to read the sentences he had scribbled on a piece of paper the night before. He spoke for barely five minutes and his speech of less than three hundred words was at first widely criticized. It was said to be too brief and to be even insulting to the dead, but, in time, Americans came to realize that this was one of the most moving and powerful speeches of all time. Here are Lincoln's actual words:

Fourscore and seven years ago our fathers brought forth, on this continent a new nation conceived in liberty and dedicated to the proposition that all men are created equal.

Now we are engaged in a great civil war testing whether that nation, or any nation so conceived and so dedicated, can long endure. We are met on a great battlefield of that war. We have come to dedicate a portion of that field as a final resting-place for those who here gave their lives that that nation might live. It is altogether fitting and proper that we should do this.

But, in a larger sense, we cannot dedicate, we cannot consecrate, we cannot hallow this ground. The brave men, living and dead, who struggled here, have consecrated it far above our poor power to add or detract. The world will little note nor long remember what we say here, but it can never forget what they did here. It is for us the living rather to be dedicated here to the unfinished work which they who fought here have thus far so nobly advanced. It is rather for us to be here dedicated to the great task remaining before us – that from these honoured dead we take increased devotion to that cause for which they gave the last full measure of devotion – that we here highly resolve that these dead shall not have died in vain, that this nation under God shall have a new birth of freedom, and that government of the people, by the people, for the people, shall not perish from the earth.

GIBRALTAR is a peninsula, known as the Rock, at the most southerly point of Spain and about 14 miles (22 km) from the coast of Africa. Connected to the Spanish mainland by a narrow isthmus, it is a powerful naval base, with a town on the western side. Gibraltar was captured by the British and Dutch under Admiral Sir George Rooke in 1704 during the War of the SPANISH SUCCESSION and withstood a historic siege from 1779 to 1783 during the AMERICAN WAR OF INDEPENDENCE, when General Sir George Eliott held it for over three and a half years against a combined Franco-Spanish force equipped with floating batteries. It was ceded to

Gibraltar besieged by the Spaniards in 1782

Britain by the Treaty of Utrecht, 1713, renewed by the Treaty of Versailles, 1783.

During both World Wars it was a point of vital strategic importance for control of the Mediterranean. Since the 1950s Spain has claimed the return of Gibraltar on the grounds that the British, in granting the Gibraltarians domestic self-rule, have broken the Treaty of Utrecht. Britain would probably have ceded the colony but for the fact that the civilian population, largely non-Spanish, have expressed a strong preference to remain as they are.

GILBERT, Sir Humphrey (*c.* 1530–83), Elizabethan soldier, pioneer colonist and stepbrother of Sir Walter RALEIGH. He entered the service of ELIZABETH I, served as a captain in Ireland and fought against the Spaniards in the Netherlands. Interested in colonization and the discovery of the North-West Passage, he published a *Discourse to Prove a Passage by the North West to Cathay and India* in 1576, and two years later the Queen gave him a charter to 'occupy and possess' any remote lands 'not actually possessed of any Christian prince'. At his own expense he fitted out an expedition in 1578, which failed, and it was not until 1583 that he sailed from Plymouth with five ships to Newfoundland.

Here, in the first serious attempt to colonize North America, he proclaimed himself Governor at St John's, issued leases of land and a code of laws. Sailing southwards to establish another settlement, he lost one of his ships while exploring the coast near Cape Breton and decided to return to England in the little frigate *Squirrel*, of only 10 tons, accompanied by the larger *Golden Hind*. In bad weather off the Azores he refused to leave the frigate to go aboard the other vessel and was last seen on deck, with a book in his hand, crying out 'unto us in the *Hind*, ''we are as near to heaven by sea as by land'''. Suddenly, the lights of the *Squirrel* disappeared, as she and her commander were swallowed up by the sea.

GLADSTONE, William Ewart (1809–98), British statesman, Prime Minister and leader of the Liberal Party, was born at Liverpool, the son of a wealthy Scottish merchant. Educated at Eton and Oxford, he almost entered the Church, but decided upon a political career and first entered Parliament as a Tory in 1832. He became Colonial Secretary and followed PEEL in supporting Free Trade and repeal of the CORN LAWS. Under Lord Aberdeen (1852–55) he made his reputation as Chancellor of the Exchequer and in 1859, decided to serve under PALMERSTON, partly because he agreed with his pro-Italian policy and partly because of his own intense rivalry with DISRAELI. This was the vital move that was to make him leader of the Liberal Party.

In 1868 he became Prime Minister for the first time, holding office until 1874, a period which saw his disestablishment of the Irish Church, the Irish Land Act, the 1870 EDUCATION ACT, Cardwell's Army reforms and the Ballot Act to make voting secret. In foreign affairs, he kept out of the FRANCO-PRUSSIAN WAR, took no action when Russia introduced warships into the Black Sea and accepted the International Court's ruling against Britain in the ALABAMA DISPUTE. In spite of many reforms, his measures provoked much opposition and his rival Disraeli returned to office in 1874.

Gladstone retired to his religious studies, but re-emerged to arouse the nation with his denunciation of the Bulgarian Atrocities (1876) by the Turks. In the famous Midlothian Campaign he passionately attacked Disraeli's foreign policy with such success that he became Prime Minister for the second time in 1880. During the next five years he had to wrestle with problems in Ireland, where disorder compelled him unwillingly to adopt stern measures, in Egypt, where he was blamed for not sending troops in time to save General GORDON, and in South Africa, where he gave the Boers independence in the Transvaal.

1886 saw him Prime Minister for the third time and he now introduced his cherished measure to promote IRISH HOME RULE. It split the Liberal Party, some of whom voted with the Conservatives to defeat the Bill in the House of Commons. Gladstone resigned, but in 1892 the 'Grand Old Man', as he was called, now in his eighty-third year, became

Prime Minister once again, determined to solve the problem of Ireland. His second Home Rule Bill passed the Commons but was decisively rejected by the Lords, causing him effectively to retire from politics. Even at the end of his life he showed his old vigour in criticizing naval expenditure and denouncing the Armenian Massacres (1896) in Asia Minor.

Gladstone was the greatest Liberal politician of his century. Stern, self-righteous and deeply religious, he was a thunderous orator, whose duels with Disraeli fascinated Parliament and the country. He was an outstanding Chancellor of the Exchequer and a reformer whose measures earned him the name of 'the People's William'. In his sympathy for oppressed peoples like the Irish and the Bulgarians he was ahead of his time, so that his liberal ideas and moral attitude aroused much opposition.

GLORIOUS REVOLUTION (1688–9) was the overthrow of JAMES II, followed by a constitutional settlement that changed the position of the monarchy in Britain.

Through disregarding the laws of the land, keeping a standing army and appointing Roman Catholics to high positions, James II made it clear that he intended to force the country back to Catholicism. The birth of his son in June 1688 provided a Catholic heir to the throne, and this event prompted a small group of leading men to invite William of Orange (husband of James II's daughter Mary) to come over to save the English Constitution and Church (see WILLIAM III and MARY II).

William landed at Tor Bay on 5 November 1688 with an army of 30,000 men and moved slowly inland. His banner proclaimed 'A Free Parliament and the Protestant Religion'. James, who had intended to fight near Salisbury, found that his army was too unreliable to offer battle and that many of his supporters, including his best general, Lord Churchill (later Duke of MARLBOROUGH), had deserted to William. In London, learning that his daughter ANNE had fled, his nerve broke and he attempted to escape to France. Captured, he was allowed to escape again and to find refuge at the court of LOUIS XIV.

After some delay and confusion, a convention of MPs and City of London councillors met in February 1689 and offered the throne jointly to William and Mary on conditions set out in a Declaration of Rights. This document, made into a Statute as the Bill of Rights (1689), began with the wrongful acts of James II, including suspension of laws, levying money without consent of Parliament and keeping a standing army in peacetime. Parliaments were to be frequent and freely elected, with free speech for Members. Lastly, Roman Catholics and those married to Catholics were to be barred from the Crown.

In accepting these terms, William became a constitutional monarch. Hereditary succession was preserved in the person of Mary, daughter of James II, but the idea of Divine Right was abandoned. Parliament made sure of its control by insisting that the King's ministers should submit an annual estimate of expenditure and obtain consent for every tax. This was the origin of the modern Budget. By the Mutiny Act (1689) troops might be kept under military discipline for only one year; hence the Act had to be renewed annually, and this compelled the King to summon Parliament every year. The Triennial Act (1694) provided for a General Election at three-yearly intervals.

A Scottish convention offered the crown of Scotland to William and Mary on condition that the Presbyterian Church should be re-established and this was accepted, but Ireland declared for James II, so that the Revolution was established there by William's victory at the Battle of the Boyne, 1690.

GOLD RUSH, Australian. The first significant discoveries of gold were made in 1851 near Bathurst in New South Wales, but far greater finds soon occurred in Victoria. A dramatic 'gold rush' then took place, as workers of every kind abandoned their jobs and set off for the 'diggings'. Then, as the news spread across the world, adventurers from Britain, America and Europe poured into Melbourne. Thousands of Chinese entered Australia; towns like Bendigo, Ballarat and Castlemaine became famous names and the population of Victoria leapt up from 77,000 in 1851 to about 200,000 in 1853, with some 80,000 roaming the goldfields.

To try to control the situation and to pay for the cost of goldfield administration, Governor La Trobe imposed a gold-seeker's licence of £18 a year. This caused great resentment among the miners and led to the tragic episode of EUREKA STOCKADE (1854), when a number of miners resisted the police and

Australian gold prospectors

Panning for gold in California

the military and were killed. The gold rush spent itself in a few years, as the easily won gold ran out and mining came to be carried on by companies with resources to sink shafts. Some of the great camps, whose inhabitants had numbered thousands, became ghost towns; others survived to become rural centres of farming districts.

A second gold rush occurred after gold was found at Coolgardie in Western Australia, with far richer discoveries at Kalgoorlie. Much the same conditions occurred· as diggers hurried into the near-desert area, but this time there was no tragic clash with the authorities, though many of the miners died from typhoid. As in Victoria the population rose dramatically, from about 50,000 to 180,000 ten years later.

GOLD RUSH, Californian, began in 1849, after gold had been discovered in a river-bed near a saw-mill at Fort Sutter. Up to this time California had been quiet ranching country with an American population of only a few hundred; then in 1848 Mexico (defeated in the MEXICAN WAR of 1846–8) ceded the province to the United States. In his message to Congress President Polk mentioned the newly-found riches and the Gold Rush was on.

Thousands of fortune-seekers set out on the 'Golden Trail', some across the fever-ridden Panama

Isthmus, some by clipper round Cape Horn and the majority by the land route across the Mississippi, the Great Plains and the Rocky Mountains. Two-thirds of the miners were Americans, while the remainder came from Europe, Asia and Australia. All of them, exploited on the way by shippers, guides, mapmakers and storekeepers, made for the canyons and gulches where gold dust could be washed out in pans and troughs. In 1849 over 10 million ounces of gold were mined and in 1852, the peak year, 81 million ounces. The effects were dramatic. While the mountains were filled with lawless, roaring camps, San Francisco sprang up overnight to become a boom city, a metropolis surging with energy, vice and riches. California itself grew so fast that in 1850 it was added to the Union as a State.

GORDON, Charles (1833–85), British general, who served in the CRIMEAN WAR and earned the nickname 'Chinese Gordon' for his brilliant leadership of Chinese imperial troops during the Taiping rebellion (1863–4). From 1874 to 1880 he spent long periods in the Sudan, opening up the country and governing it with outstanding skill. In 1884 the British government sent him to the Sudan to evacuate the Egyptian forces there, for the country had been overrun by rebels led by a religious fanatic called the Mahdi. Gordon reached Khartoum, where

he inspired the besieged garrison to hold out for five months. He felt that the government would be bound to send a relief force and this would enable him to defeat the Mahdi; however, just two days before the relief force did arrive, Khartoum's defences were stormed and Gordon was killed. The British people were grief-stricken at the death of a popular hero and many regarded GLADSTONE as little short of a murderer. He had delayed sending the relief force because he believed that Gordon was deliberately disobeying his instructions to withdraw from the Sudan.

GORDON RIOTS (1780), a violent uprising of the London mob which began as an anti-Catholic demonstration. An Act had been passed giving Catholics certain citizen rights, whereupon Lord George Gordon, a mentally deranged Protestant fanatic, organized a procession to present a demand to Parliament to repeal the Act. The mob got out of hand, burned Catholic homes, set fire to property, looted liquor stores and broke open the jails. The rioters terrorized the capital for a week, until GEORGE III called in the soldiers to restore order. Over two hundred persons were killed and, although some of the ringleaders were executed, Lord Gordon himself was acquitted of high treason. He died insane in Newgate Prison in 1793.

GRANT, Ulysses S. (1822–85), American general and 18th President of the United States, was born in Ohio, and after being trained at the military academy of West Point he entered the US army. Having served in the MEXICAN WAR, he resigned his commission in 1854 to take up farming. On the outbreak of the CIVIL WAR in 1861 he joined the

Federal side and was appointed colonel of a Missouri infantry regiment. Quickly proving himself an able soldier, he captured Fort Henry and Fort Donelson and won the two-day battle of Shiloh in 1862. In the following year he launched a great attack on Vicksburg, which he captured, taking 31,000 prisoners.

Now a major-general, he defeated General Bragg at Chattanooga and in March 1864 LINCOLN made him Commander-in-Chief of all the Union armies. His plan was to keep up a relentless pressure on the enemy, and in a series of bloody engagements he broke the Confederate resistance, captured Richmond and forced LEE to surrender at Appomattox on 9 April 1865. He had brought the great struggle to an end and, as commander of more than a million men, had shown courage, inexhaustible energy and a grim plodding determination to achieve victory at all costs.

He was elected President for the Republicans in 1868 and again in 1872, but his eight-year term of office was one of the most unsuccessful in American history. No one doubted that Grant himself was honest, but he was too trusting and easygoing to check corruption, and his administration was marred by a succession of scandals involving members of Congress and Grant's close associates. After he retired from the Presidency, he accepted a partnership in a banking firm, only to be swindled out of all that he possessed by the other two partners. To earn money he wrote his autobiography, *Personal Memoirs*, a clear modest account of his military career.

GREAT TREK (1836–7) was a series of movements north out of Cape Colony (South Africa) by Boer farmers who wanted to free themselves from British

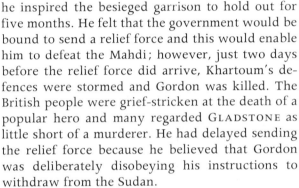

Trekkers crossing the Drakensberg Mountains

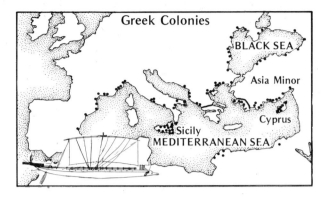

Greek Colonies

rule. They resented a law of 1828, called the 50th Ordinance, which gave Hottentots equal rights with Europeans; they felt cheated by the abolition of SLAVERY, 1833, and they thought the British government gave them no protection against Bantu warriors on the frontier.

So groups of trekkers under leaders such as Piet Retief, Uys and Pretorius, began moving north in covered waggons pulled by teams of oxen. They travelled across the veld for about 300 miles (480 km), some of them settling beyond the Orange River and others going further north across the Vaal into the region which became the Transvaal. Here they had to fight the Matabele and drive them out. One main group, led by Retief, crossed the Drakensberg Mountains into Natal, where the Zulus massacred them. Other Boers arrived, however, to defeat the Zulus and occupy the area. The British annexed Natal in 1843. Thus the Great Trek led to penetration of the interior and to a division of South Africa into four states; two British (the Cape and Natal) and two Boer (the Orange Free State and the Transvaal). It also of course deprived the Africans of large areas of land.

GREEK COLONIES. In Ancient Greece an increasing population and a shortage of good land caused a large-scale colonization movement. It began in the 8th century BC and lasted about two hundred years. With wives, children, gods and customs, Greeks would set off to southern Italy, Sicily, Asia Minor or the Black Sea. In a suitable place they would found a new city, which strictly speaking was not a 'colony', since it was independent of its mother-city. Nevertheless, it was natural to set up trade between the parent-city and its 'offspring'; Corinth, for instance, kept in close touch with the great city-state of Syracuse, which its citizens had founded in Sicily.

The rise of new powers to east (Lydia, Assyria) and west (Carthage, Etruria) checked further Greek expansion. However, colonies were founded as far afield as Spain, the south of France, North Africa, Egypt and Cyprus. In this way Greek influence and culture spread throughout the Mediterranean.

GREEK WAR OF INDEPENDENCE broke out in 1821, when Greek patriots rebelled against the Turks, who had ruled their country as part of the OTTOMAN EMPIRE almost continuously since the 15th century. The rebels suffered defeat at first, but in Morea, a region of southern Greece, they made such headway that the Turkish Sultan called on his powerful vassal MEHEMET ALI of Egypt for help. When the Egyptian troops under Ibrahim Pasha appeared to be bent on wiping out the Greek population, Russia intervened by sending a warning note to Turkey. Canning, the British Foreign Secretary, then formed an agreement (Treaty of London 1827) with Russia and France to mediate on behalf of the Greeks. British warships joined Russian and French squadrons to form a combined fleet, which annihilated the Turkish-Egyptian fleet

The Battle of Navarino

in Navarino Bay (1827). A French army ousted Ibrahim from Morea and Russia declared war on Turkey. After some modest gains the Tsar was ready to make peace, and by the Treaty of Adrianople (1829) the Sultan recognized the independence of Greece. The new state was smaller than the Greeks had hoped, for it did not include Crete, Samos and Thessaly, but they had to be satisfied for the time being. In 1832 the crown was accepted by Prince Otto of Bavaria, who thus became the first King of Greece.

GREGORY I (*c*. 540–604), known as Gregory the Great, an Italian monk, was consecrated Pope in 590. The Roman Church owes to him her public services, ritual and sacred chants and he is looked on as the father of the Church. He reformed the clergy in Gaul, sent missionaries to Spain and St AUGUSTINE to Britain.

GREY, Sir George (1812–98), British colonial governor and Premier of New Zealand. After spending three years exploring north-west Australia he was appointed Governor of South Australia (1841–5), where he was so successful that he was then sent to govern New Zealand. He managed to defeat or pacify the Maoris and to buy great areas of land for settlement. New Zealand's constitution of 1852 was largely his own creation. After a period as Governor of Cape Colony he returned to New

Zealand in 1861 to bring the MAORI WAR to an end, in spite of quarrels with the settlers and his generals. Recalled in 1868, he again returned to New Zealand in 1870, where he spent the rest of his life in politics, becoming premier from 1877 to 1879.

Grey was the most outstanding figure in New Zealand's history in the 19th century and the country's one able governor. Intelligent, cultured and possessed of great influence with the Maoris, he was also a despot who did not hesitate to bend the truth to suit his own purposes. As a politician he was a popular orator who put forward many reforms, including manhood suffrage, but he lacked the ability to get on with colleagues.

GREY, Lady Jane (1537–54), 'nine days' Queen' of England (1553), was the daughter of Henry Grey, Duke of Suffolk, and Frances Brandon, whose mother, Mary, was the sister of HENRY VIII. Thus Jane was great-granddaughter of Henry VII, and all her troubles stemmed from her closeness to the throne. As a child she became the ward of Lord Seymour, who hoped to marry her to EDWARD VI, but Seymour fell and after his execution the Duke of NORTHUMBERLAND compelled her to marry his son Lord Dudley against her own wishes.

As Edward VI lay dying, Northumberland worked on his fears that if Princess Mary (later MARY I) succeeded to the throne she would destroy the Protestant religion, and Edward agreed to leave the crown to Lady Jane. He died eight days later, and on 10 July 1553 Northumberland had Jane proclaimed Queen of England. But the country rallied to Mary and on 19 July Jane's 'reign' came to its end. She was arrested and sent to the Tower of London, but it was understood that, although she was found guilty of treason, Mary would not allow her to die. However, when her father became involved in Wyatt's unsuccessful rebellion her fate was certain and she was executed on Tower Green on 12 February 1554. Jane was well-educated, highly intelligent and an ardent Protestant; she seems to have possessed all the Tudor obstinacy and determination that characterized Henry VIII and her cousins, Mary and Elizabeth.

GUESCLIN, Bertrand du (*c*. 1320–80), was a poor and ugly Breton knight who rose to become Constable of France and the most famous French warrior during the HUNDRED YEARS' WAR. After

distinguishing himself in innumerable engagements against the English, he defeated the King of Navarre, enemy of Charles V of France. Charles twice ransomed du Guesclin when he was captured by Sir John Chandos and EDWARD THE BLACK PRINCE. Made Constable of France in 1370, he used new tactics against the English longbowmen, refusing to make massed charges but attacking their flanks and employing cannons to blast them from a distance and to demolish castles. By these methods he recovered nearly all the territory won by EDWARD III and the Black Prince. He died fighting against the mercenary companies that were pillaging the countryside.

GUILDS (*or* Gilds) were companies of persons who banded together for religious, charitable and business reasons. They generally mean the merchant and craft guilds which flourished in the Middle Ages, especially in England, Germany and city-states like FLORENCE.

In England the 'guild merchant' came into existence soon after the Norman Conquest. It was originally composed of both merchants and artisans, who, with royal permission, formed the guild to regulate the borough market and fair, to fix tolls paid by outsiders and to punish cheats and bad workmen. This old style of guild lasted longest in the smaller boroughs, but in bigger towns, especially London, many separate, rival guilds were formed, whose merchants all followed one particular trade, such as the vintners, mercers, drapers, goldsmiths and grocers. Members of these merchant guilds or companies were chiefly dealers who sold what others produced; many became very rich and they filled important offices, such as that of Lord Mayor and Sheriff, and they were the main employers of labour.

A medieval town in which trade was controlled by the guilds

Craft guilds (also known as 'mysteries') were brotherhoods of skilled artisans, such as weavers, tanners, cutlers, tailors and cordwainers (shoemakers), mostly master-men, who met together to manage everything to do with each particular craft. They fixed prices and standards of workmanship, as well as wages and working hours for their journeymen and apprentices. Members made payments into a fund to help their fellows in time of trouble and to look after widows and orphans; they also supported their local church and took part in festivals and pageants. Members of a guild often inhabited a particular district or street; hence Ironmonger Row and Cordwainer Street.

In the 14th century, as the gap widened between masters and workmen, the journeymen began to form their own fraternities to obtain better wages and hours, though in England they did not succeed in becoming fully free from control by the masters' guilds. Many craft guilds survived until the second half of the 18th century, but with the coming of new industries and the factory system their usefulness and influence disappeared.

GUNPOWDER PLOT was a conspiracy to blow up the Houses of Parliament on 5 November 1605, when King JAMES I was to have been present at the opening of Parliament. With the accession of James I Roman Catholics had hoped to be allowed to worship freely, but they were bitterly disappointed when even harsher penalties were introduced against those who held to the Catholic faith. Robert Catesby and Thomas Percy (who had declared he would kill the King as early as in 1603) hatched a plot to blow up Parliament in order to kill all the country's leaders. An armed uprising and foreign aid would then bring about a Catholic triumph. Catesby's principal accomplices were his cousins, Robert and Thomas Winter, and Francis Tresham, Sir Everard Digby, John Grant, Ambrose Rokewood, John Wright and Guy Fawkes, a daring Yorkshireman who had been serving in Flanders with the Spanish forces.

In May 1604 the conspirators hired a house next to the House of Lords and began to dig a tunnel from the cellar, but were halted by a massive foundation wall. Fawkes then discovered that there was another vault or cellar right under the House of Lords and this was available for hire as a coal and timber store. By May 1605 thirty-six barrels of gunpowder had been placed in the vault and concealed under coal and faggots; the conspirators then dispersed, some, including Fawkes, to the continent to enlist supporters.

As the date for the murder drew near, someone, probably Tresham, sent an anonymous letter to Lord Monteagle, warning him to stay away from the opening of Parliament. On 26 October Monteagle showed the letter to the King's ministers and it was decided to wait a few days to let the plot ripen. Catesby was warned that the secret was known, but believing that no notice would be taken of the letter he decided to go ahead and told Fawkes to remain on guard at the cellar. A search on 4 November revealed the barrels of gunpowder and Fawkes, still at his post, was arrested and taken to the Tower. Under torture, he held out bravely and did not reveal the names of the conspirators until he learned that Catesby, Percy and Wright had died at bay in Staffordshire, while the rest were wounded and arrested. Eight conspirators and a Jesuit priest were executed and Tresham died in the Tower.

The Gunpowder Plot caused an upsurge of hysterical hatred against the Catholics and severer penalties against their religion. Roman Catholics in general and their priests had had no part in the conspiracy, but a handful of fanatics delayed religious toleration for centuries.

GUSTAVUS ADOLPHUS (1594–1632), King of Sweden (1611–32), who raised Sweden to the status of a great European power, was the son of Charles IX. He came to the throne at the age of seventeen and quickly recovered territory from Denmark lost by his father. In 1617 he ended a war with Russia, by which Sweden received a large part of Finland and Livonia. Next he defeated Sigismund of Poland in a long difficult war that ended in 1629, giving him possession of the Prussian Baltic ports and a foothold on the mainland of Germany. By now he had made the Baltic 'a Swedish lake'.

Meanwhile, this gifted king, with his minister Oxenstierna, reformed his country's government, developed its iron and copper industries and encouraged commerce and education. He himself was a brilliant linguist who spoke eight languages, a statesman who towered above his contemporaries, an energetic commander and a trainer of soldiers who influenced the arts of war. He provided his men with uniforms, organized them in small regiments, deploying the infantry in ranks only three deep and training them to march, load and fire faster than the enemy. He introduced lighter muskets and more mobile field artillery, while teaching his cavalry to charge home with the sword, instead of using pistols and retiring to reload.

In 1630 Gustavus entered the THIRTY YEARS WAR as Protestant champion, partly because of his sincere religious views and partly because he feared that the imperial forces of the Catholic League, advancing across Germany, would threaten his Baltic possessions. By a series of spectacular victories he drove the imperialists back, beat their general, Tilly, at Breitenfeld (1631), took Mainz and, in the following year, pursued and killed Tilly at Ingolstadt. To save Vienna, the Emperor put Wallenstein at the head of a new army, which met the Swedes at Lützen, near Leipzig. Fighting with heroic fury, the Swedes were victorious, but, as he led a countercharge, Gustavus himself was killed. He left one child, his daughter Christina, who succeeded to the throne of Sweden.

GUTENBERG, Johann (*c.* 1398–1468), German printer, who is regarded as the inventor of printing with movable type. Born in Mainz, he went to Strasbourg in about 1428 and was engaged on work for which he borrowed money from friends. It may have been for his printing-press. Back in Mainz a rich burgher named Fust lent him money in 1450, but brought an action against him five years later and probably secured the press and, with the assistance of a printer named Schöffer, printed various books. Gutenberg seems to have continued printing, and his Latin Bible of 1455 (known as the *42-line Bible* because it was printed in two columns each of 42 lines) is said to have been the first book wholly printed with movable copper type. A number of other works have been credited to Gutenberg, but no books bearing his name as printer are known.

Gutenberg's printing press

H

HABEAS CORPUS ACT (1679) was passed in CHARLES II's reign to make sure that the Government would not keep political opponents in prison without trial. This right to personal liberty was supposed to have been granted by MAGNA CARTA but it had often been ignored. The Act meant that persons arrested could demand trial at the next sessions and that, after that time, a judge must grant a *Writ of Habeas Corpus* (which means 'you must have the body') requiring the persons in charge of the prisoner to release him.

In emergencies the Government can suspend *habeas corpus*. This has happened in times of disturbance and national danger, as in the Jacobite rebellion of 1745, during the French Revolution and the First World War.

HADRIAN (76–138), Roman Emperor (117–138), was brought up in Spain, like his guardian the Emperor TRAJAN. After holding important positions in Rome and military commands, he succeeded Trajan in 117. The Empire's eastern frontiers were under attack, so he abandoned territories which Trajan had taken, made peace with Parthia and strengthened the defences of Upper Germany. Unlike most emperors, he spent nearly all his reign visiting the provinces; on his first great tour (121–6) he went to Gaul, Germany, Britain (where he ordered the building of HADRIAN'S WALL), Spain, Sicily and Greece; on a second tour (128–134) he visited Asia Minor, Syria, Palestine (where JERUSALEM was rebuilt at his order), Arabia and Egypt. His aim was not to expand the Empire but to establish peace and order behind strong frontiers. A great builder of palaces, temples and libraries, a poet, musician and writer, who introduced many reforms into the Roman world, his character was a mass of contradictions. Mean yet generous, cruel yet kind, he was nevertheless one of the most capable rulers who have ever lived.

HADRIAN'S WALL, parts of which still exist, runs across northern England from Wallsend at the mouth of the river Tyne to Bowness-on-Solent, a distance of 80 Roman or $73\frac{1}{2}$ English miles (118 kilometres). The wall was ordered to be built during the visit of the Emperor HADRIAN in 122, its purpose being to mark the northern frontier of the Empire, to serve as a defence against the barbaric tribesmen of Caledonia and as a base for garrison troops. At least 10,000 soldiers worked for five years (122–6) to build the wall, which, when completed, was made of stone (turf was used for the

Hadrian and a mile-castle on his wall

western stretch, but this was soon replaced by stone). It stood about 20 feet (6 m) high, with a rampart walk wide enough for two soldiers to march abreast. The wall was strengthened by sixteen forts for troops, with smaller forts ('mile-castles') a mile apart, each having a gateway wide enough for a cart, and two signal turrets to each mile. A great ditch was dug along the northern side, while to the south a road ran between the wall and the *vallum*, a ditch with earth banks.

Under the next Emperor, Antoninus Pius, a second wall of turf was built further north (140–158), but this had to be abandoned some forty years later and Hadrian's Wall again became the northern frontier. It was crossed by the barbarians on a number of occasions when the Roman troops were temporarily withdrawn and was finally abandoned in 383.

HAIG, Douglas, Earl (1861–1928), field-marshal who was Commander-in-Chief of the British forces on the Western Front from 1915 to 1918. A professional soldier, he had served in the Sudan, BOER WAR and India, before taking command of the 1st Army Corps at the outbreak of the FIRST WORLD WAR. He succeeded Sir John French as Commander-in-Chief in December 1915. Haig had the difficult task of commanding a huge army engaged in trench warfare, where tactical movement was impossible, yet the public clamoured for victories, and he was hampered by the Prime Minister LLOYD GEORGE, who distrusted him and would probably have had him dismissed but for the support of King GEORGE V. At the Battle of the Somme (1916) the British

suffered casualties of half a million, and in 1917 Haig launched the Passchendaele offensive, which cost a further 300,000 casualties. To his critics he was a heartless incompetent commander who squandered thousands of lives in useless frontal attacks; to others he was the dedicated soldier whose steadfast tenacity won through to the end. In 1918 he withstood the German offensive, and when the chance came to counter-attack smashed through the Hindenburg Line and drove on almost to the frontier of Germany. In retirement, as president of the British Legion, he devoted the rest of his life to helping disabled soldiers.

HAILE SELASSIE (1891–1975), Emperor of ETHIOPIA, was known as Ras Tafari before his coronation in 1930. Prior to that he had fought two campaigns to remove rivals to his throne. For five years he introduced reforms aimed at modernizing his backward country, but in 1935 Ethiopia was invaded by MUSSOLINI's army and annexed to the Italian crown. Haile Selassie fled to Britain, but in 1941, with the help of the British and South African troops, who defeated the Italians, he regained his throne.

From that time the Emperor seems to have continued to work for reform, but at a slow pace. In 1955 he granted Ethiopia a new constitution and five years later suppressed an attempt to overthrow him. A man of great dignity and courage, he remained on good terms with the leaders of the new African states and also with the West, but in 1974, he was overthrown by a military revolution and placed in confinement. His opponents claimed that he was an autocrat who had enriched himself and his numerous relatives while Ethiopia was suffering from poverty and famine.

Hammurabi and the pillar on which his laws were inscribed

HAMMURABI, King of BABYLON, who reigned from about 1792 to 1750 BC, was one of the greatest rulers of ancient times. By defeating the Elamites and neighbouring city-states, he secured the whole of the Sumerian plain, the Land of the Two Rivers, and exercised a firm, benevolent rule over his cities and provinces, sending out messengers with his orders inscribed on clay tablets. His Code of Laws was remarkably advanced for its time; women were to be respected and allowed to own property, slaves had rights and free-born children were to attend school. There were regulations for merchants' profits and doctors' fees, and punishments for bad workmen, thieves and wrongdoers.

HAMPDEN, John (1594–1643), Parliamentary leader in the struggle with CHARLES I, he came to be looked on as a popular hero and staunch upholder of English liberty. A cousin of Oliver CROMWELL, he entered Parliament and first became well known when he went to prison in 1627 for refusing to pay

the King's forced loan. His most famous act of defiance was his refusal to pay £1 Ship Money on his inland property in Buckinghamshire (1637); he lost his case in court but won a moral victory and Ship Money was eventually declared illegal. As leader of the opposition to the King, he was one of the Five Members whom Charles tried to arrest in 1642, and when the CIVIL WAR broke out he took an active part in raising the parliamentary army. He was killed in a skirmish with RUPERT's cavalry at Chalgrove Field in 1643.

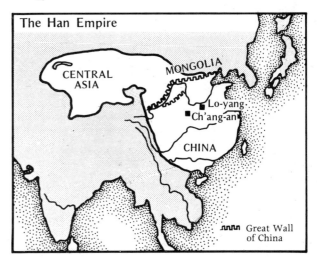

The Han Empire

CENTRAL ASIA — MONGOLIA — Lo-yang — Ch'ang-an — CHINA

ᴧᴧᴧᴧ Great Wall of China

HAN Dynasty in CHINA lasted from 206 BC until AD 220. It was founded by Liu Pang, who, together with his successors, placed great emphasis upon the teachings of Confucius (551–479 BC). They believed, for instance, that rulers should exist for the good of the people and they therefore tried to rule in a just and benevolent manner. Taxes were reduced and an imperial university and an efficient civil service were founded. This was a period of imperial expansion, when China's borders were extended and, under the Emperor Wu Ti (140–87 BC), Korea was conquered, the northern barbarians defeated and trade links established with India and indirectly with Rome.

During the four hundred years of Han rule literature and history flourished, a national library was founded and scholars produced one of the world's first dictionaries. In the field of science, astronomers observed sunspots, predicted eclipses, recorded earthquakes and made a sundial and a calendar to measure time. This period also saw the appearance of glazed pottery, lacquer and fine sculpture.

HANNIBAL (247–183 BC), Carthaginian general, was the son of Hamilcar, who took him to Spain as a boy and made him swear eternal enmity to ROME. In 221 Hannibal became Commander-in-Chief of the Carthaginian army and spent the next two years conquering southern Spain. By capturing Saguntum, a town allied to Rome, he brought about the start of the Second Punic War (*see* CARTHAGE).

In 218 Hannibal led his army, which included a number of elephants, over the Pyrenees, through Gaul and across the Alps into Italy, to complete one of the most astonishing military feats in history. Although he had lost half his army on this perilous march, he defeated the Romans on the river Trebia and, in the following spring, crossed the Apennines to destroy the main Roman army by Lake Trasimene. With small numbers and no siege-engines he had no hope of taking Rome itself, so he moved south to ravage the countryside and raise the Italians against their overlords. At Cannae (216) he routed a much larger Roman army to win one of the most complete victories of all time, yet after this triumph his fortunes began to decline. Though the south of Italy supported his cause, his home government denied him reinforcements, while the Romans could still raise large armies. Moreover, their general Quintus Fabius Maximus adopted new tactics, avoiding battle but shadowing the Carthaginians and harassing their movements.

Nevertheless, Hannibal maintained himself and his dwindling army for years, winning campaigns by superior tactics and holding on in the south in the hope that his brother Hasdrubal would arrive to reinforce him. Hasdrubal succeeded in crossing the Alps in 207 but was defeated and killed at the Metaurus, so Hannibal retreated to the mountains, where he held out for four more years. In 203, hearing that Carthage was threatened by the Roman commander Scipio, he returned to Africa to take command of an ill-trained army and was heavily defeated at Zama (202).

Hannibal was still only forty-six and he now took control of Carthage as chief magistrate, reforming its government so effectively that the city was able to pay the heavy tribute demanded by Rome. After seven years, alarmed by this prosperity, the Romans demanded Hannibal's surrender; he went into exile, first to the court of Antiochus of Syria, then to Prusias King of Bithynia. Learning that Prusias intended to hand him over to the Romans, this military genius, who had held out for fifteen years in a hostile country against able generals and superior armies, committed suicide by taking poison.

HANOVER was a state in north Germany, lying between the rivers Elbe and Weser, whose ruler was known as the Elector because of his right to take part in the election of the Holy Roman Emperor. Hanover was of no particular importance in European affairs until the Elector George Louis became King of England as GEORGE I in 1714. His succession was due to the fact that his mother Sophia had been made heir to the throne by the Act of Settlement (1701), which barred Roman Catholics. Sophia was the daughter of James I's daughter, Elizabeth, who married the Elector Palatine in 1613. Sophia died before Queen ANNE, so her claim was inherited by George.

The Hanoverian monarchs in Britain were the first four Georges and William IV. They retained the Electorate (indeed George I and George II much preferred it to England), but in 1837, when VICTORIA came to the throne, Hanover passed to Ernest Duke of Cumberland, because the Salic Law forbade the accession of a woman. In 1866, having sided with Austria and suffered defeat in the AUSTRO-PRUSSIAN WAR, Hanover became part of the kingdom of Prussia.

During the 18th century the British connection with Hanover led to increased trade and to involvement in continental affairs. Hence Britain took part in the War of the AUSTRIAN SUCCESSION (1740–8), and in the SEVEN YEARS WAR (1757–63) GEORGE II made a pact with FREDERICK THE GREAT to protect Hanover from French attack.

HANSEATIC LEAGUE was an alliance of north German cities in the Middle Ages. It was at its most powerful in the 14th and 15th centuries, when its members numbered about eighty-five cities, including Hamburg, Lübeck, Bremen, Cologne, Brunswick and Danzig, with great 'factories' or trading centres in London, Bruges, Bergen and Novgorod. The League's wealth originated in the Baltic trade with Russia and, at its height, it traded with all the countries of western Europe, controlled much of the cloth trade, exercized strict discipline over its members and was stronger than most of the monarchs with whom it did business. Its decline set

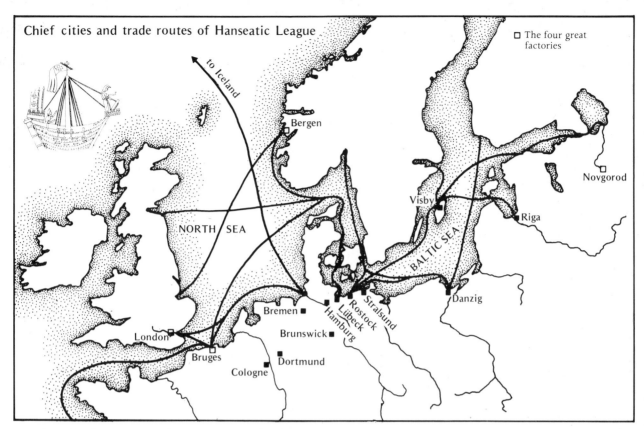

□ The four great factories

to Iceland

Bergen

NORTH SEA

Visby

Novgorod

Riga

BALTIC SEA

Danzig

Stralsund
Rostock
Lübeck
Hamburg

Bremen

Brunswick

London

Bruges

Dortmund

Cologne

in when the discoveries of COLUMBUS and VASCO DA GAMA changed the main trade routes; in addition, the Dutch and the English increased their sea-going trade.

HAPSBURGS (*or* Habsburgs) were members of the ruling house of Austria, which played a dominant part in Europe for nearly seven hundred years. The first prominent Hapsburg was Rudolph I, who was elected Emperor of the HOLY ROMAN EMPIRE in 1273; successive dukes made themselves the most powerful of the German princes, and from 1438 to 1806 the Emperor was always, with one exception, a Hapsburg. Under the Emperor Maximilian (1493–1519), who married Mary of Burgundy, the family's interests spread into western Europe and Maximilian's grandson, CHARLES V, ruled an empire that stretched from the New World to the Danube.

After Charles retired, the Hapsburg empire was divided; PHILIP II ruled Spain, the Netherlands, Italy, and the Americas, while his brother Ferdinand I acquired the Austrian lands, and the title of Emperor. In the 17th century, while the Spanish side of the family declined, the Emperor led the

Below Emperor Maximilian with his family, including his grandson the future Emperor Charles V (*centre*)

121

fight against Protestantism, besides resisting the Turkish advance into Europe. Throughout the following century the Austrian Hapsburgs were engaged in a losing struggle with the French BOURBONS, but they gained territory in Italy. NAPOLEON put an end to Hapsburg power in Germany, but it partially recovered after his fall. However, the Emperor FRANCIS JOSEPH (1848–1916), faced with the rise of Prussia and loss of Italy, had to concentrate on retaining his rule over Austria-Hungary. At the end of the FIRST WORLD WAR this empire broke up and the power of the Hapsburgs came to an end.

HARDIE, James Keir (1856–1915), founder of the Labour Party in Britain, was born into poverty in Lanarkshire, Scotland. He started to earn his living at the age of seven and at ten was working in a coalmine. Although he had no schooling, he taught himself to read at home and as a young man became a well-known lay preacher. Chosen to lead a miners' protest against a cut in wages, he was dismissed and black-listed by the mine-owners, so he turned to journalism for a living. He organized a union of the Ayrshire miners and was appointed secretary of the Scottish Miners' Federation.

In 1892 Hardie was one of three Labour men elected to Parliament and he made his celebrated entry to the House of Commons, wearing not formal dress but a cloth cap and a workman's suit. In the following year he founded the Independent Labour Party, whose main aims were to spread socialism and influence the trade unions. He lost his seat at West Ham in 1895, but was returned for Merthyr Tydfil in 1900 and remained its Member until his death. He was the first Chairman of the Parliamentary Labour Party. Widely respected for his dignity and sincerity, Keir Hardie was a convinced pacifist

who opposed both the BOER WAR and the FIRST WORLD WAR. He also supported the SUFFRAGETTE movement and advised its members on tactics.

HARGREAVES, James (died 1778), an English weaver from Blackburn, Lancashire, invented the Spinning Jenny in about 1764. This invention enabled one person to spin seven threads simultaneously. Hargreaves' fellow-spinners destroyed his machine so he moved to Nottingham and set up a spinning-mill there.

HAROLD II (*c.* 1022–66), SAXON King of England for only one year, was the son of Earl Godwin of Wessex and brother-in-law of EDWARD THE CONFESSOR. During the latter part of the Confessor's reign Harold, who had distinguished himself as a warrior and statesman, practically ruled the kingdom. In 1064 he was wrecked on the coast of France and held captive by Duke William of Normandy (later WILLIAM I), who tricked him into swearing an oath to support William's claim to the throne of England. However, in January 1066 Harold was chosen King by the WITAN, and during that summer he kept an army and a fleet at readiness to deal with Duke William's projected invasion. In September Harold Hardrada of Norway and Tostig, Harold's traitorous brother, landed in Yorkshire with an army, whereupon Harold marched north and completely defeated the invaders at Stamford Bridge. Three days later William landed unopposed in Sussex. Instead of gathering an overwhelming force, Harold dashed back to the south, outdistancing his infantry and the half-hearted northern earls. Nor did he wait for reinforcements from the west, but drew up his tired troops on Senlac Hill, near HASTINGS, and offered battle to the Normans. On 14 October 1066, in a desperate day-long engagement, the Saxon army was destroyed and Harold himself slain.

HARVEY, William (1578–1657), the English physician and discoverer of the circulation of the blood, studied medicine in Padua and built up a prosperous practice in London. As a doctor at St Bartholomew's Hospital and lecturer in surgery at the College of Physicians, he was able to carry out dissections of bodies and he reached his conclusions about the circulation of the blood as early as 1616. It was, however, not until 1628 that he published

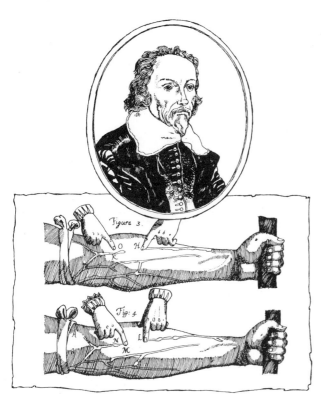

Harvey and a diagram from his book on the circulation of the blood

his account, which contradicted ancient theories and for a time made Harvey an object of ridicule and abuse. His reputation soon recovered and he was made Physician-in-Ordinary to Charles I. Having been present at the Battle of Edgehill (in charge of the King's sons), he spent the years of the CIVIL WAR at Oxford and afterwards returned to London to find that a hostile mob had destroyed his home and all his medical papers and specimens.

Harvey's discovery was complete, except for his inability to realize the existence of capillaries, owing to the fact that the microscope had not yet been invented. He is regarded as the founder of modern medicine, and an annual lecture in his honour is still given at the Royal College of Physicians in London.

HASTINGS, Battle of, was fought on 14 October 1066 between the English or SAXON army, led by King HAROLD, and Duke William of Normandy's invasion force (see WILLIAM I). Both armies were probably about nine or ten thousand strong.

Harold, who had hurried south from York after his victory at Stamford Bridge, took up position on a ridge called Senlac Hill, about 6 miles (11 km) from Hastings. His royal troops, the Huscarls, dismounted to fight on foot; they held the front line; several ranks of shire levies were massed behind and another body of Huscarls grouped themselves round the King and the standard of Wessex in the centre. The Saxons' main weapons were battle-axes and spears. Duke William's army, which had to attack uphill, consisted of infantry, armoured cavalry carrying spears and swords and a force of archers.

The battle began with the archers firing their arrows, to which the Saxons had no answer. Next the Norman infantry attacked, but were driven back and chased downhill, contrary to Harold's orders, by some of the Saxons, who were cut to pieces by the cavalry. However, the shield-wall was re-formed and throughout the afternoon William launched heavy attacks with his armoured knights. The old story of his luring the Saxons out of position by a feigned flight is probably untrue. It seems more likely that the Normans managed to break the line in places and to pour cavalry through the gaps to spread panic among the levies. Many fled, but the Huscarls stood their ground, fighting to the last around their dying king, who had been wounded in the eye by an arrow. By nightfall William had gained a complete victory.

Thus, in a single day, Harold, most of his nobles and the finest men in England were slain. One battle delivered the kingdom into the hands of William the Conqueror and changed the course of history.

HASTINGS, Warren (1732–1818), first Governor-General of British India, went to Calcutta at the age of eighteen in the service of the EAST INDIA COMPANY. He rose rapidly to important positions, and in 1772 became Governor of Bengal, which had been ruled badly since CLIVE's departure. A year later, after Lord North's Regulating Act, he was

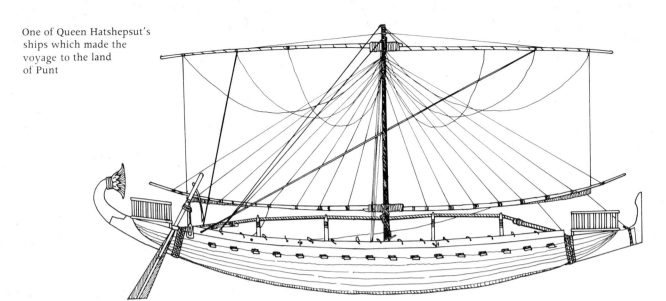

One of Queen Hatshepsut's ships which made the voyage to the land of Punt

appointed Governor-General with a council of four. One of these was Philip Francis, who opposed him at every turn and with whom he fought a duel. Hastings introduced reforms into the lawcourts and taxation system, besides taking steps to encourage education and Anglo-Indian understanding.

During the American War of Independence, when the French stirred up opposition to the British, he sent armies to hold Bombay and Madras, seized ports to prevent the French using their fleet, strengthened Oudh as a buffer state against attack on Bengal by the Mahrattas and managed to break up a hostile confederacy of Indian princes.

Without doubt he saved British rule in India, but after his return to England in 1785, his enemy Francis, aided by the politicians, Burke and Fox, had him brought to trial on charges of 'high crimes and misdemeanours'. He was principally accused of executing a Hindu banker, of hiring out Company troops to the Nawab of Oudh and of ill-treating the Begums (princesses) of Oudh to extract money from them. His trial before the House of Lords lasted seven years and ended with his complete acquittal, but the costs left him a ruined man. However, the Company granted him a large pension, though he received no honours from his country, apart from being made a Privy Councillor.

It now seems clear that Hastings was not particular what he did under pressure, when he felt he was serving British interests, but, unlike some officials, he made no effort to amass a fortune for himself.

HATSHEPSUT, Queen of EGYPT of the 18th Dynasty, reigned for some twenty years until about 1482 BC. On the death of her husband Thotmes (or Tuthmosis) II she became regent for her young stepson Thotmes III, but soon took complete control of the kingdom. She seems to have ruled well and to have pursued a peaceful policy of fostering trade and the arts. Her steward Senenmut directed the building of a magnificent temple in her honour and it can still be visited at Deir el-Bahri. At her death or overthrow Thotmes III assumed power and, perhaps in revenge for being thrust aside by his stepmother, had her name hammered out of monuments and buildings which she had erected.

HAWKINS, Sir John (1532–95), son of a Plymouth merchant, went on trading voyages as a young man to the Canaries and Spain, where he got on good terms with Spanish merchants and officials. These contacts may have caused him to see the possibilities of slave trading. At all events, in 1562 he commanded the first of his three expeditions, sailing to the Guinea coast to pick up Negroes whom he sold to Spanish settlers in the West Indies. On the third voyage (1567) his ships were treacherously attacked by the Spaniards at San Juan de Ulua, from which he and his cousin DRAKE barely escaped with their lives.

Hawkins played a mysterious role in unmasking the Ridolfi Plot (1571) to assassinate Queen ELIZABETH and place MARY QUEEN OF SCOTS on

William Rufus. Henry, known as 'Beauclerc', was clever, tight-fisted and a harsh capable ruler who kept close control over the Exchequer and compelled barons and commons to obey his laws. He won the support of Englishmen through his marriage to Matilda, daughter of Queen MARGARET of Scotland and a member of the old Saxon royal house, and they fought with him when he invaded Normandy and, at Tinchebrai, defeated and captured his brother Duke Robert.

After Henry's son and heir William was drowned in the *White Ship*, he forced the barons to agree to accept his daughter, the Empress MATILDA, as heir to the throne. On his death, however, they dishonoured their oath and chose STEPHEN to be king.

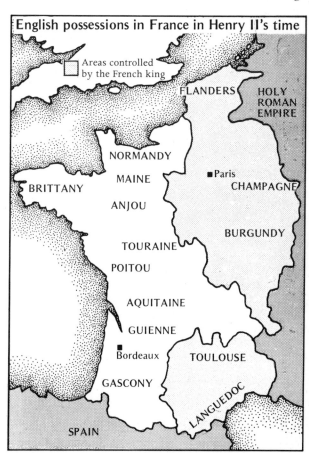

English possessions in France in Henry II's time

Areas controlled by the French king

FLANDERS
HOLY ROMAN EMPIRE
NORMANDY
MAINE
Paris
CHAMPAGNE
BRITTANY
ANJOU
BURGUNDY
TOURAINE
POITOU
AQUITAINE
GUIENNE
Bordeaux
TOULOUSE
GASCONY
LANGUEDOC
SPAIN

the throne. Having hoodwinked the Spanish ambassador into believing he was an ardent Catholic willing to betray his country, he obtained information which he passed on to BURGHLEY, who was then able to arrest the plotters. Hawkins, the tough sea-captain, was clearly a clever schemer, a man of many gifts. Appointed Treasurer of the Navy in 1573, he built a fleet of warships that were faster, more manoeuvrable and more heavily armed than traditional fighting ships of the time, and he himself commanded the *Victory*, one of his new ships, and took part in all the engagements as the ARMADA sailed up the Channel in 1588. By his work in the shipyards he had done more than any man to bring about the defeat of Spain and Lord Howard knighted him on board the *Ark Royal*.

In 1590 Hawkins led an expedition to attack Spanish shipping off the Azores, but he met with only partial success. Then in 1595 came his last voyage, a disastrous venture in joint command with Drake. The two great captains did not agree and the Spaniards, warned of their coming, were well prepared. The attack on Puerto Rico failed, but by that time Hawkins had fallen ill and he died at sea in November 1595.

HENRY I (1068–1135), King of England (1100–35), WILLIAM I's youngest son, succeeded his brother

HENRY II (1133–89), King of England (1154–89), was the son of Geoffrey of Anjou and the Empress MATILDA, daughter of Henry I. At eighteen, he inherited his father's lands of Anjou, Maine and Touraine; he already ruled Normandy and by his marriage to Eleanor of Aquitaine in 1152 he added

Poitou and the great Duchy of Aquitaine to his possessions. His invasion of England and agreement with STEPHEN to be recognized as his heir brought him the English crown in 1154, by which time his possessions stretched from the borders of Scotland to the Pyrenees.

This dynamic self-willed man speedily restored order in England, compelling the barons to pull down the castles they had built without royal permission and introducing an efficient system of justice with assizes, travelling judges and trial by jury. In the task of restoring the royal authority, he had the assistance of Thomas BECKET, his Chancellor from 1154 to 1162. Becket virtually ruled the kingdom during Henry's absences abroad, when he was incessantly touring his vast possessions and protecting them against attack by the French. Wishing to obtain control over the Church, he caused Becket to become Archbishop of Canterbury, but this appointment led to their tragic quarrel and Becket's murder in 1170. For his part in the crime Henry had to do penance and give up all idea of reducing the power of the Church (*see* PAPACY).

His latter years were saddened by the disloyalty of his sons, Henry, Geoffrey and Richard (*see* RICHARD I), who, encouraged by their mother, rebelled against him. In 1178 he defeated them all and then pardoned them for their disobedience, but they soon resumed their plotting. In 1189 Richard and PHILIP AUGUSTUS of France attacked Henry suddenly and forced him to accept humiliating terms. It is said that, lying ill in a castle at Chinon, he learned that his favourite son JOHN had joined the conspiracy, upon which he turned to the wall broken-hearted, and died.

HENRY III (1207–72), King of England (1216–72), succeeded his father King JOHN at the age of nine and did not commence to rule until 1232. When he did so, it became evident that this pious learned youth was also a weakling who lacked the capacity to command respect. As a result, although his reign was a notable period for church building (Henry built the present Westminster Abbey), for the foundation of colleges and the arrival in England of the FRIARS, it was, also, a period of extravagance and civil war. The barons rebelled and, after the King's defeat at Lewes, Simon de MONTFORT ruled the country until he, in turn, was defeated and

killed at Evesham. For the rest of Henry's reign the kingdom was governed by his son, the Lord Edward, who eventually succeeded his father as EDWARD I.

HENRY IV (1367–1413), King of England (1399–1413), was known as Bolingbroke before he came to the throne. A son of JOHN OF GAUNT, he was exiled by his cousin RICHARD II, but at an opportune moment landed in Yorkshire, saying he had come to claim his father's estates. Many of the barons joined him in a rebellion, and when Richard II returned from Ireland he found no one willing to fight for him. He was deposed in favour of Henry and murdered soon afterwards. As king, Henry had to face the problems of being a usurper; he failed to defeat the Scots and had to deal with OWEN GLENDOWER's uprising in Wales, as well as with the rebellious Percies of Northumberland. With the help of his son, Prince Henry (later HENRY V), he overcame his difficulties, but, worn out by illness and care, this shrewd resolute man died before he was fifty.

HENRY V (1387–1422), King of England (1413–22), the eldest son of. HENRY IV, had seen plenty of fighting during his father's reign and, to strengthen his position on the throne by waging a popular war, he reopened the HUNDRED YEARS' WAR with France and won the brilliant victory of AGINCOURT in 1415. But it took him three years of hard campaigning to conquer Normandy and most of northern France. By the Treaty of Troyes (1420) the defeated French king, Charles VI, gave him his daughter in marriage and agreed that Henry was the heir to the throne of France. However, only two months before he would have succeeded his father-in-law Henry died of camp fever. In some ways he was the hero-king of popular legend – brave, pious,

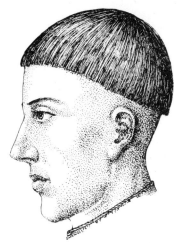

thoughtful and just – but, on occasion, he could display heartless cruelty towards the enemy and to the LOLLARDS, whom he persecuted.

HENRY VI (1421–71), King of England (1422–61), was the son of HENRY V and Catherine of France. Before he was a year old he was proclaimed King of England and, on the death of his mother's father, King of France. During his childhood his uncles, the Dukes of Gloucester and Bedford, ruled England and the French possessions for him, but after Bedford's death in 1435 the HUNDRED YEARS' WAR with France went badly and by 1453 only Calais was left to the English.

By this time England was in a state of disorder, due partly to the return of soldiers from France and an uprising called Jack Cade's Rebellion and partly to the rivalry between the houses of York and Lancaster, whose supporters began to arm their followers. Henry, who became mad on several occasions, was unable to restrain the nobles or to contend with his domineering wife, Margaret of Anjou. Nor, when the Wars of the ROSES broke out, did he take a significant part in the fighting, for this pious weakling was no soldier. He was captured by the Yorkists at Northampton, recaptured by his wife and, after their defeat at Towton, became a refugee in Scotland.

EDWARD IV assumed the crown in 1461 and poor half-witted Henry, taken prisoner in Lancashire, was lodged in the Tower. WARWICK 'the Kingmaker' briefly restored him to his throne in 1470, but after Warwick's death in battle and the final defeat of the Lancastrians he was put to death in 1471.

Henry's sole achievements were the founding of Eton College, and King's College, Cambridge; his gentle, saintly character caused some of the common people to regard him as a martyr.

HENRY VII (1457–1509), King of England (1485–1509), won the throne by defeating RICHARD III at Bosworth Field, bringing to an end the Wars of the ROSES. First of the Tudor monarchs, he was born in Wales, the son of Edmund Tudor, Earl of Richmond, and Margaret Beaufort, a descendant of JOHN OF GAUNT. He had become the last Lancastrian claimant to the throne when HENRY VI was murdered and, for safety, had gone to live in France.

Once he had gained the throne, his policy was to make it secure for himself and his family. So he married Elizabeth of York to put an end to the Yorkist-Lancastrian feud and he dealt swiftly with Yorkist plots and the two imposters who claimed the throne, Lambert Simnel and Perkin Warbeck. Realizing that an impoverished king was weak, he amassed a fortune by various means, including forced 'loans' and heavy fines on those who displeased him. Wealth enabled him to overawe the nobles, since they were well aware that he could hire an efficient army to carry out his wishes. He also used his money and wits to advance the power and dignity of the Crown, keeping a regal court and marrying his son Arthur to Catherine of Aragon and his daughter Margaret to JAMES IV of Scotland. At his death he left his son a well-run kingdom with a full Treasury. Henry supported learning, trade and exploration; he built the Henry VII Chapel in Westminster Abbey and encouraged the CABOTS to go on their voyages of discovery. This cool-headed unsmiling monarch may have lacked the magnetism of his son HENRY VIII, but he was certainly very much shrewder.

HENRY VIII (1491–1547), King of England (1509–47), was nearly eighteen when he came to the throne, the very image of a Renaissance prince,

handsome, athletic and adept in music, languages and poetry. He was also vain, selfish and extravagant. The fortune which his father left him was speedily spent on lavish display and on a campaign in France that resulted in one hollow victory. At this time his chief minister was Cardinal WOLSEY.

Shortly after his accession Henry had married his brother's widow Catherine of Aragon, but when she failed to provide him with a male heir he instructed Wolsey to obtain for him a divorce. For political reasons the Pope delayed giving a decision (1527–9) and finally refused. But, with the assistance of Archbishop CRANMER, Henry put Catherine aside and married Anne Boleyn. He went on to attack the Pope's authority in England and, in 1535, to have Parliament declare that the King was the Supreme Head of the Church in England. Between 1536 and 1539 Henry and his minister Thomas Cromwell closed down the monasteries, confiscated their wealth and sold their lands. By this time Henry had developed into a cruel tyrant; anyone who aroused his suspicion or displeasure was likely to be executed, and those who died included nobles, ministers, prelates and two of his six wives, Anne Boleyn and Catherine Howard.

Yet his subjects regarded him with awe; he had defied the Pope and monarchs abroad; his kingdom was orderly and obedient; Wales and Ireland had been subdued; Scotland had been twice defeated, at FLODDEN (1513) and Solway Moss (1542); and when FRANCIS I of France went to war with England the fleet which Henry had built was strong enough to protect the kingdom.

At the end of his life Henry made careful plans for the government of the land after his death until his son Edward came of age. He chose a council of ministers, some of them Catholics and some holding to the new Protestant faith; there would be no violent changes, no extreme policies. But although men obeyed him trembling while he was alive, they disobeyed him as soon as he was dead.

HENRY IV (1553–1610), King of France (1589–1610), known as Henry of Navarre, was one of the greatest French monarchs. Son of the heiress of Navarre, he was brought up a Protestant and as a youth became leader of the French HUGUENOTS in the wars of religion. His marriage to Margaret of Valois, sister of the French King, provoked the massacre of ST BARTHOLOMEW (1572). After much

Henry IV at the Battle of Ivry

fighting Henry III recognized him as his successor, and in 1589 Navarre became King. But the Catholic League, aided by Spain, would not accept a Protestant, so Henry had to fight for the kingdom. He was victorious at Ivry and Arques but could not take Paris. Declaring that 'Paris was worth a Mass', he changed his religion in 1593 and became a Catholic, thus winning the support of most of his countrymen.

For the rest of his life Henry devoted himself to restoring law and order and prosperity to his country. With his minister Sully he curbed the nobles, improved trade and, by the Edict of Nantes, gave toleration to the Huguenots. He was assassinated by a religious fanatic.

HENRY THE NAVIGATOR (1394–1460), Prince of Portugal, a son of John I and Philippa, daughter of JOHN OF GAUNT. After distinguishing himself in a campaign against the MOORS of Morocco, he was made governor of the Algarve in southern Portugal and there, at Sagres, he built an observatory and a school of navigation. He sent out expeditions which discovered the Madeira Islands, explored the

Azores and pushed down the west coast of Africa. He believed that it would be possible to find a sea route to India and, although this was not achieved in his lifetime, he undoubtedly provided inspiration and training for the men like DIAZ and VASCO DA GAMA, who advanced the world's geographical knowledge and built Portugal's colonial empire.

HINDENBURG, Paul von (1847–1934), a German general who, on the outbreak of the FIRST WORLD WAR, came out of retirement to win the battles of Tannenberg and the Masurian Lakes against the Russians in 1914. He was transferred to the Western Front in 1916 and given supreme command of the German armies, a post which he held to the end of the war. He conducted the German retreat in 1918 and recommended the abdication of the Kaiser WILLIAM II.

Despite Germany's defeat, Hindenburg remained a hero to his people and in 1925 he was elected President of the German Republic. Von Papen, a leading politician, persuaded the old man to appoint HITLER (whom he despised) as Chancellor in 1933 and he died in the following year at the age of eighty-seven. Hitler then combined the offices of President and Chancellor.

HIROSHIMA, a Japanese town with a then population of about 250,000 on which the first atomic bomb was dropped by an American Superfortress B-25 on 6 August 1945. The explosion and fire devastated an area of over 4 square miles (10 km²), killing about 80,000 persons, though this figure rose to 140,000 within a year, as radioactivity took effect. Three days later a second atomic bomb was dropped on the city of Nagasaki, with similar dire results, whereupon the Emperor Hirohito ordered his forces to surrender and the SECOND WORLD WAR came to an end.

It has been said in justification that the use of these atomic bombs brought about the end of the war and thereby saved the lives of thousands who would have otherwise been engaged in further fighting and the invasion of Japan. On the other hand, it was known at the time the decision was taken to drop the bomb that the Japanese government was about to ask for peace terms.

Hiroshima was completely rebuilt within five years of the disaster.

HITLER, Adolf (1889–1945), was born in Austria, the son of a customs official. He did poorly at school and went to Vienna, where he led a miserable existence, taking casual work and sleeping in doss-houses. In this unhappy period he probably formed his violent opinions and passionate hatred, particularly of Jews.

From 1914 to 1918 he served in the German Army, winning the Iron Cross but not rising above the rank of corporal. 1919 found him in Munich, where he joined an obscure political group and became known as a spell-binding orator, who blamed Germany's defeat and suffering on Jews, Communists and traitors. By 1921 he had won control of the party, now called the National Socialist German Workers Party (the NAZIS).

Believing that the German Weimar Republic was about to collapse, Hitler, with his supporters Röhm, Göring and LUDENDORFF, made his first attempt to seize power in 1923. This was the *Munich Putsch*, a complete fiasco, which resulted in Hitler being arrested and sent to prison. But his impassioned harangues at his trial were widely reported; they made him a national figure.

Out of prison after a year, he rebuilt the Nazi Party, so that by 1928 it had twelve seats in the Reichstag (parliament), and when the economic collapse of 1929–30 brought Germany's recovery crashing to ruins (*see* the Great DEPRESSION) Hitler and his friends seized their chance.

In their fear and bewilderment people were ready to listen to this frenzied orator, who said he knew the causes of their troubles and how to cure them. In 1930 he stood against HINDENBURG for

the Presidency and two years later, when 230 of his followers were elected to the Reichstag, he was at the head of Germany's biggest single party. The ex-corporal could no longer be ignored and von Papen, head of the Nationalist Party, persuaded Hindenburg to accept Hitler as Chancellor. He at once demanded new elections. The Reichstag building was mysteriously burnt down; the Nazis pinned the blame on the Communists and with their strong-arm squads arresting and terrorizing opponents the elections were held in an atmosphere of public alarm. With Nationalist support, the Nazis won a big enough majority to give Hitler dictatorial powers, and within a year Germany was a one-party state. Nazis held all the key positions and their opponents were dead, fled abroad or in concentration camps.

In August 1934 Hindenburg died and Hitler proclaimed himself President, Chancellor and Commander-in-Chief of the German Army. His position was unassailable and he began to carry out his policy to make Germany strong. Rearmament was introduced, secretly at first, and then openly. He withdrew Germany from the LEAGUE OF NATIONS, restored conscription in defiance of the Treaty of VERSAILLES, and in 1936 sent troops to occupy the demilitarized Rhineland. His generals were appalled by the risk, but the gamble came off, because Britain and France made no move. He next used the SPANISH CIVIL WAR to try out new weapons and planes on FRANCO's side, and his friendship with

MUSSOLINI was expressed in the Rome-Berlin Axis.

He must now expand Germany's frontiers, and after tanks had crossed the Austrian border he announced the *Anschluss*, i.e. that Austria was part of the German Reich. Next he demanded the Sudetenland, a German-speaking part of Czechoslovakia, and so great was the fear of war which he had aroused that Britain and France meekly gave way to his demands at Munich. But he had not finished. In March 1939 he seized the remnant of Czechoslovakia and then he made demands on Poland for the port of Danzig and the Polish Corridor.

Shaken by the guarantee which Britain and France gave to Poland, he decided to swallow his hatred of the Soviet Union and made a non-aggression pact with STALIN. Having removed the danger of Soviet help to the Western powers, he was ready to make his *Blitzkrieg* (lightning war) on Poland and the SECOND WORLD WAR broke out in September 1939.

For two years Hitler's triumphs confirmed the Germans' belief in his genius. Their armies overran Poland, Norway, Denmark, Holland and France with masterly ease; Britain certainly held out, but Yugoslavia and Greece fell like the others and Hitler ruled an empire bigger than Napoleon's. Then in June 1941 he took the astonishing decision to invade Russia. Doubtless he expected his invincible armies to sweep all before them and by conquering European Russia win the farmlands, oil and minerals which the 'master race' required. He almost succeeded. By November the Germans were within 30 miles (48 km) of Moscow, but winter and Russian resistance brought them to a halt. However, with Hitler in command on all fronts, 1942 brought further successes as STALINGRAD was reached and in Africa ROMMEL was almost in Egypt. That was the peak of Hitler's triumphs, for after the defeats at Stalingrad and Alamein there were to be no more victories anywhere.

By 1943 it was clear that Germany could not win, but it was impossible for Hitler to contemplate defeat. A group of generals and others came to the conclusion that there was only one way to end the war, and in 1944 occurred the July Plot to assassinate Hitler. He escaped death and took a bloody vengeance not only on the conspirators but on thousands of others who might have been tempted to take the same course.

As the Allies closed in on Germany, Hitler's mind seems to have given way. No longer in touch with the people, unable to comprehend their disastrous situation, he became so cut off from reality that he called for Germany's complete destruction because it had failed him and his dreams. As the Russians entered Berlin he killed himself in the air-raid shelter under the Chancellery on 30 April 1945.

HITTITES, a people of the Ancient Near East who rose to power in Asia Minor and built the Hittite Empire, which for many years rivalled the empires of Egypt and Assyria.

By about 2000 BC the Hittites were a civilized people using cuneiform (wedge-shaped) writing. Their leading kingdom, Hatti, whose capital was called Hattusas, conquered its neighbours to found the First Hittite Empire (*c.* 1900–1650 BC). During this period King Mursil I captured BABYLON and overthrew the last of HAMMURABI's line.

The Second Hittite Empire (1400–1200 BC) became the greatest power in Western Asia; Hittite armies conquered all Syria, defeated the powerful Mitanni people and campaigned for years against the Egyptians. They fought the great battle of Kadesh in 1286 BC, when both sides claimed victory. In view of the rising power of the ASSYRIANS they made a peace treaty, sealed by the marriage of RAMESES II to a Hittite princess. It was not long, however, before the empire began to break up, due to the Assyrians and to the arrival of the Peoples of the Sea.

The Hittites seem to have been skilled iron-workers, architects and city-builders; they possessed a literature and a humane code of law; in warfare they understood fortification and made effective use of light horse-drawn chariots.

HOHENZOLLERNS, a German dynastic family which became the royal house of Prussia and imperial Germany. The family traced its origins back to the 9th century, when it owned a castle at Zollern in Swabia. Hohenzollerns were Burgraves of Nuremberg, and in 1415 Burgrave Frederick VII was given Brandenburg by the Emperor; the family prospered and by the 17th century was the leading Protestant house in Germany. In 1701 the Elector of Brandenburg became King of Prussia, and under FREDERICK the Great Prussia rose to become a major power in Europe. Hohenzollern-HAPSBURG rivalry persisted for many years, until BISMARCK united Germany under the Hohenzollern king of Prussia. After Germany's defeat in 1918 Kaiser WILLIAM II abdicated and the Hohenzollern dynasty in Germany came to an end.

HOLY ROMAN EMPIRE was founded by CHARLEMAGNE in the year 800. It was meant to be a revival of the Roman Empire, blessed by the Pope and Christian ideals. In practice it was a loose and fluctuating union of German and north Italian kingdoms and duchies. During the Middle Ages there occurred a long drawn-out struggle between the Emperor and the Pope (*see* PAPACY). Masterful emperors often appointed and deposed popes and, from time to time, a pope like Gregory VII (Hildebrand) would excommunicate and humble the emperor.

A number of German princes, called Electors, had the privilege of electing the Emperor. In 1273 they elected Rudolph of Hapsburg, and thenceforward the Holy Roman Empire became very largely the possession of the HAPSBURG family.

In the 16th century CHARLES V, whose vast possessions included Spain, the New World, the Netherlands, Austria, Hungary and much of Italy, besides the Empire, tried to restore its glory. But he failed to do so and it remained basically German. It was much weakened by the THIRTY YEARS WAR (1618–48), and the Emperor's power declined further as Austria and Prussia rose in importance.

When NAPOLEON dominated Europe, he insisted on the abolition of the Holy Roman Empire and Francis II, the last emperor, resigned in 1806. But by that time the Empire had long since ceased to have any real meaning.

HOOVER, Herbert (1874–1964), 31st President of the USA, was born into a Quaker family in Iowa. He trained as a mining engineer and had made himself a fortune by 1914. When the First World War broke out, he became chairman of the relief organization set up to help Belgium, and when America entered the war he was made food administrator for the United States. After the war he directed American Relief in Europe, organizing supplies of food and clothes for the needy countries.

As a Republican, he was elected President in 1928 and soon had to deal with effects of the Stock Market crash of 1929 and the ensuing DEPRESSION. Hoover thought that trade would naturally revive and he became very unpopular because he opposed the idea of government aid to the unemployed. Hence, in the 1932 Presidential Election he was heavily defeated by Franklin D. ROOSEVELT. Hoover again helped with international relief during and after the Second World War.

Fur trapper for the
Hudson's Bay Company

HUDSON'S BAY COMPANY was founded by Prince RUPERT and several others in 1670, when Charles II granted a charter for exclusive trading rights in northern Canada. Fur-trading posts were built and there was fierce rivalry with the French until Britain's right to the area was recognized by the Treaty of Utrecht, 1713, which ended the War of the SPANISH SUCCESSION. Cut-throat competition occurred later between the Company and a rival concern, the North West Company, but when the two were merged in 1821 they had a fur-trading monopoly. Difficulties arose as immigrants wanted to settle in the Company's vast hunting areas, and in 1869 it sold its territorial rights to the Canadian government for £300,000. The Company continues to trade to this day.

HUGUENOTS is the name given to French Protestants, followers of CALVIN, in the 16th and 17th centuries. During the reigns of Francis II (1559–60) and Charles IX (1560–74), when CATHERINE DE MEDICI was the power behind her sons, a religious war broke out between the Huguenots, led by the Prince of Condé and Admiral Coligny, and the Roman Catholics, led by the family of the Guises.

On ST BARTHOLOMEW'S Day 1572 Coligny and thousands of fellow Huguenots were murdered. In the civil war that followed the Huguenot leader was Henry of Navarre, heir to the French throne. After his accession as HENRY IV he turned Catholic, but granted freedom of worship to the Huguenots by the Edict of Nantes (1598). LOUIS XIV revoked the Edict in 1685, ordering persecution of the Huguenots and closure of their churches. Thousands of them therefore fled to Britain, Germany and

Switzerland, where their industry and business skill made them valuable citizens. The Huguenots regained religious freedom at the time of the FRENCH REVOLUTION of 1789.

HUNDRED DAYS (March–June 1815) refers to the period during which NAPOLEON was at liberty, from his escape from Elba to his defeat at WATERLOO. It began with a triumphant march from the south of France to Paris, but enthusiasm for the returned Emperor soon began to dwindle. The French people were reluctant to believe his promises of constitutional government and the Allies were equally doubtful about his supposed peaceful intentions. They re-formed the Grand Alliance and after WELLINGTON and Blücher had defeated Napoleon at Waterloo they sent him into permanent exile on St Helena.

HUNDRED YEARS WAR (1338–1453) between England and France was begun by EDWARD III of England. The English King had to pay homage to the French King for the fief of Gascony, and this led to ill feeling. On the death of Charles IV, Edward claimed the French throne through his mother

133

Isabella, but the French rejected his claim and chose Philip of Valois (Philip VI) as their king. Philip angered Edward by sending aid to the Scots and sheltering David Bruce when he fled to France. Finally, Edward supported the Flemish cloth-weaving cities in a rebellion against their overlord, the Count of Flanders, who appealed to *his* overlord, the King of France. Philip declared that by his action Edward had forfeited Gascony, and this was the immediate cause of the war.

The principal events of the war were as follows: the English won the sea battle of Sluys in 1340, fought an indecisive campaign in Brittany (1342), won a great victory at Crécy (1346), and starved Calais into surrender in 1347. The truce that followed was prolonged by the BLACK DEATH.

The war reopened in 1355, by which time John II had succeeded Philip VI. Edward III's son EDWARD THE BLACK PRINCE ravaged the south of France and won an overwhelming victory at Poitiers (1356), capturing King John, who promised to return all the possessions once held by HENRY II. When the French refused to accept this promise, Edward laid waste the north of France. By the Treaty of Brétigny (1360), he gave up his claim to the French throne in return for large gains and a huge ransom for King John.

The war broke out again in 1369, and for the next seven years the French were generally successful. Their leader Bertrand du GUESCLIN realized that the English owed their successes mainly to their longbowmen, so he declined to meet them in pitched battles, but outmanoeuvred them and made such effective use of cannons that he won back all the lost territories, except Calais and an area round Bordeaux. During this period the English fleet was badly beaten at the battle of La Rochelle (1372).

By reviving Edward III's claim to the French throne, HENRY V renewed the war in 1415 when he invaded France and won the battle of AGINCOURT. Aided by the Burgundians, he conquered Normandy and other areas, forcing Charles VI to make peace. By the Treaty of Troyes (1420) Henry was to marry the French King's daughter and succeed him as King of France. However, Henry died in 1422, just before Charles, whereupon his infant son HENRY VI was proclaimed King of France and actually crowned in Paris. The Dauphin, who assumed the title of Charles VII, suffered a series of defeats at the hands of the Duke of Bedford, but the situation was dramatically changed by JOAN OF ARC. She defeated the English at Patay and Orléans (1429) and had Charles crowned at Rheims. Although she was burned as a witch in 1431, the war continued to go against the English. The great Duke of Bedford died, the Burgundians changed sides and the French retook Paris. Steadily they recovered their provinces, and by a crushing victory at Castillon, near Bordeaux, in 1453, won back Guienne and brought the war to an end. It left France ravaged but united and the English with nothing except the town of Calais.

HUNTER, John (1728–93), a Scot from Kilbride, Lanarkshire, was one of the greatest surgeons of all time. He came to London to join his brother William, a gifted anatomist, who founded a school of anatomy in Great Windmill Street. After service in the British Army, John practised surgery in London, gave lectures, conducted experiments and built up a famous museum containing over 30,000 specimens. He is said to have found surgery merely a technical method and to have left it a branch of scientific medicine.

I

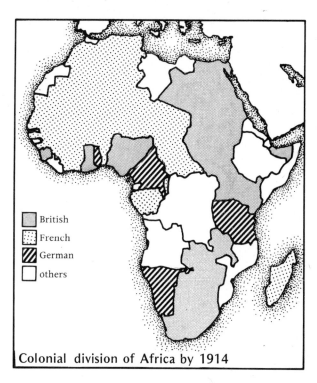

Colonial division of Africa by 1914

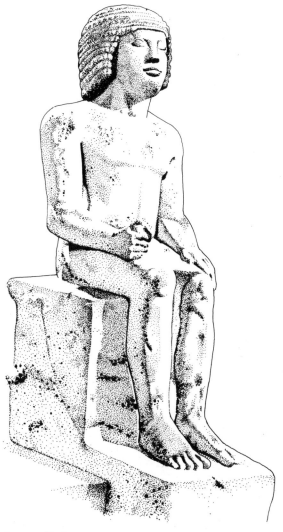

Statue of Imhotep

IMHOTEP was vizier and architect to the powerful King Zoser of EGYPT during the time of the Old Kingdom. In about 2700 BC at Sakkara, near modern Cairo, Imhotep built the Step PYRAMID, using stone blocks instead of mud bricks. It was probably the world's first stone building and it is still standing today. Imhotep, who was also famed for his knowledge of healing, was later revered as a god.

IMPERIALISM meant originally the rule of an emperor. Hence, Ancient Egypt, Assyria, Persia, Rome and Macedon were all imperialist powers, ruling subject peoples. In more recent times imperialism has come to mean colonial rule by some of the more powerful countries of the world, such as Spain and Portugal from the 16th century, Britain, France and Holland from the 17th century onwards and many other countries, including the USA, Germany and Italy, in more recent times. Imperialism was specially prevalent in the second half of the 19th century, when most of the European powers took part in the 'scramble for Africa' and large areas of Asia also came under imperialist rule. Since the Second World War imperialism has almost passed away, as colonial peoples have acquired independence, mostly peacefully but in places by force. It could be held that the Soviet Union, dominating as it does the countries of eastern Europe and a great tract of Asia, remains the last great imperialist power.

INCAS were American Indians of Peru, a ruling class or tribe whose emperor was known as 'The Inca'. In about the 12th century they emerged from the Peruvian highlands to settle in the fertile valley of Cuzco; then, during the 15th century, the

Incas carrying gold to ransom Atahualpa

Emperor Pachacuti founded the Inca Empire by establishing his rule over all the tribes of Peru through conquest or persuasion. His son Topa Inca expanded the empire to include Ecuador, Bolivia and northern Chile. He died in 1493 and his son Huayna Capac, with no further conquests needed, lived in magnificent style until the arrival of the first Europeans, who brought with them an illness (probably smallpox or measles) which killed him and many of his people. Civil war then broke out between his sons Huascar and Atahualpa.

Thus when the Spanish adventurer PIZARRO arrived in Peru with a small force of soldiers he found the empire in disarray. By treachery he and his men killed most of the leading nobles, captured Atahualpa and eventually put him to death (1533). Huascar was already dead and the ordinary people, lacking leaders, put up little resistance to the Spaniards. In a very brief period the Inca Empire was completely destroyed. The Incas ruled their subject peoples with extraordinary efficiency, dividing them into groups of families under a headman, who in his turn took orders from higher officials commanding many groups until, at the top, Inca nobles served as provincial governors and members of the Supreme Council. The Emperor was all-powerful, but he seems to have been a benevolent despot and the subject peoples did not hate their overlords in the way that the Mexican tribes hated the AZTECS. Land was shared out so that every family could support itself; widows, the sick and the old were cared for, and food stores were set aside against times of scarcity.

The Incas built roads and bridges throughout the Empire, constructed irrigation works and organized a postal system with relays of swift runners. Their capital Cuzco and other towns astonished the Spaniards by their magnificence. The Incas worshipped several deities, but their principal god was the Sun, from whom the royal family was supposed to be descended. Human sacrifice only occurred in times of emergency, such as a famine or the Emperor's illness. This remarkable people, so advanced in many ways, had no written language, no money and no knowledge of the wheel.

INDIAN MUTINY (1857–8) may be traced to several causes. Reforms introduced by Lord Dalhousie (Governor-General 1847–56) and innovations such as railways and the telegraph had upset traditional Indian ways of life; the caste system seemed to be threatened and there was fear that Christianity would be forcibly introduced; reverses in the AFGHAN and CRIMEAN WARS had weakened belief that the British were invincible; and, finally, the introduction of a new cartridge,

Indian cavalry attacking British soldiers during the Mutiny

136

said to be greased with cow or pig fat, gave offence to both Muslims and Hindus.

The Mutiny broke out at Meerut on 10 May 1857, when native soldiers killed their European officers, marched to Delhi, took the city and proclaimed the aged Mogul Emperor as their leader. The rising spread to Oudh, the Ganges Valley and Central India, but the Punjab, under John Lawrence, remained loyal, while the princes and the Indian people as a whole held aloof. At Cawnpore the British garrison and civilians were massacred by order of Nana Sahib, but at Lucknow, capital of Oudh, a small force held out for weeks until saved by General Havelock. But his troops could only strengthen, not relieve, the defenders. Meanwhile, Delhi was retaken and towards the end of the year Sir Colin Campbell arrived from England to relieve the Lucknow garrison, capture the city and, by cautious methods, suppress the mutiny. Sir Hugh Rose recovered Central India in the spring of 1858, but resistance continued in parts of Oudh until the end of the year.

The Mutiny was not a national rising. It was an attempt to throw off British rule by a few ex-rulers, their followers and the Bengal army. The chief result of the Mutiny was to bring an end to government by the EAST INDIA COMPANY, for in August 1858 Queen Victoria signed the Act which transferred the government of India to the Crown.

INDIAN NATIONAL CONGRESS was founded in 1885 in order to draw together educated and informed persons and eventually to become a parliament. From the outset it was essentially a Hindu movement, for the Muslim body was the Muslim League. Up until the 1920s Congress stood mainly for a greater share in government, but thereafter, under GANDHI's leadership, it became the nationalist movement demanding independence. After this was achieved in 1947, the Congress Party became the major political party in India.

INDIANS, NORTH AMERICAN, known as Red Indians and Redskins, were the original inhabitants of the continent. They are thought to have numbered about a million when the white man first came to North America and at that time they followed a Stone Age way of life, marvellously adapted to the plains and woodlands. Organized into many separate tribes and speaking a variety of languages, they mostly lived in villages under their chiefs and were skilful hunters who also practised simple farming.

There is ample evidence that the Indians were at first disposed to be friendly to the white settlers, trading pelts and furs in exchange for knives, blankets, kettles, guns and alcohol. During the 18th-century rivalry between the French and the British, certain tribes took sides and fought alongside their white allies; the Algonquin and Huron tribes sided with the French, since their enemies, the Iroquois, were the friends of the British. In South Carolina, too, the British could count on the friendship of the Creek and the Chickasaw Indians and, generally speaking, it was not until the second half of the 18th century that the Indians came to see the white man as their implacable enemy. From about 1760 the frontier, moving ever westward, was bitterly contested for over a hundred years, during which time the Indians, outnumbered and usually out-witted, steadily lost ground.

In 1811 the Shawnee Indians, under their chief Tecumseh, made a stand but were defeated at Tippecanoe Creek. Then, as farming advanced towards the Mississippi, tribes like the Cherokee, Chickashaw, Chocktaw and Seminole Indians migrated to new hunting grounds west of the river. But the white men followed remorselessly, crossing the Plains and the Rockies, pouring into areas where gold had been discovered, organizing cattle trails and killing the buffalo, on which the Plains Indians depended for all the necessities of life.

It was the US government's policy to concentrate the Indians into reservations, guaranteed by treaty. But these reservations dwindled in size and were constantly occupied by incoming settlers. The area known as Indian Territory, for example, was set aside as the home for forty tribes, yet in 1899 it was opened to white settlement and in 1907 it became the state of Oklahoma.

Some of the more warlike tribes, like the fierce Blackfeet, Comanches, Sioux and Apaches, resisted the white man's advance and attacked his settlements. The white men struck back. In 1864 occurred the Sand Creek Massacre when several hundred Cheyenne under their chief Black Kettle were slain by the Colorado Militia. Efforts to soothe Indian feelings with 'guaranteed' hunting-grounds were disregarded by pioneers and gold prospectors, and in 1875 the Sioux, on the warpath, wiped out

Steel mills at Merthyr Tydfil in Wales in 1817

CUSTER'S force at Little Big Horn. This disaster provoked massive retaliation and total defeat for the Sioux and their allies.

Many other tribes, including the Nez Percé, the Flatheads, the Comanches, the Blackfeet and the Navajo Indians, were forced from their lands, subdued and herded on to reservations. The Apache chief GERONIMO led one of the last campaigns against the white men, but he was defeated and exiled by 1886. Five years later a detachment of the 7th Cavalry murdered over three hundred Sioux in a virtually unprovoked attack at Wounded Knee Creek. After this there was no more resistance from the Indians.

INDUSTRIAL REVOLUTION. It is not easy to say when the Industrial Revolution began or ended, but the term is usually taken to mean the changes which took place in Britain between about 1770 and about 1830. These important changes in methods of work and in people's lives arose from the invention of machines, increased production of coal and iron, use of water and steam power, the building of factories and rise of a wage-earning class working in them and living in industrial towns.

Clearly there is no precise date for the origins of such changes; factories had their beginnings in the workshops of Tudor and Stuart times; John Kay of Bury invented his Flying Shuttle as early as 1733. HARGREAVES' invention of the Spinning Jenny in 1764 was a crucial event and so was the setting up of ARKWRIGHT'S factory using water power at Cromford in 1771. It was the adaptation of James WATT'S steam-engine to drive machinery (from 1781) that led to large-scale factory production; CARTWRIGHT'S power-loom speeded the process. The practice of bringing large numbers of people together to work in one building was particularly suitable for the cotton industry, but it soon spread to the woollen trade and other industries. Use of steam power meant that factories and factory towns sprang up near to the coalfields, and therefore much of industry became concentrated in the midlands and the north. Houses for the workers were built as speedily and as cheaply as possible and these rapidly became slums.

These inventions and new methods of work resulted in a tremendous increase in Britain's trade and wealth, which grew still greater as the country came to be provided with an efficient network of RAILWAYS. More goods were produced than ever before; more workers had regular wages and food, so that the population increased rapidly. Even so, the benefits of this revolution in production were not shared evenly. Wages may have been higher in industry than in agriculture, but they were still too low and hours of work too long for wage-earners to lead healthy lives. Rapid industrialization produced fortunes for some, a rising standard of living for a great part of the nation and squalor and misery for the less fortunate.

INNOCENT III (1161–1216) was the greatest of the medieval popes, a man of outstanding ability and determination who exercised authority over practically all the kings and princes of his time (*see* PAPACY). It was he who excommunicated King JOHN of England and subsequently annulled MAGNA CARTA; he also made Otto of Brunswick Emperor and later put FREDERICK II in his place. At various times England, Sicily, Ireland, Aragon and Portugal belonged to him as papal fiefs (*see* FEUDAL SYSTEM). He called the Fourth CRUSADE (1202–4) and the Albigensian Crusade against a body of French heretics, besides summoning a great council of churchmen called the Fourth Lateran Council (1215).

A heretic condemned by the Inquisition on his way to execution

INQUISITION normally means the searching out and punishment of heretics by the Roman Catholic Church. It dates from the 13th century, when Pope Gregory IX appointed inquisitors, usually Dominicans, to deal with heresy. The inquisitor would tour a district and hold an enquiry, encouraging heretics to confess. Those who did so at once would be given light punishment; then, after about thirty days' grace, trial would take place of accused persons who had not confessed. From 1252 torture could be used to extract confession and those found guilty could be sentenced to imprisonment, loss of property or death by burning.

The Spanish Inquisition, whose first Grand Inquisitor was called Torquemada, was set up by FERDINAND AND ISABELLA; it was finally abolished in 1820.

IRISH HOME RULE, meaning self-government for Ireland, began as a movement in 1870 when Isaac Butt founded the Home Rule Association. Butt was succeeded as leader by Charles Stewart PARNELL, who obstructed parliamentary business at Westminster in order to draw attention to Irish grievances. GLADSTONE, realizing that his measures to help Ireland were not enough, became converted to Home Rule and introduced Home Rule Bills, one in 1886 which was defeated in the Commons, and one in 1893 which was rejected by the House of Lords.

Liberals mostly supported Home Rule and in 1912 the Prime Minister Asquith introduced a third Bill. When the Lords defeated it, Asquith secured its passage in three sessions of the Commons, thus by-passing the Lords. Opposition from Ulster, led by Sir Edward Carson, almost resulted in civil war, as Ireland became divided into two armed camps. The Bill was made law in 1914, but its operation was suspended because of the outbreak of the First World War.

By the time the war ended the situation had changed through the rise of the Sinn Fein Party and demands for complete independence. After a period of warfare and terrorism LLOYD GEORGE's government passed the Government of Ireland Act (1920) providing for separate parliaments for Ulster and the South, which became the Irish Free State. It was renamed Eire by De Valera in 1937, and eleven years later the last links with Britain and the Commonwealth were severed when Eire became the Republic of Ireland. But the country was still partitioned and in 1969 a bitter struggle broke out in Ulster, which was still continuing in 1976.

ISLAM is the religion of the Muslims preached by the prophet Mahomet or Mohammed. He was born at Mecca in Arabia in about 570, took to a life of prayer and meditation, acquired enemies and fled to Medina, where he attracted a band of devoted followers. Claiming to be God's special messenger, he won so much support that by the time he died in 632 all of Arabia had been converted to the new

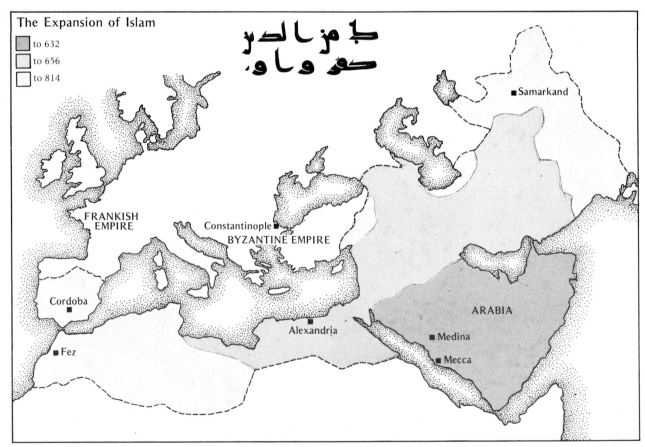

The Expansion of Islam

- to 632
- to 656
- to 814

FRANKISH EMPIRE

Constantinople
BYZANTINE EMPIRE

Samarkand

Cordoba

Fez

Alexandria

ARABIA

Medina

Mecca

Islamic faith. His successors, known as caliphs, inspired Arab armies to carry out Mahomet's desire to convert the world to his faith, so that from about 635 to about 800 the Arabs swept across the Near East, into Egypt, through North Africa and into Spain. In the East Islam conquered the Persian Empire and spread to parts of India, but the Byzantine and Frankish Empires checked Islam's entry into Europe. The Arabs (or Moors) who conquered Spain pushed into France, but were decisively defeated by Charles Martel, chief of the Franks, at Poitiers in 732, causing them to retire behind the Pyrenees. Charlemagne campaigned in Spain against the Moors without winning any major success.

In about 1000 Turkish tribes from central Russia began to press into the Near East and India; they adopted the Islamic faith and were followed by a particularly ferocious tribe, the Seljuks, who overran Persia and Asia Minor, including the Holy Land. Their ill-treatment of Christian pilgrims led to the First Crusade (1096–9) and the founding of the Crusader kingdoms in Palestine. Christians in the Middle Ages referred to their Muslim enemies as Saracens.

At its greatest extent the Islamic Empire stretched from the Atlantic to India, with millions of devout followers of Mahomet. When the tough, almost invincible warriors conquered an area, they usually settled down and built fine cities. They farmed well, encouraged industry and trade, revived learning and became expert in mathematics, science and literature, at a time when most of the rulers of Western Europe could barely read or write.

Islam embarked on a further period of conquest after the Ottoman Turks captured Constantinople in 1453, won possession of the Byzantine Empire and pushed into Eastern Europe. In 1521 Suleiman the Magnificent captured Belgrade and took Hungary and most of Rumania. For many years the Hapsburg Emperors, the Pope and the city of Venice were preoccupied with the task of stemming the Turkish advance. It was eventually checked by Don John of Austria's victory at Lepanto in 1571. In the 17th century the Ottoman leaders declined, and in 1683 John Sobieski of Poland defeated the Turks near Vienna and cleared them out of Austria. After this, although Islam remained one of the major religions of the world, there were no more waves of conquest.

IVAN the Terrible (1530–84), Tsar of Moscow, succeeded as Grand Duke Ivan IV at the age of three. His mother died when he was seven and the boy was brought up in a brutal atmosphere; ill-treated by the *boyars* or nobles, he came to hate them all his life.

At sixteen Ivan demanded to be crowned Tsar (Emperor), the first Russian to assume that title, and from 1550 to 1560 he ruled well with the aid of his advisers of lowly origin. In this period he pushed Muscovy's borders east of the Urals by conquering Kazan and Astrakhan. Hoping to establish links with the West, he received Richard Chancellor, the merchant-adventurer, and made a commercial treaty with England. The port of Archangel was built to help trade, but Ivan's attempts to secure a Baltic outlet by conquering Livonia were not successful.

The deaths of his wife and a favourite son seem to have so upset Ivan's neurotic character that from 1560 he ruled like an insane tyrant. He had the saintly metropolitan (bishop) of Moscow strangled, killed his cousin and struck his own son so savagely that the boy died. His worst atrocity occurred in and around the city of Novgorod, where, on suspicion of a conspiracy, he spent five weeks destroying every building and systematically murdering the inhabitants. Ivan IV was a man of great ability, who anticipated the ideals of Peter the Great, but he was also a cruel and immoral tyrant.

J

JACKSON, Andrew (1767–1845), 7th President of the USA, the son of a Scottish-Irish immigrant, was reared in poverty and trained for law on the Tennessee frontier. In charge of the Tennessee troops during the WAR OF 1812, he defeated the Creek Indians at Horseshoe Bend and made himself a national hero by routing the British at New Orleans (1815). When the Seminole Indians made raids from Florida, then a Spanish possession, Jackson defeated the Seminoles and, against orders, invaded Florida. As a result Spain sold Florida to the USA and Jackson, known as 'Old Hickory', became its Governor.

In 1828, when he defeated John Quincy Adams for the Presidency, his election was received with wild enthusiasm. To the ordinary citizen this was the triumph of the self-made man, a Westerner who had fought for his country and who represented the democratic spirit of the times. Jackson was certainly hostile to social privilege and to the wealthy bankers and speculators of the East. He was also a strong nationalist, who despised men who put State interests above those of the country. During his two terms of office (1829–37) he destroyed the Second Bank of the United States (thereby causing a severe financial panic) and firmly insisted that South Carolina should not be allowed to nullify a tariff law passed by Congress. As President he was an active leader, directing policy with the aid of his personal advisers known as the 'kitchen cabinet'. At the end of his second term he retired to Nashville, Tennessee.

JACKSON, Thomas 'Stonewall' (1824–63), American Confederate general, was born in Virginia and educated at West Point. As an artillery officer, he distinguished himself in the MEXICAN WAR, and when the CIVIL WAR broke out he joined the Confederates and commanded a brigade at the first battle of Bull Run (1861). It was there that his dour defence won him the name of 'Stonewall' Jackson. During the Shenandoah Valley campaign of 1862 he won victory after victory by brilliant tactical skill, and he gave LEE the closest and most loyal support in Northern Virginia at the battles of Antietam, Fredericksburg and Chancellorsville (1863). In the last battle he died after being accidentally shot by his own men, a tragedy and a mortal blow to the Southern cause. He was a general of the rarest quality, beloved by his men ('Remember Jackson!' became their battle cry) and held in high honour by all who knew him: 'such an executive officer the sun never shone on', was Lee's judgement of his fellow general.

JACOBINS were the most extreme group during the FRENCH REVOLUTION. From 1789 they met at the Jacobin Club in Paris in a disused monastery of Dominican (Jacobin) monks, where they expressed revolutionary ideas and had them passed on to the public. ROBESPIERRE became the leading spokesman, and in 1793 Jacobin clubs sprang up in all large French cities; but after Robespierre's execution they were closed down, and the Jacobin Club in Paris ceased to exist from November 1794. The term 'Jacobin' continued to be used to describe a person with extreme left-wing views.

JACOBITE REBELLION OF 1715 took place shortly after the accession of the first Hanoverian king of Great Britain, GEORGE I. Jacobites were numerous in the west of England, in Lancashire and in the Highlands of Scotland and their best hopes lay in simultaneous risings, backed by foreign troops and the presence of the Old Pretender, James Edward, son of JAMES II. However, with LOUIS XIV on his death-bed, there was no prospect of French help and the Pretender gave the Earl of Mar orders to raise the rebellion in Scotland without waiting for the English Jacobites to move. But he did not come over to lead his supporters.

Mar raised the Highlanders, but showed little military skill at the indecisive battle of Sheriffmuir and, lacking victory, the clansmen soon drifted away. The belated appearance of the Pretender did nothing to rally his supporters and he returned to the continent within a month. Meanwhile, in Lancashire a force of Jacobites had seized Preston briefly, but were soon forced to surrender, so that the 'Fifteen' petered out in dismal fashion.

Scottish Highlanders at the Battle of Culloden

JACOBITE REBELLION OF 1745, known as the 'Forty-five', was led by the Young Pretender, Prince CHARLES EDWARD STUART, against the Hanoverian rule of GEORGE II in Scotland and England. Disappointed in his hopes of French support, Charles Edward landed with only seven companions at Moidart in July 1745. He speedily won over the Cameron and Macdonald clans, occupied Edinburgh and defeated Sir John Cope at Prestonpans. In November he invaded England with a force of about 6,000 men, took Carlisle and advanced through Lancashire to Derby, which he reached on 4 December. By that time it was clear that there was no prospect of a French invasion or of a general uprising by the English Jacobites; the chieftains refused to continue the march to London, and on 6 December the rebels began the retreat northwards, with the Duke of Cumberland in pursuit. At Glasgow the Prince received reinforcements which enabled him to defeat a government army at Falkirk, but Cumberland came on remorselessly into the Highlands and at Culloden, near Inverness, in April 1746, he totally defeated Charles Edward's tired army. The Prince escaped from the battlefield and after many adventures as a hunted fugitive secured a boat to carry him to France and into exile for the rest of his life.

In the Highlands Cumberland punished the rebels with savage cruelty, hunting them down and burning their crofts. Nearly a hundred leaders were executed, so that the clan system and the authority of the chieftains were broken.

JAMES I (1394–1437), King of Scotland (1406–37), son of Robert III, was captured as a boy by the English when on his way to safety in France. He was kept a captive for eighteen years, during which time he accompanied HENRY V to the wars and married Joan Beaufort, a lady of the court In Scotland James ruled well, bringing in many reforms, subduing the unruly Highlanders, forcing the nobles to obey the law and calling a parliament, which he hoped would work like the English parliament. These measures caused discontent among the nobles and in February 1437, during festivities at Perth, James was assassinated by Sir Robert Graham. On that evening occurred the celebrated act of heroism by Catherine Douglas, who thrust her bare arm through iron loops to serve as a bar to the door in order to delay the murderers and give the King time to hide. James, besides being a stern and capable ruler, was a poet, a scholar and an athlete; he founded St Andrews University.

JAMES II (1430–60), King of Scotland (1437–60), was only a child when his father JAMES I was murdered, and during his minority the nobles behaved with their usual violence and greed. When he began to rule, he showed his father's spirit, restored law and order and tamed the Douglases. Taking advantage of the Wars of the ROSES, he decided to recover Roxburgh Castle from the English, but was killed when a siege gun blew up in his face.

JAMES III (1451–88), King of Scotland (1460–88), was only nine when his father JAMES II died. Bishop Kennedy governed the country wisely for him until his death in 1465, after which young James was seized by the Boyd family. However, he overthrew the Boyds, married Margaret of Denmark (thereby gaining the Orkney and Shetland Islands) and made a treaty of friendship with EDWARD IV of England. Unfortunately, the nobles took no interest in his taste for music, architecture, astrology and alchemy, and they were angered because he liked to rely on a council of low-born advisers. They rebelled against him, seized his eldest son and proclaimed him Governor of Scotland. After the battle of Sauchieburn, near Stirling, the King was found dead in a mill, stabbed by an unknown hand.

JAMES IV (1473–1513), King of Scotland (1488–1513), was brought to the throne by nobles who rebelled against his father JAMES III. He soon proved himself a capable ruler, who increased the royal authority, improved justice, laid the foundations of a navy and raised a force to control the Highlands. Although he had supported Perkin Warbeck (an imposter who claimed the throne of HENRY VII), he came to the conclusion that it would be wiser to abandon the age-old enmity with England, and in 1503 he married HENRY VII's daughter Margaret Tudor. The marriage did not affect Scotland's old friendship with France, and James was able to cut quite a figure in European politics, sending aid to the Queen of Denmark, advice to the citizens of Lübeck and the Duke of Guelders. After HENRY VIII came to the English throne, James found himself courted by Louis XII of France, who asked him to invade England when Henry was on the point of sailing to France. The temptation was too much to resist, and in August 1513 James crossed the border at the head of a splendid army, only to be totally defeated by the Earl of Surrey at the Battle of FLODDEN. With some 10,000 of his men James was killed, leaving as heir to the throne a boy not two years old.

JAMES V (1512–42), King of Scotland (1513–42), became king at the age of one, when his father JAMES IV was killed at FLODDEN. His mother Margaret Tudor, who soon married the Earl of Angus, offended the Scottish nobles by her pro-English policy and they brought over from France the Duke of Albany to act as regent. After a period of strife, James escaped from Angus's clutches, drove him into England and, at sixteen, began to reign. Although he was hard put to control the nobles, he showed his father's zeal for justice.

He married Magdalen, the daughter of King FRANCIS I of France, and after her death in 1538 a second French princess, Mary of Guise. This French alliance displeased his uncle, HENRY VIII, and so did his refusal to throw off the Pope's authority. Henry decided it was time to teach his nephew a lesson, but his invading army was badly mauled by the Scots. James ordered his nobles to follow the retreating Englishmen, but when they did so they were attacked and severely beaten at Solway Moss. The news so depressed James that he died a few days later, leaving the kingdom to his baby daughter MARY QUEEN OF SCOTS.

JAMES I and VI (1566–1625), King of Scotland (1567–1625) and England (1603–25), was the son of MARY QUEEN OF SCOTS and Lord Darnley. After his mother's abdication when he was one, he was brought up by various guardians and tutors, who

As king of Scotland one of his principle aims was to do nothing to offend his cousin ELIZABETH. So he made an alliance with England and did not try to avenge his mother's execution (1587). He was rewarded in 1603 with the news that on her death-bed Elizabeth had named him as her successor.

Thenceforward, the main events of his reign were the Hampton Court Conference, when he quarrelled with the Puritans, the GUNPOWDER PLOT (1605), the end of the Spanish War and execution of RALEIGH, the marriage of his daughter Elizabeth to the Elector-Palatine, the sailing of the MAYFLOWER (1620) and the protracted struggle with Parliament.

The English Parliament was affronted by the theory of Divine Right; the nobility resented James's liking for favourites and penniless Scots; his sale of Monopolies harmed trade and his pro-Spanish policy offended the Protestants. Not all of James's difficulties were his own fault, but he lacked dignity and tact; he had no understanding of men and he was unsuccessful in almost everything he attempted at home and abroad. He deserved his title, 'the wisest fool in Christendom'.

JAMES II (1633–1701), King of Great Britain (1685–88), the second son of CHARLES I, escaped to France at the end of the CIVIL WAR, served in the French and Spanish armies and returned to England at the Restoration. As Lord High Admiral he commanded the Navy during the DUTCH WAR and fought in the sea battles of Lowestoft and Sole Bay. By his first marriage to Anne Hyde, daughter of Clarendon, the Lord Chancellor, he had two daughters, Mary and Anne, both brought up as Protestants and both destined to become Queen of England. In about 1670 James became a Roman Catholic, and his second marriage to Mary of Modena, aroused anxiety because he was heir to the throne, since CHARLES II had had no legitimate children. A movement arose to exclude him from the throne and he had to go into exile in Brussels and Edinburgh (1681–5).

Yet there was no outcry when he succeeded his brother in 1685, and Parliament voted him a comfortable income. Perhaps the ease with which he suppressed two rebellions – MONMOUTH's in England and Argyll's in Scotland – led him to suppose he could do as he pleased. At all events, he maintained a large standing army, stationed troops

gave him a good education, little affection and a great deal of stern religious teaching. For years the boy was a puppet in the hands of violent nobles, but he grew up to outwit them and to rule Scotland better than most of his ancestors. He was clever, ungainly, conceited about his learning and generous to his friends; he believed in the Divine Right of Kings (i.e. the theory that kings, being appointed by God, were above criticism) and he wrote two books on the subject.

uproar when it became known that Mary of Modena had borne a son, so there was now a Catholic male heir to the throne. At this a group of leading men wrote to William of Orange (later WILLIAM III), inviting him to come over to save the Constitution and the Protestant religion.

William landed with an army in 1688 and James, unable to trust his troops and deserted by his best general, fled to the continent (*see* GLORIOUS REVOLUTION). He returned briefly to Ireland but was defeated at the Boyne (1690) and this formerly brave soldier again lost his nerve and fled. He died in exile in France.

on Hounslow Heath to overawe London, appointed Catholics as army officers and to official positions and issued the Declaration of Indulgence that would have given tolerance to Catholics. When six bishops and the Archbishop of Canterbury protested at having to read the Declaration in church, he had them put on trial. The country was in an

JAPAN seems to have been first settled by people from Siberia called Ainus, and the nation emerged from a mixture of Ainus, MONGOLS and other Asians. Their history begins with the Emperor Jimmu (possibly 660 BC), from whom all the emperors are said to be descended.

In AD 552 the Buddhist religion was first introduced into Japan; it spread rapidly and there followed, from about 680, the so-called Fujiwara

Incident in the Heiji War of 1159, which began the struggle between the Taira and Minamoto families

era, lasting four centuries, when the Fujiwara family ruled the country. Its sons acted as statesmen, its daughters as wives of the emperors. In this period, when the capital was moved to Heian (modern Kyoto), literature, art and fine building flourished.

During the 11th century the Taira family took over power, but they were ousted in 1185 by their enemies the Minamoto family. The Emperor became a sacred but shadowy figure and real power rested with a noble called the Shogun. The Hojo family was the next to rule Japan, and in 1281 when the Emperor of China, Kublai Khan, tried to assert his authority the Japanese won a great naval victory off Kyushu. An era of civil war among the nobles led to the rise of the SAMURAI warrior class and there next emerged the Tokugawa family, whose Shoguns ruled from 1603 to 1867.

At first foreigners were welcomed, so that trade was started with Portuguese, Dutch and Spanish merchants and Jesuit missionaries made many converts to Christianity; but reaction set in. Christians were murdered and foreigners almost completely excluded. Nevertheless, during this period of isolation, Japan enjoyed peace and prosperity under the Tokugawas. In 1853 the arrival of an American naval force under Commodore Perry led to treaties being signed with the USA, Russia, Britain and Holland. Anti-foreigner riots were followed by the downfall of the Tokugawa Shogun, but under the great Emperor Meiji (1867–1912) Japan emerged from her isolation and feudal state. The Emperor took on real authority, the *samurai* lost their power and foreigners were employed to modernize the army, the navy, farming, education and public services.

In 1894 Japan went to war with China over Korea and speedily won a decisive victory. Then, in 1904–5, she astonished the world by completely defeating imperial Russia. Overnight Japan had become a major power, soon linked by treaty and agreement to Britain, the USA and Russia.

During the FIRST WORLD WAR Japan joined the Allies, and in 1915 took advantage of China's weakness to make the notorious 'Twenty-One Demands' for control of Chinese affairs. Between the wars, when Japan's industrial and military strength advanced rapidly, there was bitter enmity with China. Japanese troops invaded Manchuria in 1931, and by 1939 they had captured nearly all China's principal cities and had taken control of the richest provinces.

The outbreak of the SECOND WORLD WAR saw Japan an 'Axis' partner of Germany and Italy, and in December 1941 her military leaders, headed by General Tojo, decided to attack the US Pacific base at PEARL HARBOR. There followed two triumphant years, when Japanese forces took Hong Kong, Malaya and Singapore and conquered the Dutch East Indies, Borneo, the Philippines and most of Burma. But America's recovery brought disastrous naval defeats and loss of island bases, which led to the bombing of the Japanese mainland and to complete surrender after the dropping of atomic bombs on HIROSHIMA and Nagasaki (1945).

Since the war, after a period of Allied occupation under General MacArthur, Japan, still loyal to the Emperor Hirohito, has pursued a peaceful policy, while becoming one of the world's leading industrial powers.

Jefferson and his house at Monticello, which he designed

JEFFERSON, Thomas (1743–1826), the third President of the USA, held office from 1801–9. Born in Virginia, he studied law, became opposed to rule by Britain and was chief author of the DECLARATION OF INDEPENDENCE, 1776. He later served in Congress, was Minister in Paris (1785–9) and returned to America as the first Secretary of State. He disliked the idea of a strong federal government, yet, as President, he was responsible for the LOUISIANA PURCHASE (1803). During his second term of office (1805–9) he succeeded in keeping America out of the war in Europe. After his retirement he founded the University of Virginia. Jefferson was essentially a thinker, scholar and writer; he was not an efficient governor of Virginia and was so inefficient a farmer that he died in poverty. He believed in freedom for the common man (by which he meant landed yeoman, not uneducated labourers), freedom of the press and religion, freedom from great inequalities of wealth; he was a democrat, who hoped America would remain a rural nation.

JENKINS'S EAR, War of (1739), was fought between Britain and Spain, mainly in the Caribbean. British merchants and sea-captains had long persisted in doing more than the agreed amount of trade (one shipload) with the Spanish colonies. When a ship *was* caught carrying on unauthorized trade, Spanish coastguards were inclined to deal roughly with the crew. The Opposition to WALPOLE taunted him for not protecting English seamen and they brought into the House of Commons, a Captain Jenkins, who produced from a box an ear, supposed to have been cut off in a fight with the Spaniards. This incident aroused such war fever that Walpole was obliged to declare war on Spain.

The sea-fighting began with some minor British successes and the capture of Portobello, but the fleet was in poor condition and an attack on Cartagena on the Spanish Main failed. The war became merged in the much greater War of the AUSTRIAN SUCCESSION (1740–8).

Jenkins's Ear helped to bring down Walpole, who resigned in 1742. It occasioned his famous remark, when hearing the enthusiastic noise that welcomed the war, he muttered 'They are ringing their bells now, but they will soon be wringing their hands!'

JERUSALEM had been occupied by the Egyptians long before King DAVID made it his royal city in about 1000 BC. Solomon built the Temple of Jehovah and added some massive fortifications, but the city was destroyed by NEBUCHADNEZZAR II in

Roman soldiers carrying spoils from the Temple in Jerusalem

587 BC. It was rebuilt by the Jews who returned from captivity in Babylon in about 445 BC. Spared by ALEXANDER THE GREAT, it suffered damage when captured by PTOLEMY I of Egypt and was later occupied by a Greek garrison until taken by the Romans in 65 BC. With their aid, Herod the Great constructed some splendid buildings and fortifications, but to punish the rebellious Jews the Romans razed the city to the ground in AD 70.

Rebuilt as a Roman colony named Aelia Capitolina, it remained unimportant until the Emperor CONSTANTINE built two magnificent churches there in about 326. Others were constructed during the 5th and 6th centuries, but in 614 the city was devastated by the Persians and finally captured by the Muslim Caliph Omar in 636. It remained in Muslim hands until 1099, when it was taken by the Crusaders, who made it the capital of their 'Kingdom of Jerusalem' (*see* CRUSADES). SALADIN recaptured the city in 1187; it passed into Turkish possession, was added to by SULEIMAN the Magnificent and remained in Muslim hands until finally captured by British forces in 1917.

Jerusalem, bitterly contested by Arabs and Jews during the War of Independence of 1948 (*see* ARAB-ISRAELI WARS), became a divided city, but in 1950 the Jews made it the capital of the State of Israel and subsequently gained control of the whole city.

JINNAH, Muhammad Ali (1876–1948), Indian Muslim leader who is regarded as the creator of Pakistan. Between the wars he led the Muslim community and was president of the Muslim League. Changing his earlier views, he came to demand the creation of independent Muslim states, and in 1947 took the office of Governor-General of Pakistan. He ruled the country almost single-handed until his death in 1948.

JOAN OF ARC (1412–31), a peasant girl, was brought up in the French village of Domrémy during the HUNDRED YEARS WAR. From about the age of thirteen she claimed to hear voices of saints telling her to free France from the English and to help the Dauphin Charles to be crowned king. She made her way to the Court at Chinon, convinced Charles of her sincerity and was given permission to don armour and lead an army to relieve the city of Orléans. In May 1429 she forced the English to raise the siege, and in July she was present when the Dauphin was crowned Charles VII at Rheims. After this she defeated the English several times, but failed to take Paris. In May 1430 she was captured by the Burgundians, who sold her to the English. Accused of being a heretic and a witch, she was condemned to death and burned at the stake in Rouen on 30 May 1431. She was made a saint in 1920.

JOHN (1167–1216), King of England (1199–1216), was the youngest son of HENRY II. He grew into a clever spoilt young man, who plotted against his own father and, later, against his brother RICHARD I when he was away on Crusade. He succeeded Richard in 1199 and probably had his nephew Prince Arthur murdered to remove a possible rival. This crime harmed him in the eyes of his Norman barons, many of whom deserted him, so that although John was an able soldier he lost Normandy and other French possessions to PHILIP AUGUSTUS of France. He withdrew to England, where he ruled firmly until he became involved in a quarrel with Pope INNOCENT III over the choice of Stephen Langton as Archbishop of Canterbury. The Pope excommunicated John, who promptly seized Church revenues, hired an army and went to Scotland, where he defeated William the Lion.

In 1213 John made his peace with the Pope, becoming his vassal; then, having accumulated a large war treasure and powerful allies on the continent, he set out to win back the French territories. The expedition was a failure and John returned to England to find that the barons, angered by his greed and arrogance, were determined to assert their own rights. Taking advantage of his temporary lack of money and troops, they forced him to accept MAGNA CARTA (1215), but he had no intention of keeping his promises. The Pope supported him and annulled the Charter; he collected an army and harried the barons so fiercely that they invited Louis VIII of France to come over and accept the crown. John was campaigning with furious energy when he died suddenly at Newark. He had considerable ability, but no gift of inspiring loyalty; the nobles, who hated him personally, were quite ready, on his death, to accept the authority of his baby son.

JOHN OF GAUNT (1340–99), so called because he was born in Ghent, Flanders, was the fourth son of EDWARD III of England. He married first Blanche of Lancaster and their son became King HENRY IV. Through his later marriage to Constance, daughter of Pedro the Cruel of Castile, he claimed the throne of Castile, but in an expedition to Spain failed to oust his rival. An ambitious man, he was unpopular in England and was perhaps unfairly blamed for the troubled state of affairs during the reign of his nephew, RICHARD II. He supported WYCLIFFE and the LOLLARDS against the established Church. By his third wife, Catherine Swynford, he had three sons, known as the Beauforts, and from the eldest descended Henry Tudor, who defeated RICHARD III and became King HENRY VII.

JONES, John Paul (1747–92), the American naval hero, was born John Paul on an estate near Kirkcudbright, Scotland, where his father was a gardener. At twelve John Paul went to sea as apprentice on a Whitehaven vessel; in due course he made several voyages to America, including two on a slaver, and was appointed captain by the age of twenty-one. For some reason, possibly because he accidentally killed a mutinous seaman at Tobago, he left the sea, added Jones to his name and began a new life in America.

In 1775, when the AMERICAN WAR OF INDEPENDENCE broke out between Britain and the colonies, Jones was commissioned as a lieutenant by the Continental Congress. As commander of the *Providence* and then of the *Alfred* he cruised along the eastern seaboard inflicting much damage on British shipping and fisheries. In 1777, as a captain, he sailed the *Ranger* to Brest and thence to Whitehaven, where he made a surprise attack on the port and later captured the British sloop *Drake*. Next year the French, now at war with Britain, furnished him with a small squadron of warships, whose flagship he renamed the *Bonhomme Richard*, and with

this force he attacked shipping in British waters. Off Flamborough Head he fought a desperate battle with the much superior *Serapis*, forcing the British man-of-war to surrender before his own crippled flagship sank.

After this exploit Jones spent much time in Paris, where he negotiated prize money for the ships he had captured; then he returned to America to be presented by Congress with a gold medal.

In 1788, appointed rear-admiral in the Russian navy, he took part in operations against the Turks in the Black Sea. Russian officers intrigued against him and he was recalled to St Petersburg, leaving soon afterwards for Paris, where he died in 1792. More than a century later his body was discovered there, and in 1905 a fleet of American warships carried it to Annapolis, Maryland, where it now rests in the United States Naval Academy.

JULIUS CAESAR (102–44 BC), Roman general and dictator (*see* ROME), was born into an impoverished branch of an aristocratic family; he entered politics

the last forces of the Senate in North Africa. Back in Rome, as undisputed master of the Roman world, Caesar was appointed dictator for ten years. Pompey's sons made a last stand in Spain but were utterly defeated by the great general at Munda in 45. He was not to wield supreme power for long. He had many enemies and a conspiracy, headed by Brutus and Cassius, was formed to rid Rome of a man who seemed to have become too powerful. On 15 March 44 he was stabbed to death near Pompey's statue in the Senate house.

Caesar was undoubtedly ruthless and ambitious; whether his rule would have been a complete tyranny it is impossible to say, but the effect of his career was to change the Roman Republic into government by one ruler. He was one of the foremost generals in history, a great orator and a writer whose accounts of his campaigns are wonderfully clear and direct.

JULY REVOLUTION was an uprising in Paris in July 1830 which forced Charles X, last of the BOURBONS, to give up his throne. Since his accession in 1824 he had provoked liberal opposition, and the 1830 revolution in France sparked off similar uprisings in Belgium, Switzerland, Poland, Germany and Italy. In France Charles X was replaced by Louis Philippe, whose reign, lasting until the REVOLUTION OF 1848, is often called the July Monarchy.

JUSTINIAN (483–565), one of the greatest Byzantine emperors, ruled from 527 to 565 and restored, at least for a time, the power and unity of the Roman Empire (*see* BYZANTINE EMPIRE). A man of enormous drive and energy, he was a good judge of men and his great generals, Belisarius and Narses, won back Africa from the VANDALS and Italy from the Goths. Successful wars were waged against the Persians and the tribes of the Danube plain. As a Christian emperor, Justinian summoned a general council of the Church and rigorously persecuted heretics. He was also a great legislator, issuing many new laws and collecting and revising Roman laws.

His most trusted counsellor was his wife Theodora, a remarkable woman, who had been an actress and dancer before he married her. She shared in the government of the Empire, crushed a rebellion with ruthless cruelty and gave generously to the poor.

and as a young man spent money lavishly (he probably obtained it from his millionaire friend, Crassus) to win popular favour. In 61 he went as governor to Farther Spain, where he first showed his talent for war. Back in Rome, he became consul in 59 and formed a partnership or triumvirate with Crassus and Pompey, a successful general. He then received the coveted governorship of Gaul, and the years 58–50 were spent mostly in a series of brilliant campaigns in which he conquered Gaul, defeated the Germanic tribes and made two expeditions to Britain.

The death of Crassus left Pompey and Caesar rivals for supreme power, and in 49 Caesar marched his victorious legions towards Italy, defied the Senate and entered Rome. Pompey fled, so Caesar hurried to Spain to defeat his supporters and then crossed to Greece where he routed Pompey at Pharsalus in 48 BC. Pursuing his rival to Egypt, he found that Pompey had been murdered and, after a love affair with CLEOPATRA and a victorious campaign through Syria and Asia Minor, he defeated

K

KEMAL, Mustapha (1880–1938), who called himself 'Kemal Atatürk', was the founder of modern Turkey. A soldier who fought in the BALKAN WARS and commanded the Turkish forces in the FIRST WORLD WAR at Gallipoli and in Syria, he emerged at the end of the war as his country's foremost general. Determined to lead Turkey's recovery from defeat, he set up a provisional government in 1920 and drove the Greeks from Smyrna. The sultanate was abolished in 1922 (*see* OTTOMAN EMPIRE), and by the Treaty of Lausanne (1923) Kemal secured better terms than the original Turkish peace settlement. He then established the Turkish Republic with himself as President, an office he held until he died. In order to modernize his country he ruled as a dictator, forcing the people to accept Western customs and ideas; among many reforms, he introduced the Latin alphabet, greater freedom for women, better education and modern industries.

KENNEDY, John F. (1917–63), 35th President of the USA, was the second son of Joseph Kennedy, the ambassador to Britain in 1938–40. Educated at Harvard and the London School of Economics, he served as a naval lieutenant in the Pacific during the Second World War and was decorated for bravery. In 1946 he entered Congress as a Democrat and six years later was elected to the Senate. When he stood for President in 1960, his programme called the New Frontier and his air of idealism gave him a narrow victory over Richard Nixon.

As President he brought an atmosphere of glamour and optimism to politics, but during his brief career he was not in fact markedly successful. He had wide public support, but failed to persuade Congress to accept a number of domestic reforms. In foreign affairs, after the fiasco of the Bay of Pigs invasion of Cuba (1961), he got on well with KRUSHCHEV, the Russian Premier, but was unable to bring the COLD WAR to an end. When the Russians introduced Soviet missiles into Cuba, Kennedy imposed an embargo on Russian shipments, which seemed certain to lead to war. However, Krushchev backed down and agreed to withdraw the missiles. Kennedy's greatest achievements were the Nuclear Test Ban Treaty of 1963 and his readiness to promote good relations between the US and other countries. In VIETNAM he increased American support for the South Vietnam regime.

While on a tour of Texas, President Kennedy was murdered in Dallas on 22 November 1963. An ex-Marine named Lee Oswald was arrested, only to be shot dead by a seedy character, Jack Ruby. It was widely rumoured that there had been a plot to kill Kennedy and that Ruby had shot Oswald to silence him. A commission, set up to discover the truth, reported that there was no plot and that Oswald was the sole assassin.

KERENSKY, Alexander (1881–1970), was a Russian lawyer who became Prime Minister of Russia in 1917 after the February Revolution. After the Tsar NICHOLAS II had abdicated Kerensky, a moderate socialist, tried to carry out two impossible tasks, to create a democratic state and persuade the Russians to go on fighting the Germans. In November 1917 his government was overthrown by the BOLSHEVIKS and Kerensky fled abroad, first to Paris and then to the US, where he died in 1970.

KING, Martin Luther (1929–68), an American clergyman and Negro civil rights leader, was born in Atlanta, Georgia, the son of a Baptist preacher. After education at Morehouse College and Boston University he himself became a Baptist minister and, from about 1955, a leader of social protest against segregation laws. Although he was frequently arrested, imprisoned and ill-treated, he never ceased trying to improve racial relations by peaceful means. He was in prison in 1960 when the presidential candidate, John F. KENNEDY, spoke out on his behalf, and in 1963, when leading a protest march on Washington, he delivered a speech beginning 'I have a dream . . .', a piece of oratory so moving and powerful that he became a figure of more than national importance. For his work and his books, *Stride towards Freedom* and *Strength to Love*, he was awarded the Nobel Peace Prize in 1964, but four years later, when organizing a Poor People's March, he was shot and killed by an assassin at Memphis, Tennessee. His murder was followed by an outbreak of Negro violence throughout the USA, which he would have utterly condemned.

KINGSFORD-SMITH, Sir Charles (1897–1935), who is regarded by some as the greatest of all the pilots who pioneered the world's air routes, was born near Brisbane, Australia. In 1928, with three others, he flew across the Pacific from America to Australia in the *Southern Cross*; in 1929 he and his partner flew from Australia to Britain in 12 days 14 hours, and a year later he crossed from Britain to America and went on to circumnavigate the world. Other flights included Britain to Australia (1930, 7 days) and Australia to America (1933), when he again crossed the Pacific. In 1935, with two other airmen, he set out to break the record from Britain to Australia in *Lady Southern Cross*; they reached Baghdad and passed over Calcutta en route for Singapore but were never seen again.

KNOX, John (died 1572), attended Glasgow University, but little is known of his life until 1544 when he became a disciple of George Wishart, the Lutheran preacher. Wishart was burnt at the stake for heresy in 1546 and Knox took refuge in St Andrews Castle with the murderers of Cardinal Beaton, who had persecuted Wishart. Taken prisoner, Knox was condemned to the French galleys by Mary of Guise, mother of the child MARY QUEEN OF SCOTS. He suffered eighteen months imprisonment before going to England, where he became one of EDWARD VI's chaplains. On Mary Tudor's accession as MARY I he fled to Geneva, where he studied under CALVIN.

He returned to Scotland in 1555 to preach Calvinism with great vigour, but although he made converts he was forced to go abroad again until 1559. In that year he was invited back by the Scottish nobles, and his powerful preaching led to a revolt against the Catholic Queen Regent, so that,

with English help, the French were driven out. By 1560 Calvinism had been adopted as the Scottish religion and Knox was practically ruling the country. This was the situation when Mary Queen of Scots arrived from France, a Catholic who was ready to tolerate her subjects' religion. Knox, however, was not prepared to accept her faith; he lectured the Queen and, after Darnley's murder, repeatedly denounced her and her court.

Mary's abdication and flight to England meant the overthrow of Catholicism in Scotland. Knox's work was done, for he had firmly established the stern religion of Calvin and turned Scotland into a Protestant country. He continued to preach and direct religious affairs until his death. Knox was a fierce unbending reformer, a preacher of magnetic power and an idealist who would have used the confiscated Catholic wealth for the good of the Church and the common people, whereas, in fact, it was seized by the nobles. His celebrated book *First Blast of the Trumpet against the Monstrous Regiment of Women* was an attack on Mary Tudor and Mary of Guise.

KOREAN WAR (1950–3) resulted from the division of Korea (previously held by the Japanese) into Russian-occupied North Korea, with a Communist government, and American-occupied South Korea with a right-wing government. This division had occurred in 1945 when Soviet troops entered Korea after Russia declared war on Japan. In 1949 the occupying forces withdrew, and in the following year a North Korean army suddenly crossed into the South and captured Seoul, the capital. President Truman referred the matter to the UNITED NATIONS' Security Council, which named North Korea as the aggressor and asked member countries to send troops to help South Korea. (Russia was boycotting the Council at the time and so was unable to veto this decision).

General MacArthur, commanding a UN army composed chiefly of American troops with contingents from, eventually, twenty-one countries, including Britain and the Commonwealth, halted the North Koreans, then drove them back with enormous losses. He advanced into North Korea itself, destroyed its defences and had called for a surrender to end the war when the Chinese intervened. Attacking in force, they compelled Mac-Arthur to retreat to the 38th parallel, and caused him to call for an all-out attack on China itself; he also publicly defied President Truman, who courageously dismissed him from his command. Further Chinese offensives were held and then driven back by the UN army, which managed to regain all South Korean territory. A truce was called in July 1951 and, although outbreaks of fighting occurred during the next two years of talks, a ceasefire was agreed in 1953.

As a result of the war Korea remained divided almost exactly as before; the country was devastated, some 3 million Koreans are said to have lost their lives and the Americans suffered 142,000 casualties, including 33,600 killed.

KRUPPS, the great armament firm at Essen, Germany, was built up by Alfred Krupp (1812–87), who developed his father's forge into a vast iron and steel works that by 1914 employed 80,000 workers and exported guns of every type all over the world.

During the FIRST WORLD WAR the firm had practically the monopoly of German arms production. Post-war limitation of German armaments brought a decline in profits, causing the chairman, Gustav Krupp von Bohlen, to become an ardent supporter of HITLER.

During the SECOND WORLD WAR Krupps made use of slave labour from occupied countries and

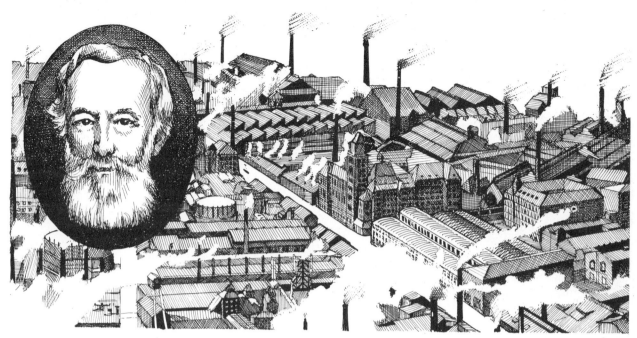

Alfred Krupp and part of his vast steel works at Essen

this resulted in Gustav's son, Alfried Krupp, being sentenced to twelve years imprisonment and loss of his fortune by the Nuremberg court (1948). The firm was to be dispersed. However, Alfried was released in 1951, his wealth was returned to him, along with £25 million compensation. The dispersal order has never been fully carried out.

KRUSHCHEV, Nikita (1894–1971), rose from peasant origins to become a leading official in the Communist Party in Russia. STALIN died in 1953, and within two years Krushchev had outmanoeuvred his rivals to become First Secretary of the Party and the strongest man in the Soviet Union. He startled the world by denouncing his former master Stalin as a military bungler and mass-murderer, and for a time gave the impression of being a genial man of the people, whose aim was to make life more pleasant in his own country and to ease the tensions of the COLD WAR. His action in removing the missile bases from Cuba seemed to point to an era of peaceful coexistence, especially when it was followed by a treaty banning nuclear tests. But in 1970 he was suddenly relieved of his post of Prime Minister and First Secretary. He then retired into obscurity in the country, where he died in the following year.

KU KLUX KLAN, an American secret society, was formed in 1865 to reassert white superiority in the South by terrorizing Negroes. Led by a Grand Wizard and officers with such names as Grand Dragon, Titan, Kludd, it pursued its activities for only about five years, but was revived in 1915. Its enemies then included Jews, Catholics, liberals and recent immigrants, who were terrorized by threats, arson, the burning of fiery crosses, beatings and lynchings. In the 1920s its influence was very widespread, but the Klan declined during the Depression years, only to re-emerge in the 1950s when the civil rights movement began to be active.

L

LAFAYETTE, Marie Joseph Paul (1757–1834), went to America at the age of twenty to help the colonists in the AMERICAN WAR OF INDEPENDENCE against Britain. He distinguished himself in several battles, became a friend of WASHINGTON, went back to France to raise more assistance for the American cause and took a prominent part in the Battle of Yorktown.

From 1782 in France, although an aristocrat, Lafayette campaigned for social reform; he treated the peasants well on his own estates, demanded a national assembly and, on taking his seat as a deputy in the States-General of 1789, became one of the leaders of the FRENCH REVOLUTION. He supported the storming of the Bastille, organized the National Guard and took command of the army, but his position was never easy, since the extreme revolutionaries despised his humane attitude, while the Royalists hated him for his reforming zeal. After commanding the army against Austria (1792), he returned to Paris to defend the monarchy, but was deserted by his troops and declared a traitor, so he fled, was captured by the Austrians and held prisoner for five years.

Released by Napoleon, he returned to France, but, disliking the Emperor, retired to his estates. Under the Bourbons he became a leader of the opposition, made a triumphal visit to America (1824–5) and briefly commanded the National Guard during the JULY REVOLUTION of 1830. To the end of his life he continued to press for reform and to keep in touch with liberals everywhere. Lafayette, though brave, was not a good general nor did he possess great ability as a politician and administrator; but he cared passionately for humanity and liberty, had the gift of winning popularity and tried hard to deserve it. No foreigner has ever won so much warm admiration from Americans.

Durham Cathedral, one of the great Norman cathedrals begun while Lanfranc was Archbishop of Canterbury

LANFRANC (c. 1005–89) was an Italian who became Prior of the monastery at Bec in Normandy. Duke William (later WILLIAM I of England) made him Abbot of Caen and, after the Conquest, brought him to England to be Archbishop of Canterbury (1070). Lanfranc proved to be a most zealous reformer, who corrected the slack ways of the Anglo-Saxon Church and monasteries; he brought able Norman bishops and priests to England, built schools and churches and supported William's refusal to accept undue interference by the Pope in English affairs.

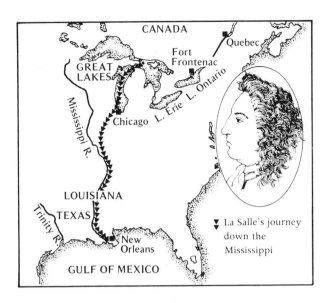

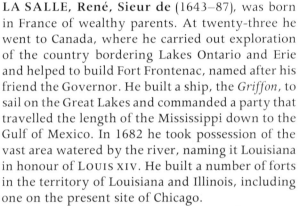

▼ La Salle's journey down the Mississippi

LA SALLE, René, Sieur de (1643–87), was born in France of wealthy parents. At twenty-three he went to Canada, where he carried out exploration of the country bordering Lakes Ontario and Erie and helped to build Fort Frontenac, named after his friend the Governor. He built a ship, the *Griffon*, to sail on the Great Lakes and commanded a party that travelled the length of the Mississippi down to the Gulf of Mexico. In 1682 he took possession of the vast area watered by the river, naming it Louisiana in honour of LOUIS XIV. He built a number of forts in the territory of Louisiana and Illinois, including one on the present site of Chicago.

During a visit to Paris he was appointed governor of Louisiana by the King and he set out in July 1684 with a fleet of four ships and four hundred men to establish the new colony. The expedition was a total failure, for the commander of the fleet refused to obey La Salle's orders and the mouth of the Mississippi was missed, so that a landing had to be made in Texas. The commander returned to France, leaving La Salle with one ship and only forty-five colonists. After some time he set out in hope of reaching the river and travelling on to Illinois, but his own men treacherously killed him near the Trinity River in Texas. His brother and seven survivors eventually reached Quebec.

LAUD, William (1573–1645), a churchman and strong supporter of CHARLES I, became Bishop of London in 1628 and Archbishop of Canterbury in 1633. A small sharp-tongued man of tyrannical disposition, he introduced some much-needed reforms into the Church, insisting on more orderly and dignified services and putting a stop to money-lenders and rogues using St Paul's Cathedral as a place of business. But he was hated for his rigorous persecution of Puritans and others who did not conform to the services of the established Church. When he and Charles I tried to force the Scots to use a new Prayer Book based on the English one, they provoked a war that compelled Charles to recall Parliament. Laud's enemies in the Long Parliament had him impeached in 1641 and imprisoned him in the Tower. Three years later, during the CIVIL WAR, he was condemned to death by attainder (i.e. without trial) and executed on Tower Hill on 10 January 1645.

LAWRENCE, Thomas Edward (1888–1935), who is popularly known as 'Lawrence of Arabia', went to Mesopotamia and Syria as an archaeologist before the First World War; he learned to speak Arabic, and by adopting Arab dress was able to pass as an Arab. On the outbreak of war he went to Cairo to work in military intelligence, and in 1916 was sent into Arabia, where he became the moving spirit in the Arab revolt against the Turks. He established a close understanding with the Arab leaders, especially with Emir Feisal, led daring attacks on the Damascus-Medina railway, struck south to open a route to Akaba and advanced with Feisal to reach Damascus before the British under Allenby (1918).

After the war Lawrence was deeply disappointed

by what he felt was the Allies' betrayal of promises of independence given to the Arabs. His contribution to the defeat of the Turks may have been exaggerated, but he had become a legend and, mainly to evade publicity, he enlisted in the ranks of the RAF (1922) under the name of Ross, then joined the Tank Corps and was transferred back to the RAF. He changed his name to Shaw in 1927, left the RAF in 1935 and shortly afterwards was killed when his motorcycle crashed. He told the story of the Arab revolt in *The Seven Pillars of Wisdom* (1926) and he also translated the *Odyssey*.

LEAGUE OF NATIONS came into being on 10 January 1920; its formation had been regarded as absolutely essential by the American President Woodrow WILSON, but Congress rejected his view and the USA never became a member. Forty-two states had joined by the end of the year and the membership later increased to over sixty states. Japan and Germany resigned in 1933, Italy in 1937. Russia became a member in 1934.

The League Covenant bound member nations to respect each other's independence and to reject war as a way of settling disputes. Sanctions could be used against any state breaking the Covenant and these varied from trade bans to the use of armed force. The League was also concerned with arms reductions, human rights, labour conditions, public health, drugs, slavery and the Court of International Justice. The official headquarters was at Geneva.

On several occasions the League was able to prevent war, as in 1921 when Yugoslavia invaded Albania and in 1925 when Bulgaria attacked Greece. Various disputes were settled and mandates (protective agreements) were arranged for countries such as Palestine, Syria and the former German colonies in Africa.

The League ran into difficulties when powerful nations ignored its decisions or simply withdrew their membership, and its prestige never recovered from its failure to prevent the Italian conquest of ETHIOPIA. When Japan occupied Manchuria, the League imposed no economic sanctions and took no military action to expel Japanese troops from Chinese territory. The fact was that for various reasons – self-interest, weakness, distance – member states were not prepared to do much more than pay lip-service to the principles of the League. Its last meeting was held in 1946, by which time it had already been replaced by the UNITED NATIONS.

LEE, Robert E. (1807–70), was born in Virginia and educated at West Point Military Academy. He distinguished himself in the MEXICAN WAR and when the CIVIL WAR broke out, although opposed to secession, he felt he owed allegiance to his native state and therefore joined the Confederates.

As commander of the Army of Northern Virginia he won a series of victories over the Union armies, including the Seven Days Battle that saved Richmond, Second Bull Run, Fredericksburg (1862) and Chancellorsville (1863). An invasion of Maryland was, however, a failure in 1862 and Lee was hard put to extricate his army after Antietam. When he advanced into Pennsylvania, he met defeat at GETTYSBURG (1863), but again conducted a skilful retreat to Virginia, and through 1864 and 1865 engaged in an epic struggle with General GRANT.

Despite inferior numbers and supplies, he held his own until Grant took Petersburg and Richmond; he then surrendered at Appomattox on 9 April 1865. Lee, who had not been given supreme command of the Confederate armies until February of that year, was a masterly and chivalrous general and his partnership with 'Stonewall' JACKSON, his second-in-command, was one of the most brilliant in the whole history of the war. He later became president of Washington College and was buried in the college grounds.

LEICESTER, Earl of (Robert Dudley, *c.* 1532–88), was the son of John Dudley, Duke of NORTHUM-BERLAND, who was executed for placing Lady Jane GREY on the throne in 1553. Leicester was in the Tower for a time, but on ELIZABETH's accession she made him her favourite and would probably have married him, had he been free. He was, however, married to Amy Robsart, whose mysterious death suggested that he had had her murdered; after this scandal Elizabeth gave up all idea of marrying him and, though he remained her favourite, she was too astute to allow him much influence in public affairs. Leicester probably possessed a great deal of charm, but he was a vain, shallow, aggressive personality, without much real ability. His sump-tuous entertainment of Elizabeth at Kenilworth was in keeping with his character, but when she put him in charge of an expedition to Holland (1585) he proved to be so incapable that she recalled him. When the Spanish invasion threatened he was captain-general of the army at Tilbury, and it may have been he who suggested to Elizabeth that she should make her famous address to the troops. He died shortly after the defeat of the ARMADA. Leicester, whose love affairs infuriated the Queen, secretly married Lady Sheffield in 1573 and bigamously married the Countess of Essex in 1578.

LENIN, Nikolai (1870–1924), whose real name was Vladimir Ilyich Ulyanov, was the leader of the RUSSIAN REVOLUTION and founder of the Com-munist state. He was the son of a schools inspector, and as a student he took part in revolutionary activity, for which his brother was executed. Lenin himself was banished to Siberia for a time, and he became a leading BOLSHEVIK until forced to live abroad in exile. But he kept in close touch with his followers until 1917, when he returned to Russia from Switzerland, being allowed to pass through Germany by the Germans, who rightly believed that he could overturn the government.

With TROTSKY Lenin organized the Russian Revolution of October 1917, made peace with Germany, suppressed all other parties and conduc-ted the Civil War against opponents of the Revolu-tion. By 1921 he was master of Russia, and in order to restore the shattered country he introduced his New Economic Policy, allowing a limited amount of private enterprise before the introduction of com-plete COMMUNISM.

Although he fell ill, Lenin's hold on the Party and on the people's affection was so great that there was never any question of replacing him before his death. Ruthless and utterly dedicated to the success of the Revolution, Lenin nevertheless had a kindlier side to his nature than many of those, like STALIN, who followed him.

LINCOLN, Abraham (1809–65), the 16th President of the US, was born in a log cabin in the backwoods of Kentucky. His father, a farmer, moved about restlessly and for a time the family lived in the forests of Indiana, where young Abraham became an expert woodsman. He had no regular schooling, worked on the river-boats and tried his hand as a storekeeper, postman and mill-manager before a friend encouraged him to study law. This was the turning-point in his career; it roused all his energies and latent ability, so that he rapidly became an attorney and built up a successful legal practice in Illinois. In 1834 he was elected to the Illinois legislative assembly and in 1846 to Congress, but he only served one term, being more interested in law, it seemed, than in politics. In 1842 he married Mary Todd, but the marriage did not prove to be a happy one; of their four sons only one survived childhood.

LEPANTO, Battle of (1571), fought in the Gulf of Corinth between two fleets of oared galleys, resulted in the total defeat of the Turkish navy by an allied fleet commanded by Don John of Austria, half-brother of PHILIP I of Spain. To check the aggressive power of the OTTOMAN EMPIRE, Pope Pius V formed a league that included Spain, Venice, Genoa and Naples; Don John's victory ended the legend of Turkish invincibility at sea. This was the last naval battle in which oared ships played an important part; the allied victory was largely due to the introduction by Venice of a new ship, the *galleass*, a heavy galley with three lateen sails.

LEWIS AND CLARK, whose full names were Captain Meriwether Lewis and Lieutenant William Clark, were two American officers sent by President JEFFERSON to explore the vast country lying west of the river Missouri. They left St Louis in May 1804, moved up the Missouri by canoe, crossed the Rockies and reached the Pacific in November 1805. They returned a year later with valuable scientific collections and observations, having travelled nearly 10,000 miles (16,000 km) through uncharted country. Yet they had lost only two of their company and one of these through desertion. This epic journey was to provide a route to the west for thousands of migrants and it opened up the country for fur-trading in competition with British traders.

Lewis and Clark sight the Rockies

It was the question of extending SLAVERY into the new Western territories that brought Lincoln back into politics. In 1858 he stood as Republican candidate for the Senate in opposition to Stephen Douglas, who had introduced a Bill allowing the new states to introduce slavery. Lincoln lost the election, but he so distinguished himself in a series of public debates with Douglas that he was now a national figure, and in 1860 the Republicans chose him as their Presidential candidate. He was elected by a decisive majority.

The new President was exceptionally tall, nearly 6 ft 4 ins (1m 98), with long ungainly limbs, a dark complexion and coarse black hair. He possessed remarkable strength and patience; he was gentle, humorous and so fair-minded that he was known as 'Honest Abe'. Although he disliked slavery, he made it clear that he had no intention of interfering with it in those states where it was already legal, yet on his election seven Southern states left the Union and formed the Confederacy; others followed and it was this that led to the outbreak of the CIVIL WAR. Lincoln stated bluntly that no state had the right to leave the Union and he was prepared to use force to maintain this view. Thus, when the Confederates captured Fort Sumter in April 1861, Lincoln called for seventy-five thousand volunteers to take up arms to save the Union.

During the first two years of the war the North suffered several defeats and Lincoln was much criticized for his conduct of affairs. But he stuck to his task with great patience and calmness, taking whatever powers he deemed necessary, especially as Commander-in-Chief, leaving Congress to approve his actions afterwards. In 1862, on his own authority, he declared free all the slaves in the rebellious states. When he found in Ulysses GRANT a general who could win victories, he gave him complete support, and as the war turned in favour of the North and he himself was re-elected President he felt strong enough to refuse any solution to the war except a restored union and total abolition of slavery. Yet he never called for vengeance or uttered one vindictive word against the Southerners; he spoke of 'binding up the nation's wounds' and of treating former enemies 'with malice towards none, with charity for all'.

On 9 April 1865 the Southern general Robert E. LEE surrendered to Grant. The war was practically over and on 14 April Abraham Lincoln had taken his seat in Ford's Theatre in Washington when a fanatical Southerner, John Wilkes Booth, entered his box and shot him at point-blank range. Lincoln, the one man great enough to have found solutions for his country's post-war problems, died the next day.

LINDBERGH, Charles (1902–74), won world fame by making the first solo flight across the Atlantic. On 20 May 1927 he flew his single-engined Ryan monoplane *The Spirit of St Louis* from New York to Paris in thirty-three hours. He received rapturous welcomes everywhere, many honours and the rank of colonel in the American army. Later he made a number of survey flights for trans-Atlantic and trans-Pacific air routes. In 1932 his baby son was kidnapped and murdered in horrifying circumstances. Lindbergh tried to keep America out of the Second World War, but after PEARL HARBOR he served with the US Air Force.

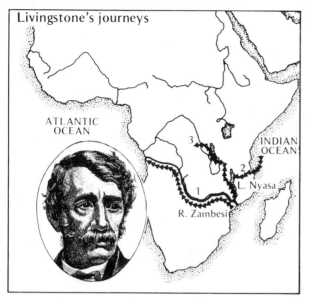

Livingstone's journeys

ATLANTIC OCEAN

INDIAN OCEAN

L. Nyasa

R. Zambesi

LIVINGSTONE, David (1813–73), was born at Blantyre in Scotland; from the age of ten, he worked in a cotton factory, but educated himself so that he was able to study medicine. In 1840 the London Missionary Society sent him out to Bechuanaland in South Africa, where he worked for ten years as a missionary, often accompanied on his journeys by his wife and children. He then made up his mind it was his duty to open up the unexplored interior of Africa, alone except for native porters and guides. In 1852–6 he crossed Africa from the Atlantic to the Indian Ocean, tracing the course of the Zambezi River and discovering the Victoria Falls. In 1858–63 he explored eastern and central Africa, discovering Lake Nyasa and seeing for himself the disastrous effects of the slave trade carried on by the Arabs.

His third great expedition lasted from 1865 to 1873, when he travelled vast distances in search of the sources of the Nile; he suffered from fever and many hardships and, in Europe, was given up for lost until dramatically discovered at Ujiji by H. M. STANLEY. By this time his health was ruined and soon after he had set out on yet another expedition his servants found him dead. They carried him and his journals 1,000 miles (1,600 km) to Zanzibar and his body is buried in Westminster Abbey. Livingstone's travels, made known to the public through his books, aroused enormous interest and con-

vinced Europeans that great opportunities awaited the white man in Africa. Livingstone himself hoped that his journeys and writings would lead to the spread of Christianity and to the stamping out of the slave trade. Though he took a paternal attitude towards the Africans, he loved and respected them and believed that they would soon be able to take their place in the modern world.

LLEWELYN I (1173–1240), known as 'the Great', was Prince of Gwynedd (North Wales). He married Joan, daughter of King JOHN, who, after quarrels, forced him to submit in 1211, but Llewelyn later recovered all his losses, captured Shrewsbury and defied English armies during HENRY III's reign. He united Wales, married his children into powerful Marcher families and, in the latter part of his reign, pursued a peaceful policy. In 1239 he abdicated in favour of his son Dafydd (David) and retired to a Cistercian monastery.

LLEWELYN II (died 1282), grandson of LLEWELYN the Great, was himself known as 'the Last'. He inherited the kingdom of Gwynedd that had shrunk to Snowdon and Anglesey, but during the Barons' War in HENRY III's reign he recovered lost territories and made himself lord of north and south Wales. He supplied Simon de MONTFORT with Welsh troops. When EDWARD I came to the throne, the situation changed; he demanded that Llewelyn pay homage to him, and, when he refused, launched a major attack on Wales with three armies. Llewelyn, trapped in the mountains of Snowdon, was forced to surrender in 1277 and make a humiliating peace. In 1282 he led a revolt against the English, but was killed in a skirmish near Builth in central Wales. His death marked the end of Welsh independence.

LLOYD GEORGE, David (1863–1945), British Prime Minister, who was popularly known as 'the Welsh Wizard' and 'the Man who won the War', was brought up in poor circumstances in North Wales. His uncle, a shoemaker and lay preacher, encouraged him to study, so that he qualified as a solicitor and in 1890 entered Parliament as Liberal MP for Caernarvon.

As an opponent of the BOER WAR, he was highly unpopular for a time, but was brought into the Cabinet in 1905 as President of the Board of Trade, becoming Chancellor of the Exchequer in 1908. His

'People's Budget' of 1909, which introduced super-tax and taxation of land values, aroused furious opposition and provoked a crisis when the Lords rejected the Budget. This led to the Parliament Act of 1911, which restricted the power of the Lords. As Chancellor Lloyd George introduced some important reforms, including OLD AGE PENSIONS (1908) and, with Winston CHURCHILL, the National Insurance Act of 1911, which brought in sickness and unemployment benefits.

In August 1914 he was opposed to war, but the German attack on Belgium (*see* FIRST WORLD WAR) caused him to change his mind and as Minister of Munitions (1915–16) he transformed production of armaments. In December 1916 he contrived to overthrow Asquith, the Prime Minister, on the grounds that he was not conducting the war with efficiency and vigour. Lloyd George then became Prime Minister and remained in office until 1922. He showed great energy as a war leader, instituted a war cabinet, insisted on convoys at sea and secured a single military command under the French general Foch. He did not get on with HAIG, who, he considered, squandered troops needlessly.

After the war he took a prominent part in the Paris Peace Conference and in the resettlement of Europe by the Treaty of VERSAILLES. But at home his position weakened; the Coalition Government was dominated by Conservatives, and most of the Liberals distrusted him for his treatment of Asquith, so that he was a leader without a party. In 1922 he fell from power over the Chanak crisis, when he appeared to mishandle a tense situation in a quarrel between Greece and Turkey. The Conservatives withdrew from the Coalition, forcing Lloyd George to resign. He never held office again.

His reputation had been damaged by a scandal over the sale of titles in the Honours List and by his acquisition of the Lloyd George Party Fund; he was undoubtedly the cleverest politician in the House, a man of the utmost brilliance, but to many people he appeared to be tricky and unreliable. In 1929 he put forward a plan to solve the country's economic problems, but it was disregarded, and in 1940 he refused to join Churchill's government, partly on account of his age and partly because he wanted a negotiated peace with HITLER.

LOLLARDS, in the 14th and 15th centuries in England, were followers of the teachings of John WYCLIFFE. It was his disciples, the 'poor preachers', rather than Wycliffe himself, who were responsible for the rapid spread of Lollardy. In the eyes of the Church Lollards were heretics, for they did not believe in transubstantiation (the miraculous changing of bread and wine into the body and blood of Christ) nor in altars, images, pilgrimages or saints. They thought that wars and the riches of the Church were wrong. Hence, as heretics, they were persecuted and some were burnt at the stake. At the beginning of the movement Lollards included many of the gentry, but for the most part they were humble folk, artisans, poor clerics and labourers. After the execution of Sir John Oldcastle (1417) in Henry v's reign, the Lollards lost support and ceased to have much importance.

LONG MARCH (1934–5) was an epic journey by Chinese Communists during their conflict with the Kuomintang or Nationalist Party led by CHIANG KAI-SHEK. In 1931 the Communists under MAO TSE-TUNG had established a Chinese Soviet Republic in Kiangsi Province in the south, but after three years of warfare Chiang Kai-shek succeeded in sealing off the province. To avoid annihilation, the Communists decided to break out and in October 1934 began the 8,000-mile (13,000 km) march to Shensi Province in the north-west. Thousands perished on the march across difficult mountain country, some of which was uninhabited desert. Chiang's armies followed but never managed to catch up with the main force of Communists, who were able to organize a strong defensive position in Shensi.

LOUIS IX (1214–70), King of France, who was known as Saint Louis from his piety. He ruled as an absolute monarch but greatly improved justice in

poor general, he was defeated in Egypt, taken prisoner and held to ransom. He returned to France in 1254, imposed order on his warring nobles and made just peace settlements with England and Aragon. In 1270 he embarked on a second crusade, which was diverted to Tunis, where he died of plague. He was the greatest of the medieval kings of France.

LOUIS XIV (1638–1715) became king of France at the age of five and took effective control of his kingdom from 1661. Thus for over half a century he was absolute ruler of France and the dominant personality in Europe. His aim was to extend the 'natural' frontiers of France to the Rhine, chiefly by conquering the NETHERLANDS, a policy which was resisted for years by England, Holland, Sweden and Austria. Though his generals won many victories, Louis never succeeded in realizing his life's ambition, and in the War of the SPANISH SUCCESSION (when his aim was to put his grandson on the throne of Spain) his armies suffered heavy defeats at the hands of MARLBOROUGH. By the end of his reign France was practically bankrupt.

The 'Sun King', as Louis was called, lived in

the country, built hospitals and encouraged education. In 1242 he defeated an invasion army of HENRY III of England, and having taken the Cross set out on his first CRUSADE in 1248. Brave, but a

Louis XIV and the palace of Versailles

exotic splendour in the magnificent palace which he built at Versailles. Here the French aristocracy had to attend the monarch and take part in an endless succession of ceremonies and banquets; here too writers, artists and musicians created a golden age of French literature and art. Shrewd, dignified and industrious, Louis was a despot who had no understanding or sympathy for the common people. His extravagance and their sufferings were to lead eventually to the FRENCH REVOLUTION.

LOUISIANA PURCHASE (1803), the biggest land sale in history, doubled the size of the USA when France sold a vast area of about 830,000 square miles (2,125,000 km^2) stretching from the Mississippi westwards to the Rocky Mountains and northwards to Canada. Louisiana had been ceded by France to Spain in 1762, but in 1800 Napoleon forced the Spanish government to give it back. He had some idea of developing an American Empire until President JEFFERSON stated bluntly that if the French took possession of New Orleans the US would at once ally itself to Britain. Napoleon, knowing that another war with Britain was about to break out, decided therefore to fill his war chest by selling Louisiana for $15 million. The deal was

negotiated in Paris by Talleyrand, the French minister and Livingston, the American minister, assisted by James Monroe.

LUDDITES were workers who banded together to destroy steam-powered looms, lace machines and stocking-frames in the period 1811–18. Prices were high, wages low and unemployment was on the

Luddites attacking a factory

165

increase, so the workers tended to blame their troubles on the new machines. The Luddites first made their appearance in the hosiery areas of Nottinghamshire and spread to the textile districts of Yorkshire and Lancashire. The damage done in Luddite riots was considerable until the government brought in the death penalty. The Luddites were supposed to be named after Ned Lud, an apprentice who had smashed a stocking-frame in a rage.

LUDENDORFF, Erich (1865–1937), German general who was a close partner of HINDENBURG in the FIRST WORLD WAR. They shared the credit for victories over the Russians in 1914 and from 1916 virtually directed the war. Ludendorff is said to have been responsible for unrestricted U-boat warfare, for returning LENIN to Russia and for the harsh terms of the Brest-Litovsk treaty. When the Allies began their advance in July 1918 his nerve broke; he advised peace negotiations and in October fled to Sweden in disguise. After the war he attached himself to extreme nationalist groups, became one of the first NAZIS and took part with HITLER in the Munich Putsch of 1923. Later he broke with Hitler and founded his own anti-Semitic group, but it had little influence.

LUTHER, Martin (1483–1546), the German Protestant reformer (*see* REFORMATION), was born in Saxony of peasant parents. A clever boy, he attended university, took his degree and then entered an Augustinian monastery. He was ordained priest in 1507 and later became a professor at Wittenberg University. In 1510 he visited Rome and was dismayed by the wealth and corruption there.

When the Dominican monk Tetzel came to Germany to sell indulgences for the remission of sin, Luther nailed to the church door at Wittenberg Castle a paper in Latin attacking the sale of indulgences (1517). A translation spread rapidly through Germany, and Luther refused to recant or to obey a papal summons to Rome. In 1520 he wrote three pamphlets questioning the teaching of the Church and urging German princes to cast off the Pope's supremacy. For this he was excommunicated, but he publicly burned the Bull of Condemnation before a large crowd of supporters. He continued to preach with tremendous fire and to win converts to his belief that the Gospel was the

only true source of religious teaching and that salvation came to men through the love of God. In 1521 the Emperor CHARLES V, at the Diet of Worms, called on Luther to recant, but he refused and, although outlawed was protected by Frederick of Saxony, in whose castle at Wartburg he carried out his great work, his translation of the New Testament into German.

His rebellion against the Church aroused widespread support, though some of his followers carried the reform movement further than he wished. Indeed, when the German peasants used his teachings as a reason for revolting against their serfdom in the PEASANTS' WAR (1524–5), Luther supported the princes when they put down the revolt without mercy. In 1525 he married Catherine von Bora, a nun who had left her convent under the influence of his teaching. They lived happily together for the rest of his life, but in the meantime the religious war continued between the German states accepting Luther's reforms and others remaining Catholic. The conflict was ended, at least for a time, by the Peace of Augsburg, nine years after Luther's death.

M

MACADAM, John (*or* McAdam, 1756–1836), a Scottish engineer, invented a cheap and effective method of surfacing roads. He used a layer, 10 to 12 inches (25 to 30 cm) thick, of stones, preferably granite, each about one inch (2·5 cm) long and wide. This layer was put on the subsoil of the road and was finished off with a topping of fine stone chips, which the iron-rimmed coach wheels ground into powder. Washed down by rain, the powder bound the stones together and helped to produce a springy road surface. In 1815 Macadam was appointed surveyor-general of roads at Bristol, where he successfully put his theories into practice. His method was widely adopted and in 1827 he became general surveyor of metropolitan roads. Parliament made him a grant of £10,000.

MACEDON, a kingdom in northern Greece, is chiefly remembered because it produced ALEXANDER THE GREAT. His father, Philip II, built up an invincible army, whose power lay in the *Macedonian phalanx*, a dense formation of soldiers armed with exceptionally long pikes. By his victory at Chaeronea (338 BC) Philip won control of Greece and was succeeded in 336 by Alexander, who conquered the PERSIAN EMPIRE and spread Greek civilization through the near East.

After his death the Macedonian Empire split into three parts, EGYPT, Syria and Greece, where Antigonus, in Macedonia, ruled the country. After a period of anarchy Philip V restored order, and in 215 was strong enough to send help to HANNIBAL in his war with ROME. This action and Philip's alliance with Syria made the Romans determined to crush Macedon, and in 197 BC their army routed the Macedonian phalanx and Macedon became a vassal state under Rome.

MACQUARIE, Lachlan (1761–1824), was a Scottish soldier who had risen to the rank of colonel when he was sent to Australia to succeed Captain Bligh as Governor of New South Wales (1809). Energetic, honest and warm-hearted, he set to work

to bring order and progress to a community that was corrupt and not far from collapse. He treated the convicts with humanity, employed many of them to build roads and lay out the city of Sydney and several towns. Himself an ardent traveller, he encouraged exploration and enlarged the colony. His policy of treating deserving ex-convicts as the equals of free settlers and officers aroused hostility and led to endless complaints about the way in which he was managing public affairs. Worn out by the strain of his thankless task, Macquarie resigned in 1821 and returned to Britain, where he soon died. During his governorship he had changed the demoralized penal settlement into a flourishing colony and he is rightly known as the 'Father of Australia'.

MAGELLAN, Ferdinand (*c.* 1480–1521), entered the service of King Emanuel of Portugal and distinguished himself on expeditions to the East Indies and Morocco. In 1514, having fallen into disfavour for some reason, he went to offer his services to the court of Spain. After he had put forward a plan to reach the Spice Islands of the East Indies by sailing west, CHARLES V provided him with a fleet of five small ships and a crew of about 275 officers, volunteers and seamen. Magellan sailed from Seville on 10 August 1519 and wintered off the coast of Patagonia, where he had to suppress a mutiny. In 1520 he guided the fleet through the dangerous 360-mile (575 km) long strait that bears his name and entered the ocean which he named the Pacific. With a starving crew, he sailed on for ninety-eight days reaching Guam, thus discovering the Philip-

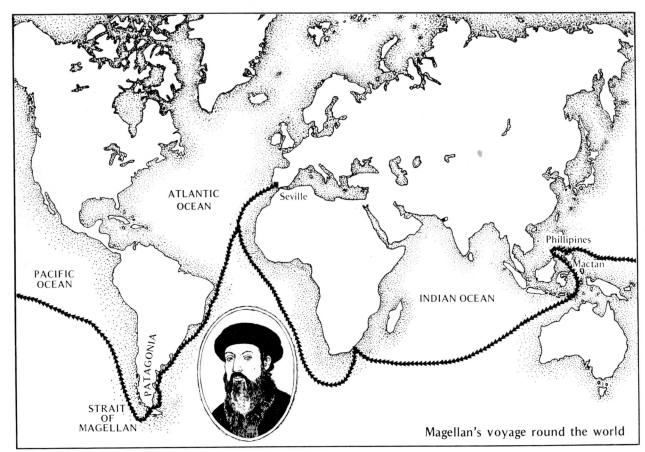

ATLANTIC OCEAN

Seville

PACIFIC OCEAN

Phillipines

Mactan

INDIAN OCEAN

PATAGONIA

STRAIT OF MAGELLAN

Magellan's voyage round the world

pine Islands, and was killed on the island of Mactan when he intervened in a quarrel between local princes. One ship only, the *Vittoria*, reached Spain on 6 September 1522, with thirty-one survivors on board, the first vessel that ever sailed round the world.

MAGNA CARTA (1215) was the document granted by King JOHN at Runnymede to the English barons. HENRY II had earlier set up a powerful system of government and the barons, while not wishing to overthrow it, wanted to prevent it being used in the tyrannical fashion which John had adopted. By 1214 the King had suffered defeat in France, he had no allies except Pope INNOCENT III, and no money with which to hire mercenaries. The time was therefore ripe for the baronial uprising, which, in the following year, forced John to agree to redress their grievances.

The Charter is divided into sixty-one clauses, providing for the liberty of the Church, the city of London and various ports and towns, for protection against abuses of the royal power, for strict administration of justice, for one standard of weights and measures, for the protection of life, liberty and property and the upholding of various feudal rights and customs. One group of clauses demanded that taxes required the consent of a baronial council, and this resulted eventually in the principle of parliamentary consent to taxation. The 39th clause said that freemen should be judged by their equals according to the law of the land, and, although the barons were concerned only with their own class and not with the common people, this clause came to be regarded as vital to the rights of all Englishmen.

In fact, the importance of Magna Carta lay far more in what people thought it meant than in what it actually said. It came to stand for the rights of all men; it bound the king to rule according to law and became of fundamental importance to the development of law and government in countries, including the United States, which base their system on the English one.

The great Manchu emperor Ch'ien-lung (reigned 1736–96)

Maori chiefs signing the peace treaty of Waitangi
(1840) with the white settlers

MANCHUS or Manchu Tatars were tribesmen who invaded China from the north in the 17th century and overthrew the MING Dynasty. By 1644 they had captured Peking and established the Ch'ing dynasty, which lasted until 1911.

MAORI WARS occurred in New Zealand, largely between 1860 and 1872. Their cause was the white settlers' demand for land, which the Maoris increasingly refused to sell. The position was complicated by the fact that Maori land belonged to the tribe as a whole and not merely to those who happened to occupy it.

The Maoris' obstruction of land surveyors led to the Taranaki War of 1860–61, an indecisive struggle that was followed by a truce. Sir George GREY came from Cape Town to take over as Governor, but even his prestige did not prevent a renewal of fighting in 1863. The Waikato War, in which the followers of King Tawhiao took part and the imperial troops were commanded by General Cameron, ended after the battle of Orakau, where the Maoris put up a heroic though hopeless resistance. There followed a period of guerrilla warfare waged by Maori religious fanatics called the *Hau hau* (1864–8) and a last campaign led by Te Kooti (1868–70).

Hostilities petered out by 1872, when the fierce old chief Wiremu Kingti submitted, but Tawhiao, who withdrew inland to what was known as King Country, did not submit until 1881.

In these wars, in which casualties were not heavy (Maori deaths are thought to have been about 2,000), the Maoris showed much courage and skill in bush skirmishes and in defending strongpoints, but in the long run they could not sustain a war against better-armed regular troops, who were supported by colonial forces, notably the Forest Rangers. As a result of the wars three million acres of Maori land were confiscated, and between 1865 and 1892 the Maoris sold a further seven million acres. Thus, as far as the settlers were concerned, colonization was able to proceed unhampered by native resistance.

MAO TSE-TUNG (born 1893) came from farming people in Hunan province and was involved in revolutionary activities from an early age. In 1918 he became a librarian in Peking, and, a convinced Marxist (*see* COMMUNISM), he joined the Chinese Communist Party when it was founded in 1921. Back in Hunan as a Party organizer, he became certain that the peasants, not the urban workers, would play a crucial role in the coming revolution. This view was not welcomed by the Party leaders, but Mao was able to pursue an independent line and with a small band of followers to organize a

peasant uprising in Hunan. Defeated, he withdrew to the mountains, founded the Kiangsi Soviet and, with Chu Teh, held out against attacks by CHIANG KAI-SHEK'S nationalist forces (the Kuomintang) until 1934. Mao then undertook the epic LONG MARCH, leading the remnants of his supporters from Kiangsi to Shensi in the north-west. During the next ten years he built the party into a peasant-based disciplined organization, which came to terms with Chiang Kai-shek in order to fight the Japanese.

During the Civil War (1946–9) Communist forces overcame the Kuomintang and after Chiang Kai-shek's final defeat Mao was elected chairman of the People's Republic. Subsequently he tended to keep in the background, leaving government to his subordinates, while remaining China's venerated leader, the father of the Communist revolution.

MARATHON, Battle of (490 BC), occurred when the Persian army of DARIUS I landed at Marathon about 26 miles (42 km) north-east from ATHENS. They were opposed by an Athenian army aided by a thousand men from the city of Plataea, but the Spartans declined to send help. When the Persians delayed their attack, the Athenians, although out-numbered, charged with such fury that they broke the enemy's ranks and forced the survivors back to their ships. After the battle Pheidippides, who had fought all day, is said to have run all the way to Athens to tell the people that their city had been saved. He delivered the message and fell dead from exhaustion.

MARCO POLO (c. 1254–1324), a Venetian, made the immense journey mostly overland from Italy to China in company with his uncles, who had earlier visited Peking (see YÜAN Dynasty). The Emperor Kublai Khan offered Marco, then aged twenty-one,

The marble bridge over the Yellow River which impressed Marco Polo on his first journey for Kublai Khan

a post in his service and the young man stayed for seventeen years in China, working for the Khan, travelling the country and filling several important posts. He became Governor of the city of Yangchow, Imperial Commissioner on a tour to Yunnan and Burma and Envoy to Ceylon. Eventually, the Khan allowed the three Polos to return home; they went by sea via Singapore, Ceylon and the Persian Gulf, for they had to escort a Mongol princess to the court of the ruler of Persia.

They reached Venice after twenty-three years' absence, bringing wealth with them in the form of precious stones. A year later Marco Polo was cap-tured in a sea-fight against the Genoese; to while away the time in prison, he wrote a description of the almost totally unknown Empire of China. His account was derided and it was many years before Europeans discovered the truth of his description of a great civilization.

MARCONI, Guglielmo (1874–1937), was born at Bologna, Italy, the son of a wealthy Italian father and an Irish mother. He received a good education and from boyhood showed a keen interest in electrical research. Using primitive instruments he succeeded in transmitting wireless signals a dis-tance of two miles (3 km) by 1896, the year in which he went to England to further his experi-ments and to receive help and advice from the engineer-in-chief of the Post Office. He set up a company in London, had two wireless stations built, so that by 1898 wireless messages were sent across the English Channel and between warships.

Marconi at work with his wireless apparatus

Marconi's greatest triumph came in 1901, when he established radio communication between Poldhu, Cornwall, and St John's, Newfoundland. He was awarded the Nobel Prize for Physics in 1909, served Italy in the First World War, and in 1919 his company set up the world's first broadcasting station at Chelmsford in Essex. He received various honours in his own country and during his later years took part in some of the activities of the Italian Fascist Party.

MARGARET (died 1093), Queen of Scotland and Saint, was the sister of Edgar Atheling (chosen by the Saxons as king after HAROLD's death), with whom, after the Norman Conquest, she fled to Scotland. There she married Malcolm III and three of their sons became kings of Scotland. Her daughter married HENRY I of England. Margaret introduced new customs and manners into the Scottish court, encouraged the founding of monasteries and schools and cared for pilgrims and the poor. She was made a saint in 1251.

MARIA THERESA (1717–80), Empress, was the daughter of the Emperor Charles VI. By the Pragmatic Sanction, which the principal European powers promised to observe, her father appointed her as his heir to the Austrian lands. In 1736 she married Francis of Lorraine, and on her father's death in 1740 she became Queen of Hungary and Bohemia and Archduchess of Austria. Most of the continental powers at once put in claims to her dominions and FREDERICK THE GREAT of Prussia

seized Silesia. This provoked the War of the AUSTRIAN SUCCESSION (1740–8) in which Maria Theresa defied her attackers, but was unable to recover Silesia and some lands in Italy. However, her rights were admitted and her husband was elected Emperor.

During the ensuing period of peace, she introduced financial reforms and encouraged agriculture and commerce so successfully that Austria, impoverished at her accession, became a prosperous country. Throughout her reign she was ably assisted by her minister Kaunitz. She had not forgiven Frederick for the theft of Silesia and she won over France to join Austria in attacking Prussia in the SEVEN YEARS WAR (1756–63), but failed to regain the province.

Later she joined Prussia and Russia in the first partition of Poland (1772) in order to share the booty, but, if this seems unprincipled, it must be said that she was by now governing with her son Joseph, and the decision was probably his. Maria Theresa was a majestic and dominating personality, a woman of undaunted courage and energy, who won the affectionate loyalty of her subjects.

171

Marie Antoinette on her way to the guillotine

him and for a time he was in prison and for years stripped of all offices; however, William recognized his ability and before his death chose him to take over leadership of the Grand Alliance (Britain, the Netherlands and Austria) against France.

When Anne became queen in 1702, the Marlboroughs' fortunes rose high, for Sarah completely dominated her amiable mistress and Marlborough, as Captain-General, was given great power at home and abroad. During the next ten years his masterly diplomacy held the Grand Alliance together, while his gifts as a general in the War of the SPANISH SUCCESSION brought him some of the greatest victories in history. His task was difficult because of jealousies among allies and because the Dutch, concerned for their country's safety and understandably nervous of LOUIS XIV's military power, hampered his strategy and prevented him more than once from engaging the enemy in what could have been decisive battles.

MARIE ANTOINETTE (1755–93), Queen of France, was the daughter of the Emperor Francis I and MARIA THERESA. At the age of fifteen she married the Dauphin, afterwards Louis XVI, who was devoted to her, but her irresponsible behaviour and extravagances made her extremely unpopular. She was derided as 'the Austrian'. After the outbreak of the FRENCH REVOLUTION, she continued to hope for foreign aid and to scheme for the restoration of the monarchy. In 1791 she, her husband and children attempted to flee, but were arrested at Varennes and returned to Paris. Thenceforward, she suffered imprisonment, separation from her family and vile accusations, but at her trial her dignity and courage impressed even those who were determined upon her death. She was guillotined on 16 October 1793.

MARLBOROUGH, Duke of (John Churchill, 1650–1722), the son of an impoverished Cavalier, entered the service of James, Duke of York after the Restoration, served in the army and at CHARLES II's court, and at twenty-eight married the beautiful and imperious Sarah Jennings, lady-in-waiting to Princess Anne, later Queen ANNE.

JAMES II raised Marlborough to the peerage and made him a general, but at the GLORIOUS REVOLUTION of 1688 Marlborough put the Protestant religion before the King and went over to the side of William of Orange. WILLIAM III never trusted

In 1704, to prevent the French taking Vienna, Marlborough marched the Anglo-Dutch army from the Low Countries to the Danube, joined forces with Prince Eugene of Savoy and won the tremendous victory of BLENHEIM. Little happened in 1705, but in the following year he won the battle of Ramillies and conquered practically all the Spanish Netherlands. With Eugene he won the battles of Oudenarde (1708) and Malplaquet (1709), but they were not able to invade France itself. By this time England had become tired of the war and the tactless domineering Sarah had lost her influence over Queen Anne, who dismissed her in 1710. Marlborough's fall soon followed. Accused of prolonging the war for his own benefit and of enriching himself from public funds, he was dismissed from his command. GEORGE I reinstated him as Captain-General in 1714, but his health gave way and he was stricken with paralysis for several years before his death.

Opinions vary about Marlborough. Some writers have pointed to his desertion of James II and to his love of money and advancement. However, it is now generally agreed that he was not guilty of dishonesty. He was handsome, extraordinarily charming, possessed of immense patience and, for his time, unusually concerned for his soldiers, who loved him and called him 'Corporal John'. Of his military talents there can be no doubts; he ranks with the greatest commanders of all time, and it was said of him that he never fought a battle that he did not win and never besieged a fortress that he did not take.

MARX, Karl (1818–83), the founder of modern international COMMUNISM, was a German Jew, who studied law at Bonn and Berlin universities and then edited a paper, which was closed down for its attacks on the government. He married and went to Paris and then to Brussels, where, with his lifelong friend and disciple Frederick Engels, he issued the *Communist Manifesto* (1848), a masterpiece of propaganda, ending with the celebrated watchwords 'Workers of the world unite! You have nothing to lose but your chains!' For its attack on the state, religion and culture, he was expelled from Brussels and in 1849 settled permanently in London.

There, living in poverty but helped by Engels, he studied history and economics in the Reading Room

of the British Museum and in 1864 founded the International Working Men's Association, later known as the First Communist International. In 1867 he published the first volume of *Das Kapital*, the book that was to become the Communist 'Bible'; the second and third volumes were edited by Engels after his death. Ignoring poverty and ill health, Marx continued to hope for the revolution, which eventually came, not in industrialized England, but in Russia. He died in London and was buried in Highgate cemetery.

MARY I (1516–58), Queen of England, was the daughter of HENRY VIII and Catherine of Aragon. After Henry's divorce she was separated from her mother, deprived of rank and declared illegitimate, but she clung to the Catholic faith and during the reign of her brother EDWARD VI steadfastly refused to recognize the new religion. On his death, she faced NORTHUMBERLAND's conspiracy with Tudor determination, gathered an army in East Anglia, rode to London and was acclaimed queen by popular consent. She began cautiously, releasing imprisoned Catholics but refraining from persecution of Protestants; however, her proposed marriage to PHILIP II of Spain was highly unpopular and led to Wyatt's Rebellion, which was rigorously put down.

In 1554 Mary married Philip, and with the arrival of Cardinal Pole into England she devoted herself to her mission of restoring the Catholic religion. The old ceremonies and Latin services were brought back, papal supremacy was restored and the statute for burning heretics was revived. During the next few years some three hundred people were burned, but the martyrdoms only served to strengthen the Protestant faith. Meanwhile, Philip had left England and Mary, bitterly disappointed in her hopes of a child, became seriously ill. She died in 1558, saddened by the loss of Calais in a Spanish war in which England had no interest. She was an intelligent, courageous and obstinate woman, neither vengeful nor cruel, who believed she was acting rightly for the true religion. She failed to understand the English people and the strength of Protestantism.

MARY II (1662–94), Queen of England, was the elder daughter of JAMES II by his first wife, Anne Hyde. Brought up a Protestant, she married her cousin William of Orange in 1677, and eleven years later ascended the English throne as joint sovereign with her husband after the GLORIOUS REVOLUTION (1688) had overthrown her Catholic father. Although WILLIAM III was the dominant partner, he trusted her with the government of the country during his absences in Holland and was grief-stricken by her early death from smallpox.

MARY QUEEN OF SCOTS (1542–87), the daughter of JAMES V of Scotland and Mary of Guise, was born while her father lay dying after the disaster of Solway Moss. A queen when a week old, she was sent to France as a child to be educated and in 1558 she was married to the Dauphin, who succeeded his father as Francis II in the following

year. When Francis died in 1560, his mother, CATHERINE DE MEDICI, made it clear that Mary was no longer welcome at the French court, so she returned to her native Scotland, where John KNOX was playing a dominant role. The REFORMATION was in full swing, but Mary made no attempt to interfere with the new religion, merely insisting that she should be free to worship as a Catholic. At this stage she had the people's support.

Renowned for her beauty, she was charming, intelligent and talented, but she was less fortunate than her cousin ELIZABETH, for she never had a wise counsellor to whom she could turn for advice. After considering several princes as a husband, she finally chose her cousin Lord Darnley, the nearest heir after her to the thrones of Scotland and England. Darnley proved to be an arrogant weakling and Mary, who soon came to despise him, gave her confidence to her Italian secretary Rizzio. On 9 March 1566 Darnley and his friends murdered Rizzio in Mary's presence, but she pretended to forgive him and their son James (later JAMES I and VI) was born in June of that year. A few months later Darnley fell ill and was lodged in a house near Edinburgh which, on 10 February 1567, was blown up and Darnley was found dead in the garden. Suspicion fell on the Earl of Bothwell, a new favourite of the queen, but he was acquitted by a court that was overawed by his armed followers. After this he carried off Mary to Dunbar and married her. The Scottish people, horrified to learn that their Queen had married her husband's murderer, demanded her removal; the nobles would not support her and her army melted away, so, on 24 July, she abdicated in favour of her infant son.

In the following year she escaped from her island-prison and raised a small army, but defeated by the Regent Moray at Langside she fled to England to seek the protection of Queen Elizabeth. She found herself, in fact, a prisoner for the rest of her life, since Elizabeth and her advisers regarded it as too dangerous to allow her to be at liberty, the focus for Catholic hopes. Plot followed plot and it was finally alleged that Mary had agreed to the assassination of Elizabeth (*see* BABINGTON PLOT). True or not, she was tried and sentenced to death, though it was some time before Elizabeth could be persuaded to sign the warrant of execution. Eventually she did so and on 8 February 1587 Mary was beheaded at Fotheringay Castle. Worn out by the strain of nineteen years' imprisonment, she met her end with matchless courage and dignity.

MASON-DIXON LINE is the boundary line separating the states of Maryland and Pennsylvania, which was surveyed between 1763 and 1767 by the English astronomers Charles Mason and Jeremiah Dixon. The line came to mark the boundary between the slave and the free states before the American CIVIL WAR and between the North and the South. The area south of the line was often called 'Dixieland'.

MATILDA (1102–67), Empress, only daughter of HENRY I of England, married the German Emperor Henry V. The English nobles promised that they would accept her as queen, but on Henry's death they preferred her cousin STEPHEN, chiefly because they hated her second husband, Geoffrey of Anjou. Matilda came to England in 1139 to recover the throne, made good progress and was about to be crowned queen when the Londoners, angered by her arrogance, drove her from the capital. Civil war dragged on for years, but the death of her chief supporter, Robert Earl of Gloucester, was fatal to Matilda's cause. She left the country in 1147, but her son, HENRY II, established himself as Stephen's successor. The brave, haughty empress retired to Normandy, ending her days as a pious friend of the poor.

A player of the Mayan ritual ball game honours the sun

MAYAS were American Indians who inhabited the Yucatan peninsula, consisting of most of modern Guatemala and Belize (former British Honduras). There, in tropical rain-forests, this mysterious people raised great stone cities, ruled by priests and nobles, supported by maize-growing peasants. The first great era of Mayan culture lasted from about AD 300 to 900; during this period, cities such as Tikal, Copan, Palenque and Uaxactun were built with massive temples and many-roomed palaces, ornamented with rich carvings. In Tikal two vast pyramid temples were surrounded by some three hundred and fifty lesser temples and mansions covering an area of six and a half square miles (16 km²). Great upright stones were carved with symbols relating to astronomy and time, for the Mayas had worked out a calendar and, alone among Amerindian peoples, possessed a form of writing. They were also good mathematicians, with a system of counting in twenties. They made pottery, stone axes and many ornaments of gold, greenstone, jade and copper.

In about 900 this lowland civilization collapsed, possibly because of a revolt by the peasants against the priests; building ceased and the jungle swept over the cities. On the higher sunny uplands of Yucatan there developed a second flowering of Mayan culture from the 9th century. The temples and buildings were less lofty, though cities like Labna and Uxmal contained majestic palaces and broad plazas. From about 975 Toltecs from Mexico entered the area and came to rule it, bringing Toltec gods, human sacrifice and war. The dominating city up to 1200 was Chichen Itza and afterwards, to about 1400, Mayapan. By the 15th century decline had set in, but the Mayas put up a fierce resistance to the Spaniards. For many years practically nothing was known of the Mayas, until interest was aroused in the 19th century by the discoveries of John L. Stephens, an American diplomat and traveller.

MAYFLOWER, the ship which carried the PIL-GRIM FATHERS to America, was, in 1620, an old vessel of 180 tons and about 90 feet (27m) long. After the *Speedwell* sprang a leak, the pilgrims had to return to port and at Plymouth, they all crowded aboard the *Mayflower* – seventy-three male and twenty-nine female colonists, including some children. During the voyage, which lasted sixty-five days, the ship was severely buffeted in a storm, so that a main beam cracked and had to be secured by a great screw which happened to be on board. The *Mayflower* reached Cape Cod, near Boston,

Massachusetts, early in November 1620; the colonists all went ashore at Plymouth on 11 December and the ship later returned to England. In 1957 the *Mayflower II*, a replica of the original ship, sailed from Plymouth, England, to celebrate the 350th anniversary of the founding of the first permanent English settlement at Jamestown, Virginia. She reached Cape Cod in fifty-four days.

MAZZINI, Giuseppe (1805–72), was born in Genoa, when it had been absorbed by Sardinia. In about 1830 he joined the Carbonari, a revolutionary secret society, was arrested and exiled. He then founded his own society, 'Young Italy', which aimed at a united Italian republic. For trying to stir

up revolution he was exiled for twelve years to London, where he became known as the most tireless political agitator in Europe. He returned to Italy in 1848 and became leader of the triumvirate which took control of the Roman Republic and held the city for nine months until a French army restored the Pope (*see* REVOLUTIONS OF 1848). Mazzini went back into embittered exile to plan risings in several Italian cities but he had no success. He supported GARIBALDI, but hated CAVOUR and considered it disgraceful when Italy became united under a king; he would have no dealings with the new kingdom and died in Pisa, where he was living under an assumed name. A political dreamer and sincere idealist, Mazzini aroused Italian nationalism and, in his own fashion, paved the way for a united Italy.

MEDICI FAMILY were for many years the leading citizens and rulers of FLORENCE. Their great wealth, which came principally from banking, was founded by Giovanni (*c.* 1360–1429), whose son Cosimo earned the name Pater Patriae (Father of his Country) through his skilful control of the city's affairs and support for the arts. He founded an academy and libraries, erected many splendid buildings and gathered around him scholars, painters and sculptors.

After Cosimo's death leadership of Florence fell to his grandson, Lorenzo the Magnificent (1449–92), who encouraged Michelangelo, Botticelli and other artists and scholars, while trying to promote peace among the Italian states. Florence, now the greatest centre of RENAISSANCE learning and art, was torn by feuds; Lorenzo escaped assassination in 1478, but his brother was killed. Towards the end of his life he was unpopular in the city, and the family's wealth declined due to his neglect of the Medici Bank. Under his incompetent son Piero Florence was sacked by the French and Piero was driven out. However, Giuliano, another of Lorenzo's sons, restored the family influence and a third son became Pope Leo x.

In the 16th century the Medicis showed less ability: Lorenzo II (1492–1519) was a feeble ruler, who passed on his faults to his son Alessandro, Governor of Florence after the city had surrendered to the Emperor CHARLES V in 1530. Cosimo I became Grand Duke of Tuscany in 1569, a title held by members of the family until the male line died out in 1737. Among the Medicis who were linked by marriage to royal houses were CATHERINE DE MEDICI (1519–89), who married Henry II of France, and Marie de Medici (1573–1642), wife of Henry of Navarre (HENRY IV of France) and the regent of France for her son Louis XIII.

MEHEMET ALI (*or* Mohammed Ali, 1769–1849), an Albanian soldier, was sent to Egypt in 1801 as an officer of the OTTOMAN forces that co-operated with the British in driving out the French. By 1806 he had emerged as Pasha of Cairo, with the approval of the Sultan. He crushed his former allies, the Mamelukes, in 1811 and became undisputed master of upper Egypt. He campaigned in Arabia and won control of the Sudan, though his son Ibrahim was completely defeated at Navarino in 1827, when he sent him with a fleet to help the Turks against the Greeks during the GREEK WAR OF INDEPENDENCE. In return for his aid the Sultan gave Crete to Mehemet Ali, who promptly demanded Syria as well; when this was refused, he conquered the province and marched on Constantinople, only to be checked by the European powers. Eventually he was defeated near Beirut and had to abandon Syria, but in 1841 he secured recognition as hereditary Pasha of Egypt. In that country he introduced reforms in agriculture, trade and industry, improved communications and irrigation, reorganized the army and founded schools. He has been called the founder of modern Egypt. In 1848 he resigned in favour of his son Ibrahim.

MERCIA, one of the Anglo-Saxon kingdoms (*see* SAXONS), was situated in the midlands and, at its greatest extent, stretched from the river Humber to the Thames (excluding East Anglia) and to the Welsh border. It first came to prominence under Penda (632–54), a heathen king and a great warrior, but the kingdom reached its peak during the reign of King OFFA (757–96). He held authority over both WESSEX and Northumberland and was respected by continental rulers, including CHARLEMAGNE. After his death Mercia came under the rule of Egbert of Wessex, and in 874 was overrun by the Danes.

MEXICAN WAR (1846–8) arose out of friction between the USA and Mexico, whose dictators had appeared to threaten the weak republic of Texas. In 1845 Texas accepted the offer to be annexed by the USA, which therefore became involved in a boundary dispute with Mexico. President James K. Polk sent troops to Texas under General Zachary TAYLOR, who took up position on the Rio Grande, where he was attacked by a Mexican army in April 1846. In a brilliant campaign Taylor captured Monterrey and defeated the Mexicans in the hard-fought battle of Buena Vista (1847). Meanwhile, another American army under Winfield Scott landed at Vera Cruz, pushed westward to defeat the Mexican President Santa Anna, and capture Mexico City. The war ended by the Treaty of Guadalupe Hidalgo, by which Mexico acknowledged the annexation of Texas and for a small sum ceded the disputed Texan territory, New Mexico and California. Young officers, later to be famous, who distinguished themselves in the Mexican War included Ulysses S. GRANT, Jefferson DAVIS and Robert E. LEE.

MING Dynasty of CHINA (1368–1644) was founded by Chu Yüan-chang, who raised an army of revolt against the ruling MONGOLS and fought them for twelve years until, in 1368, his general Hsü Ta captured the capital Cambaluc, later Peking. Chu, who now proclaimed himself Hung Wu, built a new capital at Nanking and brought back Chinese laws and culture, which had declined under the Mongols. The second great Ming emperor was Yung Lo, who moved the capital to Peking and built the Imperial City with the Forbidden City inside it. Yung encouraged trade and education; he also had a gigantic collection of Chinese writings made and he sent seven naval expeditions to countries as far away as Cambodia, Ceylon, Persia and Africa. Yung's reign ended in 1424 and during the next two centuries, when there were no outstanding rulers, Ming China received a growing number

A Ming warrior

of voyagers, traders and missionaries from Europe. The period is especially famous for the production of Ming pottery, which used two or even three colours of glazes on a single piece. After three centuries the Ming dynasty was overthrown by the MANCHUS, an invading people from the north-west.

MINOAN CIVILIZATION was a pre-Greek civilization on the island of Crete which lasted from about 2000 to 1400 BC. The Minoans were sea-traders, who probably came originally from Asia Minor; they traded extensively with Egypt, the Near East and the Aegean Islands, using their wealth to build unfortified palaces at Knossos, Mallia and Phaestus.

The palace at Knossos covered nearly six acres, with courts, halls, antechambers, bathrooms and a throne room. The walls were covered with brilliantly realistic pictures and the palace had a remarkably modern drainage system for its tanks, baths and latrines. Minoan pottery was among the most beautiful ever made and many examples have been excavated by archaeologists.

A remarkable feature of this early civilization was the use of writing, chiefly it seems for palace records and accounts. The Minoans worshipped a nature goddess, whose symbol was a double axe, and they seem to have enjoyed bull-fights and displays of spectacular gymnastics.

Earthquakes occurred in about 1700 BC, causing the palaces to be rebuilt and new towns to be founded. Mycenaeans occupied Knossos from about

A Minoan painting at Knossos illustrating
gymnasts performing with a bull

1475 BC (*see* MYCENAE), and soon after 1400 the
great palace was mysteriously destroyed, possibly
by earthquake or by invaders, and the Minoan
civilization ended.

MONASTERIES, for Christian monks, began to
develop when hermits gave up their solitary lives
in order to live in a community. The early Irish
monasteries were collections of small huts sited
close to a wooden church. An Italian monk, St
Benedict of Nursia, founded the Benedictine Order
in the 6th century, giving it a set of Rules which
were observed (and still are) in monasteries throughout Europe. He divided the monks' day into three
parts – the church services, study and learning, and
work in the garden and fields. Wherever they were
built, Benedictine monasteries were organized in
much the same way, the monks living under the
rule of an elected abbot (or, sometimes, a prior)
while officials such as the sacristan, almoner,
cellarer, chantor and librarian, carried out specialist
tasks.

From time to time during the Middle Ages new
Orders appeared, usually in an attempt to return to
a simpler, stricter way of life. The most important
of these were the Cistercian Order, whose monasteries were usually built in remote places and
whose monks became great sheep-farmers, the
Cluniac Order, a very strict one founded in 910 at
Cluny in France, the Order of the Augustinian
Canons, and the Carthusian Order, whose monks
lived in separate cells, meeting in church and at
meals, but rarely speaking. Monasteries for women
were usually called nunneries and there were some
double-houses for both monks and nuns. The word
'convent' really means a religious community, and
'monastery', strictly speaking, refers to the buildings only.

Large monasteries of the Benedictine and Cistercian Orders were built on more or less similar lines;
the greatest building was the church, in which
services took place at regular intervals by day and
night throughout the year; on its southern side were
built the cloisters, covered walks with access to the
Chapter House (for meetings), Refectory or dining-
room, Dormitory, Abbot's Lodging, Buttery, Bake-
house, Kitchen, Warming-room etc. The Infirmary
or hospital and the Almonry and Guest-house were
usually separate buildings. In the grounds there
would be gardens, barns, stables, a fishpond and a
cemetery. The monastery's layout enabled the
monks to carry out the work for which it had been
founded, that is, to worship God, to help the poor
and the sick, to assist travellers and to preserve
learning.

In England, at the time of the REFORMATION,
HENRY VIII closed down over eight hundred
monasteries of various types, confiscating their
land and accumulated riches. This took place
between 1536 and 1540, while in Scotland the
monasteries disappeared or were sacked during the
next fifty years.

MONGOLS, a nomadic people of Mongolia, emerged from obscurity in the 13th century, when GENGHIS KHAN (1162–1227), at the head of hordes of mounted tribesmen, conquered a vast empire. He captured Peking in 1215 and then turned west to sweep across Afghanistan and Persia into Russia. At his death the empire was divided between his three sons, Ogotai, Jagatai and Tuli, who, with a grandson named Batu, extended the conquests to Hungary, Baghdad, Syria and further into China. Another grandson of Genghis, the great Kublai Khan (died 1294), established the Mongol or YÜAN Dynasty in China, which lasted until 1368.

In Europe the dreaded Mongol cavalry were known as the Golden Horde, and the Pope appealed to all kings and princes to unite against this terrible foe, who devastated whole countries like a scourge. One of the most celebrated Mongol chieftains was Timur or Tamerlane, who ruled from Samarkand. At the height of their power the Mongols (who are also known as Tatars or Tartars) dominated territories stretching from China to Austria, from India to the Baltic, but after 1260 the empire was no longer directed by one leader; rulers became supreme in their own states, quarrels broke out and the unity of the empire was destroyed.

After their campaigns the Mongol warriors liked to return to the grasslands of Mongolia, where their sacred capital was called Karakorum, leaving groups

behind to rule the conquered lands. While it lasted, the empire was held together by the military strength of the invincible cavalry, by a system of posts that provided swift communication and by loyalty amounting to reverence towards Genghis Khan and his family.

MONMOUTH, Duke of (James Scott, 1649–85), was the illegitimate son of CHARLES II by Lucy Walters. Charles was extremely fond of the handsome but not very talented young man, made him a duke and in 1670 Captain-General of the army. His charm, his mercy towards the rebelling COVENANTERS and the progresses he made about the country made him very popular, all the more so because he was a Protestant, whereas the heir to the throne, James Duke of York, was known to be a Roman Catholic. For putting himself forward as the Protestant candidate to the throne, Monmouth was banished for a time and was in Holland when his father died. Persuaded to invade England, he landed at Lyme Regis to raise a Protestant insurrection against JAMES II and was proclaimed king at Taunton. He failed to capture Bristol and his pitifully inadequate forces were routed at Sedgemoor on 6 July 1685. Monmouth was captured and executed nine days later.

Monmouth's Rebellion was followed by the 'Bloody Assize', when in west country towns Lord Chief Justice Jeffreys sentenced three hundred persons to death and nine hundred to transportation for their part in the uprising, some of them for quite trivial reasons.

Opposite NELSON's death on board the *Victory* at the Battle of Trafalgar

MONROE DOCTRINE is an important principle of the USA foreign policy. Its origin was a statement sent as a message to Congress by President James Monroe in 1823, in which he declared in effect that any attempt by European powers to interfere in the American hemisphere would be considered as dangerous to the peace and safety of the USA. At the time rebellions against Spain and Portugal in the South American colonies (*see* BOLIVAR) aroused fears that there might be a large-scale European invasion and a revival of colonial activity. There was also the possibility that Russia might try to extend her Alaskan territory. The Monroe Doctrine of 'Hands off the American hemisphere' has been restated many times by US presidents.

Seal of Simon
de Montfort

MONTFORT, Simon de (*c.* 1206–65), Earl of Leicester, the son of a celebrated French knight, came to England in 1229; he was one of HENRY III's favourites and married the King's sister Eleanor. De Montfort served the king as governor of Gascony, which he ruled with order and efficiency that were not present in England. He became leader of the barons against the King, forcing Henry to accept the Provisions of Oxford (1258), whereby the royal powers were largely taken over by the barons. Civil war broke out in 1264 and de Montfort won a great victory at Lewes, capturing the King and becoming for a year virtual ruler of England.

His position was, however, far from secure and the barons began to desert him; hence he summoned representatives to his Parliament of 1265, hoping to win additional support to counter the loss of the nobles. He ordered two knights to be elected in each shire-court and two burgesses in towns favourable to his cause; this has been called a great step forward in the development of the English parliament, though de Montfort did not invent the idea of elected members and his parliament was not representative of the whole country.

At Evesham in 1265 de Montfort was defeated by Henry III's son, Prince Edward (later EDWARD I). De Montfort was killed and his body, hacked to pieces, was distributed to various towns as a warning. Arrogant and ambitious though he was, he won the affection of the common people, who long remembered him as the 'good Earl Simon'.

MONTGOMERY of Alamein, Viscount (Bernard Montgomery, 1887–1976), was born in London, the son of a bishop; he entered the army, served in the First World War and, as a regular soldier, held various commands between the wars. In 1939–40 he commanded the 3rd Division and was present at the DUNKIRK evacuation. He then became a corps commander in England and made a name for himself as a leader so positive and demanding that he appeared to some to be a martinet.

In August 1942 he was appointed commander of the British 8th Army in North Africa under General Alexander, and in the following November at El Alamein he won a great victory that was a turning-point of the war. He then pursued ROMMEL's army across Libya and Tripolitania and in March 1943 won another victory at the battle of the Mareth Line. Having driven the Germans out of North Africa, he led the 8th Army to Sicily and into Italy before being recalled to England to help plan the NORMANDY INVASION. In June 1944 he led the Allied armies in Normandy under the overall com-

Opposite Scene on Normandy beach after the D-Day landings (painting by Barnet Freedman; *see* NORMANDY INVASION)

mand of General EISENHOWER and, despite friction with some of the American generals, he pressed across France and into Germany with the 21st Army Group to accept the surrender of the German armies at Lüneburg Heath in May 1945.

After the war he was appointed Chief of the Imperial General Staff and given a peerage; from 1951 to 1958 he was Deputy Supreme Commander of NATO forces in Europe. Montgomery had a flair for personal leadership; he took over a tired, dispirited army and made it into a splendid fighting force, devoted to himself. It could be said that he was an exhibitionist, a cautious general who was lucky to come to the top at the time when Allied productivity was turning out all the weapons and materials that were needed for victory. Nevertheless, he seized his chance with both hands and he gave Britain what the country needed so badly after years of struggle and defeat – victory and a popular hero.

MONTROSE, Marquess of (James Graham, 1612–50), Scottish nobleman, opposed CHARLES I's high-handed attitude towards the Scottish Church and became a COVENANTER. However, disgusted by the extremists in the national movement, he went over to the King and during the CIVIL WAR raised the Highland clans and won a number of victories over the covenanting forces. In the Lowlands he was defeated at Philiphaugh in 1645 and escaped abroad. When he heard of the King's execution, he is said to have sworn an oath to avenge him; at all events, he landed in Caithness with a small army, was defeated at Carbiesdale and

later betrayed by Macleod of Assynt. He was hanged in Edinburgh before the gaze of Argyll, his life-long enemy, but on his way to execution the great Marquess, a fine soldier, who was a man of tolerance and humanity, bore himself with the utmost courage. Years later, after the Restoration, his head and severed limbs were given solemn burial in St Giles's Church, Edinburgh.

MOORS are a people of North Africa who gave their name to Morocco. Their region was conquered by the Arabs in 707 and the Moors, converted to ISLAM, then invaded Spain, where Cordova became the centre of an advanced civilization. The Moors of Spain excelled in the study of science, mathematics and philosophy and did much to preserve the learning of the ancient world.

After many years of warfare with the Christians of Spain, they retired in 1238 to Granada in the south, where their kingdom was subject to Castile. FERDINAND completed the conquest of Granada in 1492 and soon afterwards the Moors were expelled from the country.

MORE, Sir Thomas (1478–1535), made a reputation as a lawyer and a scholar before being called to

Sir Thomas More with members of his family

Court by HENRY VIII, who made a personal friend of him and sent him abroad on state missions. When WOLSEY fell into disgrace for failing to secure the royal divorce, More was appointed Lord Chancellor, but he could not approve of Henry's marriage to Anne Boleyn and was conspicuously absent from her coronation. He resigned from his post in 1532, but he was too important for Henry to ignore and was therefore summoned to take the oath required by the Act of Succession that Anne was the true queen of England and that her children would be legitimate. More's refusal to swear the oath led to his arrest on a charge of treason. He was lodged in the Tower, found guilty and executed in 1535, his last words being, 'I die, the King's loyal servant, but God's servant first'. He was made a saint in 1935.

Sir Thomas More was one of the most attractive characters in history; a good husband and loving father, a gentle tolerant man, whose friends included ERASMUS, the Dutch scholar. Among his writings his most famous work was *Utopia*, an account of an imaginary and ideal island.

MORSE, Samuel (1791–1872), the inventor of the telegraphic system, was born in Massachusetts and in his youth was more interested in art than in science. He studied art in England and after his return to America became president of the National Academy of Design from 1826 to 1843. From 1832 he worked on electromagnetism, carrying out experiments until in 1837 he was able to interest the firm of Messrs Vail, iron and brass workers, in his system of telegraph. There was still a long struggle ahead of him and an unsuccessful trip to Europe before Congress authorized the construction of a telegraph from Baltimore to Washington. This was first used in 1844 and Morse subsequently established in court his right to the invention. The original Morse Code was devised in 1837 with Alfred Vail.

MOSES, the great Jewish lawgiver, prophet and judge, was born in Egypt probably during the reign of RAMESES II (*c.* 1292–1225 BC), when the Hebrews were living there as slaves. Moses, who was brought up as an Egyptian prince, led his people out of captivity by way of Sinai, Kadesh and Moab (where he died) towards the Promised Land of Canaan. For forty years he was their inspired leader and was the founder of the Jewish religion.

MUSSOLINI, Benito (1883–1945), the Italian Fascist dictator, was born in northern Italy, the son of a blacksmith and a schoolmistress. As a young man he went to Switzerland, where he was arrested for revolutionary activities, and on his return to Italy became well-known for his extreme socialist views. He was an excellent journalist and in 1914 he founded and edited *Il Popolo d'Italia*, which strongly urged Italy to enter the war against Germany. He himself served in the army, was wounded in a firing accident and then resumed his editorship. In 1919 he founded the Blackshirt movement and soon became a major figure in Italian politics. His success was easy to understand. Italy was dissatisfied with the outcome of the war; the country was suffering from poverty, unemployment, strikes and riots. Mussolini promised order and reform; his gangs of thugs attacked the Communists and Socialists with such violence that he became virtually master of Milan and his tactics and promises won the support of landowners, industrialists, police, politicians, the middle classes and many of the ex-soldiers.

In 1922 his 'March on Rome' bluffed King Victor Emmanuel III into inviting Mussolini to form a government; 'He is brutal enough to restore order and intelligent enough to govern,' remarked the King. For a time the government was fairly moderate, but the murder of Matteotti, the Socialist leader, in 1924, which was attributed, perhaps wrongly, to Mussolini's orders, put an end to any possibility of co-operation from the Left. By 1925 Mussolini was dictator of Italy, a big-jawed bombastic figure who radiated energy and drive as he went about the country, making speeches, opening new factories, railway-stations and drainage schemes, and rallying the people with such slogans as 'Obey, Believe, Fight'. For a time things did improve; economic difficulties lessened, employment improved and Italy seemed to be more efficiently governed; there was however a good deal of corruption, which Mussolini (never himself interested in wealth) did nothing to check.

In his desire for military glory, he embarked on the invasion of ETHIOPIA (1935), and its success convinced him of his own power, of the feebleness of the Western democracies, which had opposed him without doing anything, and of the advantages that could be gained from alliance with HITLER's Germany. His popularity was now at its peak and thereafter it began to decline, for the Italian people did not care for the German friendship nor for the help which Mussolini sent to FRANCO in Spain.

In 1940 he made the disastrous decision to enter the SECOND WORLD WAR. That Italy was not ready for a major conflict was soon seen, when in Africa General Wavell defeated a much larger Italian army, when the Greeks routed Mussolini's vaunted legions, and when Ethiopia was lost. His health began to fail and as the war went from bad to worse the King had him arrested in July 1943 and imprisoned in a hotel in the remote Abruzzi mountains. Then came his dramatic rescue by a German parachute captain, who took him to Germany, where Hitler welcomed him but made it clear he was now a very junior partner. He returned to Italy to set up a new Fascist government in the north, but this was short-lived and there was nothing for it but flight in a small German convoy. Partisans stopped the cars, recognized Mussolini and, after some delay, shot him and his mistress Claretta Petacci and took their bodies to Milan, where they were exhibited to the public, hanging by their feet.

Thus the Italian dictator came to his inglorious end. He had possessed great vitality, cunning and brutality; he was by no means wholly wicked and he possessed some likeable human qualities; he was however a vain, superficial poseur, whose defects brought suffering to his country.

MYCENAE, one of the most ancient cities of Greece, dates from about 2000 BC. Surrounded by massive walls, it stood on a hill overlooking the Argive plain and it was from Mycenae that Agamemnon and his warriors set out for TROY through the Lion Gate. Up to the 15th century BC MINOAN influence was strong, but after the occupation of Knossos in about 1475 BC, the Mycenaeans came to the peak of their power and probably exercised rule over the Greek mainland and Crete.

In about 1200 BC, probably soon after Agamemnon's return from Troy, the city was destroyed by unknown invaders. It never recovered its power, for in the 11th century BC the Dorians, a warlike people from the north, overran the area and by the 5th century Mycenae was part of the city-state of Argos. In 1876 the German archaeologist Schliemann excavated the shaft graves, discovering an amazing collection of weapons, vases, gold, jewellery and the so-called gold 'Mask of Agamemnon'.

The Lion Gate at Mycenae

N

NAPOLEON I Bonaparte (1769–1821) was born at Ajaccio, Corsica, only a year after the French had taken the island from the Italian republic of Genoa. His father disliked the change, but nevertheless sent his son to a military academy in France, and at fifteen Napoleon was commissioned in the French army. He later accepted the principles of the FRENCH REVOLUTION and in 1793, as a captain of artillery, was responsible for the capture of Toulon from Royalists helped by British warships. This brought promotion and entry into the political scene of Paris, where he saved the government by turning guns on crowds of angry citizens and was rewarded with command of the French army in Italy (1796).

A general at twenty-six, he immediately inspired a dejected army and by sheer brilliance totally defeated the Austrian and Sardinian forces. The French government, taken aback by the returned hero's high-handed attitude, were relieved to see him depart to Egypt in order to win an overseas Empire and cut the British route to India. NELSON's destruction of the French fleet ruined his plans, and hearing that the government in Paris was tottering he abandoned his army and returned to France. There, by the people's vote, he became First Consul, the real ruler of the country, and after defeating the Austrians at Marengo (1800) he turned his energies to home affairs.

Working at a pace that exhausted his ministers and subordinates, he gave France a system of government that has lasted, little changed, to this day. Trade, agriculture, education and science were encouraged and careers opened to men of ability, rich or poor. He gave the country new roads, canals, and, above all, a code of laws that established a firm system of justice. In 1804, when he became Emperor of the French, he had no rival; France was secure and he could have ruled for the rest of his life had he not chosen to devote his talents to war.

His plan to invade England was foiled by lack of seapower, so he marched east to defeat the Austrians at Ulm, to smash the armies of Russia and Austria at Austerlitz (1805) and to destroy the

Napoleon on board the *Bellerophon* on his way to St Helena as a prisoner in 1815

Prussians at Jena. He was now astride Europe, able to make and unmake kings as he pleased, to rob and oppress peoples who had earlier welcomed the French as champions of liberty.

As his ambition grew, he set up a dynasty, placing his brothers and a sister on the thrones of Spain, Westphalia, Holland and Naples. In 1809 he divorced his wife Josephine for having failed to provide him with an heir, and married Marie-Louise, daughter of the Austrian Emperor. Their baby son was made King of Rome.

In order to break Britain, Napoleon tried to stop all her trade with Europe, and when Spain and Portugal disobeyed his orders he became involved in the disastrous PENINSULAR WAR. Meanwhile, Tsar ALEXANDER I had become defiant, so Napoleon marched the Grand Army into Russia, only to lose half a million men in the terrible retreat from Moscow (1812). This disaster encouraged Europe to rise against the tyrant and force him to abdicate. In 1814 he was exiled to the island of Elba, from where he escaped a year later and returned to Paris in triumph. His soldiers welcomed him back, but the Allies refused to listen to his promises of peace and goodwill; they gathered their armies and defeated him at WATERLOO on 18 June 1815. He was imprisoned on the island of St Helena in the south Atlantic and died there of cancer six years later.

Napoleon was arguably the greatest general who ever lived. A brilliant strategist, he would concentrate whole armies on the enemy's weakest point and he made masterly use of artillery and cavalry to complete the destruction begun by his columns of infantry. He possessed in full the great commander's power to inspire his troops, but it could be said that they had little to beat in Europe, being opposed by unwilling conscripts led for the most part by second-rate generals. As a man he possessed dynamic energy and an overpowering magnetism, but he was domineering, callous and utterly selfish.

NAPOLEON III (Louis Napoleon Bonaparte, 1808–73) was the son of Louis, a brother of Napoleon I. Eager to keep alive the family name, he wrote pamphlets to foster the Napoleonic legend and during Louis Philippe's reign made two attempts to seize control. On the second occasion (1840) he was sentenced to life imprisonment, but he escaped after five years and went to London. Taking advantage of the REVOLUTION OF 1848, he

returned to France and was elected first to the Assembly and then to the presidency of the republic. He quickly took control of the army and placed his supporters in posts of authority, so that he was able to carry out his famous *coup d'état* of 1851, when he dissolved the Assembly and assumed dictatorial powers. By now he was immensely popular and in 1852 he took the title of Emperor.

The Second Empire lasted eighteen years. It was a time of glamour and splendour, of achievement, advance and workers' discontent. Paris, scene of the 1867 Exhibition, was transformed into one of the world's loveliest capitals, and at Court the fascinating Empress Eugénie presided over a scene of glittering extravagance. Louis Napoleon, intelligent and cultured though he was, did not possess the capacity to rule France practically single-handed and to carry out an active foreign policy. He involved France in the CRIMEAN WAR, in North Africa and Italy, generally to her advantage, but his attempt to foist a monarch on the Mexicans ended in disaster. In 1870 he was tricked by BISMARCK into declaring war on Prussia, quite unaware that the French army was much weaker. The FRANCO-PRUSSIAN WAR was soon over. Defeated at Sedan in September, Napoleon was obliged to surrender to the Prussians, and after his release he went into exile in England and died there.

NAPOLEONIC WARS took place in Europe between 1799, when NAPOLEON I assumed personal rule of France, and 1815, the year in which he was finally defeated.

The wars began with Napoleon's victory over the Austrians at Marengo (1800). He ended this campaign with the Treaty of Lunéville (1801) and then made the Peace of Amiens (1802) with Britain, which had been at war with revolutionary France for nine years.

Hostilities broke out again in 1803, when Britain declared war and Napoleon seized Hanover. His preparations to invade England had to be finally abandoned after the Battle of TRAFALGAR (1805), but he then defeated Austria at Ulm (1805), took Vienna and overwhelmed an Austro-Russian army at Austerlitz (1805). He next routed the Prussians at Jena, while at Eylau and Friedland he defeated the combined Prussian-Russian armies, compelling Tsar ALEXANDER I to sign the Treaty of Tilsit (1807).

In 1808 Napoleon annexed Spain and placed his brother Joseph on the throne. This led to the PENINSULAR WAR, in which the Duke of WELL-INGTON, commanding a British army supported by Portuguese and Spanish allies, withstood the French for several years and eventually drove them out of Spain.

Although this war put a heavy strain on France's military strength, Napoleon still continued his campaigns elsewhere. Having defeated Austria at Regensburg and Wagram (1809), he tried to break Britain by excluding her goods from Europe. The Continental System, as this plan was called, exasperated Russia and led to a situation in which Napoleon decided to launch his invasion of 1812. On the Retreat from Moscow five-sixths of his army perished, but he himself reached France, where he set about raising fresh armies to face practically all the nations of Europe. A coalition of powers, headed by Prussia, Russia, most of the German states and Austria, put an army of half a million men into the field, and after a series of battles won a decisive victory at Leipzig (1813). Napoleon withdrew across the Rhine into France, followed by the Allies, while Wellington, having cleared the French out of Spain, was advancing on Paris from the south. In these circumstances Napoleon surrendered (1814) and was sent to the island of Elba.

In the following year he escaped and returned to France. During the HUNDRED DAYS he raised yet another army with the intention of defeating the Prussians and British, who were the only Allies ready to meet him. At WATERLOO, on 18 June 1815, the French army was routed and Napoleon fled to Paris, where he abdicated for the second time. In October he was taken to St Helena to spend the rest of his life in exile.

Opponents in the Napoleonic Wars: (*left*) British private of the Coldstream Guards; (*right*) Grenadier officer of Napoleon's Imperial Guard

NASSER, Gamal Abdel (1918–70), a regular soldier in the Egyptian army, distinguished himself in the 1948 ARAB-ISRAELI WAR. In 1952 he was one of the leaders of the rebellion which overthrew King Farouk and installed General Neguib as Prime Minister of the Egyptian Republic. Two years later

he took Neguib's place and subsequently became President of his country and also of the United Arab Republic.

He introduced many reforms and managed to obtain foreign help, including the financing of the Aswan Dam by the USA. However, his friendship with the USSR and the purchase of arms from Czechoslovakia caused the USA to withdraw assistance. At this Nasser nationalized the SUEZ CANAL (1956) and emerged triumphant after the withdrawal of the British and French invasion forces. This episode brought him enormous prestige in the Arab world and he is generally regarded as the greatest Egyptian statesman since MEHEMET ALI.

The German imperial eagle holding the Nazi swastika

NAZIS was the popular abbreviation of the German name for members of the National Socialist Workers' Party, of which HITLER became the leader. The Nazis stood for opposition to the Communists and, eventually, to socialists and liberals, but the principal objects of their hatred were the Jews, whom they persecuted without mercy. After Hitler came to power the Nazis gained control of the police, banned newspapers and books with which they disagreed, dissolved other political parties and trade unions, instituted a Ministry of Propaganda and founded concentration camps, to which their opponents, or anyone thought likely to be an opponent, were sent. The Nazi emblem was the swastika, a crooked cross.

NEBUCHADNEZZAR II, Chaldean King of BABYLON (c. 605–562 BC), defeated the Egyptians at Carchemish (605) and conquered Syria and Palestine. In 587 he captured JERUSALEM, destroyed the temple and carried off thousands of captives to Babylon. He rebuilt the city of Babylon in magnificent style with massive walls, a fabulous palace and the celebrated Hanging Gardens.

NEHRU, Pandit Jawaharlal (1889–1964), Prime Minister of India from its independence in 1947 to his death, was educated in England at Harrow and Cambridge. He became a barrister and, in politics, a fervent nationalist, who was totally opposed to British rule. He was secretary of the India Home Rule League and president of the INDIAN NATIONAL CONGRESS. A devoted supporter of GANDHI, he spent thirteen years in prison for subversive activities, but his opposition was to the British government, never to British people, and he recognized the British contribution to Indian progress. As Prime Minister he was a strong supporter of the Commonwealth and an opponent of war and of foreign entanglements. At home his principal aim was rapid industrialization combined with improved social welfare.

NELSON, Horatio, Viscount (1758–1805), son of a Norfolk clergyman, joined the Navy as a midshipman at the age of twelve. In his early years he saw service in the West Indies, the Arctic and the East Indies; though slight of build and delicate looking, he was a captain of a frigate at the age of twenty and already known to his superiors as a brave and dashing officer. He served for several years in the West Indies, where he married Frances Nesbit, a widow, in 1787, and afterwards spent five years on half-pay ashore in Norfolk.

On the outbreak of the war with France in 1793 he was given command of the battleship *Agamemnon*, and in operations against Corsica he lost his right eye. Serving under Admiral Jervis at the Battle of Cape St Vincent, Nelson carried out a brilliant manoeuvre that led to the rout of the Spanish fleet, but not long afterwards he lost his right arm during an expedition against Santa Cruz in the Canary Islands (1797). When NAPOLEON sailed for Egypt, Nelson swept the Mediterranean in search of him and eventually found the French fleet at anchor in Aboukir Bay, near Alexandria. He boldly sailed into the Bay at night to destroy the fleet and put an end to Napoleon's dream of an eastern empire.

During two years in command of a squadron in the Mediterranean Nelson fell deeply in love with Lady Hamilton, wife of the British Ambassador at Naples. His love for her, disapproved of by a great many people, lasted to the end of his life. In 1801 at Copenhagen Nelson, with Sir Hyde Parker, destroyed the Danish fleet to prevent powerful forces joining Napoleon; then, after the Peace of Amiens (1802), he was able to enjoy his first rest ashore for years.

A year later, when war broke out again, he was appointed Commander-in-Chief in the Mediterranean, hoisting his flag in the *Victory*, in which he was engaged in a long blockade of Toulon. The French fleet escaped in March 1805, sailed to the West Indies and returned to Cadiz; Nelson, having conducted a long chase in vain, came back to England, but learning the whereabouts of the enemy fleet he re-embarked on the *Victory* and arrived off Cadiz on 28 September. At last the combined French and Spanish fleets emerged and on 21 October 1805 Nelson brought them to battle off Cape TRAFALGAR. Just before the action he sent his famous signal, 'England expects that every man will do his duty'. During the hard-fought battle he was fatally wounded, but lived long enough to know that he had won a complete victory. His last words were 'Thank God, I have done my duty'. He was carried home in the battered *Victory* to be buried in St Paul's Cathedral to the profound sorrow of his sailors and of the nation.

NERO (AD 37–68) succeeded his stepfather CLAUDIUS as Emperor of ROME in 54. Under the influence of his tutor, Seneca, he behaved well, but after he murdered his mother Agrippina and his wife Octavia Seneca was unable to restrain him. In his admiration of Greek culture, Nero liked to perform as actor and musician and he was accused of idly playing the lyre during a disastrous fire in Rome. To avert suspicion of having caused the fire himself, he accused the Christians and had hundreds

Coin of Nero

murdered (*see* CHRISTIANITY). He then taxed the provinces heavily in order to rebuild Rome. In 68 the generals in Gaul and Spain revolted against his bloodthirsty rule and named Galba as Emperor in his stead. The Senate supported them and Nero committed suicide.

NETHERLANDS, or Low Countries, consisted for centuries of a number of provinces making up the modern countries of Holland and Belgium. In the Middle Ages cities such as Bruges, Ghent, Antwerp, Ypres, were flourishing centres of trade, especially of the wool industry. From 1384 the Netherlands belonged to the dukes of Burgundy, and in the following century to Spain, as part of the Hapsburg Empire of CHARLES V.

Under PHILIP II of Spain the Netherlands fought for freedom and the Protestant religion, a bitter struggle that lasted until 1648, when Spain recognized their independence (*see* DUTCH REVOLT). William Prince of Orange, known as WILLIAM THE SILENT, had done more than any man to win this freedom; however, ten of the southern provinces retained the Catholic religion and Spanish rule (1648–1713), which was followed by that of the Austrians (1713–94). At the beginning of the 18th century the Netherlands and their British allies fought a long and ultimately successful war against LOUIS XIV's France. At the close of that century all the provinces were overrun by NAPOLEON's troops, but on the fall of Napoleon they became the kingdom of the Netherlands. In 1830 the southern provinces formed the kingdom of Belgium while the north retained the name of Holland.

NEWTON, Sir Isaac (1642–1727), was born in Lincolnshire and educated at Trinity College, Cambridge. He studied mathematics, especially calculus, the nature and properties of light and the laws of gravity. He invented a reflecting telescope and discovered the laws affecting the movements of planets, the action of the moon on the tides and many other things. His book, *Principia*, has been called 'the greatest single work of science in the world'.

To the end of his life Newton remained the most modest and gentle of men; often he did not bother to record his remarkable discoveries and he frequently solved mathematical problems that had baffled the best brains in Europe.

NICHOLAS II (1868–1918), the last Russian Tsar, was the son of Alexander III and cousin of GEORGE V of Britain, whom he closely resembled. A kindly, affectionate man, he was nevertheless opposed to progressive and democratic ideas. The main events of his reign were the Franco-Russian alliance, the defeat of Russia in the war with Japan (1904–5) and the revolution of 1905, which compelled Nicholas

to allow a parliament, or Duma, to meet, and to improve civil liberties. The period 1906–14 was one of steady improvement in Russia, but after the outbreak of the FIRST WORLD WAR Nicholas took over command of the armed forces, leaving the government in the hands of the Tsarina Alexandra and RASPUTIN. Following the RUSSIAN REVOLUTION of February 1917 he abdicated and was shot with his family by the BOLSHEVIKS in the following year.

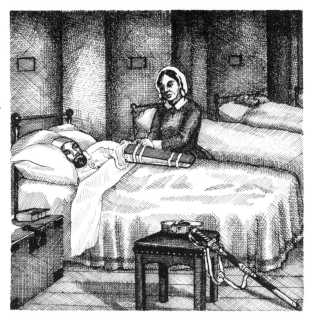

Florence Nightingale attending a wounded soldier in the hospital at Scutari

NIGHTINGALE, Florence (1820–1910), the daughter of wealthy English parents, who did not wish her to work or take up a career, nevertheless managed to visit hospitals on the continent and obtain training as a nurse. In 1853 she became superintendent of a London hospital for women, and after the outbreak of the CRIMEAN WAR she offered to go out to Scutari to nurse the wounded. With money, supplies and thirty-eight nurses, she established a hospital that was cleaner and better run than any military hospital of the time; she overcame the opposition of Army medical authorities, saved countless lives and returned to England a popular heroine. From an invalid's couch she spent the rest of her long life campaigning for a trained nursing service and for improvements in public and army health. She founded institutions for training nurses at St Thomas's and King's College Hospitals, London.

NORE MUTINY (1797) occurred in May a month after the less serious mutiny at Spithead. At a critical point in the war with France the sailors of the North Sea fleet demanded better treatment and a fairer division of prize money. Led by Richard Parker, they threatened to blockade the Thames, starve London and surrender their ships to the enemy. The government refused to give way and most of the sailors abandoned Parker and returned to obedience to their officers. Parker and a few ringleaders were hanged and the ex-mutineers, sent to join Admiral Duncan, who had been bluffing the Dutch with a three ship blockade, speedily proved their loyalty by fighting bravely in the Battle of Camperdown when the Dutch fleet was destroyed.

NORMANDY INVASION, the Anglo-American seaborne invasion of Europe during the SECOND WORLD WAR began on 6 June 1944 ('D'-day). A great flotilla of ships and landing-craft, supported by massive naval and air forces, conveyed in the first instance over 150,000 Allied troops from southern England to the beaches of Normandy.

The invasion, known as 'Operation Overlord', had been mooted since 1942 and was planned in meticulous detail. To some it seemed that the 'Second Front' had been too long delayed, but it is difficult to see how it could have been attempted earlier. General EISENHOWER was appointed the Supreme Allied Commander, while the naval, army and air forces all came under British command. General MONTGOMERY was appointed Commander-

in-Chief of the Anglo-American ground forces, Admiral Ramsay commanded the naval forces and Air Marshal Leigh-Mallory the air forces.

Prior to the invasion heavy air attacks were made on the Pas de Calais area to deceive the Germans into thinking that the attack would be made on that part of the coast. Hence, the seaborne landings preceded by airborne landings were made on the Normandy beaches with practically no interference, except from the weather, which was unusually bad for June. The German defences came under the supreme command of Field Marshal von Runstedt, with Montgomery's old enemy, Field Marshal ROMMEL, commanding the sixty divisions that were to oppose any invasion. Despite their preparedness, the landings took the Germans by surprise. Local defence forces put up fierce resistance on the beaches, especially on the one called 'Omaha', where the Americans encountered a German division on an anti-invasion exercize. However, the effect of the dummy attacks and of the Allies' almost total air superiority delayed Rommel's concentration of forces into the invasion area.

Thus by the end of D-day the Allies had secured a foothold in Europe. All five beaches were held and, although the penetration had not been as deep as had been hoped, a base had been won from which it would be possible to pursue the three main objectives of the landing. These were to strike up the Cotentin Peninsula and capture the port of Cherbourg, to press inland to secure landing-grounds for aircraft and to attract to Caen the maximum weight of enemy armour.

By the end of June these objectives had been realized. The Americans reached Cherbourg on 25 June, the British were engaging two-thirds of the Germans' total armoured strength around Caen and the American commander, General Patton, had already begun his drive inland. By July the Allies had landed over 1,500,000 men, a colossal army supplied with stores landed at the artificial harbour called 'Mulberry' and with fuel supplied by an oil pipe-line known as 'Pluto'. Paris was captured on 24 August, Brussels was reached on 3 September, Antwerp on the 4th and the German frontier on the 12th.

The Normandy Invasion had proved to be a triumph of planning, courage and military skill. It confronted the German General Staff with what they had always feared – a war on two fronts. With the Russian victories in the east, it brought about Hitler's downfall and Germany's defeat.

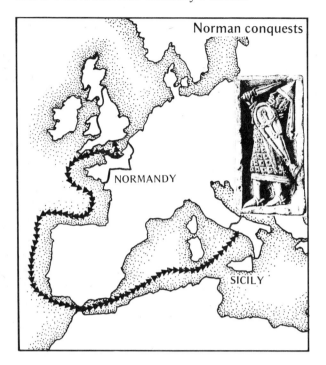

Norman conquests

NORMANDY

SICILY

NORMANS came from Scandinavia and the name is identical with Northmen and Norsemen (*see* VIKINGS). From the 8th century these hardy warriors raided Western Europe, and then in 911 a Norman chief named Rollo acquired part of France, which became known as Normandy. In the 11th century, under WILLIAM THE CONQUERER, they invaded and conquered England, at about the same time as another force of Normans defeated the Saracens in Sicily, where they established a Norman kingdom. Others won lands in southern Italy.

Normans from France and Italy played leading roles in the First CRUSADE (1096–9) and in setting up the Crusader kingdoms in Palestine. Wherever they went, the Normans were noted for their energy, ruthlessness and military skill; they were great builders of castles and churches and some were pious churchmen. Their system of holding land in return for service came to be known as the FEUDAL SYSTEM.

NORTHUMBERLAND, Duke of (John Dudley, *c.* 1502–53), was an able soldier, who rose to a

position of almost complete power behind the boy-king EDWARD VI. Ruthless and unscrupulous, he realized that he would be ruined if the Roman Catholic princess MARY came to the throne, so he married his son Guildford Dudley to Lady Jane GREY, and persuaded Edward to name Lady Jane as his successor. On Edward's death Northumberland made Lady Jane queen of England, but a popular uprising in favour of Mary brought about his downfall. He was speedily arrested and executed for treason. Another of his sons, Robert, became Elizabeth I's favourite, the Earl of LEICESTER.

NUFFIELD, Viscount (William Morris, 1877–1963), began work as a boy in a bicycle shop. On his own account he turned to making bicycles; then in 1904 he opened a garage, and by 1912 this self-taught engineer had built his first Morris-Oxford car. He visited America to study FORD's mass-production methods, and after the First World War introduced similar methods into his Cowley works, which turned out a stream of new Morris models even during the DEPRESSION years. After the Second World War he produced the Nuffield tractor, and following the Austin-Morris merger in 1952 he became the British Motor Corporation's chairman and then its president. By this time immensely rich, he had already given away huge sums, mostly to hospitals and for medical research. He set up the Nuffield Trust to help the Special Areas (hard hit by the Depression), founded Nuffield College (1937) at Oxford and the Nuffield Foundation (1943) for medical, scientific and social research. When he reached the age of eighty he had given away £27 million and no longer owned the great motorcar firm which he had started.

O

obtained in 1829, and O'Connell, having entered Parliament, took up his next great cause, repeal of the Union of England and Ireland. In 1844 he was imprisoned for sedition, and after his release a few months later his health broke down and he took little more part in Irish affairs.

Coin of Offa

OATES, Titus (1649–1705), son of a preacher, was expelled from school and two Cambridge colleges before taking holy orders and becoming a naval chaplain. He was dismissed for ill conduct, as he was from a Roman Catholic college in France. He next appeared in England in 1678 with the story of the Popish Plot to murder CHARLES II and set James Duke of York (later JAMES II) on the throne. This tale suited the political purposes of the Earl of Shaftesbury and others, who worked up an anti-Catholic panic, in which innocent persons were imprisoned and executed, while Oates concocted accusations and obtained a pension of £600 and a suite of rooms at Whitehall. A Whig parliament tried to bring in a Bill to exclude James from the succession, but Charles sent him abroad and dissolved Parliament. The anti-Catholic fury died down and when James II came to the throne Oates was punished with flogging and life imprisonment, but on the accession of William and Mary this scoundrel recovered his liberty and pension.

O'CONNELL, Daniel (1775–1847), a lawyer and Irish patriot, formed the Catholic Association (1823) to campaign for Catholic Emancipation. This was

OFFA (died 796), King of MERCIA, raised his kingdom to a position of supremacy over other English kingdoms of the time, including WESSEX. He seems to have ruled an area that included London and Kent, southern and central England to the Welsh border and northwards to Northumbria. He dealt with CHARLEMAGNE on almost equal terms and made a trade treaty with him. Offa's Dyke, running from the Dee to the Severn, is a great earthwork and ditch constructed by Offa to mark the Welsh-Mercian frontier.

OLD AGE PENSIONS in Britain were introduced in 1908 when Asquith was Prime Minister of a Liberal government and LLOYD GEORGE was Chancellor of the Exchequer. The idea of financial help for the elderly poor had been put forward for more than twenty years by politicians such as Joseph Chamberlain and social reformers such as

Charles Booth and Seebohm Rowntree. The 1908 Budget provided that at seventy a single person should receive 5 shillings (25p) a week and married couples 7 shillings and 6 pence (37½p), provided their income was less than £26 a year for single persons and £39 for a couple. Some five million persons benefited from the small but valuable pension, and the cost was met from general taxation, since there was as yet no insurance plan. From 1948 old age pensions became payable after the age of sixty for women and sixty-five for men.

OTTO I (912–73), known as Otto the Great, was the creator of a strong German state. He reigned from 936 to 973 and was crowned Holy Roman Emperor in Rome. By winning a great victory over the Magyars of Hungary in 955, he freed Germany from their raids; Poland, Bohemia and Denmark paid tribute to him, while, in the west, he exercised a kind of protectorate over France. On two occasions he invaded Italy, where he compelled the Romans to promise they would elect no pope without the Emperor's consent (*see* PAPACY). Indeed, he deposed one pope (John XII) and replaced him with his own nominee (Leo VIII). Otto's policy was to unite Germany under the Emperor, reducing the power of the dukes, ruling through bishops and counts and allying himself to the Church, which he kept under his own control.

OTTOMAN EMPIRE dates from about 1300 when the Ottoman Turks, a tribe related to the SELJUK TURKS, overran Asia Minor and penetrated into Europe. Their capture of Constantinople, capital of the BYZANTINE EMPIRE, in 1453 gave the empire its capital and the place of residence of the Sultan. His armies subjugated Serbia, Bulgaria, Macedonia and Greece in the 14th and 15th centuries; then they penetrated Italy and, in the 16th century, conquered Syria and Egypt.

The empire reached its peak of splendour in the reign of SULEIMAN the Magnificent (1520–66), who defeated the Hungarians and laid siege to Vienna. Cyprus and Crete were acquired, but from the last quarter of the 16th century the Sultan's power slowly declined. The Ottoman navy suffered a decisive defeat at LEPANTO (1571) and the empire was challenged by the HAPSBURGS and by the

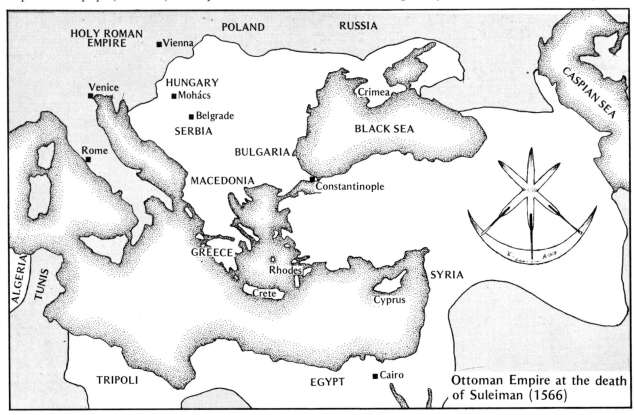

Ottoman Empire at the death of Suleiman (1566)

Russians, who waged a series of wars to obtain access to the Black Sea and to push back the Turkish frontiers.

Greece won her independence in 1830 (*see* GREEK WAR OF INDEPENDENCE), but the CRIMEAN WAR (1853–6) propped up the empire for a time, because France and Britain supported the Sultan against the Tsar. However, in the second half of the 19th century Egypt and most of the Ottoman possessions in south-east Europe broke away from the Sultan's rule. The BALKAN WARS (1912–13) further reduced his power, and by 1913 he was left with only a small strip of land in Europe. After the First World War and Turkey's defeat, the empire came to an end, with the sultanate itself being abolished in 1922.

OWEN GLENDOWER (*or* Owain Glyn Dwr, *c.* 1359–1416), leader of the last Welsh rebellion, took up arms when, in a quarrel with Lord Grey of Ruthin, he was denied justice by HENRY IV. The rebellion spread rapidly until the whole of Wales was ablaze, and Owen, whose guerrilla tactics baffled the English armies, laid claim to the crown of Wales. He allied himself to the Mortimers, the Percies and Charles VI of France, who sent a force of 3,000 men, which advanced with the Welsh to Worcester. Owen's alliance failed and his forces were broken up by Prince Henry (later HENRY V), the warrior son of Henry IV. By 1407 Owen Glendower was on the run and, as the rebel cause grew

weaker, he lost his strongholds at Aberystwyth and Harlech. Refusing to surrender, he went into hiding. How or where he died is uncertain, but he remains a Welsh hero.

OWEN, Robert (1771–1858), was born in Newtown, Wales, and went to London as a boy to work in a draper's shop. He moved to Manchester and at twenty had his own spinning mill; later he became sole manager and co-partner of New Lanark cotton mills in Scotland. The INDUSTRIAL REVOLUTION was in full swing and Owen became concerned about workers' long hours and low wages. He introduced many reforms, such as better housing, improved pay, a company shop and a school that was run on remarkably progressive lines. He had much to do with the passing of the Factory Act (1819), but his reforms and sceptical views on religion aroused opposition, which finally caused him to leave New Lanark in 1828. He had been in America earlier, in 1825, when he founded New Harmony, an ideal community in Indiana, but it failed, as did similar projects elsewhere. From 1829 to 1834 he helped to promote the co-operative movement and then tried to set up a great national trades union federation. Towards the end of his life most of his projects failed, he lost all his money and came to be looked on as a crank. He was in fact a reformer ahead of his time and most of his ideas have since been accepted. He has been called 'the father of British Socialism'.

Robert Owen and the New Lanark cotton mills

P

PALMERSTON, Viscount (Henry Temple, 1784–1865), is chiefly remembered as an aggressive Foreign Secretary, whose attitude to foreigners was typical of Victorian 'cocksureness'. In his long career he spent sixty years in Parliament, was in office for fifty years (mostly as Secretary at War and Foreign Secretary) and was Prime Minister for nearly ten (1855–8, 1859–65).

The following are some typical examples of his foreign policy: he played a leading part in securing the independence of Belgium (1830–31) and the election of Leopold of Coburg (Queen Victoria's uncle) as king; he bullied China in 1840 when its government wanted to prevent the import of opium from India, and he forced it to cede Hong Kong and to open five other ports to British shipping; in 1856, when China seized a British ship, the *Arrow*, on a charge of piracy, he extracted £4 million in compensation; earlier, in 1850, he threatened Greece with war when Don Pacifico, a Maltese Jew and therefore a British subject, claimed damages for the loss of property in a riot in Athens.

'Firebrand' Palmerston, as he was called, got into disfavour with Queen VICTORIA and the Prime Minister (Lord Russell) for not consulting them over foreign policy, and he was forced to resign when he ignored the views of the British government and warmly congratulated NAPOLEON III on his seizure of power in 1851. However, 'Pam' was soon back in office. Strongly anti-Russia, he brought the CRIMEAN WAR to a successful conclusion after he had become Prime Minister in 1855.

PAPACY means the office or position of the Pope, the Bishop of Rome. As head of the Roman Catholic Church, he played a leading role for centuries in the history of Western Europe. The first pope was St Peter, whose powers were handed on to his successors down to the present day. Since his time, there have been more than two hundred and fifty Popes, some of whom have had to contend with one or more rivals, known as 'anti-popes'.

Among outstanding popes who influenced the early course of history were GREGORY I, 'the Great', who sent St AUGUSTINE to England in 596, and Leo III, who crowned CHARLEMAGNE Holy Roman Emperor at Rome in 800. The placing of a crown on an emperor's or king's head may have led to the feeling that the crown was granted by the Pope or by one of his subordinates. At all events, there grew up a belief that the authority of the Pope was supreme over all men, including kings and princes.

This belief did not go unchallenged. WILLIAM I, a good son of the Church, would not allow the Pope to interfere in his newly won realm, but it was on the continent that a far greater struggle took place between Emperor and Pope (*see* HOLY ROMAN EMPIRE). The Emperor OTTO I actually deposed Pope John XII in 963, but the Papacy, weak and often corrupt, grew in strength until, in 1077, Pope Gregory VII humiliated the Emperor Henry IV, forcing him to wait barefoot in the snow at Canossa in order to acknowledge the Pope's authority. No matter that Henry had his revenge later; Canossa stood for papal superiority.

Masterful popes followed. There was Urban II, who proclaimed the First CRUSADE in 1095, bidding the princes of Western Europe put aside all other concerns and set out for the Holy Land. There was also Alexander III, whose orders even the formidable HENRY II of England had to obey, including doing penance for the murder of BECKET. Perhaps the most powerful of all the medieval Popes was INNOCENT III, who launched the Fourth Crusade in 1202, deposed the Emperor Otto IV and exacted obedience from the headstrong King JOHN. Somewhat later, Innocent IV (1243–54) made war on the

Opposite The Emperor JUSTINIAN with attendants, shown on a mosaic in the church of San Vitale which he built at Ravenna

MAXIMIANV

Emperor FREDERICK II and completely defeated him.

This papal supremacy lasted for a great many years, but during the 14th century, when popes lived in exile at Avignon in France for over sixty years and when later there were rival popes each claiming to be the true descendant of St Peter, men's faith began to weaken. Attitudes changed, the force of nationalism grew stronger and the RENAISSANCE affected ways of thinking, so that the Papacy had to meet its greatest challenge in the REFORMATION.

PARNELL, Charles Stewart (1846–91), entered Parliament in 1875 and at once devoted himself to securing IRISH HOME RULE. As president of the Land League, he worked for lower rents and an end to ownership of land by absentee landlords. So great was his hold on his countrymen that he was called 'the uncrowned king of Ireland', and after a spell in jail for, allegedly, inciting violence he arrived at an understanding with GLADSTONE, who saw the need for Home Rule. The murder of Lord Cavendish (Chief Secretary for Ireland) in Phoenix Park in 1882 upset their plans; a Home Rule Bill was rejected and in 1887 Parnell was charged by *The Times* with having been concerned in crimes committed by the Land League. The accusation was based on a forgery, but it weakened his influence and this was practically destroyed when the husband of Kitty O'Shea, with whom Parnell had been in love for several years, brought a divorce suit. In the moral climate of the time Parnell was ruined as leader of the Irish party, and he lost the support of Gladstone and the Roman Catholic Church. He married Kitty O'Shea in 1891 and died soon afterwards.

Opposite Lorenzo de MEDICI, the RENAISSANCE prince and patron, shown as one of the Three Kings in a painting done for his palace in Florence by Benozzo Gozzoli

Pope Boniface VIII (1294–1303), whose insistence on papal supremacy led to the decline of the papacy

PASTEUR, Louis (1822–95), a French chemist studying fermentation in beer and wine, discovered the existence of micro-organisms (germs) in the air and this led to heat treatment of beer and milk known as *pasteurization*. His work also led Joseph Lister, the British surgeon, to use antiseptics in surgery. Pasteur demonstrated the value of inoculation against chicken cholera, anthrax and rabies.

PATRICK, Saint (died *c.* 460), the son of Christian parents, was born somewhere near the Severn estuary, perhaps in south Wales, towards the end of the Roman occupation of Britain. Captured by Irish pirates when a boy, he was sold into slavery in Ulster, but after several years managed to escape and return home. He studied for the priesthood in Gaul and was eventually sent by the Pope to Ireland as a missionary. With his band of priests, he travelled the country, converting the Irish and organizing the building of churches. His *Confession*, in which he describes his mission, is the only authentic British document of the 5th century.

PEARL HARBOR, Hawaii, the main Pacific base of the US navy, was attacked by some three hundred Japanese carrier-based aircraft on 7 December 1941, when no state of war existed between the USA and Japan. Seven battleships out of eight were sunk or put out of action and many aircraft on nearby airfields were destroyed, but, by good fortune, a substantial part of the US fleet was at sea. 4,500 men were killed, wounded or missing. The attack, which took the American defences completely by surprise, was intended to give the Japanese the naval superiority which they required in order to launch their campaigns of conquest in south-east Asia. The United States declared war on Japan two days later and on Germany on 11 December.

PEARY, Robert Edwin (1856–1920), the American admiral and explorer, made eight Arctic voyages and on 6 April 1909 was the first man to reach the North Pole. Accompanied by his Negro servant Mathew Henson and four Eskimos, he made the 500-mile (800 km) journey from Cape Columbia in Grant Land, travelling by sledge so fast that at one stage he covered 130 miles (200 km) in two days without skis.

PEASANTS' REVOLT (1381) in England began in Kent, where a mob of peasants, led by Wat Tyler, marched to Maidstone to release John Ball, a popular preacher, from jail. The causes of the revolt lay in the general distress among the poor, discontent at the Statute of Labourers, which since the BLACK DEATH (1348) had forbidden workers to seek higher wages, and at attempts to enforce and even increase feudal burdens and dues. The peasants seized Rochester Castle, sacked Canterbury, sent messages to raise the men of Essex, Hertfordshire, Surrey and Norfolk and marched to London.

There they got out of hand, looted the City and murdered the Lord Treasurer and the Archbishop of Canterbury. At a parley, arranged at Smithfield in the presence of the young king RICHARD II, Walworth, the Lord Mayor, stabbed Tyler to death, whereupon the King's presence of mind prevented a massacre. On promises of pardons and reform, the leaderless peasants went home but, once dispersed, punishment was dealt out to many of those who had taken part in the rebellion. However, the landlords in general refrained from drastic measures and the villeins, though never set free by law, gradually gained their freedom, so that serfdom died out.

PEASANTS' WAR (1524–5) began in the Black Forest, Germany, where the peasants rose against the nobles, demanding, in Twelve Articles, various reforms including the right to elect their clergy, to hunt wild game, to fish and to be freed of villein service. In central Germany the peasants were particularly successful under the leadership of a fanatic named Münzer, until defeated by the forces of the Swabian League supported by LUTHER, whose own revolt had originally encouraged the uprising. At Frankenhausen the peasant army was routed, Münzer and thousands of the insurgents were killed and the revolts collapsed.

PEEL, Sir Robert (1788–1850), is chiefly remembered because, as Home Secretary, he founded the Metropolitan Police Force (whose constables were known as 'Bobbies' or 'Peelers') and, as Prime Minister, he secured the repeal of the CORN LAWS. A Tory, who was expected to protect farming by maintaining the Corn Laws, he nevertheless became convinced that British farming no longer needed protection and that a potato famine in Ireland made it essential to admit cheap foreign corn into the country. Hence, in 1846, supported by the Whigs and some of his own colleagues, and in the Lords by the Duke of WELLINGTON, Peel put through the repeal. He was immediately defeated in the Commons by manoeuvres carried out by DISRAELI and his friends. He resigned and never held office again.

PELOPONNESIAN WAR (431–404 BC), the great struggle between ATHENS and SPARTA, began when Athens interfered in a quarrel between Corinth and two of her colonies. Since Corinth was an ally of Sparta, no more excuse was needed for war. In fact, the real cause was the long-standing rivalry between the two states, Sparta, the dour land power, and Athens, the prosperous maritime state with its empire called the Delian League.

The war falls into three periods; for ten years each side ravaged the other's territory for part of the year; plague weakened the Athenians, PERICLES died, the tanner, Cleon, took over leadership, but the Spartans did not exploit their advantage, so both sides accepted the peace of Nicias (421). The

German peasants, flying their banner with a boot, take a nobleman prisoner during the Peasants' War.

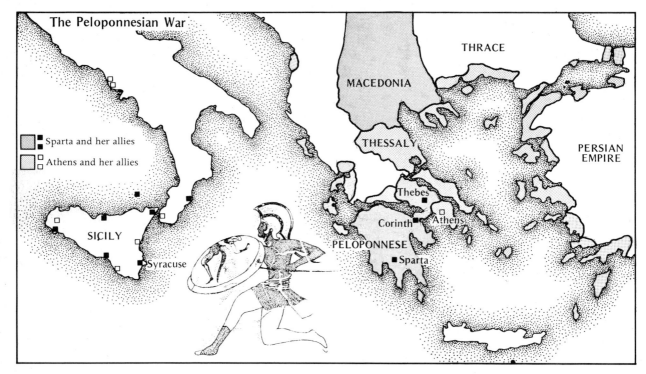

The Peloponnesian War

Sparta and her allies

Athens and her allies

THRACE

MACEDONIA

THESSALY

PERSIAN EMPIRE

SICILY

Syracuse

Thebes

Corinth   Athens

PELOPONNESE

Sparta

truce, violated more than once, lasted until 415, when the Athenians, anxious to expand their maritime power westwards, sent an expedition to Sicily to attack the Corinthian colony of Syracuse. At this, the Spartans sent help to the Syracusans, who trapped the Athenian fleet in their harbour, destroyed the ships and wiped out the expeditionary army (413 BC).

This disaster introduced the third stage of the war, for it encouraged the Athenian allies to desert and Persia to intervene on the side of Sparta, which was naturally delighted to have an ally with a fleet to tackle the Athenians at sea. Nevertheless, the final stage lasted surprisingly long, from 412 to 404, for the cautious Spartans never tried to capture Athens by assault and the Athenians, though torn by quarrels and misgovernment, achieved some successes. The end came in 405 BC when Lysander, the Spartan admiral, captured the entire Athenian fleet at Aegospotami and cut off the city's food supply. After a siege Athens surrendered in the following year.

PENINSULAR WAR (1808–14). When NAPO- LEON ousted the Portuguese royal family and put a French king on the throne of Spain, he provoked a rebellion that gave Britain the opportunity to land an army in Portugal and get to grips with the French. Sir Arthur Wellesley (later Duke of

Spanish guerrillas attack French soldiers during the Peninsular War

WELLINGTON) defeated General Junot at Vimiero in August 1808, causing Napoleon himself to come to Spain for a short time, during which Sir John Moore was killed at Corunna. In 1809 Wellesley drove Marshal Soult out of Portugal and won the battle of Talavera; that winter, he constructed a deep system of fortifications around Lisbon, called the 'Lines of Torres Vedras', which the French were unable to pierce. When their starving troops withdrew, Wellington (as he had become) followed them into Spain, where he won the bloody battle of Albuera (1811). Assisted by Spanish guerrillas, he next stormed Ciudad Rodrigo and Badajoz, beat 40,000 Frenchmen at Salamanca and entered Madrid. His army was not strong enough for him to remain there, so he returned to Portugal. However, in 1813 he was able to take the offensive after Napoleon had withdrawn troops from Spain to try to make up for the disastrous losses in Russia; this time he advanced right across Spain, beat the French at Vitoria and drove them across the border into France, where he finally defeated Soult at Toulouse (April 1814).

Wellington's success was largely due to his skill in organizing supplies in a barren land, to his use of troops in line to deal with the French attacks in column and to the help he received from local people and guerrillas, who hampered French communications and supplies.

PENN, William (1644–1718), son of Admiral Sir William Penn, became a Quaker in 1668 and was several times imprisoned for his preaching and writings. His father's death brought him a fortune and a claim against the Crown for £16,000, in payment for which he accepted from CHARLES II a grant of land in North America. There he founded, in 1681, the state of Pennsylvania for his persecuted fellow-Quakers. By 1683 some three thousand Quakers had gone out to settle there, a treaty of friendship was made with the Indians and Philadelphia was established as the capital. Penn returned to England in 1684 to continue his work to help Quakers; he was back in Pennsylvania in 1699–1701, then again in England where he suffered ill health and lost most of his money before he died in 1718.

William Penn's treaty with the Indians

The Penny Black (1840),
the world's first
adhesive postage
stamp

Pepys holding
a volume of
his diary

PENNY POST (1840) in Britain was devised by Rowland Hill, a reformer who wrote a pamphlet pointing out the advantages of a uniform rate for letters. The cost of mail up to that time had been heavy; it varied according to distance and had to be paid by the receiver of the letter. This caused letters to be sent through private hands or to be smuggled through Post Office channels. Hill proposed a charge of one penny a letter, no matter what the distance, the charge to be paid by the sender, who would buy a stamp. Parliament adopted his scheme in 1839 and it came into force in the following year. The result was a vast increase in mail, with great advantages to business firms, politicians and causes such as the anti-CORN LAW movement.

Other countries quickly followed Britain's lead, and official adhesive stamps were first issued in Brazil in 1843, in the USA in 1847, in Australia (New South Wales and Victoria) in 1850, in Canada in 1851 and in South Africa (Cape of Good Hope) in 1853. By 1870 stamps were being issued by 108 countries, and treaties had been arranged so that pre-paid letters could also be sent abroad. This led to the Universal Postal Union, founded in 1874.

PEPYS, Samuel (1633–1703), entered the public service through the influence of his cousin Montagu, later Earl of Sandwich. He went on the voyage that brought CHARLES II to the throne in 1660, the year in which he became Clerk 'of the Acts' to the Navy and began the celebrated diary which he was to keep in secret for nine years. Pepys rose steadily in reputation and wealth, for though he took advantage of money-making opportunities he worked hard, mastered his job and was a zealous reformer of abuses in the affairs of the navy. Although his period of office coincided with such episodes as the Medway Disaster during the DUTCH WAR, he carried out drastic and far-reaching reforms and was largely responsible for making naval service into a professional career for officers.

In 1679, at the time of the Popish Plot (see OATES), Pepys was accused of being a papist and imprisoned for a time in the Tower. He then had to watch the ruin of his work as the navy was completely run down for five years. However, before the end of Charles II's reign, he was back in favour and able to restore the strength and morale of the service. After the GLORIOUS REVOLUTION of 1688 he was again in trouble and was dismissed from his office. He went into retirement to devote himself to his splendid library, to the company of his many friends and the meetings of the Royal Society, of which he was twice President. Pepys's Diary is a fascinating record of life in London and at Court, and of the work, interests and weaknesses of a young man making his way in the world.

PERICLES (*c.* 490–429 BC), son of Xanthippus, came into prominence as a young man in ATHENS after the defeat of the Persians. A democrat, who was opposed to the aristocrat Cimon, he became the leading citizen of Athens for more than thirty years. With the aid of his friend Phidias, the sculptor, he carried through a policy of beautifying the city

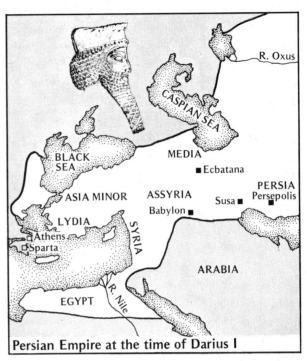

Persian Empire at the time of Darius I

with splendid buildings including the Parthenon. He supported the Thirty Years Peace with SPARTA (445), and when war did break out managed to persuade the Athenians to adopt defensive siege tactics on land and to rely principally on their sea power. In 430 plague broke out in Athens, carrying off Pericles's two sons and most of his friends; he himself died in the following year. During his leadership Athens reached the peak of her artistic glory and prosperity; he had many enemies jealous of his power, but he was a man of courage, dignity and honour.

PERSIAN EMPIRE. The Persians appear to have been nomads who moved from the steppelands of Asia to settle in the land known as Persia (modern Iran). There they displaced the Elamites and joined forces with their kinsmen, the Medes, to defeat the ASSYRIANS. In 553 BC the Persian CYRUS THE GREAT overthrew the Medes and moved his capital from Susa to Ecbatana. He then conquered Lydia, Asia Minor, BABYLON and Syria, in addition to extending his power eastwards. After his death in battle (529 BC), his son Cambyses conquered EGYPT, so that the Persian Empire stretched from the Nile to the borders of India.

DARIUS I (c. 522–485 BC), the next king, campaigned in Russia for a time and then invaded

Greece, but his army was defeated at MARATHON. His son Xerxes continued this war, but met defeat at Salamis and Plataea. A number of weak rulers followed Xerxes, so that the Empire declined until Artaxerxes III (359–338 BC) succeeded in restoring its power. However, shortly after his death and during the reign of Darius III Persia was attacked by ALEXANDER THE GREAT, whose victories at Issus and Arbela (331 BC) were so overwhelming that Persia became part of the Macedonian Empire.

PETAIN, Philippe (1856–1951), made his reputation as the general commanding the defence of Verdun in the FIRST WORLD WAR. Later he had to cover up the French army's weakness after the mutinies of 1917, and between the wars, as Marshal Pétain, he eagerly supported the defensive and ultimately useless Maginot Line that was to protect France from German attack. With the French collapse in 1940 the aged Marshal became head of government, accepting defeat and making little resistance to German demands. He directed the Vichy regime (which ruled unoccupied France) until virtually replaced by Pierre Laval. After the war he was condemned to death for treason, this being commuted to life imprisonment. He died in captivity, always protesting that he had done his best to serve France and defend her people.

PETER THE GREAT (Peter I, 1672–1725), son of the Tsar Alexi, led a wild and perilous youth, while his older sister Sophia ruled as regent, but he later drove her into a convent and ruled jointly with his idiot half-brother Ivan. He gave Ivan precedence but kept all the power to himself.

Peter's first concern was to organize the army on European lines and build a navy. Lacking a seaport, except Archangel, he attacked Turkey (*see* OTTOMAN EMPIRE) and captured Azov on the Black Sea (1696). Eager to find out about Western civilization, he set out with an embassy, visiting Prussia, Hanover and Amsterdam, where he worked as a shipwright. He spent three months in England, working on ships in the dockyard at Deptford, and returned to Russia taking with him about five hundred English engineers, surgeons, artificers, seamen and artillerymen. In Moscow he put down a revolt with barbaric cruelty, forced the nobles to adopt European dress and ideas, reorganized the Church and forced peasants into the army or into labour battalions.

In 1700 he declared war on Sweden and after many defeats from Charles XII his generals beat the Swedes at Poltava in 1709. Russia thereby gained a strip of the Baltic coast, where Peter built the port of St Petersburg (now Leningrad), a city that was the wonder of the world for its splendour and the speed with which it was built. Meanwhile, he again attacked Turkey, this time losing Azov, but by 1721 he had made peace with Sweden and had won three Caspian provinces from Persia.

He toured Europe a second time in company with the Tsarina Catherine, his former mistress, a slattern whose appalling manners shocked the Courts of Paris and Vienna as much as the behaviour of Peter himself, whom they regarded as an insane gorilla. He was certainly a monster of cruelty, a man with no understanding of justice or dignity, but when he died at the age of fifty-two he had made Russia into a modern power, having given her an army and a navy, factories, schools, industries, a system of government, an alphabet, a coinage, hospitals, museums, newspapers and a splendid capital.

PETERLOO was the popular name for a massacre which occurred on 16 August 1819 in St Peter's Fields, Manchester. A large crowd assembled to listen to a Radical speaker named Henry Hunt, when the local magistrate sent a force of yeomanry to arrest Hunt. The mounted soldiers tried to seize 'revolutionary' banners, panic broke out, swords were drawn and eleven persons were killed and hundreds injured. Peterloo was the worst instance of repression by the authorities during the period of unrest in England that followed the NAPOLEONIC WARS.

PHILIP AUGUSTUS (Philip II, 1165–1223), King of France, succeeded his father Louis VII in 1180. Throughout his reign his aim was to increase the power and territory of the French crown and he therefore supported HENRY II's sons against their father. In this way he hoped to weaken the English king's hold on his French possessions. Philip went on CRUSADE with RICHARD I, quarrelled with him and returned home to bargain with JOHN for Richard's territories; the latter's sudden return led to a long war that continued until Richard's death in 1199.

Philip then supported Arthur of Brittany against John; he conquered Normandy and by 1204 had recovered a great part of the Angevin empire. When John and his allies invaded France in an attempt to take them back, Philip won a decisive victory at Bouvines (1214). He spent the rest of his reign carrying out reforms in France and improving the city of Paris, where he built most of the cathedral of Notre Dame.

Philip II and his palace the Escurial

PHILIP II (1527–98), King of Spain (1556–98), only son of the Emperor CHARLES V, married Queen MARY I of England in 1554. He spent fourteen months in England, and after the abdication of his father in 1556 became the most powerful monarch in Europe. He defeated a league formed against him by Henry II of France and Pope Paul IV and it was during this war that the English lost Calais to France and Mary died. Failing to win the hand of her sister ELIZABETH, he married Elizabeth of France. His aim was to concentrate all power into his own hands and, as Catholic champion of Europe, to stamp out heresy.

He made much use of the INQUISITION in Spain,

but in the NETHERLANDS it produced rebellion and, finally, the independence of the United Provinces (*see* DUTCH REVOLT). In 1571 his half-brother Don John of Austria won the great victory of LEPANTO over the Turks, and in 1580 Philip annexed Portugal; these were the greatest triumphs of his reign, but in 1588 his ARMADA, sent against England, was destroyed, and in 1592 he failed to drive HENRY IV from France. Philip had much ability but he was an obstinate fanatic whose vast enterprises practically bankrupted Spain.

PHILLIP, Arthur (1738–1814), was an English naval captain when chosen to command the 'First Fleet', which transported the first batch of convicts to Australia. For many years, convicts had been transported to the American colonies, but after the War of Independence this was no longer possible. Hence, the choice of Australia. At Botany Bay Phillip decided the country was unsuitable, so he founded his settlement at Port Jackson (Sydney) on 26 January 1788. As Governor he had to contend with difficulties so great that the colony might well have perished but for his firm leadership and his compassionate attitude towards the convicts and their guards. He never doubted that New South Wales would prosper and when he returned to England in 1792 the colony was well-nigh self-supporting. He was promoted vice-admiral in 1809.

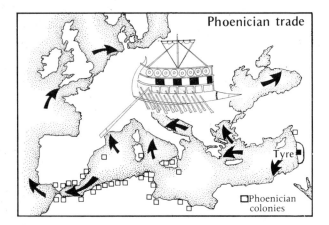

Phoenician trade

Tyre

☐Phoenician colonies

PHOENICIANS were a Semitic people originally inhabiting a narrow strip of land along the eastern Mediterranean between the sea and the mountains of Lebanon. Their chief cities were Tyre, Sidon, Byblos, Berytos (Beirut), Acre and Arvad. Probably the first navigators to sail out of sight of land, they traded throughout the Mediterranean and even beyond from about the 18th century BC. For their own industries they brought metals from Spain, Cyprus, Asia Minor and perhaps Britain, precious stones, perfumes and spices from Arabia and the East, linen from Egypt, ivory and ebony from Africa. They invented an alphabet of twenty-two signs.

The Phoenicians were under Egyptian domination until the 14th century BC; Byblos, a centre for the papyrus trade, was then the chief city. By about 1200 BC Tyre had become more important, and from this time on the Phoenicians founded colonies in North Africa (including CARTHAGE), Malta, Sicily, Sardinia, Spain, Crete, Rhodes and Cyprus. From 800 until 539 BC Phoenicia itself came under the Assyrians and Babylonians and, after them, the Persians, until it was merged into the empire of Alexander the Great.

PILGRIM FATHERS was the name given to the party of 102 Puritans or Separatists who on 6 September 1620 sailed to America in the MAYFLOWER. They had earlier fled from Scrooby in Nottingham-

shire to Leyden, Holland, but decided to seek a grant from the Virginia Company to found a colony where they would be free to worship in their own faith. The *Mayflower* carried the Pilgrims further north than had been intended and they first went ashore at Cape Cod in November. Deciding to abandon the idea of reaching Virginia, they searched for a suitable site for their settlement and landed at Plymouth on 11 December. They elected John Carver as their first governor and their leaders included William Bradford, William Brewster and Captain Standish. Huts and a Common House were built and the local Indians proved to be friendly, but lack of food and severe weather caused the deaths of nearly half the colony that first winter. In 1621 Carver died and William Bradford became governor; the ship *Fortune* arrived with stores and more colonists, so that the settlement survived and later became part of Massachusetts.

PILGRIMAGE OF GRACE (1536) was a rebellion in Yorkshire against HENRY VIII. Its leaders, Robert Aske, Lord Darcy and Sir John Constable, supported by the leading families in the north, demanded the restoration of the closed monasteries and punishment of the bishops who had supported King Henry's religious policy. On promise of a full pardon and a parliament at York, the rebels dispersed, whereupon the King had the leaders, including four abbots, arrested, tried for treason and executed. In this way Henry evaded what might have been a serious situation, and the effect of the Pilgrimage (so called because the rebels marched with banners proclaiming their religious faith) was to speed up the dissolution of the larger monasteries. Fear of accusations of treason caused practically all the abbots to surrender their property to the King.

PITT, William (1759–1806), known as Pitt the Younger to distinguish him from his father, Pitt the Elder, Earl of CHATHAM, entered Parliament at the age of twenty-two, when Lord North's government was tottering after the disasters of the AMERICAN WAR OF INDEPENDENCE. Pitt so distinguished himself in debate that Shelburne made him Chancellor of the Exchequer in 1782. This government soon fell, but the Fox-North coalition which followed was unpopular and King GEORGE III found an excuse to dismiss them and appoint Pitt to the office of First Lord of the Treasury, the equivalent of Prime Minister. He was only twenty-four and his position appeared to be hopeless; yet he withstood all the attempts to drive him from office, won the approval of the City and the admiration of the country, so that in the Election of 1784 he obtained support that kept him in power almost continuously for over twenty years.

Pitt used the years of peace to restore England's reputation and finances. A believer in Adam Smith's theory of free trade, he reduced duties on tea, spirits, tobacco and other imports, introduced various taxes on luxuries to compensate the Exchequer, put through a trade treaty with France, reformed the Treasury accounting system and drastically reduced government extravagance and graft. His India Act (1784) transferred political affairs from the EAST INDIA COMPANY to the government, while his Canada Act (1791) avoided racial dispute by dividing the country into Upper Canada (British) and Lower Canada (French). In Europe he ended England's isolation and made his views felt by foreign governments.

Pitt was a man of peace, who did not relish the challenge of war, as his father did. When war came with France in 1793 his policy to subsidize continental allies was frequently to fail, but his pre-war economies had not affected the navy, so that the victories of Jervis, Duncan and NELSON enabled Britain to continue the contest with NAPOLEON. Fear of revolutionary action caused him to bring in harsh measures, including the COMBINATION ACTS, but he also had the courage to introduce income tax to help pay for the war.

In hope of solving the problem of Ireland, Pitt decided to put through a union of the two parliaments, promising this would be followed by Catholic Emancipation, but when the King refused to agree he felt compelled to resign in 1801. He resumed office in 1804 and put together yet another coalition of European powers, only to learn that Napoleon had smashed it to pieces at Austerlitz (1805). Men said 'the Austerlitz look' never left his face and he died a few months later at the age of forty-six, murmuring 'Oh my country! How I leave my country!'. Pitt, a lonely man who never married, devoted his life to politics; he can be criticized for his reluctance to pursue parliamentary reform and abolition of SLAVERY, but he achieved much in peace, rather less in war and he won and retained the trust of his countrymen.

PIZARRO, Francisco (c. 1478–1541), the conquerer of Peru, was born in Spain and made his way to the New World as a young man. He accompanied BALBOA in discovering the Pacific and settled in Panama, where he made a partnership with a soldier named Almagro. Together they explored southwards down the west coast of South America, where they obtained information about the INCA Empire of Peru. In 1528 Pizarro returned to Spain to obtain CHARLES V's commission to conquer the unknown kingdom, of which he was to be governor and captain-general.

He returned to Panama and departed for Peru at the end of 1530 with his brothers and 180 men, leaving Almagro to follow with reinforcements. The adventurers reached Tumbez in north Peru and in 1532 arrived in Cajamarca, where they were well

received by the Inca ruler Atahualpa. In February 1533, after Almagro had arrived, Atahualpa was seized, held to ransom and murdered. Pizarro then sacked Cuzco and, helped by divisions among the Incas, conquered all of Peru by 1535. While Almagro went off to Chile, Pizarro founded Lima and other cities, but the Incas rebelled and laid siege to Cuzco, which was only relieved by Almagro back from Chile. A quarrel broke out over his inferior share of the spoils and, after a battle between the two forces, Almagro was executed in 1538. Pizarro then ruled the country until 1541, when Almagro's son and his supporters attacked his house in Lima and murdered the old conqueror.

Geoffrey of Anjou, founder of the Plantagenet dynasty

PLANTAGENETS were members of the royal Angevin house who occupied the English throne from 1154 to 1399. The name is said to have been derived from the custom of Geoffrey of Anjou, father of HENRY II, wearing a sprig of broom (whose Latin name is *planta genista*) in his cap. Thus Henry II was the first of the Plantagenets, followed by RICHARD I, JOHN and HENRY III. These are called the earlier Plantagenet kings, while the later ones were EDWARD I, EDWARD II, EDWARD III and RICHARD II. The Houses of York and Lancaster which succeeded can be considered a continuation of the Plantagenet line, in that HENRY IV was a descendant of Edward III.

PROHIBITION, a ban on all alcoholic drink, came into force by law in the United States on 17 January 1920. It had long been urged by Temperance organizations, such as the Anti-Saloon League and the Women's Christian Temperance Union, but they could have had no idea of the effect of the ban. Evading the law against drink became highly popular among ordinary citizens and big business for gangsters such as Al Capone, who controlled illegal breweries and bars known as 'speakeasies'. Police, politicians and even judges were drawn into the network of corruption; drunkenness increased, gang battles took place and it was estimated that two hundred civilians and five hundred Prohibition agents were killed during the Prohibition era. It came to an end in December 1933 when President F. D. ROOSEVELT announced the repeal of the disastrous law.

PTOLEMY was the name of fourteen kings of EGYPT who reigned from 305 to 30 BC. The founder of the dynasty, Ptolemy I, also called Soter, was a Macedonian soldier, a friend of ALEXANDER THE GREAT, at whose death in 323 he received Egypt as his share of the conquests. He declared himself king in 305 and during his reign he encouraged Greeks to settle in Egypt, developed the city of Alexandria as the new capital and started the museum and library there.

Ptolemy II, who built the great lighthouse called the Pharos, and Ptolemy III were both energetic rulers, but from the time of Ptolemy IV (221–203) there was a marked decline in the character of the kings and in the fortunes of Egypt. The last of the line, Ptolemy XIV, was Caesarion, the son of CLEOPATRA and JULIUS CAESAR; he was murdered by Octavian (AUGUSTUS) in 30 BC.

Pym with John Hampden. Both were leading Parliamentarians who opposed Charles I.

PYM, John (1584–1643), entered Parliament in 1614, and from 1625 sat as Member for Tavistock, having by this time become a leader of the Country Party which opposed the policies of CHARLES I. He supported the Petition of Right, took the leading part in impeaching Strafford and LAUD and was one of the Five Members whom Charles went to the House to arrest. As the CIVIL WAR drew near, he used his influence to keep London in a ferment and constantly to put Parliament's point of view to the citizens. In the early stages of the war, he held the Parliamentary cause together by his zeal in organizing troops and raising money and supplies. Known as 'King Pym' to his enemies, he died in London in 1643.

PYRAMIDS were the first and probably the greatest stone buildings in the world. About eighty of them were erected in ancient EGYPT during the period of the Old and Middle Kingdoms (3rd to 12th dynasties, *c.* 2700–1786 BC). The first of these tombs of the kings was the step pyramid at Sakkara, built for King Zoser by IMHOTEP.

Just west of modern Cairo at Gizeh are the three great pyramids of Cheops (or Khufu), Chephren and

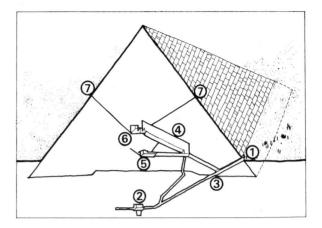

Diagram of the interior of the Great Pyramid of Cheops: 1 entrance; 2 subterranean burial chamber; 3 passage leading to this chamber; 4 grand gallery; 5 small burial chamber, the 'Queen's Chamber'; 6 large burial chamber, the 'King's Chamber'; 7 ventilation shafts

Men-kau-Ra (or Mykerinos). The largest of these, the Great Pyramid of Cheops, covers an area of over 13 acres (52,500 m²), was 481 feet (146 metres) high and was constructed of over two million huge blocks of limestone. When completed, the pyramids were faced with fine polished limestone from Tura across the Nile; this facing, which has now almost entirely vanished, caused the pyramids to gleam in the sun, pointing to the sky across which the dead king would make his last journey.

Pyramids were built on the edge of the desert, within reach of the flood waters during the inundation season; the dead king's body was conveyed by boat to a chapel, and from there, it was drawn up a quarter-mile-long (400 m) stone causeway, roofed over and walled, to the mortuary temple on the east side of the pyramid. Here it underwent ceremonies of purification and was finally placed in a sarcophagus or stone coffin in a chamber situated beneath or inside the pyramid.

Despite the utmost secrecy and precautions, the pyramid tombs were always robbed of the treasures placed beside the king. Smaller pyramids were sometimes built for royal wives and children, but nobles were entombed in flat-topped buildings called mastabas. Pyramid building ceased as the Middle Kingdom came to an end. Then, after a period of anarchy, the New Kingdom was established (1567 BC) and the kings abandoned the construction of pyramids for tombs dug in the rocks.

Q

QUISLING, Vidkim Abraham (1887–1945), a Norwegian politician, whose name has come to mean a traitor, had founded a Fascist party in Norway before the SECOND WORLD WAR. When the Germans invaded his country in April 1940, he declared himself Prime Minister and though he had only a small following he remained the leader of those who were ready to collaborate with the Germans. After the war he was tried for treason and shot.

R

RAILWAYS in Britain had their beginnings in tracks with wooden rails along which horse-drawn carts carried coal from the pits to ports and to river or canal banks. By about 1775 there were many of these tracks in England, especially in the mining districts of the north-east and south Wales. Iron rails were introduced, and in 1804 Richard Trevithick's steam locomotive came into use briefly on a track in south Wales. Opposition from workers who tended the horses caused the owners to give up locomotives, but at Wylam Colliery, near Newcastle, William Hedley and Timothy Hackworth built *Puffing Billy* (1813) and *Wylam Dilly*, two locomotives which pulled coal trucks for many years. In the following year George STEPHENSON, a Wylam man, built a locomotive called *Blücher*, and the usefulness of this engine and its successors led to the building of the world's first public railway, the Stockton and Darlington Railway, which opened on 27 September 1825.

In 1829 the Rainhill Trials were held to discover the best locomotive for use on the projected Liverpool and Manchester Railway, and in a series of

Passenger and freight trains on the Liverpool and Manchester railway at the time of its opening

test-runs Stephenson's *Rocket* proved itself the winner. The Liverpool and Manchester Railway opened in 1830, and after this private companies were formed to build railways throughout the country. At astonishing speed, tracks, stations, tunnels, viaducts and cuttings were built by gangs of 'navvies', so that between 1840 and 1850 over 5,000 miles (8,000 km) of railway were opened, and the boom continued almost unabated for the next quarter century. George Stephenson and his son Robert became the leading designers of railways, and the whole country, including Scotland and Ireland, became linked by a network of tracks. Contrary to expectations, passenger traffic proved to be more lucrative than goods, and in 1844 Parliament prescribed third-class travel at a penny a mile, thereby giving the public a mobility it had never known before. Cheap transport was an important factor in the development of the INDUSTRIAL REVOLUTION.

Britain's lead in railway building was soon followed by France and Austria, who opened their first lines in 1828, and then by Belgium, Germany, Russia, Italy and Holland in the succeeding decade. In Eastern Europe systems were developed mainly from about 1860, but the Trans-Siberian line was not completed until the end of the century.

In the USA railway building started at an early date in the northern states, and there were moves to construct a transcontinental railroad in the 1840s, but this had to wait until after the Civil War. When the Union Pacific Railroad met the Central Pacific line in Utah on 10 May 1869, New York was linked directly with San Francisco, 3,000 miles (4,800 km) away. In Canada, after many delays, the first transcontinental railroad, the Canadian Pacific Railway, was completed in 1885.

Australia's first public railway opened in 1854 but, although a number of lines were built to link the goldfields, progress was rather slow, so that Melbourne and Sydney were not linked until 1883. Interstate communication was hampered by the fact that New South Wales built a track with the standard gauge of 4 ft 8½ ins (143 cm) whereas Victoria and parts of South Australia used broad gauge of 5 ft 3 ins (160 cm) with the remaining states using 3 ft 6 ins (105 cm). The Trans-Australian Railway between Perth and Adelaide was completed in 1917 and by 1970 the same train could travel on a common gauge from Sydney to Perth.

RALEIGH, Sir Walter (*c.* 1552–1618), son of a Devonshire landowner and half-brother to Sir Humphrey GILBERT, went to Oxford University, fought as a volunteer with the HUGUENOT forces and also in the Netherlands and Ireland. He joined Gilbert in an expedition to the Azores and West Indies, before attracting Queen ELIZABETH's favour at Court. She knighted him in 1584 and later made him her Captain of the Guard, but never gave him an important position in the kingdom. From 1583 to 1589 he sent out six expeditions to plant a colony in America; later he sent others, the last in 1603, but all were failures, resulting only in the introduction of tobacco and potatoes into England and Ireland. One of his colonies he named Virginia in honour of the Queen. In 1595 he himself went in search of El Dorado, a fabulously wealthy city, also called Manoa, supposed to lie up the Orinoco River in Central America. The expedition failed, and on his return Raleigh took part in Essex's attack on Cadiz, though he later quarrelled bitterly with Essex.

After JAMES I came to the throne, Raleigh's enemies accused him of plotting against the King, and after an unjust trial he was found guilty of treason, condemned to death and then reprieved. During his imprisonment in the Tower, from 1603 to 1616, he wrote his *History of the World* and was released on his promise to find El Dorado and bring back its treasures to the King. He set sail from Plymouth in 1617, but the expedition was a disastrous failure, Raleigh's son being killed in a fight with the Spaniards at a time when James I was hoping to marry his son to a Spanish princess. Thus, when Raleigh came home, the sentence of execution was carried out and he was beheaded on 29 October 1618.

He was clever, witty and brave; a poet and writer whose sharp tongue made him enemies; he coveted power and success, but Elizabeth, much as she liked his company, did not trust his judgement. His ideas on colonies were ahead of his time, for he held that they would absorb surplus population, reduce unemployment and stimulate trade.

RAMESES II, King of Ancient EGYPT of the 19th Dynasty, reigned from about 1292 to 1225 BC. He was the son of Seti I, and early in his reign led a campaign against the HITTITES, which resulted in the great battle of Kadesh, an indecisive engagement which Rameses claimed as a glorious victory. In actual fact hostilities continued for years, until Rameses concluded a treaty with the Hittite king and married one of his daughters.

Apart from this war, a campaign in Nubia and a clash with sea-raiders in the Delta, Rameses's long reign of over sixty years was unusually peaceful, so that he was able to devote much of Egypt's wealth to building and to glorifying his own name. Among the many temples he built were the Osiris temple at Abydos, his father's mortuary temple at Luxor, the colonnaded hall at Karnak and the rock temple at Abu Simbel with the four colossal figures of himself. Statues of Rameses II have been found throughout Egypt and he did not scruple to have the names of earlier kings chiselled from their monuments and his own name put in place.

RAMESES III, King of EGYPT (*c.* 1198–1167 BC) of the 20th Dynasty, was the last great king of the New Kingdom. He led three campaigns against the Libyans and the so-called Peoples of the Sea, gaining brilliant victories and saving the country from invasion. He encouraged trade and built many temples and monuments, but there appears to have been internal trouble towards the end of his reign. Egypt, weakened by the costs of war, became less prosperous and under the remaining kings of the

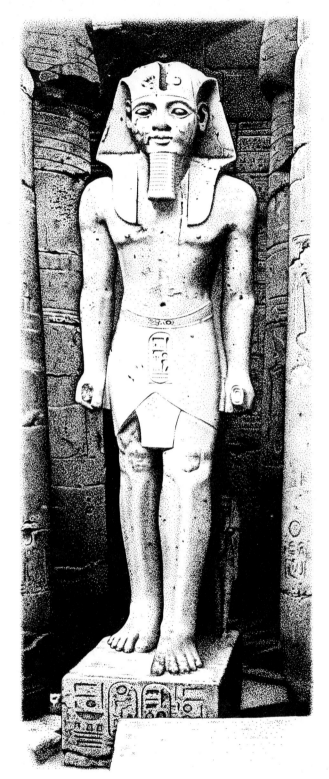

Colossal statue of Rameses II in the court of the king at the temple of Luxor

Prisoners of the Peoples of the Sea captured by the
army of Rameses III

20th Dynasty, suffered a marked decline, as power
fell into the hands of the priests of Amen.

RASPUTIN, Gregory (1871–1916), played a
sinister role in the last years of imperial Russia. Born
a Siberian peasant, his reputation as a mystic and
hypnotist brought him to the Court in 1905, where
he apparently saved the life of the Crown Prince, a
sufferer from haemophilia. Rasputin thereby gained
enormous influence over the Tsarina Alexandra,
who was unaffected by his coarse manners, drunkenness and scandalous behaviour. During the First
World War, when the Tsar NICHOLAS II was at the

front, Rasputin practically ruled Russia, dismissing
ministers as he pleased, including the Prime
Minister himself. Eventually he was murdered at
the Yussupov Palace by a party of nobles, including
members of the royal house.

RED CROSS, the organization for the relief of
suffering, was inspired by Henri Dunant, a Swiss
banker, who was moved by the suffering of the
wounded at the battle of Solferino (in North Italy,
where in 1859 a French and Piedmontese army
defeated the Austrians). Dunant's pleading resulted
in an international conference being held at Geneva
in 1864 when twenty-six nations signed the first
Geneva Convention to care for the wounded. A red
cross on a white ground was adopted as an emblem
of neutrality. Red Cross societies exist in most
countries of the world and the headquarters of the
international Red Cross Committee is in Geneva.

REFORMATION is the name given to the
religious revolution which took place in the
Western Church during the 16th century, when
much of northern Europe broke away from the

A Calvinist preacher addressing the Huguenot
congregation in the Temple at Lyons in France

authority of the Pope and the teachings of the
Roman Catholic Church (see PAPACY).

Causes of the Reformation included disgust at the
worldliness and wealth of many of the clergy, while
the RENAISSANCE led to a critical attitude towards
religion, and the invention of printing enabled reformers to spread propaganda. They stressed that
the Church had fallen away from the purity of its
early teachings and they relied on the authority of
the Bible for guidance. Many princes had long
resented papal taxation, and the greed of laymen
played a large part in the overthrow of the Catholic
Church, since kings and nobles seized the opportunity to enrich themselves by acquiring the
possessions of the Church.

There had been early movements of protest, such
as the preachings of the LOLLARDS in England in
the 14th and 15th centuries, but the Reformation is
generally regarded as having started in Germany,
where in 1517 LUTHER nailed to the church doors
at Wittenberg his attack on the sale of indulgences.
He found wide support and his opinions spread
rapidly through Germany, but the Catholic counter-
attack eventually led to the THIRTY YEARS WAR
(1618–48). At the end of this bitter struggle a com-

promise was reached, and Protestantism became the
official religion in many German states.

Lutheranism spread to the Scandinavian kingdoms of Denmark, Norway and Sweden, while in
Switzerland the Reformation made progress under
Zwingli, whose work was carried on by the Frenchman John CALVIN. Geneva became the centre for
Calvinist propaganda and a place of refuge for
exiled Protestants.

In England the annulment of HENRY VIII's
marriage to Catherine of Aragon brought about the
break with Rome, but Henry, while claiming to be
Head of the English Church, had no sympathy with
the reformers. However, under EDWARD VI the
governments of Somerset and NORTHUMBERLAND
supported the extreme Protestants. In MARY I's
reign the Church returned to obedience to the Pope,
but ELIZABETH's settlement gave supremacy back
to the monarch and established as the state religion
a Protestantism that was midway between the ideas
of Henry VIII and of the extremists of Edward VI's
reign. The Scottish Reformation was largely the
work of John KNOX whose version of Calvinism
took root as the Presbyterian religion.

The DUTCH REVOLT against Spain ended in the
Netherlands adopting Calvinism, but the Reformation had less success in France, where the HUGUE-
NOTS suffered persecution and became engaged in
wars of religion. They remained a minority, but by
the Edict of Nantes (1598) were allowed to worship
in accordance with the reformed faith.

RENAISSANCE, or Revival of Learning, was a
great movement in literature, art, architecture,
science and human behaviour that began in Italy in
the 14th century, reached its peak in the 15th
century and spread to the rest of Europe. It marks
the end of the Middle Ages and the beginning of
modern Europe.

During the Middle Ages the works of many Latin
and Greek writers were unknown, until the early
Renaissance scholars began to study and copy
manuscripts which had been neglected for centuries. All educated people could read Latin, but
Greek was little known; however, Greek scholars
came to Italy in the 15th century and others fled
there, bringing manuscripts with them, when the
TURKS captured Constantinople in 1453.

But the Renaissance was much more than the
rediscovery of classical literature and architecture.

It represented an upsurge of creative energy, of new ideas and new freedoms of thought in contrast to the fixed teachings of the Church and medieval philosophers. Men became interested in the world about them, in human nature (some writers are known as 'humanists'), in science, art and religion. The Renaissance spirit of enquiry and criticism was one of the underlying causes of the REFORMATION.

Italian cities such as FLORENCE, Milan, Padua and Venice were rich, and city life was freer and more civilized than in countries which were still mainly rural. Moreover, Italy had remained in closer touch with Greek and Roman ideas than the rest of Europe, and the Renaissance was aided by several popes who were more interested in worldly than spiritual matters. For these reasons, the New Learning first flowered in Italy; scholars translated classical works, libraries and universities were founded, Petrarch and Boccaccio in the 14th century wrote their poetry, marvellous churches and buildings were erected, and from the late 15th century artists like Leonardo, Michelangelo, Raphael, Titian and many others painted their immortal pictures. There were also gifted men like Brunelleschi, the architect, and Donatello, the sculptor. Often an artist would excel in several branches of art and knowledge; Leonardo, the great all-rounder, excelled as a painter, philosopher, athlete, inventor, engineer and naturalist.

The Renaissance spread northwards. Holland and England produced the Humanists, ERASMUS, Linacre, Colet and MORE; in France there was the poet Ronsard and the writers Rabelais and Montaigne, while in Spain Cervantes wrote *Don Quixote* (1605–15). The outstanding Renaissance artists of Flanders and Germany were the Van Eycks, the Breughels, Dürer and Holbein – who took his skill to England, where HENRY VIII saw himself as a prince of many talents and where Renaissance literature flowered in the poems of Sidney and Spenser and, above all, in the plays of Shakespeare. It was not until the 17th century that Inigo Jones brought classical architecture to England.

Every branch of science was developed, biology, chemistry, physics and astronomy – in which COPERNICUS, Keppler and GALILEO put forward new ideas – while medicine made progress that included HARVEY's discovery of the circulation of the blood.

The urge to acquire knowledge and wealth caused men to set out on voyages of exploration, principally from Spain and Portugal and, later, from England and France. Thus the Renaissance widened man's horizons in every direction, producing ideas and achievements which profoundly affected his political, religious and cultural life.

REVERE, Paul (1735–1818), the American hero whose exploit is celebrated in a poem by Longfellow, was born in Boston, son of Apollos Rivoire, a silversmith who had come to America from Guernsey. Paul served as a lieutenant of artillery (1756) and later became an ardent opponent of British authority. He took part in the BOSTON TEA PARTY in 1773 and joined the Boston Anti-British Society, whose members kept watch on the British troops at the time when the patriots were accumulating warlike stores at Concord. On 18 April 1775 800 British soldiers set out from Boston after dark, but they were seen and from his post in the church steeple Revere flashed warning lantern signals. Then he mounted his horse and rode hard across country to Lexington, warning minutemen as he went and rousing the patriot leaders Samuel Adams and John Hancock from their beds.

During the war Revere became lieutenant-colonel of artillery, and as an expert craftsman he designed the first paper money for Congress and made the first seals for Massachussetts and the united colonies. He also went to Philadelphia to make gunpowder for the war effort. Later he discovered a method of rolling sheet copper and founded the Revere Copper Company, but his greatest talent was as a silversmith, whose work fetches fabulous prices today.

Street barricades put up in Berlin during the
1848 Revolution

REVOLUTIONS OF 1848 took place in several
European countries, including France, Germany,
Austria, Hungary and Italy. The first uprising
occurred in France, where the government of Louis
Philippe and Guizot was unpopular. A demand for
social and electoral reform erupted into a revolution
in February that resulted in Louis Philippe's abdication. A republic was proclaimed, and in December
Louis Napoleon (later NAPOLEON III) was elected
president of a moderate, even conservative, government. The news of Louis Philippe's flight had
dramatic effects in Europe. Rulers of many German
states, including Prussia, hurriedly granted constitutions and reforms, but the Liberals, who
thought they had won unity and the right to a
national parliament, were speedily disappointed.
Frederick William of Prussia recovered his nerve
and the revolutionary movement collapsed.

Meanwhile, in the Austrian empire an uprising
in Vienna forced the old autocrat Metternich to
resign, while the Emperor Ferdinand lost all
authority and withdrew to Innsbruck. In Hungary
the Magyars (one of several peoples inhabiting that
country), led by Kossuth, rose against the Austrians; the Croats and Serbs rose against the Magyars
and the Czechs took up arms in their own fight for
independence. However, Prince Schwarzenberg
and the new Emperor FRANCIS JOSEPH regained

control; revolution in Vienna was crushed, and
though the Hungarians fought on until 1849 they
were defeated when the Tsar sent help to Austria.
The Magyars received brutal punishment from the
Austrian general Haynau.

In Italy 1848 seemed to bring liberty from
oppression. Rulers, frightened by the strength of
popular feeling, granted constitutions – Ferdinand
II in Naples, the Archduke of Tuscany, Charles
Albert in Piedmont and Pope Pius IX in the Papal
States. In Milan the people fought their Austrian
rulers, rebels seized control in Venice and Pius IX
fled from Rome, where a republic was declared with
MAZZINI and GARIBALDI in the forefront. But the
revolution soon faded; Ferdinand II bombarded his
own subjects; Tuscany's new constitution was cancelled; Piedmont's army met defeat and the
Austrians returned to Milan and Venice. French
troops restored the Pope in Rome, where Garibaldi
and Mazzini fled into exile. Thus the revolutions of
1848 were defeated everywhere, and the hopes of
the Liberals were completely frustrated.

RHODES, Cecil (1853–1902), was born at Bishop's
Stortford, England, and, for his health, went out to
South Africa, where he made a fortune in the
Kimberley diamond fields and in gold. He returned
to England to take a degree at Oxford University
and later entered the Cape House Assembly. In 1890
he became Prime Minister of Cape Colony, having
already secured Bechuanaland as a British protectorate. He obtained a charter for the British South

Africa Company, whose territory came to be called Rhodesia, and his aim was to establish a federated South Africa under British rule, with a railway linking British territories 'from Cape Town to Cairo'. When Kruger's Transvaal appeared to be an obstacle to his plans, he encouraged a plot to overthrow the Republic, but the failure of the Jameson Raid (1896) led to his resignation as Prime Minister. He died at Cape Town just before the end of the BOER WAR. Rhodes was a man of great ability and energy, but he was an imperialist who gave little thought to the condition of Africans in their own country. By his will he established scholarships at Oxford for students of the British Empire, USA and Germany.

Richard I and the crusader castle of Krak in Syria

RICHARD I (1157–99), King of England (1189–99), son of HENRY II, became ruler of Aquitaine as a young man and joined his brothers in rebellion against their father. In 1189 he became king of England and set out in the following year on the Third CRUSADE, journeying via Sicily and Cyprus, where he conquered the island and married Berengaria of Navarre. He was principally responsible for the capture of Acre in 1191, but he quarrelled with PHILIP AUGUSTUS of France, who returned home leaving Richard with insufficient strength to capture Jerusalem. Having made a truce with SALADIN, Richard left for England, but fell into the hands of his enemy, the Archduke of Austria. He was kept prisoner by the Emperor Henry VI until his subjects had raised a huge ransom. Having forgiven his treacherous brother JOHN, he spent the rest of his reign warring against Philip in France. He was killed when besieging the castle of Chaluz. Known as Coeur de Lion or the Lionheart, Richard was undoubtedly a brave and capable fighting-

man, but he cared for England only as a source of money for his wars and spent less than a year there during his entire reign.

RICHARD II (1367–1400), King of England (1377–99), was the son of EDWARD THE BLACK PRINCE and succeeded his grandfather EDWARD III in 1377. His uncle, JOHN OF GAUNT, ruled the kingdom for him and in 1381, as a boy of fourteen, Richard conducted himself bravely during the PEASANTS' REVOLT, when he calmed the peasants after the murder of Wat Tyler. When he grew up, he surrounded himself with favourites and behaved so irresponsibly that a party of nobles, the Lords Appellant, took over the government. A year later, in 1389, Richard seized control and ruled well for eight years, making peace with France and restoring order in Ireland.

After the death of his wife, Anne of Bohemia, he married Isabella of France in 1396, whereupon his character appeared to change and he began to rule like a tyrant. Having overthrown Parliament and taken revenge on the nobles who had earlier humiliated him, he banished his cousin, Bolingbroke, and seized the estates of Bolingbroke's father, John of Gaunt. He then departed to Ireland and in his absence Bolingbroke returned, ostensibly to claim the family lands, but soon to put himself at the head of a rebellion. Deserted by everyone, Richard was taken prisoner; he resigned the crown, which Parliament awarded to Bolingbroke as HENRY IV. Richard's end was mysterious but he was almost certainly murdered in Pontefract Castle.

RICHARD III (1452–85), King of England (1483–5), was the younger brother of EDWARD IV and supported him loyally during the later stages of the Wars of the ROSES. During Edward's reign he proved himself, as Duke of Gloucester, to be brave, charming and remarkably capable. On the sudden death of his brother in 1483, he became Protector of the kingdom and guardian of his young nephew, EDWARD V. He speedily arrested and executed the relatives and supporters of the boy's mother, Queen Elizabeth Woodville, and induced her to hand over her younger son, the little Duke of York, who was lodged in the Tower with his brother. In June Richard assumed the crown and the two boys were never seen again.

When Henry Tudor (later HENRY VII), the

Lancastrian claimant to the throne, landed in Wales in 1485, support for Richard dwindled and at the battle of Bosworth he was defeated owing to the treachery of Sir William Stanley, who changed sides. Richard died fighting with furious courage. He remains a controversial figure, for many refuse to accept the picture of him as 'Crookback', the murderous villain portrayed by Shakespeare, and they declare that the Tudors conspired to give him this evil reputation. On the other hand, the two princes *did* vanish and the man who stood to gain by their disappearance was their uncle Richard III.

RICHELIEU, Cardinal (1585–1642), was born into a noble but impoverished family in France. He entered the Church and was a bishop by the age of twenty-two and a cardinal at thirty-seven. Winning a place at the Court of the weakling Louis XIII, Richelieu rose to become Minister of State, the equivalent of Prime Minister, and his lifelong policy was to concentrate all power and authority into the hands of the King and therefore of himself. Absolute ruler of France, he never once summoned the states-general (parliament), but concentrated on curbing the power of the nobles (who hated him), on crushing every attempt to depose him and on breaking the political power of the HUGUENOTS. He captured their great stronghold of La Rochelle in 1628.

Richelieu's foreign policy was to advance French influence at the expense of Austria and Spain. Hence during the THIRTY YEARS WAR he helped Austria's enemies, including the Protestants, and declared war on Spain. He himself took the field to defeat the Spanish army that had invaded northern France.

During his career Richelieu restored the power of the French monarchy and made France a leading nation in Europe. In doing so he taxed the people heavily and denied them any form of constitutional government. He believed that his policy was in the best interests of France and asked nothing for himself, except the power to rule.

ROBERT BRUCE (Robert I, 1274–1329), King of Scotland (1306–29), was grandson of the Robert Bruce who was one of the claimants to the Scottish throne when King EDWARD I decided in favour of John Balliol (1292). He did homage to Edward I, and despite supporting WALLACE for a time fought on the English side during the siege of Stirling. However, he made a secret pact with Lamberton, Bishop of St Andrews, to defeat Edward's plans of conquest, and the turning-point in his career came in 1306 when he murdered Red Comyn, a claimant to the Scottish throne. Bruce gathered his supporters and had himself crowned King of Scotland at Scone.

Defeated by the English, he was forced to take refuge in the Highlands, eluding his pursuers with great fortitude and eventually commanding a guerrilla force, which after the death of Edward I in 1307 grew into the army with which he recovered all the great castles except Stirling. This stronghold fell after his total defeat of the English at BANNOCKBURN in 1314.

After his victory he campaigned in Ireland with his brother Edward and then invaded England to capture Berwick (1318). He continued to attack the northern counties until hostilities were ended in EDWARD III's reign by the Treaty of Northampton (1328), which recognized him as 'Robert King of Scots'. He died of leprosy, contracted during his campaigns, and was succeeded by his son David II.

Robert Bruce was undoubtedly a military genius and a capable ruler with the gift of inspiring the devotion of his people.

ROBESPIERRE, Maximilien (1758–94), the French revolutionary leader, made a reputation when a deputy in the National Assembly of 1789 as a fanatical champion of the mob and furious opponent of moderation. His impassioned speeches made him a popular hero and, as a leading member of the JACOBIN Club, he exercised considerable power in Paris. In 1791, when public accuser, he attacked the government for going to war, took a leading part in the overthrow of the monarchy and, after the execution of the King (1793), led the Jacobins to victory over the Girondins (*see* FRENCH REVOLUTION).

After their fall, he joined the Committee of Public Safety and, for a time, was practically ruler of France. He nominated the members of government committees, took complete control of the Revolutionary Tribunal, sent his opponents to the guillotine and more than anyone was responsible for the policies of the Terror. His ruthlessness led to growing alarm; no one felt safe and a coalition was formed against him that secured his arrest on 27 July 1794. He attempted suicide, but was guillotined on the following day.

ROME. According to legend the city was founded in 753 BC by Romulus and was ruled by kings until 509 BC when Tarquin the Proud was expelled. A Republic was set up, with a Senate and two annually elected consuls, though a dictator might be appointed in times of crisis; power rested with the *patricians* or nobles, but the common people (*plebeians*) eventually won the right to elect two Tribunes to look after their interests.

From 509 BC the next two hundred and fifty years were spent battling against Italian tribes, such as the Volsci, Etruscans, Aequi and Sabines and also against the Gauls (CELTS) from the north. By 396 BC the Etruscan city Veii was destroyed and the Samnites, a warlike Italian people, were beaten by by 295 BC. With the defeat of the GREEK COLONIES in Southern Italy (272 BC) Rome became mistress of the whole of Italy. There followed the prolonged struggle with CARTHAGE known as the Punic Wars, which lasted from 264 until 146 BC and ended in the total destruction of Carthage.

During this epic contest the Romans managed to acquire several provinces, including Sicily, Sardinia, Corsica, Illyricum (Yugoslavia), Spain, Tunisia, MACEDON and Greece (146 BC). In the next hundred years, they added to their possessions Asia Minor, Crete, Syria, Judaea, Cyprus and Gaul (France). They annexed EGYPT in 30 BC and CLAUDIUS sent an invasion force to Britain in AD 43.

This vast increase in territory brought great wealth and power to Rome but it also created many problems. The upper classes became greedy for riches and luxury; huge numbers of slaves, who had been captured in war, produced idleness and unemployment; the existence of a large regular army gave power to generals and eventually to the soldiers themselves, while the import of food, especially grain, from the provinces brought ruin to farmers in Italy.

This state of affairs led to political struggles and attempts at reform, notably by the brothers Tiberius and Gaius Gracchus. After they had failed, the soldier Marius (157–86 BC) reorganized the army and tried to break the power of the aristocratic Senate. His dictatorship was followed by the bloody rule of Sulla (138–78 BC), who put thousands of Romans to death. The next successful general to attain power was Pompey, who was succeeded by a much greater man, JULIUS CAESAR, whose talents and conquests carried him to a position of complete power when the Senate named him dictator for ten years. However, rule by one man was still resented by many Romans and Caesar was murdered in 44 BC.

In the civil war that followed his death Octavian, known later as Caesar AUGUSTUS, defeated Brutus and Mark ANTONY to become the first Emperor, sole ruler of the Roman world. For forty-four years he ruled this huge area with masterly skill, providing the provinces with good government, introducing many reforms and transforming Rome itself into a magnificent city, from which first-class roads radiated to the towns and cities which were built throughout the Empire. The organization created by Augustus worked so well that the Empire reached its zenith of magnificence under the fifteen emperors, good and bad, who succeeded him, from his death in AD 14 to the death of Marcus Aurelius in AD 180.

From that date, however, Rome began to decline from lack of stable government, loss of citizens,

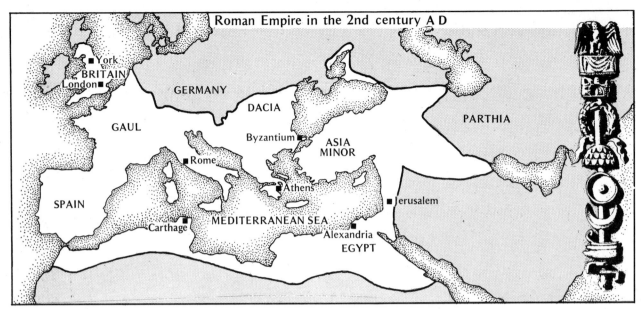

Roman Empire in the 2nd century A D

idleness and dictatorship of the legions, who made and unmade emperors as they pleased. For a time Diocletian (284–305) managed to hold the crumbling empire together, but the barbarians continued to press hard along the frontiers (*see* BARBARIAN INVASIONS) and the establishment of a new capital at Byzantium (Constantinople) by CONSTANTINE (306–37) led to the final collapse of the Roman State.

In AD 400 Italy was invaded by Visigoths, whose leader Alaric captured Rome in 410 but spared its glorious buildings; these were sacked by the VANDALS forty years later. The last of the Roman emperors in the West, Romulus Augustulus, was deposed by the Goths, who made their own leader Odoacer ruler of Italy in 476. An eastern emperor continued to rule Constantinople, but the power of Rome was ended.

ROMMEL, Erwin (1891–1944), was sent by HITLER to North Africa in February 1941 to take command of the newly formed German Afrika Korps. An able commander, who won such respect from the British that for a time they looked on him as virtually invincible, he reconquered Cyrenaica in 1941, captured Tobruk and Benghazi in 1942, and by June had advanced into Egypt as far as El Alamein. Hampered by inadequate supplies and unrealistic orders from Hitler, his army was defeated by MONTGOMERY's 8th Army in October. Rommel retreated to Tunisia and was recalled to

Europe in 1943 to take command in Italy and then in France, where he organized the construction of the Atlantic Wall. By this time he was convinced that Hitler must be removed, and those who conspired with him planned to make him head of state after Hitler's overthrow. Rommel was severely injured during an Allied air attack, and after the 20 July Plot failed to kill Hitler he committed suicide by taking poison.

ROOSEVELT, Franklin Delano (1882–1945), 32nd President of the USA, was four times elected president, an achievement unique in American history. A lawyer and a distant cousin of President Theodore ROOSEVELT, he entered politics in 1910 as a Democrat in the New York Senate. From 1913 to 1920 he served under Woodrow WILSON as Assistant Secretary of the Navy. Crippled by polio in 1921, he was never again able to walk unaided, but he overcame this handicap, returned to public life in 1924 and was elected Governor of New York State in 1928.

When he stood against HOOVER for the Presidency in 1932, his pledge of a 'New Deal' for the American people won him a sweeping victory and with great energy he at once began to put through a series of measures to combat the DEPRESSION, by promoting employment, economic recovery and confidence. He was largely successful and after re-election in 1936 he continued to press for liberal reforms at home, while pursuing a 'good neighbour'

policy abroad and urging peace upon an un-responsive HITLER.

At the outbreak of the SECOND WORLD WAR in Europe in 1939 Roosevelt declared America's neutrality, but he soon relaxed the armaments ban in order to help the Allies, and after the fall of France, as American public opinion began to change, he was able to sell destroyers to Britain and, in 1941, to put through the Lend-Lease Act to supply Britain with invaluable aid. He met CHURCHILL at sea and the two statesmen signed the Atlantic Charter, a statement of war aims. After the Japanese attack on PEARL HARBOR and America's full entry into the war, Roosevelt worked closely with the Allied leaders, meeting Churchill at Casablanca in 1943, soon after the landings in North Africa, and again in Washington and Cairo, where they discussed the Far East War with CHIANG KAI-SHEK and went to Teheran to meet STALIN. In February 1945 he was at Yalta, one of the 'Big Three' who planned the final stages of the war and the setting up of a UNITED NATIONS ORGANIZATION in the peace. His health was now failing and he died soon after his return to America.

Franklin D. Roosevelt's name is always associated with the New Deal and America's recovery from the Depression; as a liberal and a Democrat, he suffered much criticism for his domestic policies, but he continued to retain the confidence of the bulk of his countrymen to the end of his life. When war came, he had to lead cautiously, taking care not to go too far ahead of public opinion and in this he succeeded, but to many people he seemed to place too much trust in Stalin and to have been unduly suspicious of the post-war intentions of Britain and France.

ROOSEVELT, Theodore (1858–1919), 26th President of the USA, was born in New York, the son of wealthy parents of Dutch descent. A sickly child, he built up his physique by a rigorous training programme and after graduating from Harvard entered politics, but in disgust at the corruption he encountered spent two adventurous years as a cattleman in the Wild West. Back in New York, as Police Commissioner, he cleaned up the force before becoming Assistant Secretary of the Navy. Favouring war with Spain, he put the navy in a high state of readiness, but when the SPANISH-AMERICAN WAR broke out in 1898 he resigned in order to raise a volunteer cavalry unit, the famous 'Rough Riders', whom he led with courageous zest in Cuba.

As Governor of New York after the war he tackled rackets and doubtful business enterprises with such energy that the party bosses decided to get rid of him by having him returned as Vice-President, a post which normally carried practically no power. Almost immediately, however, President McKinley was assassinated (1901) and Roosevelt succeeded him for the next three and a half years. He was returned in 1904 by a huge majority for a further four years. Among his many achievements as President were the starting of the Panama Canal scheme, the ending of the Russo-Japanese War by his intervention, the cleaning up of politics and defeat of big business monopolies. In foreign affairs his declared policy was 'to speak softly and carry a big stick'.

Refusing to stand for election again in 1908, he went big-game hunting in Africa and then returned to America to stand for his new Progressive 'Bull Moose' Party, which split the Republican vote and allowed Woodrow WILSON to win the presidency in 1912. Once again Roosevelt set off on his travels, this time to the jungles of Brazil, where he fell seriously ill and came home a sick man. However, when war broke out in Europe, he attacked Wilson's neutrality policy with his old vigour, and after America entered the war he tried to get permission to serve with a division of volunteers he had raised. His four sons fought in France and one was killed in action; Roosevelt himself died in 1919, opposing Wilson to the end.

'Teddy' Roosevelt was a flamboyant character, who possessed abnormal energy and Lincoln's ability to coin memorable phrases; he did much for reform and justice and in his company nobody ever had a dull moment. In addition to his other achievements, he was a prolific writer, whose books included accounts of his adventures and his own autobiography.

ROSES, Wars of (1455–85), began in England during the reign of HENRY VI, when the rival houses of Lancaster (whose badge was a red rose) and York (white rose) took up arms in a struggle for supremacy. The Lancastrians, the party of Henry VI and his formidable wife Queen Margaret, looked mostly to the north of England for support, while the Yorkists, led by the Duke of York (Henry VI's cousin) and the Earl of WARWICK, were stronger in London and the south.

The wars fell into three phases, first, a see-saw struggle in which the Yorkists won victories at St Albans (1455) and Northampton (1460), while Queen Margaret failed to make decisive use of the Lancastrian triumphs at Wakefield (1460) and St Albans (1461). The second phase began with Edward Earl of March's victory for the Yorkists at Mortimer's Cross (1461), and this was followed by Warwick's victory at Towton (1461), after which he had March (the Duke of York's son) crowned King of England as EDWARD IV. Margaret fled abroad and Henry VI was imprisoned in the Tower until Warwick 'the Kingmaker' quarrelled with Edward IV, forced him to flee and put Henry back on the throne. In 1471, however, Edward returned to defeat and kill Warwick at Barnet, and after the Battle of Tewkesbury and the murder of Henry Edward was able to reign unchallenged until 1483.

The third stage occurred in 1485 when Henry Tudor landed in Wales, gathered an army and defeated RICHARD III (Edward's brother) at Bosworth to bring final victory to the Lancastrians and ascend the throne as HENRY VII.

The Wars of the Roses were fought by armies of nobles and hired retainers; some of the battles were murderous encounters and, as the war proceeded, the victors took to executing noble prisoners. However, there was no widespread devastation of the countryside nor sacking of towns, so that the general populace suffered little inconvenience from the war.

RUPERT, Prince (1619–82), was born at Prague, the son of the Elector Palatine Frederick V and Elizabeth, daughter of James I of England. At the

Prince Rupert and his favourite dog, Boy

outbreak of the CIVIL WAR, he went to England to serve under his uncle CHARLES I, taking command of the Royalist cavalry, which he led with great dash and recklessness. He fought in all the major battles of the war, but his surrender of Bristol in

1645 so angered Charles that he dismissed him. Cleared by a court martial, Rupert resumed command of the King's forces until obliged to surrender in 1646.

After service in France, he commanded the English fleet that supported the Royalist cause and showed considerable ability as an admiral until defeated by BLAKE in 1650. He escaped to the West Indies with his brother Prince Maurice and later went to reside in France and Germany until the Restoration (1660). Thereafter, in CHARLES II's reign, he served with his cousin James Duke of York (later JAMES II) in the DUTCH WARS, helped to found the HUDSON'S BAY COMPANY, interested himself in scientific experiments and in a method of engraving pictures on metal called mezzotint. Opinions vary about his talents as a military commander, but there can be no doubts about his courage and loyalty to the Stuart cause.

RUSSIAN REVOLUTION (October 1917) had its origins in the longstanding grievances of the peasants and workers and in the military disasters suffered by the Russian armies since 1915. Early in 1917 occurred the February Revolution, when army units in St Petersburg (Petrograd, now Leningrad) mutinied and were joined in a revolt by workers, who formed soviets or councils to take charge of affairs. Tsar NICHOLAS II was forced to abdicate and KERENSKY, a moderate socialist, formed a government whose aims were to create a democratic state and continue fighting the Germans.

Meanwhile, LENIN, leader of the extreme BOL-SHEVIKS, was brought from exile to Russia by the Germans, and that summer confusion reigned as he, TROTSKY and other leaders urged revolution, while Kerensky tried to govern. In July he seemed to have overcome the Bolsheviks and Lenin fled to Finland.

However, the defeat of a Russian offensive and the failure of other socialist parties to seize control restored the Bolsheviks' fortunes. They began to win majorities in city soviets and Lenin decided the time was ripe for an armed uprising. Moderates did not agree, but the details were left to Trotsky, who organized an insurrection of the Red Guards in Petrograd. This took place on 25 October, and owing to the fact that Kerensky had taken no effective countermeasures was completely successful. In Moscow the revolution took a little longer, but within a matter of days the Bolsheviks had become the party in power, with Lenin and Trotsky at the helm.

Red Guards with an armoured car in Moscow in 1917

S

ST BARTHOLOMEW, Massacre of (1572), took place in Paris on 24 August, St Bartholomew's Day, when the city was still full of HUGUENOTS who had come for the marriage of Marguerite of Valois to the Huguenot Henry of Navarre (later HENRY IV). A plot hatched by the Duc de Guise to kill Admiral Coligny, the Huguenot leader, was approved by the Queen Mother, CATHERINE DE MEDICI, who persuaded her son Charles IX to authorize the murder of Coligny and all Huguenot leaders. The order was given and, probably contrary to Catherine's intention, a mass slaughter took place in the early hours of the morning. Some 1,100 Huguenots perished in Paris and the massacre spread to the provinces, where thousands more were done to death. News of the massacre was welcomed by the Pope and PHILIP II of Spain, but in Protestant countries it produced a wave of horror and a determination to defend their religion at all cost.

SALADIN (1137–93), Sultan of Egypt and Syria, was born near the river Tigris, son of an official who served the SELJUK TURKS. He took part in an invasion of Egypt under Nur-eddin, was appointed vizier and, in 1174, proclaimed himself Sultan.

Garnet cross of
Saxon craftsmanship

Having received homage from the Seljuk princes of Syria, he won a crushing victory over the CRUSADERS at Tiberias (1187) and recaptured JERUSALEM. This led to the launching of the Third Crusade, during which Acre fell into the hands of PHILIP AUGUSTUS of France and RICHARD I of England. Richard defeated Saladin but was unable to reach Jerusalem, and the two leaders concluded a three years' truce. Saladin died shortly afterwards, greatly respected for his chivalry, justice and piety.

SAMURAI were members of the aristocratic warrior class in feudal JAPAN. They fought on horseback with bows and arrows, curved swords and light armour; some of them bore two swords and fought on foot. Samurai influence lasted from the 9th century for about a thousand years. Loyal to their lords, disciplined and educated, the samurai played an important role in the creation of modern Japan.

SAXONS were tribesmen from north Germany, who began raiding the shores of Roman Britain in the 3rd century and, after the withdrawal of the Romans, came as invaders in order to settle the eastern side of the country and to penetrate far into the midlands. The Saxons, whose name is said to be derived from their favourite weapon, the *seax*, a short sword, were frequently accompanied by tribesmen called Angles and Jutes.

By the end of the 6th century much of England was in Anglo-Saxon hands and areas such as Kent, East Anglia, WESSEX, Bernicia, Deira and MERCIA had developed into separate kingdoms. For many years their people were pagans, worshipping Woden and Thor, but they gradually accepted CHRISTIANITY and the authority of the Pope. Warlike and energetic, they also excelled as farmers and liked to live in family groups in villages and woodland settlements. Artistically they were skilful craftsmen in gold, silver, bronze and enamel, and after their conversion Saxon monks produced gospels and religious books famous for their brilliant illuminations. Saxon scholars, such as BEDE, were well-known to foreigners and Alcuin served CHARLEMAGNE as an adviser and founder of schools.

In the 8th century Mercia emerged as the most powerful Saxon kingdom until overrun by Egbert of Wessex, whose grandson ALFRED (871–900) withstood the VIKING raiders and preserved Christianity and civilization.

By the 10th century Saxon England was prosperous and well governed, but in 1016 it fell to CANUTE, the Dane, though that dynasty soon ended and in 1042 a Saxon king, EDWARD THE CONFESSOR, returned to the throne and was followed by the last of the Saxon rulers, HAROLD, who was defeated and killed at HASTINGS in 1066. Under the

NORMANS the Saxons remained a defeated subject race for a comparatively short time, and by the 13th century had merged with their conquerors to become the English people.

SCOTT, Captain Robert Falcon (1868–1912), commanded the *Discovery* in the Antarctic expedition of 1901–4, during which he explored the Ross Sea area and discovered King Edward VII Land. In 1910 he embarked in the *Terra Nova* on a second expedition, leading a sledge party to the South Pole, which he reached on 18 January 1912, only to find that the Norwegian explorer AMUNDSEN had beaten him by a month. On the return journey the party was delayed by blizzards and by the illness of Evans and Oates, who both died; Scott with his two remaining companions, Wilson and Bowers, perished in their tent only a short distance from a food depot. Their bodies and diaries were found eight months later.

SECOND WORLD WAR (1939–45) began on 1 September 1939, when HITLER'S Germany invaded Poland. Pledged to support that country, France and Britain duly declared war on Germany (3 September), but did nothing to help Poland, which was swiftly overwhelmed when also invaded from the east by STALIN'S Russia. There followed the 'phoney war', when little happened, apart from the Russian attack on Finland in November.

After this opening phase the main events of the war were as follows: 1940: March, Finland surrendered. April, Germany invaded Norway and Denmark; British troops were forced out of Norway. May, CHURCHILL became Prime Minister of Britain; Germans invaded Belgium and France; British army was evacuated from DUNKIRK. June, France capitulated; MUSSOLINI'S Italy entered the war. August–September, BATTLE OF BRITAIN, in which the RAF defeated the Luftwaffe; Hitler abandoned his plan to invade Britain. November, Italian troops beaten in Greece. December, British victory over Italians in North Africa; German air raids (the Blitz) on Britain.

1941: March, British naval victory at Cape Matapan. April, German invasion of Yugoslavia and Greece; British troops forced to leave Greece; ROMMEL'S Afrika Korps helped the Italians to advance in North Africa. May, Germans captured Crete; battleship *Bismarck* sunk in the Atlantic. June, Germany attacked Soviet Russia and made spectacular advances. December, Russians halted the German offensive near Moscow; JAPAN attacked PEARL HARBOR; Germany and Italy declared war on USA (*see* F. D. ROOSEVELT); Britain declared war on Japan.

1942: February–March, the Japanese captured Singapore, advanced into Burma and conquered the Dutch East Indies. May–June, American naval victories in battles of Coral Sea and Midway Island. July, German–Italian armies advanced into Egypt; Germans reached STALINGRAD. October, British victory at El Alamein (*see* MONTGOMERY). November, Allied landings in North Africa; German U-boat campaign reached its peak.

1943: January, surrender of German army at Stalingrad. May, total defeat of Germans and Italians in North Africa. July, Russian victory at Kursk; Allied landing in Sicily; Mussolini overthrown. September, Allies invaded Italy. November, Churchill, Stalin, Roosevelt met at Teheran.

1944: January, Allied landing at Anzio. April, Mussolini shot. June, Rome captured; NORMANDY INVASION. July, plot to kill Hitler. August, Paris liberated; Allied landings in south of France; Russian victories; Polish rising in Warsaw; Guam recaptured. September, Belgium liberated; British failure at Arnhem. October, Greece liberated;

American naval victory at Leyte Gulf. December, German Ardennes counter-offensive.

1945: February, Philippines reconquered. March, Allies crossed the Rhine. April, Russians took Vienna, Berlin, Prague; death of Hitler. 8 May, unconditional surrender of Germany. August, atomic bombs on HIROSHIMA and Nagasaki; Japan agreed to surrender. 2 September 1945, official end of Second World War.

SELJUK TURKS were tribesmen from the Asiatic steppes who migrated westward from about the 8th century. They were converted to ISLAM and, after some three hundred years, overran Persia, and took Baghdad in 1055. They then successfully invaded the Eastern Roman or BYZANTINE EMPIRE and established themselves in Asia Minor. It was their occupation of Palestine and ill-treatment of Christian pilgrims that gave rise to the First CRUSADE (1096–9). The Seljuk Empire declined in the 12th century and was eventually overtaken by the OTTOMAN Turks.

SEVEN YEARS WAR (1756–63) was a European conflict between France, Austria and Russia on the one side and Britain and Prussia on the other. It was a continuation of the worldwide rivalry between Britain and France and of the prolonged struggle between Austria and Prussia for Silesia.

The war began with the French capture of Minorca (1756), while in Canada General Montcalm captured Fort Oswego for France and the British failed to take Louisbourg. FREDERICK THE GREAT marched into Saxony, but was beaten by the Austrians at Kolin (1757) and the Duke of Cumberland was forced to surrender at Klosterseven. A Russian army defeated the Prussians and the Austrians entered Berlin, but Frederick extricated himself with brilliant victories over the French at Rossbach (November 1757) and over the Austrians at Leuthen (December 1757). Meanwhile, Pitt the Elder (later Earl of CHATHAM) took over the direction of Britain's war effort and in India CLIVE was victorious at Plassey.

In 1758 Frederick beat the Russians at Zorndorf, but was defeated by Austria at Hochkirch. The Prince of Brunswick won the notable victory of Crefeld over the French, and in North America the British captured Louisbourg and a number of French forts (*see* FRENCH AND INDIAN WARS).

1759, the 'Year of Victories', saw the capture of the French island of Guadeloupe, WOLFE's victory on the Plains of Abraham and the capture of Quebec, while the naval triumphs at Lagos and Quiberon Bay saved England from invasion. Prussia, hard-pressed by her enemies, was reprieved by Brunswick's brilliant victory at Minden. Even so, Frederick was defeated by the Russians and the Austrians, but he somehow managed to survive into 1760 and even to win victories with inferior numbers. This year also saw Coote's capture of Pondicherry and the end of French power in India.

Prussian fortunes were at low ebb throughout 1761 and Frederick, having lost Silesia, was near to total defeat when the death of the Tsarina Elizabeth (January 1762) brought to the Russian throne Peter III, who withdrew from the war. Frederick was therefore able to defeat the Austrians at Freiberg and to recover Silesia. By this time GEORGE II had died and his son GEORGE III showed himself anxious for peace, so the subsidies for Frederick were cut and Pitt was forced to resign. Spain entered the war on the side of France in 1762, but was beaten in the West Indies and the Philippines, by which time the other contestants were exhausted, so the war ended with the Treaty of Paris (1763). Britain gained many overseas territories including Canada, Senegal, Minorca, Florida and several West Indian islands, while Frederick the Great retained Silesia.

Children working in a coalmine before Shaftesbury's Act of 1842

SHAFTESBURY, 7th Earl of (Anthony Ashley-Cooper, 1801–85), entered Parliament and, as Lord Ashley, concerned himself with child labour and the conditions of the workers and of unfortunates such as prisoners and lunatics. He helped to prohibit chimney-sweeps from employing climbing boys (1840) and to ban the underground employment of women and children in coalmines (1842). He also took the lead in factory reform, putting through Acts to reduce hours of work. He was chairman of the Ragged Schools Union (founded to provide education for homeless urchins) and supported Florence NIGHTINGALE in her schemes for army welfare; he also interested himself in the care of juvenile offenders and in the provision of housing for the poor. A man of courage and compassion, he feared revolution and was opposed to radical ideas, believing that the poor should be helped by the rich without drastic changes to society.

SIDNEY, Sir Philip (1554–86), a nephew of the Earl of LEICESTER, attracted the favour of Queen ELIZABETH, who sent him on diplomatic missions to the Emperor Rudolph II and to the Dutch leader WILLIAM THE SILENT. He became known as a poet, and in 1585 was made Governor of Flushing and second-in-command of Leicester's army, which was raised to oppose the Spaniards in the NETHER-LANDS. Leicester showed little enterprise, but Sidney distinguished himself in several actions until fatally wounded while leading a charge at Zutphen. The story of his passing a bottle of water to a dying soldier with the words, 'Thy necessity is greater than mine', is probably true, for he was universally loved as the most noble and gallant man of his time. His poems and his pastoral romance *Arcadia* were published after his death.

SLAVERY was widespread throughout the Ancient World, since it was thought 'natural' for victors in war to make slaves of their captives, for debtors and criminals to become slaves and for 'barbarians' to sell their children to slave-dealers.

In Greece most of the inhabitants of SPARTA were slaves and even the Athenians, so keen on freedom, had no qualms about slavery. The Roman campaigns of conquest brought so many slaves to Italy that a rich man might own as many as ten thousand and the ordinary Roman citizen could afford at least one. Practically every kind of work came to be carried out by slaves, which meant that

The crossing of the Atlantic on board a slave ship

many of the native Roman working class became unemployed and had to be kept in idleness by the government. In 73 BC a slave-gladiator named Spartacus led a revolt of slaves so savage that an army of 40,000 was needed to restore order and 6,000 slaves were crucified as a warning.

In the Middle Ages slavery existed throughout Western Europe; it was common in pre-Norman Britain but died out after the Conquest. The feudal serf or villein was not the private property of a lord, but he was bound to the land and could not leave it if he wished to do so (*see* FEUDAL SYSTEM). Serfdom lasted in France until the Revolution and in Russia until the present century.

The discovery of America led to an increase in slavery, for the Europeans made slaves of the native peoples, and when these died of disease and over-work they started the African slave trade, to bring Negroes to work in the mines and plantations in a climate that was too hot for Europeans. In the 17th and 18th centuries the slave trade based on Bristol increased greatly in order to supply slaves for the cotton fields of the southern states of North America. In Britain public opinion turned against slavery, so that, thanks to the work of William WILBERFORCE and others, the trade was forbidden in 1807 and slavery was abolished throughout the British Empire in 1833.

Negroes continued to be bred and sold in certain states of the USA for work in the southern states and the slavery question came to be a principal cause of the American CIVIL WAR of 1861–5. The victory of the North brought an end to slavery in the USA. In Africa LIVINGSTONE found that Arab slave-traders had caused large areas to be deserted by the native inhabitants, who dreaded their raids. Since the 19th century slavery has been greatly reduced, but to this day may not have quite died out in some parts of Africa and the East.

SMITH, Captain John (1580–1631), was born in Lincolnshire and after an adventurous youth during which he served in the Imperial Army and was captured by the Turks, he joined the company of colonists which went out to Virginia and founded Jamestown in 1607. Smith became leader of the struggling community and while trying to obtain food by barter was captured by Indians. His life was spared, he said, by Pocahontas, the chief's daughter, who later befriended the settlers and

John Smith and a Red Indian village

married an Englishman. Smith returned to England in 1609 to write an account of his adventures and to prepare maps and leaflets for the use of travellers to America.

SMUTS, Jan Christiaan (1870–1950), was born in Cape Colony and educated at Cambridge University in England. During the BOER WAR he led commando forces against the British and later entered politics to become Louis Botha's right-hand man. He succeeded Botha as Prime Minister of the Union of South Africa in 1919. Prior to that he commanded the Allied forces that opposed the Germans in East Africa and was so respected by the British that in

1917 he was invited to join the war cabinet. He played a considerable part in the establishment of the LEAGUE OF NATIONS and was looked upon as a statesman of world stature.

He became Prime Minister again in 1939, taking South Africa into the war and becoming a confidant and adviser to CHURCHILL and other Allied war leaders. His United Party was defeated in 1948 and he then became leader of the opposition until his death. A man of vision and lofty idealism, Smuts was not always aware of everyday realities. He failed to perceive the strength of Afrikaner nationalism and was unable to do much to improve the lot of the black population of South Africa.

The Trade Label of the South Sea Company

SOUTH SEA BUBBLE (1720) is the name given to a financial crisis in Britain resulting from the collapse of the South Sea Company. To make their fortunes, its directors offered to take over much of the National Debt, paying £7 million for the privilege, an offer which caused people to think that the Company's trading prospects must be enormously profitable. In a fever of speculation its shares shot up to astronomical heights and many new companies were formed, some of them fraudulent.

In an effort to suppress its rivals, the Company spread alarm, causing panic selling and a crisis in which accusations of corruption were levelled against ministers, officials and even King GEORGE I. Sir Robert WALPOLE, out of office and apparently not involved in the affair, came to the rescue with a scheme to cut the losses and save the Whig Party from disaster. He arranged for £18 million of the Company's stock to be transferred to the Bank of England and the EAST INDIA COMPANY, and through his success in dealing with the crisis became undisputed leader of the country for the next twenty years.

Blowing up the USS *Maine*

SPANISH-AMERICAN WAR (1898). A revolt which broke out in Cuba in 1895 against rule by Spain aroused great interest in America, where sympathy for the Cubans was played up for all it was worth by the sensational press. Many people thought that the United States should intervene, and when in February 1898 an American battleship, the USS *Maine*, was blown up in Havana harbour, Congress declared war. It was soon over. An American naval squadron under Commodore Dewey destroyed the Spanish fleet in Manila Bay in the Philippines (1 May), another squadron destroyed a second Spanish fleet off Santiago in Cuba, and in

July the US army captured Santiago, where Theodore ROOSEVELT's 'Rough Riders' took part in the assault. By the peace treaty negotiated in Paris Spain ceded the Philippines, Puerto Rico and Guam to the US, and relinquished all claim to Cuba, which became an American protectorate.

SPANISH CIVIL WAR (1936–9). The election of a left-wing Republican government in February 1936 aroused opposition from Spanish army leaders, who, like many of their countrymen, were hostile to the government's socialist and anti-clerical policy. In July an army revolt occurred in Spanish Morocco, led by Generals Sanjurjo (killed shortly afterwards) and FRANCO. The rebels or 'Nationalists' transferred to the mainland, where Franco won control of the south and north-west and set up a new government at Burgos. The Republicans or 'Loyalists' moved their headquarters to Barcelona and in the fighting that raged for the next three years both sides behaved with appalling savagery.

By the end of 1936 Franco held more than half of Spain, including the vital Portuguese frontier; in 1937 he failed to take Madrid but was successful in the north. By now he was assisted by Italian troops sent by MUSSOLINI, while the Republicans received help from Russia and from the International Brigade drawn from many nations. In 1938 HITLER sent more German planes, tanks and specialist crews to aid Franco, whose forces drove eastwards to the sea and also besieged Madrid.

Early in 1939 the Republican armies began to collapse; Barcelona fell in January, and when Valencia and Madrid surrendered in March the war came to an end. The Civil War cost some three-quarters of a million lives. It aroused great bitterness and emotional feeling, especially in France and Britain, whose governments followed a policy of non-intervention, but it left Franco and his right-wing followers in power for more than thirty years.

SPANISH SUCCESSION, War of the (1702–13), arose out of the alarm aroused by Charles II of Spain's will, by which he left the whole Spanish empire to Philip of Anjou, grandson of LOUIS XIV. Britain, the United Provinces (Holland) and Austria (whose archduke, Charles, was himself a claimant to the Spanish throne) fought to prevent France becoming all-powerful, since Louis XIV and his family would control vast overseas possessions, the Netherlands, part of Italy and much of the world's trade.

The war was fought in several theatres, principally in the Netherlands and Austria, where MARLBOROUGH's brilliant victories (BLENHEIM, Ramillies, Oudenarde) led to the invasion of France. French armies were also defeated in Italy by Prince Eugene of Savoy. At sea the English and Dutch were supreme, but in Spain the Allies failed to oust Philip V from his throne. When the Archduke Charles succeeded to the HAPSBURG empire, there was no more support for the scheme to put him on the Spanish throne in place of Philip, so, with the withdrawal of Britain and the exhaustion of France, the war came to an end in 1713.

By the Treaty of Utrecht France got better terms than might have been expected after so many defeats: Philip kept Spain; Holland, much weakened by the war, recovered the Barrier Fortresses; and Austria gained Milan, Naples and the NETHERLANDS in exchange for Charles's claim to Spain; Britain gained GIBRALTAR, Minorca, Nova Scotia and the Hudson Bay territory, with the right to trade (Asiento) with Spanish America. In addition, British power and prestige had risen immensely high in Europe.

Spartan warrior

SPARTA, founded, according to legend, by Lacedaemon, stood on a plain by the river Eurotas in the Peloponnese, Greece. When, in about 1000 BC, Dorians from the north overran this region, the original inhabitants became slaves or 'helots', who were compelled to work for the intruders, henceforward known as Spartans. The local population was also made to carry out all trade and industry, for the Spartans themselves comprised a ruling warrior class of less than 30,000 persons, controlling helots and subject peoples amounting, after the subjection of neighbouring Messina, to some 600,000 souls.

Unlike ATHENS, Sparta was never a beautiful city, merely a group of villages, like a military camp. Spartan males were subjected to rigorous training from the age of six to thirty, and girls received a similar upbringing, in which courage and obedience were rated more highly than culture and intelligence. As a result of this concentration upon military prowess, Sparta was acknowledged to be the strongest city-state in Greece and the rival of Athens. After the final defeat of the PERSIANS (479 BC), Spartan arrogance caused many of the states to transfer their loyalty to Athens, but Sparta recovered her supremacy through defeating Athens in the PELOPONNESIAN WAR, which ended in 404. Hatred of her despotic rule caused her rivals to unite and she was defeated by the Thebans under Epaminondas in 371. Following the Macedonian conquest of Greece (see MACEDON), the Spartans were still strong enough to refuse to join in the Asiatic campaign of ALEXANDER, but their power was on the wane, due largely to a rapid decline in the number of citizens. Sparta fell, with the rest of Greece, under Roman power in 146 BC.

STALIN, Joseph (1879–1953), whose real name was Dzhugashvili, was a Georgian by birth, son of an artisan. At an early age he became an active revolutionary, was imprisoned and deported to Siberia, from where he escaped to spread LENIN's teachings. He met Lenin himself and attended party conferences in Finland, Sweden and England. He became the first editor of the Communist newspaper *Pravda* in 1912, when he began to use the name Stalin, meaning 'Man of Steel'. In 1917 he rallied to Lenin's side, organized his escape abroad in July, and after the success of the October Revolution (*see* RUSSIAN REVOLUTION) was made Commissar for Nationalities (1917–23). During this time he took an important part in the Civil War and developed a strong hatred for TROTSKY, while steadily increasing his power in the BOLSHEVIK Party, of which he became general secretary to the central committee in 1922. Lenin became distrustful of Stalin's character, but he died before he could bring about his downfall.

Through the 1920s Stalin gradually overcame all his rivals, particularly Trotsky, securing his expulsion from the Party, in which he himself became supreme. At this time he adopted the policy of 'socialism in one country', arguing that Russia could achieve COMMUNISM without world revolution. In his first Five Year Plan (1928–33) he forced through collectivization of farming and directed rapid development of heavy industry. In the process millions of peasants died or suffered imprisonment and the old Bolsheviks were removed in a series of purges, which became a reign of terror.

During the SPANISH CIVIL WAR Stalin sent aid to the Spanish Communists, but was careful not to become too deeply involved in the struggle. Next, after the Munich Agreement, he apparently considered an alliance with France and Britain, but astounded everyone by signing a non-aggression pact with Nazi Germany in 1939. This enabled him to invade eastern Poland and to gain territory and time at the start of the SECOND WORLD WAR before the German invasion of Russia, which he sensed to be inevitable.

When Germany did attack Russia in 1941 Stalin had himself appointed supreme commander of all the Soviet forces and as the war progressed he made contact with CHURCHILL and ROOSEVELT, meeting them at Teheran, Yalta and Potsdam to discuss the direction of the conflict and to secure his own aims at little or no cost to Russia. At the end of the war he presided over the extension of Russian frontiers and the setting up of Communist governments in Eastern Europe. Thus this enigmatic successor of Lenin established Communism in his own country and directed its extension to many other parts of the world.

Street-fighting in Stalingrad

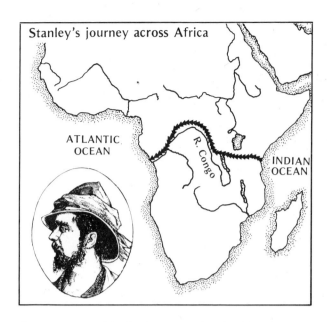
Stanley's journey across Africa

ATLANTIC OCEAN

R. Congo

INDIAN OCEAN

STALINGRAD was one of the decisive battles of the SECOND WORLD WAR. In September 1942 the German 6th Army under General von Paulus attacked this city on the lower Volga in the course of a great German drive to conquer the whole of south-east Russia. The Russians resisted street by street until November, when General Zhukov cut the German communications and besieged the besiegers. Hitler ordered von Paulus to fight to the end, and when it came, in February 1943, the Germans had lost some 200,000 men. Stalingrad was the farthest point that the Germans penetrated into Russia and their defeat caused them to withdraw from the Caucasus and to shorten their line. After Stalingrad they won no more victories.

STANLEY, Sir Henry Morton (1841–1904), whose real name was John Rowlands, was born in Wales, orphaned and harshly treated in a work-house. He worked his way to America as a cabin-boy and there took the name of a merchant who befriended him. After all kinds of adventures, including service in the American Civil War, he became a journalist and was sent by his newspaper to search for LIVINGSTONE, lost in central Africa. In 1871 he found him at Ujiji and together they explored the northern end of Lake Tanganyika.

Stanley made three more expeditions, crossing Africa from Zanzibar to the Atlantic in 1874–7 and becoming the first white man to explore the River Congo. In 1879–84 he opened up the Congo region

for King Leopold of Belgium, and on his last journey, 1887–9 he made a second crossing of the continent from west to east, when engaged in rescuing a man named Emin Pasha. When he was fifty Stanley settled in England, entered Parliament and was knighted. Brave, forceful and amazingly tough, he had survived the dangers of climate, disease and constant attacks by tribesmen and had done more to open up central Africa than any other explorer.

STEPHEN (*c.* 1097–1154), King of England (1135–54), son of Stephen of Blois and Adela, daughter of William the Conqueror, was brought up at the court of his uncle HENRY I and became King of England in 1135, after Henry died. Stephen, with the rest of the nobles, had sworn to accept Henry's daughter MATILDA as heir to the throne, but on the King's death they broke their oath. In 1139 Matilda landed in England to claim the throne, and in the civil war Stephen was captured at Lincoln, only to be exchanged later for Earl Robert of Gloucester.

Gradually, Stephen gained some kind of control and Matilda departed, but when her son Henry came over in 1153 it was obvious that he could count on considerable support. Hence, after the death of Stephen's son Eustace, it was agreed that Stephen should remain king for life and be succeeded by Henry (*see* HENRY II). Brave, generous and chivalrous, Stephen never commanded the respectful obedience of the nobles, who were able to take advantage of his insecure position.

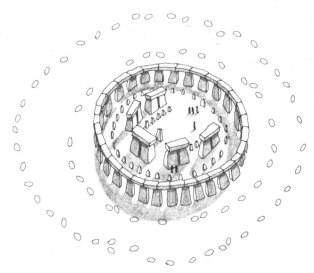

STEPHENSON, George (1781–1848), was born into poverty at Wylam, near Newcastle, and was out to work at eight years of age, so he did not learn to read and write until grown up. As engineer in charge of a pumping-engine he developed a flair with machinery, and having seen *Puffing Billy*, an early locomotive, at work at Wylam Colliery, he built a better one in 1814, called *My Lord*. Appointed engineer in charge of the first public RAILWAY ever to be constructed, which was to run from Stockton to Darlington, he laid the track, and in 1825 himself drove his locomotive *Locomotion* along the new line. This success led to the building of the Liverpool and Manchester Railway and to the victory of Stephenson's *Rocket* (1829) in the Rainhill Trials. Henceforward he and his son Robert were employed as designers of railways in Britain and abroad ; they improved on his early locomotives and were the greatest pioneers of railway development.

STONEHENGE is a great circle of tall stones on Salisbury Plain in Wiltshire, England. It stands in a circular area about 340 feet (104 metres) across, enclosed by a ditch and a bank, and seems to have been begun in about 2000 BC. The work stopped and was recommenced later in the Bronze Age when huge sandstone (sarsen) stones were set up and eighty blue stones were brought from Presley Mountains in Pembrokeshire, Wales, some two hundred miles (320 km) away. These were set up in a circle inside the outer sarsen ring, as the Blue-Stone Circle and Horseshoe. The use of lintels, with mortice-and-tenon joints, is thought to point to influence from the eastern Mediterranean and to the date of about 1500 BC, when a powerful dynasty of chiefs was ruling in south-west England.

Stonehenge faces the rising sun, and on Midsummer Day the sunrise takes place in a direct line from the centre of the circle over a single standing stone called the Hele Stone or Sun Stone. From this, it appears that the monument or temple was built by people who worshipped the sun. The popular belief that Stonehenge was associated with the Druids is almost certainly mistaken.

STURT, Charles Napier (1795–1869), the Australian explorer, was brought up in England, entered the British army and saw service against the French and Americans before being sent to New South Wales as a captain in 1826. On his first expedition of exploration, he discovered the Darling River and in 1829 followed the Murrumbidgee and Murray rivers to Lake Alexandrina, thus solving the mystery of the outlet of the Murray-Darling system to the sea. His epic return journey up the Murray in a small whaleboat in terrible conditions brought on blindness that was to afflict him at times for the rest of his life.

However, in 1838 he overlanded cattle along the Murray to Adelaide, where he held posts in the public service, and he is regarded as one of the founders of the State of South Australia. His last

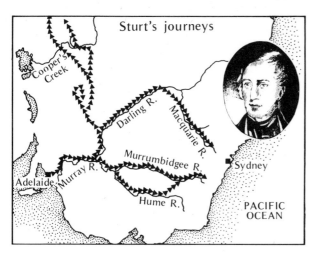

Sturt's journeys

expedition (1844–6) penetrated deep into central Australia to discover Cooper's Creek and, in place of the hoped-for inland sea, extensive deserts. Sturt's sufferings included paralysis and scurvy, but he survived and eventually left Australia in 1853 to retire to Cheltenham, England, where he died.

SUEZ CANAL runs through the Isthmus of Suez to connect the Mediterranean with the Red Sea. Such a canal may have existed in the time of Seti I (*c.* 1310 BC) and NAPOLEON contemplated constructing a canal, but it only became an attractive proposition after the development of steam navigation. Ferdinand de Lesseps, a Frenchman, obtained permission to dig a canal in 1854; the Suez Company was formed, work began in 1859 and the canal was opened in 1869. Britain took advantage of the Khedive's money troubles to acquire his share for £4 million in 1875, but effective control of the Canal belonged to the power which controlled Egypt and this fact undoubtedly led to Britain's intervention in Egypt from 1882.

The Canal is 103 miles (165 km) in length, of which 21 miles (34 km) miles are in lakes. By a convention of 1888 the Canal was never to be blockaded and was to be open to the ships of all nations, armed or unarmed, in peace or war. By the Anglo-Egyptian Treaty of 1936 British troops were to maintain defence of the Canal Zone until 1955, when Egypt assumed responsibility, which in fact she did in 1956. The property would have reverted to Egypt at the end of the ninety-nine year concession, i.e. in 1968, but for the dramatic events known as the Suez War.

Following the withdrawal of the US offer to finance the Aswan Dam because of Egypt's increasing leaning towards the USSR, President NASSER seized the Suez Canal Company's assets and nationalized the Canal in July 1956. Following an Israeli attack on the Sinai peninsula in October, Nasser ordered blockships to be sunk in the Canal. Meanwhile, France and Britain landed paratroops in the Canal Zone and moved in a seaborne force only to cease operations abruptly when Russia threatened to intervene and world opinion was strongly hostile to the aggressors.

By April 1957 the Canal was again open to shipping and compensation was eventually paid to the Suez Canal Company shareholders for the loss of their assets. However, the ARAB-ISRAELI WAR of June 1967 brought about closure of the Canal until 1975.

SUFFRAGETTES, who campaigned for votes for women, became active in Britain at the turn of the present century when the Women's Social and Political Union (1903) came to be led by Mrs Emmeline Pankhurst. Relying at first on peaceful argument, they began to interrupt political meetings and parliamentary debates, turning next to more violent demonstrations such as breaking

Mrs Pankhurst arrested on her way to petition the Prime Minister in 1908 on behalf of the suffragettes

windows, slashing valuable paintings and setting fire to buildings. The most dramatic act occurred at Epsom on Derby Day 1913, when Emily Davison flung herself under the King's horse and was killed. The suffragettes' activities changed the attitude of many of the public from mild derision to anger; they were often manhandled by hooligans and, after arrest, frequently received severe sentences. By 1910 some five hundred suffragettes had been imprisoned; in prison they usually went on hunger strike and by the so-called 'Cat and Mouse Act' of 1913 could be released when half-starved and re-arrested at any time.

At the outbreak of war in 1914 Mrs Pankhurst and her daughter Christabel called off the campaign, disbanded the WSPU and took up recruiting work. Women over thirty were given the vote in Britain in 1918, and by the Equal Franchise Act of 1928 they received the same right as men to vote at twenty-one.

SULEIMAN I (1495–1566), greatest of all the OTTOMAN sultans, ruled from 1520 to 1566 and was known to Europeans as Suleiman the Magnificent, to his own people as the Lawgiver. He greatly extended Ottoman possessions, capturing Belgrade and Rhodes, defeating King Louis of Hungary at Mohács (1526), winning large areas of eastern Asia Minor and Iraq from the Persians and forcing Austria to pay a huge annual tribute and to recognize his suzerainty over Hungary. In the Mediterranean he established naval superiority over the Christian powers and set up Algiers as a powerful corsair state on the North African shore. At Constantinople he was a patron of the arts and a poet, who had four magnificent mosques built for himself and his family. He died while on campaign in Hungary.

SUMER was the Land of Two Rivers – Mesopotamia – watered by the Tigris and Euphrates. It was here that one of the earliest civilizations in the world arose. The early Sumerians were Stone Age farmers who wove cloth and were skilful potters. New settlers came down from the north, and by about 3000 BC a number of warring city-kingdoms had grown up, such as Eridu, Ur, Larsa, Lagash, Kish, Nippur and Erech. The people lived in mud-brick houses and were ruled by king-priests whose massive temples, called ziggurats, were sacred to the local god.

In about 2500 BC Sargon of Akkad defeated the Sumerian cities and made himself lord of the country, but two centuries later his dynasty had declined and UR became the most powerful of all the city-kingdoms, controlling the whole of Mesopotamia. Its greatest ruler was King Ur-Nammu.

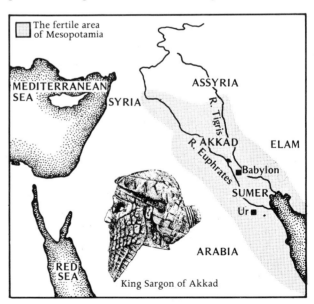

The fertile area of Mesopotamia

King Sargon of Akkad

The Sumerians, basically an agricultural people, were also keen traders, who used money and invented cuneiform (wedge-shaped) writing on clay tablets. They understood irrigation, mathematics and had a system of laws. Their dead were buried in pits or deep shafts, in which a king would be accompanied to the next world by his poisoned attendants and slaughtered oxen.

Sumer was finally crushed by the Elamites, who in turn were defeated by the Amorites, founders of the first dynasty of BABYLON. From about 2000 BC the Sumerians ceased to exist as a separate independent people.

SUN YAT-SEN (1866–1925) was born in the province of Kwangtung in China and received a Western education and medical training. He became a Christian and joined a revolutionary group whose aim was to overthrow the Manchu Emperor, but he was forced to go abroad in 1895 to Japan, America and Britain. In exile he continued to organize uprisings in China, until in 1911 revolutionaries overthrew the MANCHUS and, proclaiming China a republic, made Sun Yat-sen its president. He soon resigned in favour of Yüan Shih-k'ai, a general who seemed to have the power to hold the country together but who in fact became a dictator, and Sun, in opposing him, was defeated and forced into exile again. There followed a period of anarchy when China was in the grip of war-lords, but Sun eventually returned to Canton (1923) to be elected president of the southern republic. With Russian help he organized the Kuomintang (or National party) on Soviet lines and established the Whampoa Military Academy under CHIANG KAI-SHEK, who was to succeed Sun. Thus when Sun died in Peking the groundwork for unification of China had been laid. After his death a cult of Sun Yat-sen grew up and he became revered as the 'Father of the Chinese Republic'.

Elaborate 11th-century clock-tower built by order of a Sung emperor. It had water-driven gears and showed the movements of the planets as well as striking the time with drums and gongs.

SUNG Dynasty in CHINA lasted from 960 to 1126 (Northern Sung) and 1127 to 1279 (Southern Sung). After a period of anarchy, Chao Kuang-yin founded the Sung dynasty and made some progress in unifying the country, despite attacks by the Khitans from the north. Another northern people, the Chin, captured the Sung capital and forced the Chinese to retreat south, where Hangchow became the capital of the Southern Sung dynasty.

In this divided country the Sung rulers were not greatly interested in reconquering the lost territory; they preferred ideas and the arts – painting, poetry and ceramics, so this was a period of cultural brilliance. In addition to interest in astronomy, medicine and botany, gunpowder began to be put to military use, the abacus, a counting frame, came into use, and printing advanced from wood blocks to movable type. The Chinese civil service reached a high peak of efficiency during this period, which came to an end when Hangchow was captured by the MONGOLS under Kublai Khan.

T

A court lady of the
T'ang Dynasty

T'ANG Dynasty (618–907) was one of the greatest periods of Chinese civilization, in which CHINA was a powerful empire and a country in which the arts approached perhaps their highest level.

The second emperor, T'ai Tsung, defeated both the eastern and western TURKS, subdued Tibet and extended his control to Assam in northern India and to Korea. In government he encouraged the system of choosing his officials through civil service examinations, besides building schools and temples to Confucius. Other notable T'ang rulers were the cruel Empress Wu Chao and the Emperor Ming Huang, in whose reign China increased her trade with the outside world. Ming Huang was, however, ousted by a Tartar adventurer named An Lu-shan

in 756 and T'ang power was never restored to its former strength.

During this dynasty pottery and porcelain became more and more beautiful; T'ang sculpture, especially of horses and small terracotta figures, was superb, while many people feel that Chinese painting, with watercolour on silk, reached its peak. Printing began at this time with a Buddhist scripture printed in 868.

TAYLOR, Zachary (1784–1850), born in Virginia, entered the US army and fought in various actions against the Indians, but did not win fame as a general until he was over sixty. In 1845 President Polk sent him to Texas to protect the disputed border, and in the MEXICAN WAR that followed he repulsed the Mexicans at Palo Alto (1846), drove them across the Rio Grande and captured Monterrey. In 1847, though heavily outnumbered, he won a major victory at Buena Vista. Popular with his men, to whom he was known as 'Old Rough and Ready', Taylor was now a national figure, and in 1848 the Whigs chose him as their candidate for the presidency; in the following year he took office as the 12th President of the US. His short term was dominated by the problem of SLAVERY in the newly acquired territories, but before any decision could be made he died suddenly in 1850.

TELFORD, Thomas (1757–1834), son of a Scottish shepherd, was apprenticed to a stone-mason before going to London in 1782. He worked at Portsmouth dockyard, became surveyor of public works for Shropshire and built two bridges over the Severn. After constructing the Ellesmere Canal to connect the rivers Mersey, Dee and Severn, he moved to Scotland in 1803 to carry out a vast programme, including the building of the Caledonian Canal and over 1,000 miles (1,600 km) of roads, besides

Thomas Telford and the Menai Bridge

bridges, churches and harbours. One of his most famous works was the London to Holyhead road with the Menai Suspension Bridge; he also built part of the London docks and the Gotha Canal in Germany.

THEMISTOCLES (*c.* 523–458 BC), leader of Athenian resistance to the Persians (*see* ATHENS, PERSIAN EMPIRE), persuaded the citizens to concentrate upon building a powerful fleet and he himself commanded the squadron that won the battle of Salamis (480). After this, he outwitted the SPARTANS by contriving to rebuild the defensive walls of Athens, but the pro-Sparta faction in the city plotted his downfall and had him banished in 470 BC. He fled to Persia where King Artaxerxes received him with favour and he died in exile, a vassal of the enemy of Athens.

THIRTY YEARS WAR (1618–48), which was fought in several theatres but mainly in Germany, was a conflict between the forces of the REFORMATION and the Counter-Reformation, besides being a continuation of the struggle between the BOURBON kings of France and the HAPSBURGS, who ruled Spain and the Empire.

The war began when the vacant throne of Bohemia was offered to Frederick, Protestant Elector of the Palatinate and son-in-law of James I of England. He accepted, only to be driven out by the army of the Emperor Ferdinand II, who was resolved to restore the Catholic religion in Germany. His generals Tilly and Wallenstein won many victories over the princes, besides defeating Christian IV of Denmark, who came forward to help the Protestants. By 1629 the Emperor was triumphant all over Germany, but in the following year GUSTAVUS ADOLPHUS of Sweden took the field as Protestant champion and the tide turned. Wallenstein, feared by Protestants and Catholics alike, was dismissed; Gustavus won victory after victory, defeating Tilly at Breitenfeld (1631) and advancing into southern Germany. However, Wallenstein was recalled, and though Gustavus won the battle of Lützen (1632) he was killed and the subsequent defeat of the Protestants at Nördlingen (1634) put their cause in danger.

By this time the war had ceased to be a religious struggle and France intervened openly against the Hapsburgs, declaring war on Spain and giving support to the Swedes, the Dutch and the Germans. RICHELIEU, the French minister, played a skilful game, which was continued after his death by Mazarin. The French generals Condé and Turenne won victories over the Emperor's armies and the Swedes recovered ground in northern and central Germany, so that the imperial power declined until the Emperor Ferdinand III asked for peace. By the Treaty of Westphalia (1648) the Emperor had to accept the independence of the German princes and the limitation of his own authority; Switzerland and the United Provinces (Holland) became inde-

pendent states. Among the worst features of the war were the savagery of the fighting and the terrible devastation inflicted upon Germany.

TOLPUDDLE MARTYRS were six farm labourers of Tolpuddle in Dorset who were transported to Australia in 1834 for having taken an illegal oath in the course of forming a trade union. Led by George Loveless, they intended to join Robert OWEN's recently founded Grand National Consolidated Trade Union, and their crime in the eyes of the landowning establishment was trying to combine to obtain higher wages. Sentenced to seven years' transportation, they served only three years, owing to the outcry that arose at the injustice of their trial. After they had been granted free pardons they returned to England, one of them settling back in Tolpuddle, while the others emigrated to Canada.

TRAFALGAR, Battle of (21 October 1805), was fought off the south-west coast of Spain. Earlier in the year NELSON had pursued the French fleet

Execution of prisoners during the Thirty Years War

across the Atlantic to the West Indies and back; in August the French had taken refuge in Cadiz harbour and Nelson's object was to tempt them out to battle. On 20 October the Franco-Spanish fleet, commanded by Villeneuve, put out to sea with thirty-four ships of the line. The next day the British with twenty-seven ships came up with them off Cape Trafalgar.

Nelson's plan was to attack in two columns to cut through the enemy's half-moon formation and in this he was partially successful, though the battle became, as he had hoped, a fierce pell-mell affair, in which ships were interlocked by their rigging, so that point-blank gunnery and the crews' fighting spirit decided the issue. Eighteen of the French ships were sunk or taken; none of the rest ever fought again, but the victory cost the life of Lord Nelson, who was shot at close range by a sharp-shooter from the *Redoubtable*, close to the *Victory*, where Nelson stood on his quarter-deck, unmistakable in his uniform and decorations.

Trafalgar was one of the most decisive naval victories in history, for it removed all danger of an invasion of Britain; NAPOLEON was never able to assemble again an effective fleet to hamper Britain's trade, and British control of the seas remained absolute.

TRAJAN (*c.* AD 53–117), one of the greatest Roman emperors (he was called *Optimus* or 'best'), was born in Spain and earned a high reputation as a soldier under the Emperor Domitian. Adopted by

Domitian's successor Nerva, he succeeded him in 98 and in two campaigns defeated the Dacians and added Dacia (in Central Europe) to the Empire. In 114 he took a great expedition to the east, where he made Armenia and Mesopotamia into Roman provinces. He died on his way back to Italy and was succeeded by his adopted son HADRIAN. Trajan was a modest, dignified man who ruled firmly and well; he put down corruption, encouraged learning and beautified Rome. He laid out a splendid new Forum, in whose centre stood a great column covered with sculptures in relief commemorating his Dacian victories.

TROTSKY, Leon (1879–1940), whose real name was Bronstein, was a Russian revolutionary of Jewish parents. Exiled to Siberia for his activities, he escaped and lived abroad until returning to Russia in 1917 to work closely with LENIN to bring about the October Revolution (*see* RUSSIAN REVOLUTION). His energy and brilliant oratory were invaluable to the BOLSHEVIKS and, as commissar for foreign affairs, he negotiated with the Germans for the peace treaty of Brest-Litovsk that ended the war between Germany and Russia.

In the civil war he founded the Red Army and led it to victory, but in the process made so many enemies that after Lenin's death in 1924 his influence declined. STALIN ousted him from the Politbureau, had him exiled to Central Asia and then expelled from Russia in 1929. Trotsky continued to agitate and intrigue in several countries and this enabled Stalin to carry out purges on the pretext that Trotsky was organizing the overthrow of the Soviet regime. Sentenced to death in his absence, he found asylum in Mexico City, but was murdered there by a Russian agent in 1940.

TROY, a city on the coast of Asia Minor, is so ancient that archaeologists have discovered the remains of at least nine cities, buried one beneath another, the earliest dating from about 3000 BC. The Troy (or Ilium) of legendary fame was probably the seventh of those buried cities. The famous Siege of Troy by the Greeks took place to avenge the abduction of Helen, wife of Menelaus of Sparta, by Paris, son of Priam, King of Troy. The siege (about 1250 BC) lasted for ten years and ended with the complete destruction of Troy. On the Trojan side the chief heroes were Hector, Paris and Aeneas, while among the Greeks were Achilles, Agamemnon, Menelaus and Odysseus. The story, told by Homer and also by Virgil, is full of marvellous and supernatural happenings, but, nevertheless, it is believed to be based upon real events and upon a siege which actually took place.

TURKS originated from a vast area of Asia, stretching from the Caspian Sea across Russia to the borders of China. Millions of Turkish peoples still live in those lands, but the nomadic SELJUK TURKS migrated westwards in the 8th century. They attacked the BYZANTINE EMPIRE, and by the 11th century had established themselves in Asia Minor, Syria and Palestine. In about 1300 a powerful tribe arose, called Ottoman Turks after their first Sultan Osman (1288–1326). After relentless pressure, they captured Constantinople in 1453 and put an end to the Byzantine Empire creating in its place the OTTOMAN EMPIRE.

TUTANKHAMUN, King of Ancient EGYPT of the 18th Dynasty, succeeded AKHNATEN in about 1347 BC when he was only ten years of age. During his short reign of eight years the worship of Amen was restored to Thebes in place of the heresy of Akhnaten, but the fame of this unimportant king rests on the fact that the entrance to his tomb was concealed by diggings from the much larger tomb of Rameses VI nearby, and therefore his tomb escaped the looting that befell all the other royal tombs.

It was discovered in 1922 by an Englishman, Howard Carter, who found that the tomb consisted of four chambers containing an astonishing wealth of treasures. The mummified body of Tutankhamun lay in the innermost of three gold coffins, his head covered in a gold portrait mask. The chambers were filled with life-sized statues, chariots, couches, furniture, caskets, robes and jewellery in such quantity that it took Carter ten years to catalogue them. The sarcophagus and one gold coffin still lie in the tomb in the Valley of the Kings, while the rest of the contents are now in Cairo Museum.

TZ'U HSI (1835–1908), Empress Dowager of China, who ruled that vast country for nearly fifty years (from 1861), was a low-ranking concubine of the Emperor Hsien Feng and she bore him his only son. When he ascended the throne as a child, she quickly seized power as Empress Dowager, removing all opposition, including Prince Kung, her able brother-in-law.

The death of her son T'ung Chih might have ruined her career, but she chose a three-year-old nephew of the dead Emperor to succeed to the throne and continued to rule as regent. In 1889 this nephew, Kuang Hsü, assumed power, but the old Empress forced him to marry a cousin of her choice and still exercised such control that when he tried to introduce reforms she had him arrested and confined to an island in her palace at Peking.

She gave secret help to the fanatically anti-foreign BOXER RISING of 1900, but after its suppression belatedly recognized the need for wholesale reforms. She died one day after the Emperor, whom she was said to have murdered. Her corruption, cruelty, love of power and refusal to accept modern ideas kept China in poverty and in a state of subjection to foreign powers. This brought about the downfall of the Ch'ing dynasty and opened the way to revolution.

UV

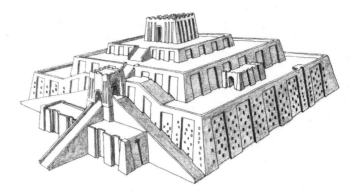

The great ziggurat at Ur

UNITED NATIONS ORGANIZATION (UNO) came formally into existence on 24 October 1945, when fifty nations signed the Charter. This world organization, like its predecessor the LEAGUE OF NATIONS, was established for the purpose of maintaining international peace and security. By 1975 137 states were members.

The principal organs of the UN are the General Assembly, which consists of all the members, and the Security Council, which has fifteen members, five of them (China, France, Britain, USA, USSR) being permanent members. In addition, there are the International Court of Justice, the Economic and Social Council, the Trusteeship Council. There are also scores of important committees and councils, such as the International Labour Organization (ILO), Food and Agriculture Organization (FAO), International Atomic Energy Agency, United Nations Education, Scientific and Cultural Organization (UNESCO), World Health Organization (WHO), the World Bank, the International Monetary Fund, the International Civil Aviation Organization, Universal Postal Union and World Metereological Organization.

UNO's permanent headquarters are situated in New York City, while the various international agencies are distributed about the world in London, Rome, Vienna, Geneva, Montreal, Berne, Washington, and Paris.

In addition to its valuable work in economic and social research, health, education, science and culture and the promotion of human rights, UNO has been active in helping to resolve international disputes and troubled situations, including Indonesia in 1949, the KOREAN WAR, the Congo (Zaïre) in 1963–4, and the ARAB-ISRAELI conflicts from 1948 until the present day.

UR, an ancient city of SUMER which stood on the river Euphrates, near the Persian Gulf, came into existence in about 3000 BC and reached its peak of prosperity about a thousand years later, under King Ur-Nammu. The main excavation of Ur was carried out in 1922–34 by Sir Leonard Woolley, who discovered the remains of many domestic houses, public buildings and a vast ziggurat or temple, dedicated to Nannar the moon god. Excavations of tombs revealed that attendants were buried with the king or queen, along with jewellery, pottery, elaborate robes and head-dresses. Thousands of clay tablets inscribed with cuneiform writing provided evidence of city life and prosperity.

Ur controlled the Sumerian empire until it was overrun by Elamites and Amorites, and the city ceased to be of importance when the Euphrates changed its course.

VANDALS were a Teutonic people of East Germany, who during the break up of the Roman Empire swarmed into Gaul and then crossed into Spain and North Africa (*see* BARBARIAN INVASIONS). Under Genseric they sacked Rome in 455, but in the following century were defeated by JUSTINIAN's general Belisarius and disappeared from history. In their heyday they were notorious destroyers of books, works of art and anything beautiful.

VASCO DA GAMA (*c.* 1469–1524), a gentleman-navigator of the Portuguese court, was chosen by King Emanuel to command an expedition of three ships that was to try to reach India via the Cape of Good Hope. He set out from Lisbon in July 1497, rounded the Cape and, despite mutinies and hurricanes, reached Calicut in India on 20 May 1498. The local ruler turned hostile and Vasco da Gama had to fight his way out of the harbour in order to return home. He went back to India in 1502 to bombard a still hostile Calicut into submission and then, after a long period of retirement in Portugal, he went out for a third time in 1524 to restore Portuguese prestige. He died on the voyage home.

VENICE, the Italian city built on islands at the north end of the Adriatic Sea, was founded in the 5th century by refugees who fled from the BARBARIANS invading the mainland. The town grew quickly and became rich from trade, especially with the BYZANTINE EMPIRE. During the period of the CRUSADES it made enormous profits from the traffic between Europe and Syria, and it was Venetians who contrived to divert the Fourth Crusade to Constantinople and to capture that city in 1204. This brought further riches from trade in the Black Sea and eastern Mediterranean, while Venetian fleets also carried silks, spices and luxury goods to western Europe.

The city was well governed by merchant aristocrats, headed by a supreme magistrate called the Doge. In the 15th century Venice reached her peak, for she controlled the main trade-route to the East and ruled wide territories on the mainland of Italy and down the Adriatic coast, besides colonies and

Above Vasco da Gama with one of the crosses he erected at landing-places along the African coast

Below The Grand Canal in Venice in the 15th century

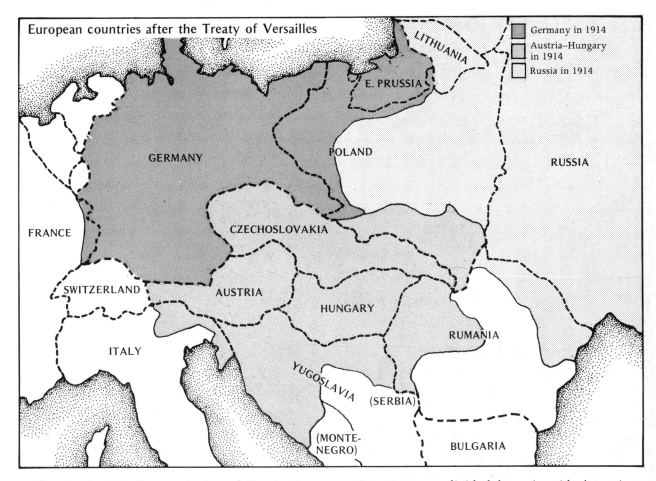

European countries after the Treaty of Versailles

Germany in 1914
Austria–Hungary in 1914
Russia in 1914

LITHUANIA
E. PRUSSIA
POLAND
RUSSIA
GERMANY
CZECHOSLOVAKIA
FRANCE
SWITZERLAND
AUSTRIA
HUNGARY
RUMANIA
ITALY
YUGOSLAVIA
(SERBIA)
(MONTE-NEGRO)
BULGARIA

trading-stations in Greece, Syria and Constantinople. Her fierce rival at this time was the other great sea-trading power, Genoa.

From about 1500 the power of Venice began to decline, due to the rise of the OTTOMAN EMPIRE and the Portuguese discovery of the Cape route to the East. In 1797 NAPOLEON compelled the last Doge to abdicate and Venice was handed over to Austria; it became part of the kingdom of Italy in 1866.

VERSAILLES, Treaty of (1919), laid down the peace settlement between the Allied Powers and Germany at the end of the FIRST WORLD WAR. By its terms Alsace-Lorraine returned to France, part of East Prussia and Silesia went to Poland, a portion of Upper Silesia to Czechoslovakia, the port of Memel to Lithuania and part of Schleswig to Denmark. Thus Germany lost one eighth of her territory and one tenth of her population, but most of the territory was merely restored to former owners.

Germany was divided by a 'corridor' to give Poland access to the sea and Danzig became a Free City. The LEAGUE OF NATIONS took on responsibility for all German overseas possessions; military service was abolished in Germany, and her army, navy and armaments industry were severely restricted. The Rhineland was to be demilitarized and occupied by Allied troops for up to fifteen years, while the Saar (whose coalmines were ceded to France) was placed under international control pending a plebiscite. Union between Austria and Germany was forbidden without the League's consent and, finally, the treaty held Germany responsible for the war and required her to pay heavy damages (reparations) to the Allies.

Excluded from the peace conference and given only five days in which to accept the terms, Germany regarded them as unjust and excessively severe. They left a legacy of bitterness of which HITLER was to take full advantage.

VESPUCCI, Amerigo (c. 1451–1512), the Italian explorer whose Christian name came to be given to America, made several voyages to the New World, shortly after its discovery by COLUMBUS. Having sailed along the coast of Venezuela in 1499, he expressed in his *Mundus Novus* (New World) letter the view that this land could not be part of Asia. The letter, widely read in Europe, caused the name 'America' to be used by mapmakers. As a reward for his services, Vespucci was appointed Pilot Major of Spain and given charge of a school of navigation set up at Seville.

Queen Victoria at the time of her Diamond Jubilee (1897)

VICTORIA (1819–1901), Queen of Great Britain (1837–1901), was the daughter of Edward Duke of Kent, and she came to the throne in 1837 at the age of eighteen after her uncle WILLIAM IV died childless. Diminutive and gay, she already possessed great dignity, so that Melbourne, her Prime Minister, found her an eager pupil; later, after her marriage (1840) to Prince ALBERT, whom she adored, she came completely under her husband's influence, learning her duties and responsibilities and setting an example of staid married life that restored the prestige of the monarchy. They had nine children and Victoria never recovered from the shock of Albert's sudden death from typhoid in December 1861.

She withdrew from public life and for a time, became unpopular in the country, yet she would not allow her eldest son, the Prince of Wales (later King EDWARD VII), any share in her responsibilities. Her obstinacy and GLADSTONE's unbending nature made their relationship difficult, but DISRAELI charmed her out of seclusion and she was delighted when he obtained for her the title Empress of India in 1877. At her Jubilees of 1887 and 1897 the whole nation gave demonstrations of loyalty and affection that almost amounted to reverence; she had become the symbol of majesty and of the age when Britain reached the summit of power and prosperity.

Victoria was shrewd and, as her reign went on, very experienced in the business of state; she frequently rebuked her ministers and sometimes refused to approve appointments, while in foreign affairs she held strong opinions, chiefly because through her children's marriages she was related to most of the ruling houses in Europe. But although she intervened in many matters, she did not really have a decisive influence on politics, and during her reign the position of the sovereign as a constitutional monarch became established.

VIENNA, Congress of (1814–15), was a meeting of the victorious sovereigns and their ministers after the defeat of NAPOLEON I in 1814 and his exile to Elba. The chief members were the four great powers, Austria, Prussia, Russia and Britain, which became the 'Five' when France was admitted in January 1815. The dominant ministers, Metternich of Austria, Castlereagh of Britain and Talleyrand of France, aimed to secure peace in Europe by ensuring a balance of power and trying to see that no country was so dissatisfied that it would go to war. They were much concerned to prevent the westward advance of Russia, whose Tsar, ALEXANDER I, generally acted as his own minister. Frederick William III of Prussia supported the Tsar's desire to recreate Poland, provided Prussia was able to dominate Germany and to gain the kingdom of Saxony.

By June 1815 the five great powers, with Sweden and Portugal, had reached agreement. Parts of Poland went to Prussia and Austria; the rest, as the kingdom of Poland, came under Russian sway; Prussia obtained part of Saxony and other considerable areas in Germany; Sweden lost Finland, but gained Norway from Denmark. The thirty-eight states of Germany were linked together in a German Confederation; the Dutch and Austrian Netherlands became one kingdom, while the perpetual neutrality of Switzerland was guaranteed. In Italy Austria regained Lombardy and Venetia, but little else was changed, except that the Kingdom of Naples was eventually restored to the Spanish Bourbon King Ferdinand. The Vienna settlement, much criticized because it ignored the national longings of many of the peoples of Europe, did ensure a long period of peace.

VIETNAM, formerly part of French Indo-China, was occupied by the Japanese during the Second World War. At its end nationalists, known as the Viet-minh, proclaimed the Republic of Vietnam and prepared to resist the French attempt to recover their colonial rule. A bitter war, lasting from 1946 until 1954, ended with the French surrender at Dien-Bien-Phu and their withdrawal from the country. Vietnam then became divided into North Vietnam, under a Communist government, and South Vietnam, a republic which looked to the United States for support. By the late 1950s serious conflict had developed between these two states, the South complaining of infiltration by Communist guerrillas and the North claiming that American interference had caused an internal rebellion.

President KENNEDY stepped up American economic and military aid to South Vietnam, but by 1965 Communist successes had brought the Saigon (Southern) government to the point of collapse when the US Congress authorized President Johnson to take action. This led to heavy bombing raids on the North by the USA airforce and to increasing involvement of American combat troops, who numbered 500,000 by the end of 1967.

Contingents of troops from Australia, South Korea, the Philippines and Thailand also took part in the war, but the Communists, receiving heavy support from the Chinese, not only withstood all pressure, but in 1968 launched an offensive that came near to capturing Saigon. This was followed by a peace conference in Paris and a temporary lull in US bombing, but the war itself, far from ceasing, spread into Cambodia in 1970.

By this time American public opinion had become disenchanted with a struggle that offered no prospect of victory and, with President Nixon pledged to bring it to an end, peace was signed in January 1973. As negotiations dragged on and American forces withdrew, the North Vietnamese troops continued their operations with increased vigour until, in May 1975, the South suddenly collapsed and the war ended with the capture of Saigon.

A Viking longship. A replica of this ship built in 1893 crossed the Atlantic in 28 days.

VIKINGS, or Norsemen, were Scandinavian sea-robbers and adventurers from Denmark, Norway and Sweden, who from about AD 800 left their farms and fishing-grounds to sail their longships on piratical voyages. Many of them crossed the North Sea to raid the coasts of England, Scotland, Wales and Ireland and from raiding they turned to conquest, acquiring most of England except WESSEX and founding settlements in Ireland, Scotland and the Isle of Man.

As they grew bolder, they ventured further afield to Spain, Morocco and Italy; they sailed up the rivers of France, conquered Sicily and took the overland route down the Russian rivers to reach Constantinople. One of the boldest Vikings, Eric the Red, discovered Greenland, and his son Leif ERIKSSON reached a land he called Vinland, which was almost certainly North America. In 911 a Viking earl founded the Dukedom of Normandy (*see* NORMANS), and it was his descendant WILLIAM I who conquered England in 1066.

The main causes of this expansion were probably the development of the longship as an ocean-going vessel and a sudden increase of population in Scandinavia, which forced the younger men to sail away in search of riches and land. To these can be added the courage, seamanship and ferocious greed of the Viking warriors.

W

WAKEFIELD, Edward Gibbon (1796–1862), a gentleman of means, was sent to prison for eloping with a schoolgirl heiress. In Newgate Gaol he studied colonial problems and wrote *A Letter from Sydney, 1829*, in which he criticized the policy of colonizing new lands with convicts and urged the government to sell land at a price poor immigrants could afford to pay after working for a time. The money from such sales would be used to help further emigration. On his release from prison Wakefield formed a colonization society and took a leading part in the founding of the colony of South Australia, which was run in accordance with his ideas. He next went to Canada in 1838 with Lord Durham and had some influence on the famous DURHAM REPORT. Then he turned his attention to encouraging emigration to New Zealand, where he was responsible for the Canterbury settlement and for those which founded Wellington, Nelson and New Plymouth He himself went to New Zealand as a colonist in 1853 and died there at Wellington.

WALLACE, Sir William (*c.* 1272–1305), the Scottish patriot, took up arms against the English after EDWARD I had taken possession of much of the country. In 1297 Wallace defeated the English at Stirling Bridge and ravaged the northern counties, but in the following year Edward beat him at Falkirk. He then went abroad to seek help, but failing to obtain it he returned to Scotland to carry on guerrilla warfare from 1303 to 1305, when he was betrayed and captured at Glasgow. Taken to London for trial, he was executed the same year and the four quarters of his body were sent to Scotland to be displayed in the principal towns.

Walpole (*left*) in the House of Commons

WALPOLE, Sir Robert (1676–1745), is generally regarded as the first British Prime Minister, though the office was not recognized in his time. He entered Parliament as a Whig in 1701 and held several important posts before becoming Chancellor of the Exchequer in 1721, when he restored confidence after the SOUTH SEA BUBBLE crisis. As Chancellor he handled GEORGE I and GEORGE II as skilfully as he managed the House of Commons, retaining power in his own hands for twenty years and elbowing rivals out of position. His aims were to maintain the Hanoverian dynasty, to promote peace at almost any price, to reduce taxes, encourage trade and put down smuggling.

In his policy of 'let sleeping dogs lie' he was highly successful, though he neglected the country's armed services and aroused virulent opposition to his one-man rule and widespread use of bribery. A man of great skill and cunning, he liked to appear as a bluff Norfolk squire who was more interested in country pursuits and hunting than in politics. He had a low opinion of human nature and reckoned that every man could be bought at a price. The outbreak of the War of JENKINS'S EAR drove him to resign in 1742, when he was made Earl of Orford and retired to his splendid house at Houghton, Norfolk, which he had filled with artistic treasures.

WALSINGHAM, Sir Francis (1532–90), politician, diplomat and head of ELIZABETH I's secret service, was an ardent Protestant, whose lifelong aims were to serve the Queen and oppose the forces of Catholicism. He became ambassador to France, 1570–3, and Secretary of State from 1573 until his death. Through spies, secret agents and bribery, he kept himself informed of affairs in the major European capitals and he managed to trap both Antony BABINGTON and MARY QUEEN OF SCOTS. He constantly urged an aggressive alliance with French HUGUENOTS and Dutch rebels (*see* DUTCH REVOLT) but, while Elizabeth valued his services, she was too cautious to adopt such a policy.

WAR OF 1812, between the USA and Britain, arose out of tensions created by the NAPOLEONIC WARS. The Americans objected to having their ships boarded and sailors seized on the grounds that they were British deserters, and American 'war hawks' alleged that the British were stirring up the Indian tribes of the north-west. Canada was a tempting prize and President Madison was persuaded to declare war in June 1812.

An attack on Canada across the border, near Niagara, failed, allowing the British under General Brock to take Detroit and several other forts; further American offensives were defeated, but on Lake Erie Captain Oliver H. Perry's 'freshwater navy' had much the better of things. At sea the British blockaded American ports, but in a number of isolated actions American frigates proved superior to their opponents.

In retaliation for the burning of Toronto, British troops set fire to Washington in 1814, and following Napoleon's abdication and the release of troops from Europe an army of veterans under General Pakenham landed in Louisiana, but were decisively beaten in the battle of New Orleans (January 1815)

The Americans repulse the British during the Battle of New Orleans

by American forces commanded by Andrew JACKSON. Unknown to either side, a peace treaty had already been signed at Ghent fifteen days earlier, by which the situation was restored to its pre-war status, so that neither side gained from this muddled and unnecessary conflict.

WARWICK, Earl of (Richard Neville, 1428–71), who became known as 'the Kingmaker', took sides with his uncle Richard Duke of York against HENRY VI, his wife Queen Margaret and the Lancastrians. In the first battle of the Wars of the ROSES (St Albans, 1455) he captured Henry VI and later escorted him to London. As Captain of Calais Warwick gained popularity and a personal following, so he was able to bring over his own troops when the war restarted in 1460. After winning the battle of Northampton, he entered London and had York's son, the Earl of March, proclaimed king as EDWARD IV.

Having beaten the Lancastrians once again at Towton and thwarted Edward IV's effort to assert himself, Warwick was all-powerful until Edward suddenly declared him and his ally Clarence, the King's brother, to be traitors. They fled to France, where Warwick came to terms with Queen Margaret, returned to England to bring Henry VI out of the Tower and make him king again. Meanwhile, Edward who had escaped to Flanders, landed in Yorkshire, collected an army and was joined by the treacherous Clarence; together they defeated and killed Warwick in the battle of Barnet on 13 April 1471.

WASHINGTON, George (1732–99), was born into a wealthy family in Virginia and as a young man he gained valuable knowledge of the frontier country through acting as a land surveyor in the Shenandoah Valley. Inheriting the family estates, he settled down as a wealthy plantation owner at Mount Vernon, and as colonel in the Virginia militia he fought against the French in the FRENCH AND INDIAN WARS. He showed outstanding courage and narrowly escaped death when Braddock's force, advancing on Fort Duquesne, was cut to pieces in 1755.

Three years later Washington resigned his command, married a rich widow and spent the next seventeen years developing his estates. As a leading Virginian he took a close interest in the worsening

George Washington at the Battle of Yorktown

disputes between the colonies and the English Crown and he was present as a delegate when Congress met at Philadelphia in 1775. Chosen to lead the American army, he modestly doubted his ability to take supreme command, but agreed to do so without pay. The task was immense. He had to weld companies of raw, often insubordinate, volunteers into a disciplined army, and through the meanness of the colonies he was constantly short of arms, food and clothing. But by his unflinching tenacity Washington proved equal to every call, until he finally brought his country to victory.

Early in the AMERICAN WAR OF INDEPENDENCE Washington compelled the British to evacuate Boston, but he had to retreat when Howe captured New York, and his victories at Trenton and Princeton were followed by defeat at Brandywine and the loss of Philadelphia in 1777. That winter he miraculously held together a starving army at Valley Forge, and when the British left Philadelphia he harassed them on the march to New York and took up position at White Plains to keep watch on the enemy for three years.

At last came the chance to strike. Learning that Cornwallis had withdrawn his army at Yorktown, Washington moved swiftly south, joined forces with the French and compelled Cornwallis to surrender on 19 October 1781. This was the last decisive engagement of the war, and when hostilities ended in 1783 the Commander-in-Chief resigned his commission and went home to Mount Vernon.

The next four years were spent in rebuilding his estates, but he did not lose touch with national affairs and in 1789 was unanimously chosen President of the republic. As Churchill wrote: 'Disinterested and courageous, far-sighted and patient, aloof yet direct in manner, inflexible once his mind was made up, Washington possessed the gifts of character for which the situation called. He was reluctant to accept office. . . . But, as always, he answered the summons to duty.'

He served two terms as President and before he retired to his beloved Mount Vernon he made a famous farewell address, warning his people against the dangers of party strife and foreign entanglements. In all history there has never been a national leader more honourable or less moved by personal ambition. He was, indeed, 'First in war, first in peace, first in the hearts of his countrymen'.

WATERLOO, Battle of (18 June 1815), was fought near a village of that name nine miles (14 km) south of Brussels. WELLINGTON, commanding an army of about 50,000 troops, half of them British, took up a defensive position behind a low ridge, with the Guards stationed at the outlying château of Hougoumont on the right, and reliable troops holding two other strong points at La Haye Sainte and La Haye. NAPOLEON, with rather more cavalry and artillery, attacked at noon with columns of infantry, which Wellington met, as in Spain, with volleys from concealed lines, followed by bayonet charges. Heavy fighting continued all afternoon, with the Guards holding out desperately at Hougoumont; after artillery bombardment, the French cavalry made four great attacks against the British centre, but the infantry squares held firm.

At about 6 pm La Haye Sainte was lost, but Wellington rallied his troops and re-formed the line, as the vanguard of Blücher's Prussian troops approached from the east. Blücher, who had been defeated at Ligny three days earlier, had withdrawn in good order, sending word that he would come to Wellington's assistance. At this crucial stage in the battle Napoleon launched a general attack, throwing in his finest troops, the Imperial

French cavalry charge the British square at Waterloo

Guard, and when this assault too was repulsed the French army disintegrated. As the Prussians broke through and took up the pursuit, Napoleon himself and his beaten troops fled in disorder. The casualties were heavy, the French losing over 40,000 men, Wellington over 15,000 and the Prussians 7,000.

WATSON-WATT, Sir Robert Alexander (1892–1973), the Scottish scientist, produced the first practical way of locating aircraft by radio. This was in 1935, and during the next few years he and a few technicians developed in secret the system which came to be known as radar. Used at first in ground stations, his invention was speedily adapted to ships, guns and aircraft, and it was said that radar contributed more than any other scientific factor to the victory over Germany in the SECOND WORLD WAR.

Watt with his steam engine

WATT, James (1736–1819), son of a Scottish carpenter, became an instrument-maker in Glasgow, where in 1763 he was asked to repair a model of a steam-engine invented years earlier by Thomas Newcomen. The engine was inefficient and extravagant in fuel, and after two years of experiment Watt

discovered that it could be vastly improved by rebuilding the engine with a separate condenser. Lack of skilled workmen to carry out his ideas, shortage of money and his own ill health might have put an end to his discoveries but for a meeting with Mathew Boulton, a manufacturer, who owned a large factory called the Soho Works, at Birmingham. The two men went into partnership to produce Watt's steam-engines, which were at first used mainly for pumping and in blast-furnaces. He went on to invent a 'rotative' engine to turn machinery and he added many other improvements, before retiring in 1800 to devote the rest of his life to experiments with machinery and chemicals.

WELLINGTON, Duke of (Arthur Wellesley, 1769–1852), arguably the greatest general Britain ever produced, earned his nickname the 'Iron Duke' through his self-control, attention to detail, and unyielding determination to win. He never lost a battle, nor even a gun. Regarded as a dull boy by his widowed mother, Lady Mornington, he was sent to a French military college, became an ensign in the British army and eventually made his reputation in India, where he defeated the fierce Mahrattas and returned to England a general.

In 1808 he went to Spain in command of an expeditionary force sent to help the Spaniards in their revolt against the French. For six years, aided by Portuguese troops and Spanish guerrillas, he conducted a series of brilliant campaigns in the PENINSULAR WAR against some of NAPOLEON's best generals and finest troops. Having beaten the French at Talavera (1809) and saved Lisbon through building the tremendous fortifications of Torres Vedras, he won victories at Albuera (1811), Badajoz, Salamanca (1812) and Vitoria (1813) before driving Marshal Soult clean out of Spain into France, where he finally defeated him at Toulouse (1814). For six years he had engaged the French without losing a battle and had deprived Napoleon of armies that he would otherwise have employed in Europe.

The Duke of Wellington, as he had now become, was given command of the Allied army that opposed Napoleon after his escape from Elba, and at WATERLOO, showing all his icy resolve, he won a desperately close but decisive victory.

He was now the most famous man in Europe and, after his return to England he entered Parliament and eventually became Prime Minister in 1828. A Tory averse to change, who regarded himself first and foremost as the servant of the Crown, he was not a success as a politician and, for a time, was intensely unpopular for his opposition to the Reform Bill. However, he had the courage and commonsense to accept the inevitable and he actually helped to carry through Catholic emancipation and repeal of the CORN LAWS.

Wellington was slightly built and of medium height, with a prominent hooked nose. He lived frugally, his speech was abrupt to the point of rudeness, but he had a dry wit and made many memorable remarks. Unhappily married, he had many women friends to whom he was a great letter writer. He ruled his troops with iron discipline, calling them 'the scum of the earth', who had 'all enlisted for drink', though he did add that it was surprising what 'fine fellows' he had made of them. Thus, his troops never loved him, as Marlborough's soldiers did, but they respected him and fought for him like lions. By the end of his life Wellington had become a national figure; loaded with honours, he died at Walmer Castle and was buried in St Paul's Cathedral at the side of Nelson.

WESLEY, John (1703–91), son of a clergyman, was educated at Oxford, where he and his brother Charles started the 'Holy Club', a group of earnest young men who were nicknamed 'methodists' because they lived by strict rules. In 1735 the Wesley brothers went to Georgia in America, hoping to convert the Indians, but having no success they eventually returned to England, where John took up his life's work as an itinerant preacher. For fifty years, he travelled five thousand miles (8,000 km) a year on horseback in all weathers to preach in churches, but mostly in the open air, in order to bring the Gospel to working people, many of whom had previously known little or nothing of the Christian religion. Helped by his brother, especially with hymn writing, and by lay-workers, the Methodists brought faith and comfort to many thousands of persons whom the established Church had never reached.

Wesley did not set out to found a separate Methodist Church and he himself remained a member of the Church of England. Into the new industrial towns of the north, into mining districts, slums, country villages and fashionable spas, undeterred by jeers, violence and the disapproval of the clergy, he carried with passionate conviction his message that Christ loved all men and would bring them salvation. His work and example inspired others to help less fortunate members of society, such as children, prisoners, lunatics, and slaves, and led to the humanitarian movement of the 19th century.

WESSEX, the kingdom of the West Saxons, founded in the 6th century, was situated in southern England and came to include the counties of Hampshire, Wiltshire, Dorset, Somerset and Devon. For a time it was subordinate to MERCIA, but Egbert (802–39) defeated the Mercians, acquired new territory and made Wessex the most powerful of the Anglo-Saxon kingdoms (*see* SAXONS). When the others were destroyed by the VIKINGS, Wessex stood alone, and under ALFRED (871–99) defeated the invaders and, in doing so, preserved Christianity and Anglo-Saxon culture. Alfred's successors conquered the territory held by the Danes, the Danelaw, and the rest of England, so that the later kings of Wessex ruled the whole country and became kings of England.

Whitney and his cotton gin

WHITNEY, Eli (1765–1825), the American inventor, designed in 1794 a machine called a cotton gin that separated the raw cotton from the seeds, a job previously done by hand, and this greatly increased the workers' output and led to a boom in cotton-growing. It also led to an increase in slave labour

in the Southern States. Whitney later designed machinery to mass-produce the components of rifles.

The emblem of the Anti-slavery Society

WILBERFORCE, William (1759–1833), when a gay and wealthy young man, underwent a religious conversion and became an ardent opponent of the slave trade (*see* SLAVERY). As an MP he demanded its abolition by law, but, although his friend PITT supported his views, the war with revolutionary France put the matter into the background. Moreover, Bills to abolish slavery passed by the Commons were rejected by the House of Lords. Wilberforce kept up his campaign, securing the support of Charles James Fox, who before his death in 1806 managed to put through a law abolishing the British slave trade. This came into effect in 1807, but the freedom of existing slaves had still to be won, so Wilberforce formed the Anti-Slavery Society, and in 1833 all slaves in British colonies were freed. Wilberforce died in that same year when the great work of his life was completed; he had also founded the Church Missionary Society and the Bible Society.

WILKES, John (1727–97), an ugly dissolute scoundrel, became one of the most celebrated champions of liberty through publishing a violent attack on GEORGE III's speech to Parliament in 1763. The attack appeared in No. 45 of the magazine *The North Briton* and the King gave orders for the arrest of Wilkes and others on a charge of libel. Claiming freedom of speech and immunity from arrest as an MP, Wilkes was released but had to flee abroad. In his absence he was sentenced to prison and expelled from Parliament, but on his return four years later he was elected for Middlesex.

Imprisoned for his old offence, he was repeatedly re-elected and as often expelled by the government, causing the London mob to riot, with 'Wilkes and Liberty!' as their battle-cry. His popularity gained him election as an Alderman of the City of London and eventually as Lord Mayor. In 1774, when the King decided to drop the matter, he returned to Parliament and became comparatively respectable in his old age.

The seal of William the Conqueror

WILLIAM I, the Conqueror (1027–87), King of England (1066–87), was the son of Robert I, Duke of Normandy, and a tanner's daughter. He succeeded his father at the age of eight and had to fight hard in his youth to establish his authority over his unruly nobles. When EDWARD THE CONFESSOR died, William claimed the English throne on the grounds that Edward, a relative, had promised it to him. But the English chose HAROLD, Earl of Wessex, whereupon William, with the Pope's blessing, assembled

an invasion army and, thanks to a certain amount of luck, defeated and killed Harold at the Battle of HASTINGS on 14 October 1066. He was crowned in Westminster Abbey on Christmas Day and, although he had to suppress several rebellions during the next few years, which he did with the utmost cruelty, he secured the kingdom by building motte-and-bailey CASTLES, by creating strong earldoms on the borders and by making a bargain with his followers that, in return for grants of land, they would give him armed support. In this way he imposed an alien aristocracy on the English, whose nobles, by the end of the reign, had lost practically all their lands.

William was brave, cunning and immensely strong; he ruled harshly, taxing the people heavily and inflicting ferocious punishment on those who rebelled or broke his Forest Laws. But, a good husband and a forgiving father to his troublesome sons, he dealt justly with those who obeyed him, reformed the English Church and, as the chronicler wrote, 'he was kind to those good men who loved God and we must not forget the good order he kept in the land'. Towards the end of his reign he ordered the great survey of England known as the DOMESDAY Book.

WILLIAM II (*c.* 1056–1100), King of England (1087–1100), second son of WILLIAM I, was known as Rufus, probably from his red face, and while he possessed his father's ruthlessness and warlike skill he had none of his virtues. He was a godless, tyrannical ruffian, who spent much of his reign quarrelling with the Church and fighting the Scots, the Welsh and the French. He forced Anselm, Archbishop of Canterbury, to flee abroad and then seized Church estates. William was killed by an arrow when hunting in the New Forest; this may have been an accident or murder carried out on behalf of his brother who succeeded him as HENRY I.

WILLIAM III (1650–1702), King of Great Britain (1689–1702) and Stadholder of Holland, was the son of WILLIAM II, Prince of Orange, and Mary, daughter of Charles I. At twenty-two he was appointed Captain-General of the Dutch forces in the struggle against France, and in 1677 he married MARY, daughter of James Duke of York, afterwards JAMES II of England. In 1688 he accepted an invitation to invade England and landed at Torbay with a small

re-form the Grand Alliance of England, Holland, Austria, Savoy and various German states. He was gathering his partners together when he suffered a riding accident and died soon afterwards.

William was never popular in England and he himself much preferred his beloved Holland. A misshapen little man, whose morose manner hid his sterling character, he carried out his bargain faithfully; England needed him in 1688 and he needed England to help him in his life's work of saving Holland from being overwhelmed by France.

WILLIAM IV (1765–1837), King of Great Britain (1830–7), the third son of GEORGE III, served in the navy and was appointed Lord High Admiral in 1827. Three years later, on the death of his brother GEORGE IV, he became king at the age of sixty-five. Good-natured and tactless, he showed commonsense during the Reform Bill crisis, and during his reign the king's position as a constitutional monarch began to become clear. He married Adelaide of Saxe-Coburg, but as they had no children he was succeeded by his niece VICTORIA.

William and Mary

force, whereupon James fled and William and his wife Mary became joint sovereigns (*see* GLORIOUS REVOLUTION). Having defeated James in Ireland at the Battle of the Boyne (1690), he subdued that country and sent an army to suppress opposition in Scotland. Two years later occurred the tragic Massacre of Glencoe, for which William was somewhat unfairly blamed.

He next went to Holland to command the Dutch army in the war of the League of Augsburg, and William, a dogged patient general, held his own in a war of sieges, recaptured Namur and by the Treaty of Ryswick (1697) obtained LOUIS XIV's recognition of himself as legal king of England (Mary had died in 1694). William, foreseeing the problem of the SPANISH SUCCESSION, made the First Partition Treaty (1698) with his old enemy Louis XIV, and when this was thwarted by the death of the little Prince of Bavaria they made the Second Partition Treaty (1700) to share the Spanish possessions between France and Austria. Louis, however, accepted the Will that left everything to his own grandson, Philip of Anjou, so causing William to

WILLIAM THE SILENT (1533–84), Prince of Orange, the Dutch national hero, was in fact a German, the son of the Count of Nassau, a Rhineland princeling. As a boy William inherited from a distant cousin great estates in France and the Netherlands, so he was sent to Brussels to be brought up at the Court of the Emperor CHARLES V. The Emperor favoured this gay, wealthy young man and made him Stadholder or governor of three provinces, and at twenty William commanded an army in a war against France.

When PHILIP II of Spain took over his father's territories, he cruelly suppressed the Protestants in the Netherlands and appointed the fanatical Duke of Alva to crush the DUTCH REVOLT, causing William to take on leadership of his adopted people. He himself was a Catholic, but he presently adopted the Protestant faith and it was at about this time that he earned the name of 'the Silent' through his prudent ability to keep his own counsel.

Outlawed to Germany, William raised an army and returned to the Netherlands to fight Alva, but his army was too small and failure seemed certain until he joined forces with the 'Sea Beggars', semi-piratical Dutch patriots, who attacked the Spaniards at sea and received secret help from ELIZABETH of England. Together they made gradual progress against the enemy, once saving the city of Leyden by opening the dykes to flood the countryside, and by 1572 William had freed the northern provinces.

He hoped to unite the entire country, but the Spaniards recovered the Catholic south, so he had to be content with the Union of Utrecht, signed in 1579, which gave independence to the north. Having spent his fortune in the struggle, he went to live simply in Delft as hereditary Stadholder and it was here that he was assassinated by a fanatic acting for Philip II. He has been called 'the wisest, gentlest and bravest man who ever led a nation' and according to the historian Motley, 'when he died, the little children cried in the streets'.

WILLIAM II (1859–1941), Emperor of Germany (1888–1918), was the son of Frederick Crown Prince of Prussia (later Frederick III) and Victoria, the daughter of Britain's Queen VICTORIA. After a military education he succeeded his father in 1888 and soon quarrelled with Germany's masterful Chancellor BISMARCK. Having dismissed him in 1890, William (who was known as the Kaiser) adopted a policy of personal rule and of giving support to the army and navy. His ambition was to strengthen Germany in Europe and to acquire an empire.

Owing to his arrogance and habit of making tactless public statements, he offended Britain, France and Russia on various occasions and kept Europe on tenterhooks for years. He certainly encouraged Austria to take an aggressive attitude to Serbia after the murder of the Archduke Ferdinand at Sarajevo in 1914, yet he did not really want a major European war. After the FIRST WORLD WAR broke out he took on the role of war leader, but in reality was no

more than a figurehead, since power had passed to the German generals.

Upon Germany's defeat in 1918 William abdicated and fled to Holland, where he lived at Doorn Castle to the end of his life. Agitation in Britain 'to hang the Kaiser' as a war-criminal fortunately died down, as people realized the absurdity of holding this man responsible for the First World War.

WILSON, Thomas Woodrow (1856–1924), the 28th President of the USA, was born in Virginia, where he graduated in law, and later became a professor at Princeton University. A fine speaker, with a sense of humour and strong beliefs in what was right, he was elected Democratic Governor of New Jersey in 1910 and speedily made his name as a reformer. This led to his nomination as presidential candidate, though the Democratic Party bosses probably expected him to be a mere figurehead who would not interfere with big business.

Once elected, however, in 1912, Wilson put through the most advanced programme of domestic reform for half a century; but he was less successful in foreign affairs. He did not understand the situation in Europe and was surprised by the outbreak of war in 1914. Convinced that war could settle nothing, he kept America neutral and was re-elected President in 1916. A year later he reluctantly asked Congress to declare war on Germany, while still hoping that peace and a lasting settlement could be reached under some form of world government or League of Nations. His famous 'Fourteen Points' for a fair peace undoubtedly influenced the Germans in their decision to ask for an armistice in 1918, and he himself led the American delegation at the Peace Conference, where he helped to draw up the Covenant of the LEAGUE OF NATIONS.

Wilson went home to present both the Treaty of VERSAILLES and the League to a hostile Congress now controlled by Republicans. When they refused to ratify the Treaty or accept US membership of the League, Wilson appealed to the country, undertaking a nationwide tour and delivering forty major speeches in twenty-two days. The strain was too great and in September 1919 he collapsed with a stroke. A cripple, unable to perform his duties, he remained in office until the next election, when the Republican candidate Harding was overwhelmingly elected.

Wilson died in 1924, bitterly disappointed by his failure to achieve his ideals. However, he did not fail completely and the short-lived League of Nations was the precursor of the present UNITED NATIONS. He was a great man, but too honest and idealist to be successful as a politician.

WITAN, or Witangemot, literally an assembly of wise men in Anglo-Saxon times, met with the king at various times to advise him. Its members included royal nobles, archbishops, bishops, ealdormen and the king's thanes. It probably met as and when the king wished, but it would also meet in emergency and to decide the succession. Thus, in 1066, the Witan named HAROLD to succeed EDWARD THE CONFESSOR.

WOLFE, James (1727–59), won Canada for Britain by his brilliant victory over the French at Quebec.

Wolfe's soldiers scaling the Heights of Abraham

He joined the army as a boy, fought at Dettingen in the War of the AUSTRIAN SUCCESSION and against the Highlanders at Falkirk and Culloden in the JACOBITE REBELLION OF 1745. At twenty-two he was a lieutenant-colonel and his outstanding ability attracted the attention of Pitt the Elder (CHATHAM) during the SEVEN YEARS WAR.

Pitt sent him to North America to help in the attack on Louisbourg and then chose him to command the expedition that was to capture Quebec. The task was a daunting one, with Quebec situated on the Heights of Abraham high above the St Lawrence river, so that a direct attack was certain to fail. Wolfe embarked his troops in small boats secretly at night; they rowed up-river and scaled the cliffs by a narrow path so that, by morning, he had over 4,000 men on the Heights.

The French commander Montcalm advanced from Quebec, and in the ensuing battle Wolfe, leading his men, was twice wounded and then hit fatally in the chest. He lived just long enough to know that he had won a decisive victory. Wolfe looked like a weakling; he was delicate, even sickly, in health, nervous and highly strung, so that he sometimes gave the impression that he was arrogant, at others that he was eccentric. But he was also a dedicated soldier who, like Nelson was determined to win glory and to die a hero.

Wolsey at Hampton Court

WOLSEY, Cardinal Thomas (*c.* 1472–1530), was the son of a butcher or grazier of Ipswich. He went to Oxford University, entered the Church and became chaplain to HENRY VII. When HENRY VIII came to the throne, he recognized Wolsey's ability and made him a Privy Councillor, from which position Wolsey advanced rapidly in power and wealth. As Bishop of Lincoln and Archbishop of York he practically controlled the English Church,

and as Lord Chancellor he directed the country's home and foreign policies on behalf of the king. In 1515 the Pope made him a Cardinal and he entertained hopes of himself becoming Pope.

In domestic affairs, during a time of inflation and unemployment, his financial policy was not successful and his own greed and luxurious style of living made him unpopular. Abroad he tried to cut a great figure, to glorify his master and to hold the balance between the Valois and Hapsburg rivals. His extravagant set-piece, the FIELD OF THE CLOTH OF GOLD (1520), achieved nothing, and in the subsequent war with France (1522–3) the English army failed to distinguish itself. Reversal of foreign policy, i.e. alliance with France and war with CHARLES V, was no more successful. Wolsey fell from power when Henry VIII gave him the impossible task of persuading the Pope (who was in the power of Charles V) to annul his marriage to Catherine of Aragon (aunt of Charles V). Dismissed from office, he returned to York, but a year later he was arrested for treason and died at Leicester on his way to London to face this charge and almost certain execution.

WRIGHT BROTHERS, Wilbur (1867–1912) and Orville (1871–1948), the first men to fly in a heavier-than-air machine, opened a shop for repairing cycles in Dayton, Ohio. Interested in the problems of flight, they made many experiments with gliders, and on 17 December 1903 at Kittyhawk, North Carolina, taking turns, they flew a machine powered by a petrol engine a distance of 284 yards (262 m). Within two years they had accomplished a flight of over twenty-four miles (39 km), but their achievement won no financial support in America, so in 1908 Wilbur went to France to demonstrate his skill and win international fame. Back in America he now obtained recognition, and in 1909 the brothers were awarded a medal by Congress. After their invention was taken up by the US army Wilbur retired from flying to devote himself to improving the Wright machine, while Orville became director of the Wright Aeronautical Laboratory.

WYCLIFFE, John (*c.* 1320–84). Little is known about this Oxford scholar until about twelve years before his death he began publishing writings attacking the Pope and the riches of some of the clergy. This attracted the support of Edward III's son JOHN OF GAUNT and of nobles at Court, who hoped they might do well if Church property was confiscated. The bishops and the Pope himself tried to silence Wycliffe, but, with John of Gaunt's protection, he was able to continue his attacks and even to challenge belief in transubstantiation, which asserts that the bread and wine become the body and blood of Christ during the Mass. This lost him some support and he was forbidden to preach at Oxford; so he retired to Lutterworth in Leicestershire, where he was rector. There he inspired a band of 'poor priests', later known as LOLLARDS, to go about preaching and, to help them, he began the first translation of the whole Bible into English. In this work he had helpers, but he himself is believed to have translated the New Testament.

Hearing of a dispute in a Chinese magistrate's court during the Yüan period

YÜAN Dynasty (or Mongol Dynasty) of CHINA was founded by Kublai Khan, grandson of the great conqueror GENGHIS KHAN. It lasted from 1279 to 1368, the MONGOLS defeating the Southern SUNG dynasty and being themselves succeeded by the MING dynasty. During this period of foreign rule the conquerors continued to use Chinese officials to administer the provinces, but they also employed foreigners, including MARCO POLO, whose account of his travels supplies us with much of our knowledge of China at this period. No major artistic changes took place, but drama flourished and novels were written for the first time; trade prospered and there was widespread use of paper money.